SUSPECT CULTURES
NARRATIVE, IDENTITY & CITATION
IN 1990s NEW DRAMA

CLARE WALLACE

þ

Litteraria Pragensia
Prague 2006

Published 2006 by Litteraria Pragensia
vytiskla tiskárna
Univerzity Karlovy v Praze,
Filozoficka fakulta
Náměstí Jana Palacha 2, 116 38 Praha 1
Czech Republic
www.litterariapragensia.com

The publication of this book has been supported by research grant MSM0021620824 "Foundations of the Modern World as Reflected in Literature and Philosophy" awarded to the Faculty of Philosophy, Charles University, Prague, by the Czech Ministry of Education.

Cataloguing in Publication Data

Suspect Cultures: Narrative, Identity and Citation in 1990s New Drama by Clare Wallace. — 1st ed.
     p. cm.
     ISBN 0-7308-124-5 (pb)
     1. Theatre Studies. 2. Irish Drama. 3. British Drama
     I. Wallace, Clare. II. Title.

Printed in the Czech Republic by PB Tisk
Typeset and design by lazarus

Acknowledgements

Many friends and colleagues have supported me as this project has taken shape. I am indebted to Anna McMullan, Ondřej Pilný, Graham Saunders, Aleks Sierz, Patrick Lyons, Alexandra Poulain, Eckart Voigts-Virchow, Peter Zenzinger, Mark Berninger Colin Clark and David Vichnar for variously sharing their time, their comments and their own work, or providing me with materials that have proved useful to my research. Research for this book has been also generously assisted by grant support from the Department of Foreign Affairs, Ireland, and the Czech Ministry of Education. In particular, I would like to thank Martin Procházka, Neil Sammells and Werner Huber for their patience in reading an earlier version of this work and for their helpful comments and suggestions. Finally, Louis Armand provided the critical encouragement and support without which this book would never have been completed—thank you.

Contents

Suspect Cultures
New Playwriting at Century's End

Suspect Culture is, of course, the name of a well-known Scottish theatre company. The term as used here, however, is figurative, flexible and deliberately plural. It is, I believe, germane given prevailing attitudes to drama, particularly within current theatre and performance studies. With the burgeoning interest in alternative forms of theatre since the 1960s, the rise of performance art and the effects of postmodernism in theatre, drama often seems an atrophied remnant of a bygone age. Johannes Birringer writing on performance and transmediality asserts that,

> The theatre of the material archive, with its national canons of plays and technical pedagogies, with its maps for the production of closed, completed and autonomous stage works, is now similar to the museum of the old masters, even though one could argue that the museum's display strategies are changing, and *mise-en-scène* making has undergone remarkable innovations during the last century both in terms of styles of directing or visual staging and in the slow hybridisation and mediatisation of theatre.[1]

Patrice Pavis, more sceptical of the discourse of postmodern theatre, has remarked how much "new dramatic writing"

---

[1] Johannes Birringer, "Interacting: Performance and Transmediality," *Monologues: Theatre, Performance, Subjectivity*, ed. Clare Wallace (Prague: Litteraria Pragensia, 2006) 297-8.

[1]

seems principally devoted to undermining or discarding the core qualities of drama having,

> banished conventional dialogue from the stage as a relic of dramaturgy based on conflict and exchange: any story, intrigue or plot that is too neatly tied up is suspect. Authors and directors have tried to denarrativize their productions, to eliminate every narrative point of reference which could allow for reconstruction of the plot.[2]

Meanwhile, Hans-Thies Lehmann has advanced the term "postdramatic theatre" to "denot[e] a theatre that feels bound to operate beyond drama, at a time 'after' the authority of the dramatic paradigm in theatre." Drama survives, but only as a "withered" organism.[3] Thus, drama at the end of the twentieth century would seem, for some commentators at least, to be "little more than a 'suspect' cultural artefact,"[4] with precious little to contribute to contemporary culture.

Yet such views have not stymied the practice of playwriting, as is evidenced by a vibrant generation of new dramatists; while the spirit of transformation, rejuvenation and provocation, associated with this generation, has been the focus of considerable critical activity. The most influential book in this respect is perhaps Aleks Sierz's survey of the new drama of the 1990s, *In-Yer-Face Theatre: British Drama Today* (2001) in which he groups a selection of young writers under the now familiar heading, "In-Yer-Face Theatre." If the status of this new wave has been questioned, what is undebatable at this stage is that throughout 1990s, and especially from 1994 onwards, theatre in the UK and Ireland was marked by the emergence of an impressive number of new, and often very

---

[2] Patrice Pavis, *Theatre at the Crossroads of Culture*, trans. Loren Kruger (London and New York: Routledge, 1992) 59.

[3] Hans-Thies Lehmann, *Postdramatic Theatre*, trans. Karen Jürs-Munby (1999; London and New York: Routledge, 2006) 27.

[4] Stephen Watt, *Postmodern/Drama: Reading the Contemporary Stage* (Ann Arbor: University of Michigan Press, 1998) 3. Watt also challenges this view.

young, playwrights. This book sets out to explore the ways in which some of the most important of these new playwrights have engaged with questions of identity, agency and representation (political, aesthetic) vis-à-vis contemporary cultural conditions of postmodernity and globalisation. Broadly this engagement might be described as adversarial or, as I would put it, suspicious, though as will be evident in the analyses that follow, their modes of engagement vary considerably.[5] In an opposing sense, 1990s drama has been viewed by some critics as an intrinsically suspect phenomenon, generated artificially by PR-hungry theatres and the media. Finally, dissemination of the new writing of the period might also been seen as a type of suspect culture that has like bacteria expanded into theatres across Europe, infecting writers, directors, dramaturges and audiences.

In contrast to the majority of studies of 1990s theatre and drama, I have set out to interrogate new writing emergent in the context of Anglophone Europe (an unwieldy way of saying Scotland, Ireland and England), which throughout this chapter is referred to somewhat imperfectly as the United Kingdom and Ireland.[6] This is not to anachronistically reassert the political

[5] Such an adversarial stance has long been the province of the avant garde and the means by which it maintains its status, as has been widely claimed. See for example Roger Shattuck, *The Innocent Eye: On Modern Literature and the Arts* (New York: Farrar, Strauss and Giroux, 1984). Louis Armand, however, highlights the way in which such an "adversarial relation" also implies a "type of parasitic relationship with the dominant apparatuses of official taste and of moral and intellectual permission." This is particularly of relevance to claims made for the avant garde nature of in-yer-face theatre. See Louis Armand, "The Organ Grinder's Monkey," *Avant-Post: The Avant-Garde Under "Post-" Conditions*, ed. Louis Armand (Prague: Litteraria Pragensia, 2006) 6-8.

[6] Evidently, devolution politically undermines the concept of a "united" kingdom. In addition, the adjective British is especially problematic with regard to the Scots and Northern Irish and its use is uneven and politically charged depending on the context. In a study on identity and politics in Scotland, for example, Ross Bond and Michael Rosie found post-devolution an increase of the proportion of the population who identify themselves as Scottish not British; however, they also discovered that such attitudes to national identity do "not map [...] political perspectives neatly" (15) See Ross Bond and Michael

fantasy of union in cultural terms or to disregard cultural specificities, but an attempt to acknowledge that flows of creative energy are rarely bounded by national borders, in particular when it comes to a public and collaborative form like theatre. Relations among these countries have long been both symbiotic and attritional. Addressing such a context inevitably generates dissonances and asymmetries, as will be discussed below; however, taking into account the considerable degree of often understated interconnectedness among the cultures, theatre traditions and theatre practitioners of these countries, it is a stance that, as I hope to demonstrate, is fruitful.

If, as Birringer contends in *Theatre, Theory, Postmodernism* (1991), "theatre's self-image permutates under pressures of experience, the changing focus of cultural and art critical discourse, and the exigencies of the political economy of which theatre is a part,"[7] then over the last decade and a half theatre in Ireland and the UK has been both responding to, and resisting, some seismic social, political and cultural shifts that have been orientated around the confluent energies of globalisation, mediatisation, postmodernity.

With the surge of publications since the late 1980s, there is now a substantial body of scholarship devoted to the examination and documentation of British, Irish and Scottish theatre, usually in their respective national contexts. The issues of shared influence, traditions or crosspollination often remain problematic, being either minimised, awkwardly accommodated or omitted. So for example, Christopher Innes (*Modern British Drama: The Twentieth Century* [2002]) neatly illustrates the former tendency when he claims, albeit not

Rosie, "National Identity in Post-Devolution Scotland," 22 July 2002 <http://www.institute-of-governance.org/onlinepub/bondrosie.html>. With respect to theatre, British tends to in fact signify English, and to discreetly ignore the Scottish or Welsh.
[7] Johannes Birringer, *Theatre, Theory, Postmodernism* (Bloomington and Indianapolis: Indiana University Press, 1991) 4.

without some justification, that apart from George Bernard Shaw, Sean O'Casey and Samuel Beckett,

> other Irish playwrights—including those from Northern Ireland—belong to a separate cultural framework. Even when their plays transfer successfully to the London stage, as with Brian Friel, Brendan Behan or Thomas Kilroy, there has been little cross fertilisation. They are addressing specifically Irish themes in a recognisably different way, and building on an increasingly well-established national tradition.[8]

The most prominent asymmetry here is the status of Irish theatre as a powerful parallel tradition which is plainly not mirrored by twentieth century Scottish drama. Paradoxically whereas studies of British, or even English, drama often make room for commentary on Irish theatre, Scotland remains largely invisible, or at best, marginal. Scottish theatre is markedly absent from Innes's extensive survey. In contrast to Irish theatre, it receives no index entry, neither do writers like Liz Lochead, Chris Hannan nor David Greig, while John McGrath is discussed only briefly in the context of agit-prop theatre.

Additionally, although Irish playwrights are acknowledged (though frequently only with an eye on national identity politics), where to place Northern Irish playwrights remains a perennial problem in texts on British drama. A patent example of the dilemma of accommodation is to be found in a British Council booklet written by David Edgar entitled, *Contemporary British Dramatists* (1992).[9] Sandwiched between sections on "National Theatres" (Scotland incognito) and "Alternative Means," one finds a section without a heading which covers Brian Friel, Anne Devlin and Christina Reid. In a later text on

---

[8] Christopher Innes, *Modern British Drama: The Twentieth Century* (Cambridge: Cambridge University Press, 2002) 3.

[9] David Edgar, *Contemporary British Dramatists* (London: British Council, 1992). Admittedly this is not a scholarly publication, but it is interesting because of this. Directed at a general readership as a showcase of British culture, it also functions as a guide to an alleged canon.

contemporary theatre practice, *State of Play* (1999), Edgar also features texts by a number of Irish dramatists (this time both Southern and Northern) and a single Scot (David Greig). Again, with the Irish the focus is primarily restricted to their negotiation of Irish identity, despite the fact that the writers themselves (including in this case Conor McPherson) tend to deny its centrality to their work.[10] David Greig's contribution to the volume, to which I will return later, treats the theme of politics and theatre, which he determinedly steers away from an exclusively Scottish frame of reference.

More recently, in his lively study of *English Drama Since 1940* (2003), David Ian Rabey demonstrates how insidious stereotypes can be resurrected in the most unlikely contexts. The book includes a chapter on Irish Drama subtitled "Twilights and Tigers," that first excuses itself as "highly selective and somewhat reductive" and then goes on to argue, in contrast to Innes, that "the interrelationship of English and Irish terms of cultural and dramatic definition" is of such significance that it cannot be ignored.[11] The chapter closes its analysis of recent Irish theatre with praise for Mark O'Rowe's *Howie the Rookie*, but in a manner that undoes the good intentions of what goes before. O'Rowe is lauded for,

> offer[ing] a glimpse of the constant possibility and "mystery" of actively discovering exhilaration alongside terror in a constantly defamiliarising landscape: perhaps the most distinctively and courageously Irish response of them all."[12]

Mystery, terror and an unfamiliar landscape may have seemed a typically Irish concoction to English travellers in the eighteenth century, but in the twenty first? The play's obvious continuities with an aesthetic of the urban underclass grit à la Irvine Welsh or the audacity of In-Yer-Face, are ignored in favour of an

---

[10] David Edgar, *State of Play: Playwrights on Playwriting* (London: Faber and Faber, 1999).

[11] David Ian Rabey, *English Drama Since 1940* (London: Longman, 2003) 147.

[12] Rabey, *English Drama Since 1940*, 165.

ambivalent truism. Conversely, Rabey is more sensitive in his treatment of Scottish theatre, discussing work by C.P. Taylor, Liz Lochead, Tom McGrath and Jimmy Boyle as an integral part of the arena of 1980s drama in Britain.

Dominic Shellard's informative *British Theatre since the War* (1999) deals with Scottish theatre briefly over three pages. Shellard surveys the development of theatre in Scotland from the founding of the Citizens' Theatre in Glasgow in 1943 and the establishment of the Traverse Theatre Club in Edinburgh in 1963, to the vital role of the Edinburgh Festival. Yet while the "vibrancy and eclecticism" of post war Scottish drama is asserted, the brevity of the section devoted to it tends to undermine claims to its significance in relation to drama south of the border.[13] Finally, as Randall Stevenson points out, Shellard's concluding suggestion that a book on post war Scottish theatre ought to be written implies that no such text exists.[14]

In contrast to such surveys of British/English drama, critical work on Scottish and Irish theatre rarely, if unsurprisingly, addresses the role or influence of English theatre. Irish theatre criticism has tended largely to explore relations between drama and Irish identity, especially since the national literary revival at the turn of the nineteenth century. Similarly, Scottish theatre criticism, as Stevenson notes, has been occupied with concerns that exclude English theatre, be they a focus on Scottish identity and history, or an interest in the influence of continental theatre on Scottish writers and practitioners.[15]

Divergent Histories

The notion that the mid-1950s was a pivotal period in the shaping of drama in Britain is commonplace to many accounts

---

[13] Dominic Shellard, *British Theatre Since the War* (New Haven and London: Yale University Press, 2000) 174-177. Hardback edition published in 1999.

[14] Randall Stevenson, "Home International: The Compass of Scottish Theatre Criticism," *International Journal of Scottish Theatre* 2.2 (2001) (online).

[15] Stevenson, "Home International," (online).

of modern British theatre.[16] Exceptionally, Ronald Hayman in *British Theatre since 1955: A Reassessment* (1979) provides an early querying of the achievements of the writers of the era, and recently dissenting opinions have been expressed in Stephen Lacey's *British Realist Theatre: The New Wave in its Context 1956-1965* (1995) and most forcefully in Dan Rebellato's *1956 and All That* (1999).[17] Nevertheless, David Edgar's approach in his introduction to *State of Play* is representative, when he claims that,

> from 1956 certainly until the late 1980s there have been wave upon wave of playwrights self-consciously addressing the social, political and cultural state of the nation in conversation with each other, and with those who followed and preceded them.[18]

In particular, discourses of power and empowerment, be they social, racial or sexual, have played critical roles throughout this period. Edgar describes how, "the first wave of 1956 playwrights [...] confronted the consequences of working-class empowerment." The second wave explored "the limits of social democracy and the welfare state," while those who followed in the 1970s and 1980s were involved increasingly with "questions of difference and identity."[19] Such compartmentalisation of course risks being more tidy than accurate, though in fairness it pinpoints a number of important and recurrent concerns. As Rebellato points out, the myth of 1956 as a moment of radical rupture with the past needs to be critiqued in light of not only

---

[16] See for example: John Elsom, *Post-War British Theatre* (1979), Christopher Innes, *Modern British Drama 1890-1990* (1992), Richard Eyre and Nicholas Wright, *Changing Stages: A View of British Theatre in the Twentieth Century* (2000) or Dominic Shellard, *British Theatre Since the War* (2000).

[17] See also Mary Luckhurst, "Contemporary English Theatre: Why Realism?" *(Dis)Continuities Trends and Traditions in Contemporary Theatre and Drama in English*, CDE 9, eds. Margarete Rubik and Elke Mettinger-Schartmann. (Trier: Wissenschaftlicher Verlag Trier, 2002) 73-84.

[18] Edgar, *State of Play*, 5.

[19] Edgar, *State of Play*, 5.

the theatre of the 1940s and early 1950s, but also in terms of the attitudes propagated by the New Wave—especially anxieties regarding theatricality, the perceived elitist intellectualism of continental theatre and homosexuality. Subsequently, it might be argued that in some critical respects the New Wave drama of 1956 marked a disavowal of particular discourses in favour of others. It is a point I will return to in my analysis of the plays of Sarah Kane, but is also one that bears implications for commentary on 1990s drama generally. Significantly the radicalism of "kitchen sink" drama, with its privileging of realistic lower class settings and speech patterns, fails to resonate in contexts where realism of this sort was already the dominant style as was the case in Scotland.[20] Thus, the narrative of the 1956 New Wave of British drama also fails to account for the situation beyond the confines of the south of England.

More immediately pertinent here are the two decades preceding the 1990s, since the theatre of these decades in both the UK and Ireland is often used as a yardstick with which to measure the accomplishments of the newcomers. In the UK, theatre benefited greatly from State subsidy from the mid-1960s to the mid-1970s. A second wave of new playwrights in England and a renaissance of Scottish drama[21] ensued, the overriding tone of which was radical and socially committed. Rabey describes the late 1970s and early 1980s as a period of "political polarisation."[22] To claim that British national identity at this time was under strain verges on understatement. The eruption of violence in Northern Ireland, the Scottish bid for Home Rule, industrial strife and race conflict, are but a few of the political co-ordinates of the era. Such a charged atmosphere

---

[20] See Stevenson, "Home International," and "Border Warranty: John McGrath and Scotland," *International Journal of Scottish Theatre* 3.3 (2002) (online). Comparable, though not identical, is Irish theatre's focus throughout the first half of the twentieth century on realistic county kitchen settings.

[21] See Bill Findlay ed., *A History of Scottish Theatre* (Edinburgh: Polygon, 1998) and Randall Stevenson and Gavin Wallace eds., *Scottish Theatre Since the Seventies* (Edinburgh: Edinburgh University Press, 1996).

[22] Rabey, *English Drama Since 1940*, 107.

gave rise to a raft of agit-prop performance groups (of which John McGrath's Scottish branch of the 7:84 Theatre Company is amongst the best known and longest surviving), and an ongoing interest in social themes among a post-1968 generation of dramatists like David Hare, Howard Brenton, Peter Flannery, David Edgar or Pam Gems.[23]

These energies notwithstanding, the most momentous socio-political factor since the late 1970s has been Thatcherite social and cultural policy and its aftermath. Adhering to an ideology of self-sufficiency and individualism, the Conservative government cut subsidies in an attempt to force theatres to fit the mould of the market. In contrast to the preceding years of extensive state subsidy, theatre was to become a product whose success, as Arts Minister Richard Luce stated in 1987, could be measured (like so much else in capitalist consumer society) only in terms of "whether or not [it] can attract enough customers."[24] Such commodification of culture (expressed by Luce in blunt monetarist fashion) has been interpreted as the outcome of earlier, apparently progressive, debates "rejecting the distinction between high art and popular art," and linked with the view that in the post-war period, the avant garde has been extinguished by the development of mass, market-led culture, which has ghettoised traditional high culture. The attacks on convention and "the patrician" of the 1960s led to the celebration of popular and commercial culture, and its academic legitimisation, in the 1970s. In turn this paved the way for the downgrading of culture in general to the lowest

---

[23] Critically the modalities of political drama have been a hub of scholarly interest in a British context. One of the leading commentators in this regard is John Bull. See *New British Political Dramatists* (1984) and *Stage Right: Crisis and Recovery in British Mainstream Drama* (1994). Most recently Rebecca D'Monté and Graham Saunders have edited *Cool Britannia: British Political Drama in the 1990s* (forthcoming in 2007).

[24] Cited in Shellard, *British Theatre Since the War*, 189.

common denominator designated by populist consumer preference.[25]

The crisis of funding in the 1980s had a distinct, tangible effect and this has been a consistent feature in many commentaries on modern British theatre.[26] Mainstream theatre underwent an unprecedented popularisation and commercialisation resulting largely in a turn to the safer financial prospects offered by adaptations of classics, Shakespeare and musicals. New work by unknown playwrights was viewed as a risk many theatres were reluctant to take. Doubtless, one might point to innovative and challenging plays by, for instance, Caryl Churchill, Howard Brenton, Howard Barker or Timberlake Wertenbaker, but some of the most renowned theatre of the 1980s arguably was produced by Andrew Lloyd Webber. Big budget musicals, created in London rather than in the USA as had been the case decades previously, of the order of *Cats*, *Phantom of the Opera* or *Les Misérables* were, as theatre historian Dominic Shellard notes, "the single most noticeable feature of the West End in the eighties."[27]

By contrast, theatre in Ireland has been extensively dominated by the discourse of national identity, originating in the late nineteenth century, and sustained by theatre practitioners, playwrights, critics and academia. From its foundation in 1904 the Irish Literary Theatre, later to become the Abbey Theatre, aimed to be a national theatre and propagated particular representations of Irish identity in opposition to a perceived, colonising English one. Lionel Pilkington has critiqued the notion that theatre in Ireland began with the Irish Literary Theatre and points to the healthy theatre

---

[25] Edgar, *State of Play*, 16-18. Edgar cites Eric Hobsbawn's *The Age of Extremes* regarding the eclipse of the avant garde.

[26] See for instance Elsom, Shellard, Eyre and Wright, as well as Vera Gottlieb and Colin Chambers eds., *Theatre in a Cool Climate* (Oxford: Amber Lane, 1999).

[27] Shellard, *British Theatre Since the War*, 190.

scene which pre-existed it.[28] Similarly, Chris Morash's *A History of Irish Theatre 1601-2000* (2002)[29] suggests a considerable expansion of the usual historical framework. In addition, the establishment of the Gate Theatre in 1928 provided the National Theatre with early competition, and in recent years, competition from other venues and companies has intensified. Nevertheless, the Abbey's status as keystone in the edifice of modern Irish drama and its continued influence cannot be denied.

The sense of continuity of debate surrounding national identity has been reinforced and prolonged by a number of factors including, among others: the size of the population and its insularity or apparent homogeneity; the steady stream of emigrants to Britain and America (which has tended to feed both nostalgic identification with, or extreme rejection of, a "motherland"); a largely agriculturally-based, rather than industrial, economy; and the often neglected cultural repercussions of the country's neutrality during the Second World War. Consequently, despite the fact that in the late 1950s and 1960s Irish theatre regained an energy absent in the previous decades thanks to the emergence of a number of dynamic playwrights, the 1950s do not bear the same resonance of revolt and cultural realignment as they did in Britain. The heritage of strict Catholicism, censorship, close Church State relations, and a frequently weak economy, in combination have meant that the politics of the welfare state, of race and racism, or of the class system (with a few rare and notable exceptions such as Sean O'Casey or, latterly, Dermot Bolger) have not been the focus of Irish theatre until more recently.

The waves of development in modern Irish theatre have, therefore, been identified as incorporating three stages: the

---

[28] Lionel Pilkington, "Theatre History and the Beginnings of the Irish National Theatre Project," *Theatre Stuff: Critical Essays on Contemporary Irish Theatre*, ed. Eamonn Jordan (Dublin: Carysfort, 2000) 27-33.

[29] Chris Morash, *A History of Irish Theatre 1601-2000* (Cambridge: Cambridge University Press, 2002).

revival period, which concluded in the 1920s, an interim period of "decline and decadence" followed by a second revival beginning gradually in the late 1950s which tapered off in the late 1980s. The third stage is the present period.[30] As opposed to some of the more experimental tendencies of Scottish or English theatre, as Anna McMullan describes:

> what is striking about the Irish theatre tradition of the last hundred years, *as it is usually perceived*, is its almost total reliance on text, and its avoidance or insulation from the performative experiments of twentieth century theatre.[31]

Among the recurrent concerns of playwrights from the 1960s to the 1980s, themes of emigration, sexual identity, religious consciousness and politics have been salient.[32] Of especial importance was the foundation of the Field Day Theatre Company in 1980 (by Brian Friel and Stephen Rea) which ambitiously aimed to destabilise deadlocked national identities by exploring a "fifth province" that would be imaginary and imaginative, rather than literal or physical.[33]

These concerns correspond to deeply-rooted issues and problems in Irish society over that period, and the 1980s, in particular, witnessed much open conflict between conservative Catholic groups and those campaigning for a more liberal, secular state. While the Conservatives in Britain moved toward the dismantling of the "nanny state" through privatisation and

---

[30] Fintan O'Toole, "Irish Theatre: The State of the Art," *Theatre Stuff*, 48. See also "Play for Ireland," *Irish Times* 12 Feb. 2000 and "Second Opinion," *Irish Times* 21 Sept. 1994. O'Toole's schema follows a generally accepted one in Irish theatre criticism.

[31] Anna McMullan, "Reclaiming Performance: The Contemporary Irish Independent Theatre Sector," *The State of Play: Irish Theatre in the 'Nineties*, ed. Eberhard Bort (Trier: Wissenschaftlicher Verlag Trier, 1996) 30. Italics mine.

[32] Christopher Murray, *Twentieth Century Irish Drama: Mirror up to Nation* (Manchester: Manchester University Press, 1997) 162-186.

[33] The notion of the fifth province is summed up by Richard Kearney in "The Fifth Province: Between the Global and the Local," *Migrations: The Irish at Home and Abroad* (Dublin: Wolfhound, 1990) 109-122.

an attempt to reintroduce a version of discipline and family values, in Ireland conservatives also attempted to control and restrict some of the changing values and practices of the 1960s and 1970s. Conservative Catholic lobby groups successfully managed to have the Constitution modified with a strong anti-abortion clause, and convincingly defeated a referendum proposing the introduction of divorce legislation. Meanwhile the State sank further into economic downturn, with soaring levels of unemployment and emigration despite considerable subsidy from the E.E.C., and in Northern Ireland the hunger strikes of the early 1980s and ongoing violence delineated a bleak future for the province (a situation that the Field Day attempted to address and culturally influence for the better).

As in Britain, funding for theatre was meagre; however the trend towards commercialisation and populism was not so prominent. With the financial resources for huge musicals unavailable and other performing arts predominantly marginalised, the play and the playwright remained at the core of Irish theatre. In the 1980s Brian Friel produced three plays, the most important being *Translations* (1980); while other writers such as Tom Murphy, Stewart Parker, and new playwrights such as Frank McGuinness, Christina Reid and Dermot Bolger mapped an impressive terrain for contemporary drama. Superficially, one might remark upon a trend towards adaptation and the classics as in Britain, however the motivating forces in context are considerably different. Adaptation of and reference to Greek tragedy in Irish theatre took on a dimension of political protest or meditation upon colonisation.[34]

Critically, national identity is still a central concern and has, since the late 1980s, been reinvigorated by postcolonial theory. In contrast to the post-war and post-imperial dispersal and confusion of the issue of national identity in Britain and in

---

[34] For an argument to this effect see Marianne McDonald, "Classics as Celtic Firebrand: Greek Tragedy, Irish Playwrights, and Colonialism," *Theatre Stuff*, 16-26.

British theatre, Irish dramatists who have "contested dominant notions of national identity" have, until recently, tended to be "recuperated into a modified but still overarching sense of 'national identity'" regardless.[35] By the end of the twentieth century, however, such an identity seemed a good deal more complicated and less predictable.

Continuities & Transformations: The 1990s
The question, therefore, is what marked the 1990s as period of significant change for theatre? It is tempting to apply to the 1990s a narrative of rupture and reformulation similar to that usually applied to the mid-fifties. Yet, as Bernhard Reitz and Mark Berninger note in their introduction to *British Drama of the 1990s* (2002), statistics indicate a continuity of the commercialisation that reshaped British theatre in the 1980s. Moreover, with respect to certain established playwrights like David Hare, the early 1990s also initially saw the continuation of anti-Thatcher political drama.[36] However, Margaret Thatcher's resignation in 1990 flagged the end of an era.

Politically and socially, dramatic alterations took place that arguably presaged the entrenchment of a pervasive postmodernity in both the UK and Ireland. These alterations implicitly signalled the disintegration of a number of political and social metanarratives that, but a decade before had seemed unassailable. By the end of the decade New Labour had taken power in Britain and the Conservative party had fallen into serious decline, devolution had redrawn the map of British politics with the inauguration of the Scottish Parliament in 1999 and the National Assembly for Wales in 1999. Finally, in Northern Ireland tentative steps towards a lasting political settlement and peace had been taken. In Ireland the old moral majority had lost its grip, the right to divorce had been narrowly accepted by referendum and Church power had

---

35 McMullan, "Reclaiming Performance," 34.

36 Bernhard Reitz and Mark Berninger, Introduction, *British Drama of the 1990s* (Heidelberg: Univeritätsverlag C. Winter, 2002) 7-11.

effectively disintegrated in a miasma of scandals. The Celtic Tiger economy brought the materialist fervour the UK had tasted in the 1980s and catapulted the Irish into a new set of dilemmas, in particular concerning immigration, human rights and the framing of a just, equitable society. The reasons behind the rapid growth of the Irish economy are well beyond the scope of this work, what is important however, is the fact that Ireland became, as Fintan O'Toole puts it, an "icon of the globalisation process"[37] apparently overnight, and was radically and irrevocably altered in little more than a decade.

In an attempt to connect these events and their implicit impact on theatre, Eamonn Jordan notes in the introduction to *Theatre Stuff: Critical Essays on Contemporary Irish Theatre* (2000):

> Under liberal capitalism, benign democracy is the defining feature. As such the ritualism of difference at the heart of theatre, seen within the realm of defiance, courage, heroic gesture, has in some ways fallen flat. Akin to this is the manner in which, at least within first world countries victimisation has in many ways begun to lose its status, in every sense of the word. Anti-Government protest plays, which were the staple of post-war British drama, have, for the moment, had their day. In a crude sense, New Labour, under Tony Blair's leadership, has led indirectly to the absence of precisely demarcated alternative politics, the dilution of oppositions and the unsatisfying postmodern concept of substitution rather than an older concept of difference.[38]

Reitz and Berninger make very similar observations, though they note how plays like Howard Brenton's *Snogging Ken* (2000) and Alistair Beaton's *Feelgood* (2001) found their political target in the practices of the New Labour regime,[39] a mere three to four years after Blair's landslide victory. Certainly since then

---

[37] O'Toole, "Irish Culture in a Globalised World," *Kaleidoscopic Views of Ireland* eds. Munira H. Mutran and Laura P.Z. Izarra (São Paulo: Universidade de São Paulo, 2003) 76.

[38] Jordan, Introduction, *Theatre Stuff*, xlvii.

[39] Reitz and Berninger, Introduction, *British Drama of the 1990s*, 12.

there has been a resurgence of political theatre of various types, as is insightfully discussed by Klaus Peter Müller in an essay in *British Drama of the 1990s*.[40] Nevertheless, throughout the decade a drift away from certain familiar metanarratives, towards more heterogeneous and contradictory political perspectives, dispersed structures of power and unstable, performative identities was definitely observable. The transformation in the theatre of the 1990s reflected these changes.

The early 1990s saw some significant new work by established playwrights—Brian Friel's *Dancing at Lughnasa*, Harold Pinter's *Party Time* and *Mountain Language*, Tom Stoppard's *Arcadia*, Caryl Churchill's *Mad Forest* and *The Skryker*, David Hare's *The Absence of War* trilogy, Frank McGuinness's *Someone Who'll Watch Over Me*—but a sea change occurred in the middle of the decade with the emergence of a new generation of writers. In addition to Martin Crimp and Marie Jones, who though influential are of an earlier generation,[41] new writers such as Gregory Burke, Jez Butterworth, Marina Carr, David Greig, Nick Grosso, David Harrower, Sarah Kane, Patrick Marber, Martin McDonagh, Conor McPherson, Anthony Neilson, Mark O'Rowe, Mark Ravenhill, Judy Upton and Enda Walsh all contributed to a re-energising of the medium.

Some points of convergence over this period for theatre in Ireland and in the UK are worth noting at the outset. As Patrick Lonergan remarks, in an essay reflecting upon the effects of globalisation on Irish theatre, the "relationships between writers, theatres and nations are changing throughout the

---

[40] Klaus-Peter Müller, "Political Plays in England in the 1990s," *British Drama of the 1990s*, 15-36.

[41] Martin Crimp's impact upon many of the new playwrights of the decade is extensive though critical attention to his work is just beginning to accumulate. Aleks Sierz's *The Theatre of Martin Crimp* (London: Methuen, 2007, forthcoming) represents the first major study of his work.

world."[42] One important dimension to this is the effective deterritorialisation that is to be seen in the traffic of playwrights and plays between Dublin, Edinburgh and London and, perhaps even more importantly, the rapid flow of plays from the UK and Ireland, in translation, throughout Europe. An outstanding example was the debut of a young English playwright of Irish parentage, Martin McDonagh, who has been claimed as part of both the English and Irish theatre. However, one might also note the ways in which Sarah Kane's and David Greig's work has become an international interest, how Conor McPherson has chosen to launch his plays more often before London audiences rather than in Ireland, how playwrights like Mark Ravenhill or Enda Walsh have had a major following in Germany, how Marina Carr's plays have been produced in the Netherlands and the USA. London remains a dominant centre for new writing; nevertheless, the path to success need not lead solely to this particular centre. Trajectories like those opened up by director Garry Hynes, who discovered McDonagh and premiered the Leenane Trilogy in Galway at the Druid Theatre in co-operation with the Royal Court in London, suggest not a unidirectional movement of influence, but a complex network of interrelations. Indeed the question of theatre, its place and its role has been innovatively addressed by the new National Theatre of Scotland which in an attempt to engage with all of Scotland (and not just the cities of the south) is multi-locational. Hence, the NTS opened in February 2006 with *HOME*, a set of ten site-specific productions in ten locations across the country.

Deterritorialisation may also be perceived at the more abstract level of cultural values and experiences. In many respects the gaps in certain cultural tendencies seem to be narrowing as a result not only of a mutual language, but also of shared popular culture, media and the spread of consumer culture. In the last decade this process, for some of the reasons

---

[42] Patrick Lonergan, "Globalization and Irish Theatre," Critical Interventions Series, Irish Writers Centre 2002 <http://www.writerscentre.ie/anthology/plonergan.html>.

described above, has visibly intensified. If it can be argued that late 1990s theatre in Ireland or Scotland has a different tone and focus to that in England, much too is shared.

A number of attempts have been made to sum up these developments in terms of a predominant theme or set of formal concerns. These provide some noteworthy insights into the nature of 1990s drama that must be acknowledged. David Edgar has argued that the upsurge in new writing since 1992 has been enabled by a number of factors which include, the influence of Tony Kushner's *Angels in America* and David Mamet's *Oleanna*; the ongoing success of playwrights like David Hare and Caryl Churchill; the self-help movement among writers; and, ultimately, the fact that writers found a subject—that of masculinity in the modern world.[43] More generally David Ian Rabey sees the drama of the decade as "collectively characterised by a more widespread emphasis on challenging physical and verbal immediacy, and bleak (arguably nihilistic) observations of social decay, severed isolation and degradation into aimlessness."[44] In contrast, Aleks Sierz has claimed what defines the new writing of the 1990s are its visceral tactics of provocation to convey a modern social critique.[45] The writers who typified Sierz's "new wave" were credited with producing a "theatre of sensation" which was "experiential not speculative" and which

> question[ed] moral norms, […] affront[ed] the ruling ideas of what can or should be shown onstage [and] also tap[ped] into more primitive feelings, smashing taboos, mentioning the forbidden, creating discomfort.[46]

---

[43] Edgar, *State of Play*, 26-27.

[44] Rabey, *English Drama Since 1940*, 192.

[45] See Aleks Sierz, *In-Yer-Face Theatre: British Drama Today* (London: Faber and Faber, 2001) chapter 1.

[46] Sierz, *In-Yer-Face Theatre*, 4.

As he notes, the period has been vividly characterised by a loss of belief in political correctness.[47] Certainly, some more "traditional" themes seem to have been submerged. Yet, political concerns are far from absent; rather they are implicit to the web of issues the work incorporates.[48] Though other labels proliferated: Cool Britannia, the Britpack, the New Brutalists and in Europe, Cool Theatre, none has had quite the impact of In-Yer-Face. Predictably enough, after an initial plethora of rhetorical flourishes, the waves of provocative new work have calmed—already at a theatre conference in Bristol in 2002, Sierz declared the In-Yer-Face theatre movement to have ended. *In-Yer-Face Theatre* is undoubtedly a vibrant and useful account of a particular phenomenon and, especially, of plays as they first were performed and received, but it is quite narrowly focused on a London theatre context and necessarily excludes writers for whom viscerality was not the determining quality.

Perhaps the most immediately apprehensible aspect of the new writing for theatre has been its vigorous marketing, especially in Britain (particularly by the Royal Court and the Bush Theatre) and a brazen trend toward labelling, which may be seen as symptomatic of pervasive trends in a developed consumer society and of a suspect postmodernity. It is hardly surprising, therefore, that this new "golden age" of theatre has its sceptics. Vera Gottlieb, in *Theatre in a Cool Climate* (1999), criticises 1990s drama in Britain for being merely a by-product of mass media, and for having "given up any attempt to engage with significant public issues."[49] She questions "whether anything new *has* happened—and if so, how significant."[50] Most importantly, she asserts that,

> all these writers are very much in touch with the malaise amongst their generation, all too aware of consumerism, but in

---

47 Sierz, *In-Yer-Face Theatre*, 39.
48 See Müller, "Political Plays in England in the 1990s."
49 Gottlieb, "Lukewarm Britannia," 212.
50 Gottlieb, "Lukewarm Britannia," 209.

effect the plays end up as "products": the "themes" of consumerism, drug culture and sexuality paralyse the plays.[51]

Similarly, Peter Ansorge, former Head of Drama at Channel 4, questions the "artistic confinement" and "small-scale" vision of much new playwriting which in his view "consists of small-cast pieces of social observation with little narrative and even less to say."[52] Speaking expressly of contemporary Irish theatre, Fintan O'Toole asserts that the prevailing tendency is "towards a dramatisation of the fragments rather than […] the whole society," and that this development is accompanied by a loss of suspense and tension. The metanarrative that apparently once was Ireland is no longer one, but a multiplicity of isolated parts which are incommensurable, a diagnosis that might equally apply to the UK. What has occurred, in O'Toole's view, is the replacement (in the Irish context) of a drama of conflict with drama of evocation.[53] More specifically still, critics like Victor Merriman condemn both the work of Martin McDonagh and Marina Carr as a celebration of a "spurious post-coloniality" which counter-productively serves to "negate the interrogation of conditions in which such images are produced and have their points of reference."[54] The implication in all these comments is that post-1980s theatre has lost direction or, more precisely, is less overtly concerned with probing material that is recognisably political or orientated towards questions of national identity. It is especially prescient that disorientation (and in particular disorientation as the result of media "interference"), long a central characteristic of postmodernism and postmodernity, emerges as a motif in the critical discourse surrounding the new dramatic writing of the 1990s. It is undoubtedly indicative of critical discontent, even anxiety, with

---

[51] Gottlieb, "Lukewarm Britannia," 212.

[52] Peter Ansorge, "Really a Golden Age?" *State of Play*, 39, 28.

[53] O'Toole, "Irish Theatre: The State of the Art," 54.

[54] Victor Merriman, "Decolonisation Postponed: The Theatre of Tiger Trash," *Irish University Review*, 29.2 (1999): 305, 317.

the perceived waning of a genre of political play (in tandem with the blurring of political agendas) and suspicion that the new drama is politically deficient, or, more precisely, ideologically regressive. Nevertheless, as will emerge in the following chapters, disorientation can operate productively and provocatively, at a thematic level and as a formal strategy with critical import.

Un/usual Suspects

In attempting to reconsider the new wave of theatre writing in the 1990s it is not my intention to debate the genealogy presented by Sierz, so much as to look at this generation of playwrights from an angle which removes the requirement for them to be In-Yer-Face or of a particular nationality. Following the work of Stephen Watt (*Postmodern/Drama* [1998]), I am interested in exploring the work of a selection of playwrights in terms of the "broader 'intertexts' of contemporary culture."[55] These intertexts, discussed below and via close analysis of specific plays, comprise dramatic heritages, theoretical texts and political events and attitudes. The playwrights discussed below are both well-known and, I would argue, have been pivotal figures in text-based theatre since the mid-1990s, although they are rarely, if ever, considered in the configuration presented here. Each has a pronounced and contrasting aesthetic and dramaturgy. As well as featuring prominently in theatre in the UK and Ireland, each has had plays produced internationally in a variety of languages and their plays continue to be produced and translated. Moreover, their work has to date generated significant critical debate. Already, monographs have been published on Sarah Kane and Conor McPherson respectively.[56] Collections of critical essays on Marina Carr's and Martin McDonagh's work have already

---

[55] Watt, *Postmodern/Drama*, 6.

[56] Graham Saunders, *"Love Me or Kill Me"*: *Sarah Kane and the Theatre of Extremes* (Manchester: Manchester University Press, 2002) and Gerald C. Wood, *Conor McPherson: Imagining Mischief* (Dublin: Liffey, 2003).

appeared,[57] while Mark Ravenhill and David Greig have been the subjects of frequent essays and articles. These playwrights constitute neither a hermetic canon nor a movement; they represent, on the contrary, a dissonant assembly of practitioners of contemporary drama whose work embodies, in particularly vivid ways, its contradictory and complementary tendencies. Certain points of contiguity emerge nonetheless: stories, storytelling and questions of value surface in McPherson, Ravenhill, Carr and Greig; trauma and extreme emotional states are explored by Kane, Carr and with a differing inflection by Greig; seams of ironic social commentary run through McDonagh and Ravenhill; while questions of authenticity and strategies of legitimation are raised by McDonagh, McPherson, Carr and Greig. Discussion of their work here is orientated around narrative and citational practices and, more broadly, questions of identity in a contemporary context. These elements interlock and interact in various ways and their patterns, I suggest, trace a number of significant tendencies in, what Drew Milne has called, the "democratic plurality"[58] of the new drama of the 1990s.

Narrative, Identity, Citation
Scholarship on the subject of narrative and narratology constitutes a vast territory.[59] To account for it is not my

---

57 Cathy Leeney and Anna McMullan eds., *The Theatre of Marina Carr: "Before Rules was Made"* (Dublin: Carysfort, 2003) and Lilian Chambers and Eamonn Jordan eds., *The Theatre of Martin McDonagh: A World of Savage Stories* (Dublin: Carysfort, 2006).

58 Drew Milne, "The Anxiety of Print: Recent Fashions in British Drama," *Crucible of Cultures: Anglophone Drama at the Dawn of a New Millennium*, eds. Marc Maufort and Franca Bellarsi (Brussels: Peter Lang, 2002) 37.

59 J. Hillis Miller remarks upon the tremendous array of theories of narrative, among which he lists Russian formalist, New Critical, Chicago school, or neo-Aristotelian, psychoanalytic, hermeneutic and phenomenological, structuralist, semiotic, tropological, Marxist, sociological, reader-response, poststructuralist and deconstructive approaches. See Miller, "Narrative," *Critical Terms for Literary Study*, ed. Frank Lentricchia and Thomas McLaughlin (Chicago: University of Chicago Press, 1990) 67.

intention and would not necessarily facilitate an understanding of the modalities of narrative pertinent to theatre, so the demarcation of narrative here is purposely selective, focusing first on some basic features of narrative structure and narrative function which may assist a broader consideration of citation, identity, intertextuality and performativity.

Though structural analysis of narrative is laden with competing terminologies the typical properties of narrative are readily identifiable. As Paul Sheehan states in *Modernism, Narrative and Humanism* (2002):

> Narrative, the process of storymaking and storytelling, is language arranged meaningfully over time. The interrelation of time, meaning and language is a complex one. Duration is bound up with *seriality*, with the organising principles of the temporal; it is temporal succession that transforms a group of events into a story. The "meaning" emitted by a group of events lies in their *causal connection*. Events are joined in series, by a process of *mutual implication* […]. Plot imposes a meaning on the events through an *immanent structure*, that though revealed at the end, has been present all along.[60]

While Martin Esslin generously describes drama as "narrative made visible,"[61] notably the framework in which narrative has been theorised and analysed has most frequently been that of literary fiction, oral culture and folktales, rather than drama or theatre. The question arises—is it appropriate or accurate to refer to narrative in theatre at all? The increasing significance of acts of narration that are frequently self-conscious and self-reflexive in post-Brechtian theatre suggests this is a field warranting investigation, as the work of many scholars has shown. Nevertheless as Pavis notes, since traditionally theatre has been "associated by critics with mimēsis (imitation of an

---

[60] Paul Sheehan, *Modernism, Narrative and Humanism* (Cambridge: Cambridge University Press, 2002) 9.

[61] Martin Esslin, *The Field of Drama* (London: Methuen, 1987) 36.

action) rather than with diegesis (narration by a narrator),"[62] narrative theory has tended to disregard it. A vivid example is to be found in the opening pages of Robert Scholes and Robert Kellogg's *The Nature of Narrative* (1966) where they state:

> by narrative we mean all those literary works which are distinguished by two characteristics: the presence of a story and a story-teller. A drama is a story without a story-teller; in it characters act out directly what Aristotle called an 'imitation' of such action as we find in life.[63]

Evidently while this restriction suits the authors' purpose in exploring the novel, it occludes the role of narrative in drama, or theatre's potential as a means and a site of the circulation of narratives, the shaping and reshaping of how stories are told. It furthermore indicates a limited notion of theatre as fundamentally mimetic.

Alternatively, Marie MacLean (*Narrative as Performance* [1988]) sees "oral narrative [...] as the begetter of [...] written narrative and staged drama" both of which are forms of "narrative performance."[64] The recognition of the performative qualities of narrative seems particularly appropriate with regard to recent theatre. One of the recurrent features of the contemporary drama treated here is that it frequently incorporates not only storytelling figures, but also self-conscious commentary on the practice and forms of storytelling, so an attentiveness to narration, its problems and its functions, is built into the plays' form and content.

McLean identifies "three complementary waves of narrative poetics" that concern primarily literary narrative: those that have explored narrative structure; those that examined

---

[62] Patrice Pavis, *Dictionary of the Theatre: Terms, Concepts and Analysis*, trans. Christine Schantz (1996; Toronto and Buffalo: University of Toronto Press, 1998) 231.

[63] Robert Scholes and Robert Kellogg, *The Nature of Narrative* (Oxford: Oxford University Press, 1966) 4.

[64] Marie MacLean, *Narrative as Performance* (New York: Routledge, 1988) 8.

narrative authority, that is "textual strategies and the relation between the teller and the telling;" and those that focus upon narrative interaction, "the relationship between teller and hearer or between *énonciation* and interpretation."[65] Preserving the terminology of Emile Benveniste, MacLean pays particular attention to "the *énonciation* of the written text and the dramatic text" arguing that, for the dramatic text, the process is always subject to doubleness. At one level the dramatic text is "reduced to a state of almost pure *énoncé*," the usual layers of explanatory material offered in a novel are absent. The reader must therefore "produce a private performance"[66] of the material in a manner less conditioned by narratorial intervention or guidance than, for instance, in the case of the reader of fiction. This view is remarkably close to what by now constitutes a truism of theatre semiotics. As Anne Ubersfeld has argued "the dramatic text is *troué*, marked with 'holes,' which in performance are filled by another text, that of the staging, the *mise en scène*."[67] This other text, the performance text, is produced by directors, actors, set designers, the theatre space and sometimes, though not always, also the author. Keir Elam sums up this relation as follows: "the dramatic text is radically conditioned by its performability [...] the written text/performance text relationship is not one of simple priority but a complex of reciprocal constraints constituting a powerful *intertextuality*. Each text bears the other's traces."[68] The final product, which is evidently subject to transformation with each performance, is a fusion of both layers.

In a more basic sense, narrative performances have some well established functions in drama. Pavis describes how classical dramaturgy regularly used narrative to report on actions that could not be staged "for reasons of decorum or

---

[65] MacLean, *Narrative as Performance*, 14.

[66] MacLean, *Narrative as Performance*, 10.

[67] See Marvin Carlson, *Theories of the Theatre* (1984; Ithaca: Cornell UP, 1993) 98.

[68] Keir Elam, *The Semiotics of Theatre and Drama* (1980; London and New York: Routledge, 2002) 191.

verisimilitude or because of technical difficulties." The effects of this are multiple: narrative may function as a streamlining device, it may facilitate narratorial commentary (modalisation) on the reported action, or it may serve, as in Brechtian theatre, as a distancing technique.[69] Implicit to the latter effects, as MacLean notes, is a potentially self-reflexive dimension, at the level of dialogue, of "performance within a performance. This is particularly clearly marked when one of the actors tells another a story. In this way, a microcosm of the narrative performance is produced within the dialogue itself."[70] A second aspect is that of "embedding," which MacLean takes from Tzvetvan Todorov's *The Poetics of Prose* (1977). Embedding involves the incorporation of "static scenes or tableaux" that function as a "frozen moment within a sequence" in order to heighten the significance of the moment. This "internalised spectacle" acts as a *mise en abyme* in which the text comments upon itself. In drama "embedded narratives" are commonly introduced by the figures of messengers, a stage narrator or onstage commentator, or by a chorus.[71] The self-conscious dimension to the use of narrative in theatre is articulated by Brecht in his definition of epic form. Epic theatre challenges dramatic form by disrupting mimēsis and short circuiting tension in various ways. While aspects of epic theatre predate Brecht's popularisation of the term, undoubtedly its heritage in anti-mimetic forms of contemporary theatre and performance is considerable.

Attitudes to the role of narrative in culture may broadly be said to reflect attitudes towards human consciousness. Thus, unsurprisingly, the emplotment of events as narrative is widely understood as a fundamentally human phenomenon.[72] Hayden White memorably asserts that "to raise the question of the

---

69 Pavis, *Dictionary of the Theatre*, 230.
70 MacLean, *Narrative as Performance*, 12.
71 MacLean, *Narrative as Performance*, 12-13.
72 In addition to Miller and Sheehan cited above, see for example Peter Brooks, *Reading for the Plot* (Cambridge, Mass.: Harvard University Press, 1984); Frank Kermode, *The Sense of an Ending* (New York: Oxford University Press, 1967).

nature of narrative is to invite reflection on the very nature of culture and, possibly, even on the nature of humanity itself."[73] As such, it is always already imbricated with questions of identity in a number of ways. So for instance, Miller in his interrogation of narrative looks not to what narrative is, but why it is so ubiquitous, why we appear to need the "same" story repeatedly, and finally, why this need is never fully satisfied. In attempting to answer these questions, he first returns to Aristotle's *Poetics* and the cathartic function of tragic drama. He recalls how Aristotle asserts that mimēsis is pleasurable because it offers orderly, rhythmic forms and learning, for which man has an affinity.[74] Narrative, in this sense, plays an important role in revealing the nature of the world to the inquisitive reader/spectator. As Miller suggests, this revelatory model "presupposes that the world has a pre-existing order and that the business of fictions is in one way or another to imitate, copy, or represent accurately that order."[75] Clearly this assumption lies behind much criticism that asserts particular stories are valuable or valueless on the basis of their representational authenticity. Evidence of this perspective is to be found especially in criticism of literatures that are allegedly circumscribed or defined by identity politics or ideologies, be they national, ethnic, racial or gender in orientation. In the context of the present study such debates over "good" or "bad" representation are most in evidence in relation to the work of playwright Martin McDonagh and, to a lesser extent, to that of Marina Carr.

A contrasting view, also surveyed by Miller, is that narrative, in fact, creates rather than merely reveals. Here, evidently, a reconnection with issues of performance can be made. Narrative, it is argued, is central to the process of

---

[73] Hayden White, "The Value of Narrativity in the Representation of Reality," *On Narrative*, ed. W.J.T. Mitchell (Chicago and London: University of Chicago Press, 1980) 1.

[74] Miller, "Narrative," 67-69.

[75] Miller, "Narrative," 69.

imposing order on the world and rendering the randomness and ambiguity of personal experience less chaotic. As Peter Brooks avers, we live

> immersed in narrative, recounting and reassessing the meaning of our past actions, and anticipating the outcome of our future projects, situating ourselves at the intersection of several stories not yet completed.[76]

This dynamic, the resistance to formlessness and the attribution of meaning, MacLean describes—alluding to Erwin Schrödinger's concept—as "negentropy."[77] The presupposition in this case is that

> the world may not be ordered in itself or, at any rate, that the social and psychological function of fictions is what speech-act theorists call "performative." [...] A story [...] makes something happen in the real world: for example it can propose modes of selfhood or ways of behaving that are then imitated in the real world.[78]

The space of narrative is, therefore, not only generative of identities and cultural values, but a space from which they may be policed, to use Miller's vocabulary, and contested. A pertinent example here might be the role of the *Bildungsroman* as the propagator of a particular form of bourgeois humanism that involves a specific notion of identity in the world.[79]

Perhaps more immediately significant in its bringing together of narrative, repetition and theatre is Marvin Carlson's contention that "drama, more than any other literary form, seems to be associated in all cultures with the retelling again and again of stories that bear a particular religious, social, or

---

[76] Brooks, *Reading for the Plot*, 3.
[77] MacLean, *Narrative as Performance*, 2.
[78] Miller, "Narrative," *Critical Terms*, 69.
[79] Sheehan, *Modernism, Narrative and Humanism*, 2-6.

political significance for their public."[80] The contours of narrative and its relations with identity can be traced to drama's movement between poles of social concerns (exteriority) and psychical concerns (interiority), and the status and rendering of character. All of which, however, become complicated, even compromised, by postmodern perspectives that tend to reject conventional narrative structures and their associated values.

Iterability, Citation & "the Haunted Stage"
In *Citation and Modernity* (1993), Claudette Sartiliot examines what she calls the "eclipse of quotation" in its Enlightenment sense, and its relation to "the advent of modernity."[81] She claims that "for modernist and postmodernist writers, quotation represents a definite break with the tradition of the nineteenth century especially, as well as a means of questioning the nature of the literary text."[82] In reviewing Sartiliot's argument here, I want to draw attention to the ways in which citation and quotation might serve in the drama in focus here.

Counter to classical definitions and theories of quotation as illustration or as ornament, modernist and postmodernist approaches to citation obscure the boundaries between the "'main' discourse" and its intertexts to the extent that "the relationship between one text and another becomes a form of complicity."[83] Notably such complicity is ludic,

> the absence of quotation marks encourages and substantiates several ruses [...] the pretence of remembering by heart, the pretence of erudition, and its correlatives, a lack of memory and distortion.[84]

---

[80] Marvin Carlson, *The Haunted Stage: The Theatre as Memory Machine* (Ann Arbor: University of Michigan Press, 2001) 7.

[81] Claudette Sartiliot, *Citation and Modernity: Derrida, Joyce and Brecht* (Norman and London: University of Oklahoma Press, 1993) 20.

[82] Sartiliot, *Citation and Modernity*, 3.

[83] Sartiliot, *Citation and Modernity*, 4-5, 20.

[84] Sartiliot, *Citation and Modernity*, 21.

Tracing the meanings of citation and quotation as they have been defined by classical rhetoric and subsequent theories, Sartiliot highlights citation as a process of "making appear, offering as an example," but also as "present[ing] to scrutiny," and as appropriation. Similarly, she unpacks the valencies of quotation as "related to the concept and convention of number and measure," as reporting, and as "the transport [of discourse] from one realm to another."[85]

Movement and displacement obviously characterise practices of citation and quotation generally. Thus Sartiliot returns to Derrida's observation that "writing and citing, writing and grafting, are closely related," to contend that he "develops a *post*classical theory of quotation as dissemination based directly on the practices of modernist texts."[86] Central to this theory of dissemination is iterability—any sign or mark, spoken or written, must be repeatable or iterable even in the absence of the addresser or addressee, in order to be comprehensible, and this inherent quality involves a rupturing of intention and meaning. Moreover, iterability implies a break with the determining authority of context:

> every sign, linguistic or non-linguistic, spoken or written (in the usual sense of this opposition), as a small or large unity, can be *cited*, put between quotation marks; thereby it can break with every given context, and engender infinitely new contexts in an absolutely nonsaturable fashion. This does not suppose that the mark is valid outside its context, but on the contrary that there are only contexts without any centre of absolute anchoring.[87]

The practice of citation demonstrates this "law of iterability," but it is also linked to memory. For Derrida, citing is a process

85 Sartiliot, *Citation and Modernity*, 22, 23.
86 Sartiliot, *Citation and Modernity*, 24, 29.
87 Jacques Derrida, "Signature, Event, Context," *Margins of Philosophy*, trans. Alan Bass (1972; Chicago: University of Chicago Press, 1977) 320.

of encryption that affirms and invigorates the discourses cited.[88] Yet, as will be evident throughout this book, citation and its manifestations in postmodernity are frequently perceived as highly ambivalent and erosive of memory.

The relations between iterability, citation, memory and theatre form the basis of Marvin Carlson's exploration of theatre, *The Haunted Stage* (2001), as a "repository of cultural memory [...] subject to continual adjustment and modification as the memory is recalled in new circumstances and contexts." Specifically, he treats the ways in which theatre is "ghosted" by "the processes of recycling and recollection":

> the retelling of stories already told, the re-enactment of events already enacted, the re-experiencing of emotions already experienced, these are and have always been central concerns of theatre in all times and places, but closely allied to these concerns are the particular production dynamics of theatre: the stories it chooses to tell, the bodies and other physical materials it utilises to tell them, and the places in which they are told.[89]

Evidently this is a diverse and complex process of rejection and reinvention, as well as appropriation and re-enactment. Implicit is the perceived status of what is inherited. Pavis insightfully describes different attitudes to heritage, inheritance and memory with regard to bourgeois, socialist and postmodern positions. He argues that with "current 'post-Brechtian'" theatre "the relationship between heritage and tradition is a question no longer of bourgeois appropriation or socialist absorption, but of intertextual use of codes and conventions."[90]

With regard to the drama of the 1990s recycling, recollection and adjustment to changing cultural conditions is pronounced and pervasive. If, according to Barthes, "the text is a tissue of

---

[88] Sartiliot, *Citation and Modernity*, 30, for discussion of citation and memory see 153-56.

[89] Carlson, *The Haunted Stage*, 2, 3.

[90] Pavis, *Theatre at the Crossroads*, 64-65.

quotations drawn from innumerable centres of culture,"[91] then Carlson contends that the dramatic text, due to the way it recycles narratives and characters, among other elements, "seems particularly self-conscious of the [intertextual] process, particularly haunted by its predecessors."[92] This is perhaps most starkly revealed when playwrights adapt or rewrite mythic narratives, legends, or earlier dramatic texts as is the case with Mark Ravenhill's reworking of Faust and *The Importance of Being Earnest*, Sarah Kane's *Phaedra's Love*, Marina Carr's Medea play *By the Bog of Cats...* and her updating of Euripides's *Iphigenia at Aulis* in her play *Ariel*. However, multiple other subtle layers of citation might be noted in formal allusions, quotations and historical references as is the case in the work of Martin McDonagh Conor McPherson and David Greig.

In addition to the mechanics of iterability in the dramatic text, Carlson's discussion of the broad range of the modality of repetition in theatre deals with the ways in which actors' reputations, staging, sets, costumes, performance traditions, even the theatre building itself may also haunt a play and affect its meanings. He remarks upon the contrasting extremes with regard to recycling among theatre cultures, how in classic Japanese and Chinese theatre codification and repetition is a central feature, while in the West the kudos of innovation and originality has lead to attempts to avoid citation altogether.[93] Neither the former, in its endeavour to exactly repeat the original and thus deny dissemination of meaning, nor the latter, in its effort to forget its origins or influences, can entirely succeed if one adheres to a Derridian understanding of communication and citation. A shift in outlook, however, has arguably occurred. In distinction to "the classical search for the preservation of particular artistic models and traditions and

91 Roland Barthes, *Image, Text, Music*, trans. Stephen Heath (London: Fontana, 1977) 146.
92 Carlson, *The Haunted Stage*, 8.
93 Carlson, *The Haunted Stage*, 11.

[...] romanticism and realism's search for unique and individual insight and expression," Carlson maintains that postmodern drama and theatre "is almost obsessed with citation, with gestural, physical and textual material consciously recycled," but in a manner different from past usages because it is overt, self-conscious and often ironic.[94] Carlson's claim is a familiar enough one but since the whole notion of the postmodern is plagued with antonymic understandings of its status and effects, and it is this context that will, in closing, be addressed.

Postmodern Contexts?

As Hans Bertens rightly notes at the beginning of his history of the postmodern idea, "postmodernism" is an exasperatingly amorphous term which for all its apparent ubiquity seems to evade sufficient specificity.[95] Perceptive histories of the contradictory fortunes of the notion of the postmodern are offered by both Bertens and Thomas Docherty; to duplicate them would be laborious and unnecessary.[96] Notably conceptualisations of the postmodern, which have emerged in increasing numbers since the 1980s, regard it variously as a cultural phenomenon (the breakdown of distinctions between high and low cultural modes, proliferation of retro-styles eclectically blended, an "anti-aesthetic" and so on), an historical periodisation (dating from approximately the late 1950s, 1968 or, according to others, from the mid-1970s[97]), a *Zeitgeist* originating in particular material economic conditions (most often in the sense of a post-Fordist consumer society).

---

[94] Carlson, *The Haunted Stage*, 14.

[95] Hans Bertens, *The Idea of the Postmodern: A History* (London: Routledge, 1995).

[96] Thomas Docherty ed., *Postmodernism: A Reader* (New York: Harvester Wheatsheaf, 1993) is perhaps the most comprehensive anthology of texts that debate the postmodern. Docherty's introduction to the reader as a whole and to each of the eight sections on different aspects of the postmodern provides a detailed and lucid account of the history of the term and the philosophical questions involved.

[97] See Bertens, *The Idea of the Postmodern*, 169.

Philosophically, it is marked by the heritage of the Enlightenment, and its alleged rejections of the Enlightenment rationalism and the humanism that shapes the modern. Aesthetically, it has conversely been touted as liberatory (an avant garde rejection of the elitist confines of modernism) and as reactionary (a return to or, worse still, cannibalisation of tradition, an art that ignores the political); politically and economically it has been associated with globalisation and laissez-faire policies, the fracturing of political metanarratives into a plurality of interest groups in forms of exacerbated relativism, the bolstering of a consumer status quo, rampant commodification, the fragmenting of communities, the highly ambivalent politics of information ownership, access and dissemination.

How then to draw something meaningful from this morass of differing perspectives? The first step I would propose, following Docherty, Bertens, Ihab Hassan among others, is to make some distinction between the two principle elements of the postmodern: postmodernism and postmodernity. Postmodernity is taken here to refer to a context that includes and exceeds postmodernism, which involves consumerism, commodification and globalisation. In other words, postmodernity denotes a cluster of social, political and cultural vectors that pertain unevenly in the Western world. These include the impact of electronic media, mass migration, the instability of the field of politics as a result of the erosion of the macropolitics of nation-states and nationalisms, and, to quote Arjun Appadurai, the "global production of locality."[98]

---

[98] Arjun Appadurai, *Modernity at Large: Cultural Dimensions of Globalization* (Minneapolis: University of Minnesota Press, 1996) 188. While postmodernism is a term, for better or worse depending on one's perspective, has taken root in the cultural sphere, it must be noted that postmodernity is much less widely adopted in other disciplines. Sociology and anthropology both tend to preserve the term modernity, and more specifically late modernity or "radicalised modernity," to describe recent developments in commodification and aestheticisation of cultures. See for instance, Anthony Giddens, *The*

Within this domain, postmodernism is a cultural phenomenon that, as Bertens notes, has been characterised by different sets of practices in different media. In *A Poetics of Postmodernism* (1988), Linda Hutcheon attempts to sketch "a flexible conceptual structure which could at once constitute and contain postmodern culture and our discourses both about and adjacent to it."[99] She argues that postmodernism cannot be regarded as a new paradigm precisely because it "works within systems it attempts to subvert," neither can it be separated from the problematics of modernism, upon which it comments. In addition, she asserts that many of the most well-known commentators on the postmodern fail to define it against existing cultural practices, relying instead on generalisations and simplifications—in particular she singles out Terry Eagleton, Fredric Jameson and Jean Baudrillard. Throughout, Hutcheon emphasises postmodernism as a contradictory practice that does not pretend to exist outside the system it comments upon and contests, but "overtly acknowledges its complicity, only to work covertly to subvert the system's values from within." Hence it both inscribes as it interrogates—a situation she describes as a "postmodern paradox." Yet it is in this self-reflexive interrogative stance that she finds postmodernism's politics as it "work[s] to instruct us in the inadequacies of totalising systems and of fixed institutionalised boundaries (epistemological and ontological)." Postmodernism accordingly does not deny history or disregard politics, as has often been claimed, but rather problematises them through ironic intertextuality, recycling and parody. Hutcheon concludes with the proposition that a poetics of postmodernism is in effect a problematics, a recurring set of "consistently

Consequences of Modernity (Cambridge: Polity, 1990) 150. Cited in Bertens, *The Idea of the Postmodern*, 236, 241-2 and 246.

[99] Linda Hutcheon, *A Poetics of Postmodernism: History, Theory, Fiction* (London and New York: Routledge, 1988) ix.

problematised issues [...] historical knowledge, subjectivity, narrativity, reference, textuality, discursive context."[100]

There is, admittedly, an element of having one's cake and eating it in Hutcheon's argumentation in which the negative aspects of postmodernism are always neutralised by their opposites. Nevertheless, Hutcheon's poetics/problematics, I would argue, at least succeeds in identifying the perimeters and characteristics of postmodernism in relation to cultural (artistic, architectural, literary) practice with a good deal more balance than has been habitual in writings on postmodernism. Although she does not discuss theatre, the elaboration of a discursively constructed reality and the reclamation of the potency of parody are useful tools with which to approach the new theatre writing of the 1990s. The lack of engagement with theatre by critical theorising and the apparent lack of impact postmodern theory has had upon drama has recently been investigated by both Stephen Watt and Kerstin Schmidt and both do much to amend the deficiency they identify, primarily with regard to American theatre.[101]

If disagreement continues as to whether terms like postmodern theatre or postmodern drama are appropriate or of value,[102] it is clear from Carlson's comments cited above regarding the postmodern stage, in theatre postmodernism has accrued a set of connotations that usually encompass the following features, or variants thereof. An anxiety regarding narrative—this may manifest itself in the fragmentation of plot and story as in the case of "postdramatic theatre," or the practices of, say, the Wooster Group or Heiner Müller, or a hyper-production of stories, testimonies and so on, as in the work of performance artists like Karen Finley or Spalding Gray.

---

100 Hutcheon, *A Poetics of Postmodernism*, 4, 224, 231.
101 Kerstin Schmidt, *The Theater of Transformation: Postmodernism in American Drama* (Amsterdam and New York: Rodopi, 2005). Watt cited above.
102 See for instance, Pavis's *Theatre at the Crossroads* (1992) and *Dictionary of the Theatre* (1996), Lehmann's, *Postdramatic Theatre* (1999), Watt's *Postmodern/Drama* (1998) among others.

An obsessive, or foregrounded, citationality—as Carlson notes, this recycling and repetition is self-consciously, self-reflexively engaged in. The erosion, or attenuation, of character—Elinor Fuchs contends that this has been an ongoing part of anti-naturalist theatre since the symbolists, claiming that modernist drama "repeatedly introduces *as a humanistic problem* its own very questioning of the human image on stage." Fuchs rather controversially concludes that if any "clear watershed" exists "between modern and postmodern in drama, it is that the postmodern normalises and shrugs off as 'merely conceptual' the sense of terror (or novelty) associated with posthumanist thinking."[103]

The new drama of the 1990s in the UK and Ireland belies any notion of such a clear division. Certain aspects of the postmodern can be identified, but it seems clear that posthumanist ideas have not been as successfully normalised or universally accepted as Fuchs proposes. Rather, in the work of each of the playwrights included here, the modern and postmodern coexist in uneasy configurations.

---

[103] Elinor Fuchs, *The Death of Character: Perspectives on Theatre after Modernism* (Bloomington and Indiana: Indiana University Press, 1996) 35.

Conor McPherson
Solitary Micronarratives

I had my health. I had resolve. But most important. Over everything else. I had a story.[1]

Before *St. Nicholas* and *The Weir* had their premieres in London in 1997 (Bush Theatre, 19 February 1997 and Royal Court Theatre Upstairs, 4 July 1997 respectively), Conor McPherson was virtually unknown. As a student he had been involved with theatre and, while completing an M.A. in philosophy, he co-founded the Fly by Night Theatre Company which produced *Rum and Vodka* in several small venues in Dublin (University College Dublin 27 November 1992, City Arts Centre, 30 August 1994).[2] In 1994, *The Good Thief* (City Arts Centre, 18 April 1994) was produced and that same year he won the Stewart Parker Award. *This Lime Tree Bower* had its first performance at the Crypt Arts Centre in Dublin on 26 September 1995 and then opened at the Bush Theatre in London on 3 July 1996. Since 1997 however, McPherson's work has attracted considerable international recognition. *The Weir*, in particular, has been widely translated and performed; the production of the play at

---

[1] Conor McPherson, *St. Nicholas* in *The Weir and Other Plays* (New York: Theatre Communications Group, 1999) 129. All quotations from *The Weir*, *St. Nicholas*, *Rum and Vodka*, *The Good Thief* and *This Lime Tree Bower* will be taken from this edition and will be cited in-text.

[2] Gerald C. Wood in *Conor McPherson: Imagining Mischief* (Dublin: Liffey, 2003) lists some earlier plays produced by the University College Drama Society between 1988 and 1992. None of these plays are in print and are likely to remain unpublished. See Wood, 9-10.

the Royal Court won the Olivier Award for Best Play. McPherson's screenplay for the film *I Went Down* (1997) was warmly received, he has directed a film version of *Endgame* (2001), as part of Michael Colgan's project to assemble all Beckett's plays on film, and he has been the recipient of numerous other awards. McPherson's involvement with cinema looks set to continue—his first full-length film, *Saltwater*, an adaptation of *This Lime Tree Bower*, was released in 2001 and a second film, *The Actors*, appeared in 2003. His subsequent plays have elicited more muted responses; *Port Authority* (New Ambassadors Theatre, 2001) and *Come on Over* (Gate Theatre, 2001) follow the patterns of monologue and monologue ensemble laid down by the earlier dramatic work; *Dublin Carol* (Royal Court Theatre, 2000) and *Shining City* (Royal Court Theatre, 2004), while dialogue based, are orientated around acts of confession. His latest play, *The Seafarer*, (National Theatre London, 2006) revisits the naturalistic setting and conversational tone crafted in *The Weir*.

Much praise has been lavished on McPherson—*The Weir*, especially, won ecstatic tributes from London critics, many of whom admired the quality and authenticity of the production. Michael Billington in the *Guardian* commended McPherson's weaving of "the Irish love of fable and the Chekhovian sense of waste," describing the play as "pure theatrical poetry."[3] The associations made here are noteworthy: McPherson delivers what an Irish playwright should—a poetically inflected yarn— while the link to Chekhov places him alongside the doyen of modern Irish drama, Brian Friel, whose reworking of Chekhov is well-known. His drama has no doubt appealed to the more conservative critical establishment in Ireland and the UK as a welcome antidote to In-Yer-Face theatre, a return to a more comfortable and pleasurable experience of theatre, reliant upon linguistic nuances rather than spectacle and violent sensation. Others have drawn attention to the prosaic nature of the plays,

---

[3] Michael Billington's comments from the *Guardian* are posted at <http://www.albemarle-london.com/weir.html>.

commenting with somewhat less enthusiasm, on their "plain-spoken and methodical" qualities and their apparent anti-theatricality.[4]

McPherson himself notes how, when his work was first produced in London, he was "identified as belonging to two completely different schools. The first was the twenty something playwrights who have recently had such media attention—Jez Butterworth, Joe Penhall, Nick Grosso, Samuel Adamson, Martin McDonagh." Additionally he "was also slotted into the so-called school of Irish writing which seemed to be 'flooding' London's theatres—Sebastian Barry, Marina Carr, Gina Moxley, Daragh Carville, Billy Roche and so on."[5] The habitual pitfalls of categorisation are well illustrated in this instance, revealing more about theatre marketing strategies in London than the work in hand which could be fairly said to straddle both "schools."

In spite of being claimed by some as the country's latest "literary giant"[6] however, McPherson's work has certainly not generated debate comparable to that surrounding plays many of his contemporaries. Surprisingly, although newspaper reviews, articles and interviews are numerous, scholarly interest has been, at best, intermittent. Mic Moroney in a lengthy essay surveying recent Irish drama in *Druids, Dudes and Beauty Queens: The Changing Face of Irish Drama* (2001) includes some consideration of McPherson, noting that "despite a mixed attempt at dramatic dialogue in *The Weir*, monologues, and the dramatic ironies of unreconstructed pathetic masculinity,

---

[4] Les Gutman, rev. of *This Lime Tree Bower* by Conor McPherson, *CurtainUp Magazine* 24 May 1999 <www.curtainup.com/limetree.html>. See also Brian Singleton's review "Am I Talking to Myself?" *Irish Times* Features 19 Apr. 2001 (online).

[5] Conor McPherson, "If You're a Young Irish Playwright, Come to London," *New Statesman* 20 Feb. 1998 (online).

[6] Alan Franks, "Ireland's Sober Voice," *Times* Features 11 Dec. 1999. Cited in Scott T. Cummings, "Homo Fabulator: The Narrative Imperative in Conor McPherson's Plays," *Theatre Stuff: Critical Essays on Contemporary Irish Theatre*, ed. Eamonn Jordan (Dublin: Carysfort, 2000) 304.

remain [his] territory."[7] A more extensive analysis by Scott T. Cummings appears in *Theatre Stuff* in which he explores storytelling in *Rum and Vodka, The Good Thief, St. Nicholas, This Lime Tree Bower* and *The Weir*. Eamonn Jordan, meanwhile, proposes an interpretation of *The Weir* as a "meta-pastoral" play that "offers a space where [contrary to the responses of many of the play's first reviewers] the charade of authenticity is contested."[8] Finally, Gerald C. Wood's *Conor McPherson: Imagining Mischief* (2003) is the first book-length study of McPherson's work both for the stage and screen.[9] In general early responses to the plays have highlighted their contribution to a "great Irish storytelling tradition,"[10] or considered their "narrative imperative."[11] Wood's text associates these qualities with a notion of theatrical mischief, suggested by McPherson himself in the Author's Note to *St. Nicholas*, to argue for the centrality of moral or, more accurately, ethical choice to the work as a whole. Yet, despite such interpretations, little (Jordan's paper excepted) has been done to investigate the nature of McPherson's formal choices or to locate his attitude to theatre within any broader context of theatre history or theory. My approach to McPherson's work is thus twofold. First, I want to tease out the formal implications of his work with monologue from the point of view of modern theatre's disruption of illusionism. Subsequently, I will consider

---

[7] Mic Moroney, "The Twisted Mirror: Landscapes, Mindscapes, Politics and Language on the Irish Stage," *Druids, Dudes and Beauty Queens*, ed. Dermot Bolger (Dublin: New Island, 2001) 269. Most recently the theme of masculinity in crisis has been explored in detail by Brian Singleton. See "Am I Talking to Myself? Men, Masculinities and Monologue in Contemporary Irish Theatre," *Monologues: Theatre, Performance, Subjectivity*, ed. Clare Wallace (Prague: Litteraria Pragensia, 2006) 260-277.

[8] Eamonn Jordan, "Narrating Authenticities in Conor McPherson's *The Weir*," *Irish University Review* 34.2 (2004): 366-367.

[9] Gerald C. Wood, *Conor McPherson: Imagining Mischief* (Dublin: Liffey, 2003).

[10] Gutman, rev. of *This Lime Tree Bower* (online).

[11] Cummings, "Homo Fabulator," 303-312. See also Dominic Dromgoole, *The Full Room* (London: Methuen, 2002) 186-189, for claims regarding McPherson's position in terms of an Irish storytelling tradition.

McPherson's use of monologue and stilted dialogue, citational and ironic elements, his appeals to the audience's credulity, and an ongoing thematics of failure in the light of Jean-François Lyotard's theory of postmodern narrative knowledge.

Anti-illusionism & the Vicissitudes of Monologue
If one of the most remarked upon aspects of McPherson's work to date has been his use of monologue, then he is but one of what seems to be a growing number of new playwrights exploring the technique—other recent examples include plays by Sarah Kane, Neil LaBute, Eugene O'Brien, Mark O'Rowe and Enda Walsh to name just a few. Few playwrights, though, seem quite so devoted to the form as McPherson; *Rum and Vodka*, *The Good Thief*, *This Lime Tree Bower*, *St. Nicholas*, *Port Authority* and *Come On Over* are all structured around a similar formal construction in which actors address/confess to the audience. Even when the plays are more conventionally naturalistic, action remains minimal, while forms of (confessional) narrative performance take the stage. In the plays which incorporate dialogue, *The Weir*, *Dublin Carol* and *Shining City*, all are structurally dependent upon characters telling their stories. In *The Weir* this happens without significant interruption, in *Dublin Carol* the central character must struggle to find willing auditors, in *Shining City* the setting is a therapist's office. As a result, McPherson plays not only upon the notion of "suspension of disbelief," but also, to paraphrase Linda Hutcheon, the discursive construction of reality and an enduring sense of provisionality, uncertainty and, ultimately, failure.[12] In a note accompanying the text of *St. Nicholas*, McPherson remarks that being creatures of reason, human beings are always in search of meaning and are driven to *make* meaning. Indeed, all his plays to revolve around this truism and, importantly, the associated ambiguities of narrative as a means of knowing and communicating.

[12] Linda Hutcheon, *A Poetics of Postmodernism: History, Theory, Fiction* (New York and London: Routledge, 1988) 4-7.

For both contemporary American and European theatre, monologue has become a much favoured formal strategy, be it in the field of drama or solo performance. Speaking of recent French theatre, David Bradby and Annie Sparks remark how,

> The prevalence of performed monologues emphasises the trend away from character and plot-led plays. Instead of the conflict between characters provided by traditional drama, these monologues rely on developing a linguistic landscape of sufficient power and fascination to hold the audience's attention.[13]

In McPherson's plays, the vulnerability of identity, aleatory and eroded plots, and the creation of rich linguistic landscapes coexist with remarkably conventional character development and everyday speech patterns. As, Brian Singleton notes, it was Brian Friel who "supplied a template" for many of the young writers testing out this form in the Irish context at least.[14] Certainly the echoes of *Faith Healer* and *Molly Sweeney*—both of which are shaped around three characters recounting events in isolation from one another—are strong in *This Lime Tree Bower* and *Port Authority*. Singleton goes on to raise the crucial question of whether such an approach is actually a denial of theatre, an attempt to make it merely "a purely literary medium."[15]

In opposition, McPherson argues that, in contrast to dialogue and confrontation, the monologue form has enabled him "to tell smaller stories in a bigger way" and made him interested in "theatre itself," especially its collusive and mischievous dimensions.[16] Though reticent about the influences that might have shaped this understanding, like Martin McDonagh he claims an early interest in David Mamet, as well

---

[13] David Bradby and Annie Sparks, *Mise en Scène: French Theatre Now* (London: Methuen, 1997) 111-112.

[14] Singleton, "Am I Talking to Myself?" (online).

[15] Singleton, "Am I Talking to Myself?" (online).

[16] Conor McPherson, interview with Wood, *Imagining Mischief*, 128.

as (predictably enough) in Samuel Beckett.[17] Yet the essence of McPherson's theatre, where "ordinary human emotions are expressed very simply,"[18] is a far cry from that of Beckett. If, as former artistic director of the Bush Theatre, Dominic Dromgoole remarked of *This Lime Tree Bower*, McPherson's work "present[s] its characters with hard modern moral choices," it is marked by a "vernacular ease."[19]

This formal commitment to unadulterated or "pure" storytelling has often been remarked, just as the hazards of such a commitment are signalled by Singleton. Nevertheless, McPherson's best plays of this period extend the prospect of storytelling theatre, being a deceptively simple mixture of revelation, complicity and duplicity that self-consciously undermines the illusion of mimetic drama with diegetic overloading. This is articulated most explicitly in *Port Authority*, where the stage directions state plainly: "The play is set in the theatre,"[20] while the play itself is purely narrative.

Wood asserts that "inspired by the organic model, new Irish playwrights are free to write with or without theatrical precedents. Creative mischief is always an option."[21] I would argue that, on the contrary, many of McPherson's ideas and practices can only take clearer shape when juxtaposed with the genealogy of preceding rejections and revisions of nineteenth century naturalistic theatre. Specifically, some significant aspects of McPherson's theatre of monologue might be collated with Brechtian epic theatre and *Verfremdungseffekt*. Though at first sight an unlikely pairing, since McPherson's drama has little in common with Brecht's politics or didacticism, the work derives many of its effects through recourse to stage techniques that are Brechtian.

---

[17] See for instance Tim Adams's interview with McPherson, "So There's These Three Irishmen…," *Observer* 4 Feb. 2001 (online). Also, Wood's interview with McPherson in *Imagining Mischief*, 123-151.

[18] McPherson, *Imagining Mischief*, 134.

[19] Dromgoole, *The Full Room*, 187.

[20] McPherson, *Plays: Two* (London: Nick Hern, 2004) 132.

[21] Wood, *Imagining Mischief*, 29.

Brecht distinguishes between "epic" and "dramatic" theatre on various levels. First, epic theatre is based on narrative rather than plot and, consequently, is process rather than end orientated. Secondly, the spectator's role is not as a participant in illusion, rather he is cast as an observer who is encouraged to take action or to face a dilemma. Brecht (in)famously abhorred the passivity of "the cowed, credulous, hypnotised mass"[22] who merely empathise with the illusions they watch on stage. Rather than being relieved of responsibility, the audience ideally should be encouraged to think. This state may be wrought through the defamiliarisation of the theatre experience to enable the establishment of critical distance. Thirdly, epic theatre is constructed as a montage of self-contained scenes; these should connect with one another, but need not do so in a linear fashion.[23] Fourthly, character should be communicated self-consciously, the actor should "quote" the character rather than "become" the character. Additionally, Brecht's plays concern ordinary, rather than exemplary characters who face moral and ethical dilemmas. Finally, as Martin Esslin describes:

> It must at all times be made apparent to the spectators that they are not witnessing real events happening before their very eyes at *this very moment*, but that they are sitting in a theatre, listening to an account (however vividly presented) of things that have happened in the *past* at a certain time in a certain place. [...] While the theatre of illusion is trying to re-create a spurious present by pretending that the events of the play are actually taking place at the time of each performance, the "epic" theatre is strictly *historical*; it constantly reminds the audience that they are merely getting a report of past events.[24]

In a similar vein, Eric Bentley describes the Brechtian stage technique as "Narrative Realism." Unlike naturalist approaches

---

[22] Bertolt Brecht, "A Short Organum for the Theatre," trans. John Willett, *Modern Theories of Drama*, ed. George W. Brandt (Oxford: Clarendon, 1998) 237-8.

[23] Brecht, "The Modern Theatre is the Epic Theatre," 227.

[24] Martin Esslin, *Brecht: The Man and His Work* (New York: Anchor, 1971) 131-2.

to staging "what the Narrative Realist does by way of omitting and selecting he intends the audience to be entirely aware of" thus drawing attention to the "'artificial' frame (the stage)."[25] Bentley goes on to defend Brecht's theatre (as distinct from his dramatic theories) as an exploration of the "fine balance and interplay between *Einfühlung* and *Verfremdung* [...]. Aristotle said: pity *and* terror. Brecht says: sympathy *and* distance, attraction *and* repulsion, tenderness *and* horror."[26] It is this tension, rather than suspense, at the heart of Brecht's drama, that McPherson intermittently captures.

Though a minor feature of Irish theatre discourse, the influence of Brecht's stagecraft in post-war British theatre has been well documented.[27] Both John Elsom and Christopher Innes mention how although several of Brecht's plays were produced in Britain in the 1930s, it was the 1956 visit of the Berliner Ensemble that proved to be a revelation for many theatre practitioners (despite the fact that the performances were in German).[28] As Innes notes Brecht's work "vividly contrast[ed] with the naturalistic approach that had dominated the British stage since Shaw, [...] offer[ing] an anti-illusionistic model for theatrical immediacy and directness."[29] Unsurprisingly, aspects of epic theatre have been adopted for a broad range of purposes from the directly political to the merely stylistic.

McPherson's work inscribes a number of points of such stylistic and formal contiguity, namely in its approach to narrative process; its problematising of the role of spectator;

---

[25] Eric Bentley, *The Brecht Commentaries 1943-1986* (New York: Grove, 1987) 59-61.

[26] Bentley, *The Brecht Commentaries 1943-1986*, 34.

[27] See John Elsom, *Post-War British Theatre* (London: Routledge and Keegan Paul, 1976), J.L. Styan, *Modern Drama in Theory and Practice 3: Expressionism and Epic Theatre* (Cambridge: Cambridge University Press, 1981), Christopher Innes, *Modern British Drama: The Twentieth Century* (Cambridge: Cambridge University Press, 2002), Dominic Shellard, *British Theatre Since the War* (New Haven and London: Yale University Press, 1999).

[28] Elsom, *Post-War British Theatre*, 113, Innes, *Modern British Drama*, 113-4.

[29] Innes, *Modern British Drama*, 114.

tensions between distancing effects of non-naturalistic acting or staging and the empathy generated by the confessional register of the narrative; and time. In each of his plays to date, varied as they may seem, the emphasis is upon process rather than plot. Characters are to serve the narratives first and foremost, and actors are instructed by McPherson, who regularly directs his own work, to "just tell the story."[30] Direct storytelling, however, is belied by the dynamics of confession, judgement, sympathy and empathy that circumscribe relations between speaker and listener, performer and spectator. The dilemmas presented invite the spectator's judgement of the choices made or not made by the characters. Yet, at the same time as the audience is drawn into this relationship, they are made aware of the collusive game, foundational to the theatre of illusion, in which "this is an actor playing a character, and he knows that we know he is, or she is, an actor."[31] As a result, much of McPherson's work, echoing Brecht's, turns on the tension between sympathy and distance, attraction and repulsion generated by these games.

Similarly, the term "Narrative Realism" can be productively applied to the monologue plays. In these pieces the presentation of character is realistic (as opposed to symbolic or expressionistic for instance), but the fourth wall is dispensed with. The characters stand, or sit, facing the audience and tell their stories. The choice of a monologue form allows for the stage space to remain undefined either physically or temporally, while whatever is described must be reconstructed in the imaginations of the audience.

In their conception of time, McPherson's monologue plays also outline a terrain proximate to that of Brechtian theatre. As Singleton indicates, one of the consequences of monologue is that it "traps [...] characters in the field of memory; they never do anything in the present."[32] Instead, again reminiscent of the

---

[30] McPherson, *Imagining Mischief*, 132.
[31] McPherson, *Imagining Mischief*, 128.
[32] Singleton, "Am I Talking to Myself?" (online).

epic form (though in a manner much more literal than Brecht's plays), past events are reported often in loosely episodic patterns. *This Lime Tree Bower*, *Port Authority* and *Come On Over* are constituted by a montage of narratives that are contiguous rather than sequential. In *St. Nicholas* a single monologue loops through a past experience, and *The Weir*, despite its naturalistic frame, is also structured around cycles of stories that ultimately overshadow any action in the play's present. In Brecht's theatre the destabilisation of chronology and of the naturalist illusion of presence should guide the spectator to a state of reflection. McPherson claims a desire to communicate with his audiences and to generate communication among them,[33] a much less defined objective than the ultimately didactic approach of Brecht.

It is this ambiguity, and possible dissensus, that distinguishes McPherson's plays from the moral underpinning of Brecht's epic theatre. This ambiguity also aligns his use of monologue and narrative with a contemporary discourse of identity, though clearly not in its most extreme posthumanist form. Current uses of monologue in theatre seem to swing between elevated (confessional) authenticity and ambivalent, dubious or possibly false communication. As Deborah Geis argues in *Postmodern Theatric(k)s* (1993), in contrast to the revelatory function of the soliloquy in Shakespeare's drama, contemporary monologues are frequently characterised by the ways in which they play "tricks." Specifically, the opportunities and difficulties monologue presents are bound up with resonances of the form and its implications. Commonly accompanied by further restrictions of the semiotic field of the stage, it focuses attention intensely upon the speaker and upon the way in which s/he expresses her or himself. Language and linguistic elements are, therefore, foregrounded. Further, the contexts for monologue in "real" life are relatively confined and are associated with various forms of performance activity.

---

[33] McPherson, *Imagining Mischief*, 133.

These might be said to fall into a number of categories: speeches, sermons, instruction and lectures; recitation and storytelling; confessions; and finally, "perversions" of these former categories in psychosis, hysteria and so on. So while it might be asserted that the monologue form is "essential" storytelling, a stripping away of dramatic illusion, it is impossible to dispel absolutely the other, highly performative, circumstances in which monologue appears or the functions it serves. Subjectivity and unreliability are, thus, inherent to the form. For Geis the contemporary monologue is less concerned with character development or narrative progress than with theatricality, parody and ambivalence.[34] Despite the apparent directness and simplicity of McPherson's work, the modalities of trickery and ambivalence are, I would argue, at its core.

Microwaved Narratives

In *The Postmodern Condition* (1979), Lyotard famously asserts that the predominant characteristic of knowledge under postmodernity is an "incredulity towards metanarratives."[35] The supposed universal or transcendent truths of western civilisation, which he refers to as meta- or grand narratives have been called into question. Lyotard describes the "modern" period as being committed to knowledge that legitimated itself

> with reference to a metadiscourse [...] making an explicit appeal to some grand narrative, such as the dialectics of the Spirit, the hermeneutics of meaning, the emancipation of the rational or working subject, or the creation of wealth.[36]

In this way, as Marvin Carlson describes, metanarratives have "provided legitimacy for a wide variety of cultural norms,

---

[34] Deborah Geis, *Postmodern Theatric(k)s: Monologue in Contemporary American Drama* (Michigan: University of Michigan Press, 1993).

[35] Jean-François Lyotard, *The Postmodern Condition*, trans. Geoff Bennington and Brian Massumi (1979; Manchester: Manchester University Press, 1984) xxiv.

[36] Lyotard, *The Postmodern Condition*, xxiii.

procedures and beliefs."[37] One of the effects of "the obsolescence of the metanarrative apparatus of legitimation," Lyotard avers, is that "the narrative function is losing its functors, its great hero, its great dangers, its great voyages, its great goal."[38] This does not imply that narrative forms are becoming extinct, however. In place of metanarrative mechanisms, a multiplicity of language games and micro- or little narratives exists; these are not legitimated through reference to metanarratives, but are provisionally "legitimated by the simple fact that they do what they do."[39] Lyotard draws upon Wittgenstein's "language games" claiming that "What [Wittgenstein] means by this term is that each of the various categories of utterance can be defined in terms of rules specifying their properties and the uses to which they can be put,"[40] denotative, performative, prescriptive and so on. Nevertheless, although narrative language games can "define what has the right to be said and done in the culture in question,"[41] they remain conditional and are often, contradictory, since they are only legitimated by the specific context of which they are a part.

The narrative form is pre-eminent in the "formulation of traditional knowledge"[42] for Lyotard. In interrogating the nature of "narrative knowledge," he associates knowledge with the capacity of forming "good" denotative and other forms of utterance—"good" being defined and accepted by a particular social circle in which a speaker operates.[43] He then goes on to outline some of the principle ways in which narrative forms bear knowledge. Stories may relate "positive or negative apprenticeships (*Bildungen*)"; as such they may function to

[37] Marvin Carlson, *Performance: A Critical Introduction* (London and New York: Routledge, 1996) 138.

[38] Lyotard, *The Postmodern Condition*, xxiv.

[39] Lyotard, *The Postmodern Condition*, 23.

[40] Lyotard, *The Postmodern Condition*, 10.

[41] Lyotard, *The Postmodern Condition*, 23.

[42] Lyotard, *The Postmodern Condition*, 19.

[43] Lyotard, *The Postmodern Condition*, 18.

sanction certain social institutions or to provide role models. The narrative form also involves "a wide variety of language games" and "the areas of competence whose criteria the narrative form supplies and applies are thus tightly woven together in the web it forms." Following from the skills required by the form itself, "the narrative tradition is also the tradition of the criteria defining threefold competence—'know-how,' 'knowing how to speak,' and 'knowing how to hear' (*savoir-faire, savoir-dire, savoir-entendre*)—through which the community's relationship to itself and its environment is played out." Finally, "narrative form follows a rhythm." This rhythm may take on the qualities of ritual, as in fixed or ceremonial storytelling. The significance of narrative is therefore not only to be found in the content of the story, but in the act of recitation, and while "the narrative's reference may seem to belong to the past, […] in reality it is always contemporaneous with the act of recitation." [44]

The prospect of comprehending a world of boundless, delegitimated micronarrative polyphony has been understood in various ways as negative, positive or, indeed, self-contradictory. Steven Connor, for instance, critiques Lyotard's argument on the basis that "it can only establish its principle of the necessary heterogeneity of forms of language-use by means of a preliminary homogenisation of [all human events] in terms of *language* itself." [45] Critics who approach Lyotard from the perspective of traditional emancipatory politics find such a limitless heterogeneity of language games is debilitating to the establishment of a coherent notion of justice and naïve with regard to the distribution of power. [46] From the perspective of

---

[44] Lyotard, *The Postmodern Condition*, 20-22.

[45] Steven Connor, *Theory and Cultural Value* (Oxford: Blackwell, 1992) 111. O'Connor goes on to discuss the paradoxical implications of Lyotard's notion of incommensurability and his "covert universalism" in some depth.

[46] See for instance Nancy Fraser and Linda Nicholson, "Social Criticism without Philosophy: An Encounter between Feminism and Postmodernism," *Universal Abandon? The Politics of Postmodernism*, ed. Andrew Ross (Minneapolis: University of Minnesota Press, 1988) 83-105.

literary studies, the demise of metanarratives has frequently been read simply as a harmonious extension of traditional liberal pluralism.[47] Bertens, critical of this latter tendency, argues that in contrast, "Lyotard promotes a radically revolutionary ethos that is that of the modern avant-garde," insisting that he "advocates a radical anti-representationalism."[48]

Though these radical implications are hardly staged in McPherson's drama, which is in many respects formally conservative, the plays tacitly demonstrate some of the principle characteristics of narrative-based knowledge Lyotard describes, with form and content woven from various narrative (language) games. If McPherson's work could be said to resist a grand narrative which might focus a singular or privileged interpretation, then like Lyotard's theory, it is dogged by the paradox that the erosion of transcendent meaning is achieved through recourse to an allegedly universal value—that of storytelling. As Cummings points out, "I have a story, therefore I am" might be considered the motto of McPherson's drama to date. *Rum and Vodka, The Good Thief, This Lime Tree Bower, St. Nicholas, The Weir, Dublin Carol* and *Port Authority* "all hinge," as Cummings says, "on personal narratives, public confessions of private sins which provide first an entertaining evening and then, upon reflection, an investigation into the nature and function of story itself."[49] This investigation is yoked to a moral dimension both in terms of what story is told and how it is told.[50]

Throughout the narratives and anecdotes, however, doubt and dissensus are persistently inscribed in the performance of

---

[47] Stephen Best and Douglas Kellner, *Postmodern Theory: Critical Interrogations* (London: Macmillan, 1991) 174-5.

[48] Bertens, *The Idea of the Postmodern*, 131, 127.

[49] Cummings, "Homo Fabulator," 303.

[50] For example, Victoria White claims McPherson to be an "amoral playwright [...] He doesn't have one particular story he needs to tell, one particular set of values he needs to prove. But he needs to tell stories." See "Telling Stories in the Dark," *Irish Times* 2 July 1998: 14.

telling. And although, as mentioned above, this intrinsically mischievous dimension to his work has been pointed out by both McPherson himself, and his commentators,[51] it has remained comparatively under-analysed.

Early Plays

Since McPherson's early work comprises few of the narrative complexities of his later plays it will only discussed in passing here. What it does offer is an effective contrast with the subsequent plays, especially with regard to monologue, serving as an index of how McPherson has developed as a playwright. While Cummings defends the "immediacy and roughness" which, in his view, makes these pieces "essentially theatrical,"[52] this is, in my opinion, debatable. Doubtless, roughness is an important characteristic of both *Rum and Vodka* and *The Good Thief*; not only are the stories fairly crude in their construction and limited in scope, but the language also is one dimensional compared to the subsequent work. McPherson does little to exploit the theatrical potential, or ambiguity of monologue in either play. The results are much closer to recitations of short stories than fully developed dramatic works. While neither of the plays is particularly original in content, a more serious criticism is that they are unadventurous with the genres or stories they, intentionally or unintentionally, cite.

Rum and Vodka is a tall tale of drunken exploits and degradation. The narrator relates a momentous, weekend-long drinking session, during which he loses his job, is unfaithful to his wife and generally debases himself in the pursuit of alcohol. A clerk in the voting registration department of the city corporation, at the age of twenty four he has a wife, two small children and a burgeoning alcohol addiction. The trigger to his alcohol problem seems to be the realisation that "this was as

---

[51] See McPherson's note to *St. Nicholas* in *The Weir and Other Plays* (New York: Theatre Communications Group, 1999) 75-76, Cummings, "Homo Fabulator,"and Wood, *Conor McPherson: Imagining Mischief.*

[52] Cummings, "Homo Fabulator," 303.

good as things were going to get" (248). The play is structured in two parts; the references are all to contemporary Dublin and the speaker's story develops in an uncomplicated, linear manner. With its wandering through the environs, pubs and clubs of Dublin the play recalls James Joyce's story "Counterparts." The instances of thematic citation between the two narratives are multiple. Farrington in "Counterparts" like the unnamed speaker of McPherson's play is a clerk in a Dublin office. His insatiable thirst similarly jeopardises his job. Like the protagonist of *Rum and Vodka*, Farrington seems only to live for drink and idle, opinionated pub talk. Both protagonists briefly lust after women from another "world"—for Farrington the theatrical lady in the yellow gloves he sees in Mulligan's pub, in *Rum and Vodka* the long-haired girl he meets first in the Stag's Head and with whom he spends the night. While Farrington returns home "humiliated and discontented" and, finally, viciously beats one of his children, the protagonist of *Rum and Vodka* eventually returns in a similar condition to sit in his daughters' room and to contemplate their "unbearable" innocence and his intolerably ordinary life. If "Counterparts" can be summarised as a modest tale of hopeless frustration, paralysis and alcohol addiction, then *Rum and Vodka* plots a very similar territory with little innovation.

Written as one unbroken monologue, *The Good Thief* rehearses a familiar modern crime narrative, with all the requisite components—love interest, betrayal and divided loyalties, violence, escape, capture and so on. The play's narrator is a "paid thug" who recounts his involvement in a botched assignment to threaten a businessman into paying protection fees which spirals beyond his control and finally results in self-imposed exile following a ten year prison sentence. *The Good Thief* is clearly generically influenced by American pulp fiction thrillers, mixed with local references. Like *Rum and Vodka* it remains formally and thematically limited.

In spite of Cummings's and Wood's enthusiasm for these early plays, the depth and sense of equivocality which have become the hallmarks of McPherson's drama, are lacking here. Nevertheless, the narrative techniques of the plays ("direct first person addresses; the confiding self-aware narrators; the anecdotal phrasings and cadences"[53]), albeit in embryonic form, presage the richer textures of the later plays.

"Let the words do the work" — Play or Employment?[54]
The three plays I will discuss in detail are *This Lime Tree Bower*, *St. Nicholas* and *The Weir* which, though in many ways very different, are connected by certain common stylistic and formal features. In each, theatrical tension is created not through action but through verbal performance, while reliance, extensively or wholly, upon monologue to generate dramatic tension implies and invokes a range of ambivalences.

This Lime Tree Bower marks McPherson's first incursion onto the London theatre scene. Like his early work, the play is composed of blocks of monologue, while directions as to stage design are absent. The play as a whole is structured around three named characters, Joe, Frank and Ray, who tell stories about recent events in their lives.

Joe is a seventeen year old, whose stories centre upon his confused efforts to impress Damien, a fellow schoolmate. The climax of his narrative occurs when he witnesses his friend raping a drunken girl they are supposed to be safely escorting home after a disco. Later, when a criminal investigation begins, Damien attempts to blame Joe.

Frank, Joe's brother, supplies details about his relationship with his father and their work in the family business. He relates his frustration with how his father has been exploited by the local city councillor and bookmaker. He decides solve his

<hr>

53 James C. Taylor, "Conor McPherson: One-Man Show," *The Simon* (Autumn 1999) <www.thesimon.com/issues/2/1/64.html>.
54 Conor McPherson in Tim Adams "So There's These Three Irishmen...," *Observer* 4 Feb. 2001 (online).

father's problem by carrying out an armed robbery of the bookie's shop. The heist is a success only because he is accidentally rescued by Ray.

Ray, a philosophy lecturer, describes a number of events. The first is a drunken one-night stand with one of his students. This is contrasted with the apparently healthy relationship he has with Carmel, Joe and Frank's sister. The next is the visit by a world famous professor to the Philosophy Department. The third is his involvement with Frank and the robbery.

A rhythm is established by the fixed order of the monologues—Joe, then Ray and finally Frank address the audience. An interval is scheduled after the first six monologues and at a crisis point in the tale of the robbery. The remainder of the play consists of four further monologues. This contains a further two climactic points: Joe's witnessing of the rape and Ray's projectile vomiting at the final Konigsberg lecture. Although stage directions indicate that the characters are aware of each other, this is made explicit only once and this aspect of the monologue structure has significant interpretive implications.

McPherson's next play, *St. Nicholas*, commissioned by the Bush Theatre, features a single speaker, a debauched and cynical theatre critic in his late fifties. Again McPherson uses the ploy of direct address and "plain" storytelling. According to directions, the stage is bare. The speaker tells of his sordid existence as a journalist, of how he falls for the lead actress in a production of *Salomé* at the Abbey and then, besotted, follows the show to London. There, after making a fool of himself by telling a lot of unconvincing lies to the cast of the play, he wanders through London and finally falls asleep in Crystal Palace Park. Having established himself as a consummate liar, the narrator proceeds to inform the audience of his meeting with a vampire, of how he takes up residence with William and his compatriots, and in return procures victims for them. During the day, the protagonist spends time in his attic room attempting to write and conversing with William about art and literature. After some time he grows tired of the arrangement and comes to despise his hosts. Among the last batch of victims he recruits is Helen, the actress on whom he had a crush. Both of them are bitten, but the protagonist summons the will to leave. Afterwards the speaker plans to return to his old life with his new story. The play's tempo is generated by the progression of the speaker's reminiscences which, following an opening loop of recollections about his past as a writer, husband and father, then develop in a relatively linear fashion following the protagonist's reported increasingly fantastic actions and related emotions. Direct verbal attacks on the audience punctuate the flow of the narrative.

The Weir, McPherson's most highly acclaimed play, is the first of his works to use dialogue in an extended manner. Set in a typical rural Irish pub, the play follows the course of a single evening and adheres to the unities of time and place. Unlike the other plays here discussed, *The Weir*, employs a conventional, naturalistic approach to the set design and incorporates regular stage directions. The characters include the barman, Brendan, three locals, Jack, Jim and Finbar and a woman, Valerie, a newcomer to the area. Conversation among the characters is low key and at times formulaic, rarely wandering far from the haven of pub chit-chat. However, as the evening wears on they begin to tell stories and the play slips back into the now familiar mode of monologue. Prompted by the businessman Finbar, Jack an ageing mechanic, begins with a traditional Irish story of fairies. Finbar follows this yarn with a description of a spooky experience with a Ouija board. Jim, an odd-job man, then recounts how years previously he met the ghost of a man for whom he had just dug a grave. Valerie concludes the tales of the supernatural by telling of the death of her young daughter and how she thought she had spoken to the dead child on the telephone. Finally, before they leave the pub, Jack narrates how he missed his chance to marry.

These synopses illustrate McPherson's penchant for the small-scale story. These are legitimated only in the act of telling or performance and the act of telling itself is multi-layered and dubious. They are tales which lay claim to no monumental significance, mythic references or universal applicability. In each play reality is constructed in a discursive manner privileging linguistic over visual elements, it is, as McPherson himself puts it, the words which are to do the work rather than the spectacle of the stage design or the characters' actions.

Of particular consequence is the way in which character in all these plays is inextricably bound to narrative. With significant physical action onstage diminished, the ways in which characters speak, their vocabularies and the rhetorical devices they employ are of utmost importance. In the telling of their stories, they talk themselves into existence. More than any detours into dialogue, the monologues in the plays make, or more accurately, *make up* meaning, and this involves implicitly the competencies enumerated by Lyotard quoted above—that is a web of language games including "know-how, knowing how to speak, and knowing how to hear (*savoir-faire, savoir-dire, savoir-entendre*)."[55]

The dynamics of narrative in *This Lime Tree Bower* are generated by McPherson's playful use of perspective both within and between the partially overlapping monologues of the three characters. The first to speak, Joe, is innocent and naïve. This impression is conveyed by both the thematic foci of his monologues and by their mode of expression. His concerns are juvenile and are revealed in simple terms with childish vocabulary and, at times, excessive honesty. The most marked characteristic of Joe's rhetoric is self-doubt and this limits his perspective on the events he relates. He is attracted to the new boy in school, Damien, because of his appearance and self-confidence. Joe only gradually learns to consider what lies beneath these superficial elements. Similarly, his sexual urges are confused. He oscillates between his adoration of Damien, masturbatory fantasies about the girls he sees in the park, and

---

[55] Lyotard, *The Postmodern Condition*, 20-22.

references to another girl, "Deborah Something," who he claims to be really interested in but has ironically "only ever seen from the side" (143).

Joe's naïvety is further indicated in the details of his monologues and these too provide a microcommentary on perspective. Two of these details are of particular significance. The first is Joe's favourite game at the amusement arcade which is a kind of rifle range. The game relies upon a classic trick of perspective—targets seem to go back into the distance when in fact they merely get smaller. Joe remarks upon this detail as if it were something peculiar or novel. Notably the game is described as "an old one" which is cheap because "no one ever played it" (156). Later, when he is waiting for Damien before they go to the disco, the rifle range perspective game is mapped onto real distance: "I saw Damien coming through the gates. [...] He was far away and very small. I thought that if I'd a gun I could have shot him. I don't know what made me think that" (170). Not only is Damien metaphorically the target of Joe's affections, he is also, as is later revealed, a threat. Joe's condensation of reference here suggests this tension. However, his concluding remark reveals his reluctance to analyse the associations he makes or to understand them.

This reluctance is further underscored by Joe's rather comical attitude towards reading. He describes how he enjoys his brother's books which are mostly "thrillers and westerns":

> I liked his books because the sentences were always short. The writers gave you the facts. In school we did books where nobody said what they meant and you had to work out what everybody wanted. [In contrast] these books knew how to be read. (156-7)

Joe wishes to avoid the complexities of interpretation, of deciphering that which is not immediately comprehensible. His perplexed lack of confidence stems from this desire and is exacerbated by the fact that nothing in his life approximates the transparent, one dimensional plots of popular fiction.

McPherson balances this artlessness with Joe's adolescent self-consciousness. His candour and self-doubt give his monologues a humorous dimension. Joe's simultaneous submission to peer pressure and consciousness of the absurdity of his actions are vividly rendered:

> I started smoking too, so I could talk to him at little break behind the religion room. It was completely fucking disgusting. You were supposed to be dying for a pull and about nine blokes would be sharing a fag. By the time it came around to you it was just a soaking wet filter. And you had to drag on it like you'd die without it. But I got to talk to Damien. (135)

Although a novice in the intricacies of communication and fabrication, Joe has a strong sense of right and wrong and he is unable to dissimulate when he knows he is "being false" (141, 142). Repeatedly, Joe's monologues indicate his dilemma of not knowing who to believe, as he puts it, in a "town full of spoofers" (155). The sense that Joe's monologues are governed by progress and development is affirmed by the closing transformation of his sense of perspective summed up by his ability to recall his mother, not as a dying invalid, but as a happy healthy person.

Ray, in stark contrast, is a misanthropic and purportedly amoral opportunist. The juxtapositioning of Joe's speeches with Ray's serves to heighten the qualities of both speakers. Ray's monologues brim with self-proclaimed *savoir-faire* and *savoir-dire*, but little *savoir-entendre*. His bravado and disingenuousness are evident in his opening anecdote when he describes waking up in bed with one of his students but pretends amnesia with regard to her identity. His yarns bristle with swearwords, sarcastic retorts and harsh judgements, and smoulder with aggression. He drinks in the student bar because "[he] hate[s] academics" (144); he despises the students who buy him drinks; he refers to the student he has slept with as "a stupid fat bitch" (147); the Head of the Philosophy Department is a "terrible gobshite" (161); even Carmel "annoy[s] the fuck out of [him]" apparently because of her sense of "assurance," but also because he suspects her superior intelligence (159-60). When not drinking himself into a stupor, seducing students, or waffling his way through staff meetings and lectures, Ray spends his time with Carmel, Frank and Joe—the only people he seems to genuinely, if sporadically, tolerate and like. Central to Ray's mode of expression are distancing devices, usually framed as wit. These function to protect him from the implications of his own actions, but also indicate a poorly masked bitterness. So for example, immediately after the robbery when Joe and Frank are on the verge of hysteria, Ray takes charge:

> I don't get upset much. But the more Joe was asking what we should do next, the more I was beginning to see what a good fucking question it was. I have that sort of philosophical training. So after driving around for a while I decided that enough was enough. It was getting stupid. I pulled over and told them what to do. (176)

In contrast to Joe's stories, Ray's narrative distinctly lacks a sense of progress. Amoral and cynical, his character is defined by stasis. Ironically, as a philosopher, a "friend of wisdom," he is resistant to new knowledge or development. As in Joe's monologues, minor details prove significant upon closer inspection. The fact that he teaches Utilitarian philosophy is of ironic consequence. John Stuart Mill defines utilitarianism as,

> the creed which accepts as the foundation of morals, Utility or the Greatest Happiness Principle, holds that actions are right in proportion as they tend to promote happiness, wrong as they tend to promote unhappiness. By happiness is intended pleasure and the absence of pain; by unhappiness, pain, and the privation of pleasure.[56]

---

[56] John Stuart Mill, *Utilitarianism*, in *Classics of Western Philosophy*, ed. Steven M. Cahn, 4th ed. (1861; Indianapolis and Cambridge: Hackett, 1995) 1132-3.

Ray in practice modifies the precedents of such a theory and assiduously applies the Greatest Happiness Principle exclusively to himself. The pursuit of pleasure, however transitory or superficial, is the motivating force in each of his monologues. Ray relishes recapitulating and reinventing his sexual and drunken exploits and his ethics are described less by his reported actions than by the ways in which they are enunciated. Just as theories of utility might be criticised for their blindness to intention or motivation, so too Ray's narrative style is characterised by a lack of reflection upon his intentions or motives. Thus, Ray learns nothing from his sexual encounter with the student, from his relationship with Carmel and her brothers, from his interaction with colleagues at the university or from the visit of the world-famous Professor Konigsberg and, as predicted, he publishes a book he claims no-one will read.

Frank's monologues stand between the *Bildungen* properties and the cynical stasis of the first two narratives. His character is clearly one of balance; this is indicated by the fact that his narrative mode is primarily denotative and mediates between the extremes of the other speakers. Frank describes his actions in a neutral style, following the plodding routine of work in the family restaurant without marked emotion. Unlike Joe, he confidently judges his small world and, in contrast to Ray, he does so without bile. Frank's perceptive tolerance is illustrated in his attitude towards his father's weaknesses for storytelling and alcohol:

> He had all these stories he kept telling over and over with little exaggerations getting worse all the time. But I never tired of them. Just before twelve, he'd have his first small one of the day. He said it helped his blood flow more easily. I'd gotten used to it, but sometimes I felt it was a bit early. (150)

Like the books he possesses, Frank is interested in facts—the fact that "Simple Simon" McCurdy is a loan shark who is destroying his father, that Reynolds might know how to get a gun, that the robbery is not discovered. He rarely speculates on his own feelings or those of others, and if he does it is only briefly and strategically. For example, when he asks Carmel to substitute for him at the chip shop for the weekend, he plays upon her feelings in order to get his own way: "She was guilty about Joe not having a mother, and she was always fighting with him. I know it was mean, but she felt it and you've got to use what you've got" (187).

While in Joe's monologue the rifle range game provides an oblique commentary on his understanding of perspective, a structural echo is found in Frank's monologue in which a real gun also provides a new sense of perspective, giving him "a feeling of power" and allowing him to "see everything very clearly" (163). Frank's reasoning is founded on the assertion that "principles will only fuck you up, because no one else is ever moral" (186), a conclusion he has reached through the example of his own blighted father. McPherson thus can be seen to plot his characters along a spectrum of values from the naïvely moralistic to the cynically amoral, with pragmatic immorality in between. Wood suggests that, in contrast to Friel's *Faith Healer*, "McPherson's play is not driven by the disparities among multiple narrators [… but rather] is a shared story."[57] However, as the above analysis shows, the play is orientated around multiple stories that coalesce at points. In addition, it is driven by disparate narrative skills and moral positions—McPherson's plotting of the three characters along this spectrum permits a more dynamic engagement with perception and performative identities than allowed by his previous work, one that is further complicated in his next play.

St. Nicholas extends this exploration of narrative, perspective and the construction of discursive reality still further. The play explicitly engages the audience in a narrative game of suspension of disbelief, related by a highly problematic narrator—a figure who normally judges what is on stage rather

---

57 Wood, *Imagining Mischief*, 24.

than performing there. The fact that the speaker is anonymous and appears to break out of character at several points in the play, sharpens McPherson's challenge to stage illusion and the established safe distance between audience and performer. This narrator literally tells a story of how he found "his" story—a type of ontological or self-legitimating micronarrative. As a gruff everyman critic, he plunges into this story directly, describing himself as a former "fat bastard" (79), and marshalling an armoury of rhetorical devices to secure credibility for an unlikely confession that turns out to be a road-to-Damascus tale about an encounter with vampires. He accosts the audience directly and aggressively, employing a variety of strategies to tell the story including description, nostalgic appeals, cynical humour, insults, self-deprecation, boasting, argument and direct refutation of disbelief. As a theatre critic, he is an articulate and confident speaker who anticipates disagreement or scepticism. Similar to the character of Ray in *This Lime Tree Bower*, he is a repulsive figure, defined by bitterness and a contempt for practically all those around him— his wife, his son, his colleagues, the people he writes about, in addition to the vampires. Moreover, in contrast to the other plays in focus here, the narrator's disdain and acerbic commentary are also turned on the audience. Consequently, the audience is never fully allowed to get caught up in the current of the narrative, but is repeatedly reminded of its performance.

The capacity for and power of judgement is thematically present throughout the play. The role and responsibility of the critic is wryly and cynically surveyed:

> I was a journalist. I was a lucky bastard. I was blessed, or cursed, whichever, with the ability to string words together. […] And that's all it was. I mean, I was intelligent, but I had no real thoughts about things. I'd never taken the care to form an opinion. I just had them." (80)

Other critics are castigated for their perpetual attempts to provide opinions: "they were always looking for an angle. Like children jumping up behind each other to see a parade" (85). To make matters worse, the speaker reminds his auditors that as a cultural arbitrator he can take advantage of "the best of everything. [He] could stand there with the cast and ruin their evening. And get paid for it" (87). Ironically, in his current role he has even replaced the cast in this equation.

On the other hand, he also recognises the parasitical nature of his profession and his perspective is warped by jealousy of those who actually create something. He feels he is dead (85) and is plagued by the realisation that he "could only write about what there was already" and has "no ideas for a story" (81). The narrator experiences a breakdown of sorts when confronted with Helen's unselfconscious sense of creative purpose. This narrative crisis is the key to the games played in *St. Nicholas*. As Cummings describes, the narrator as critic feeds, like the vampire, upon others—upon their artistic endeavours, and upon their fear of his power. Moreover, his role as storyteller may be equated with the role he fulfils for the vampire household—drawing in victims/listeners, exploiting their sympathy and feeding upon their credulity.[58] The narrator also plays upon the construction of identity through storytelling and the arbitrariness of these micronarratives that function not because they reveal a profound or universal truth, but as a process of self-performance.

It is perhaps commonplace at this stage to note how *The Weir* is a play "about" narrative. This play, in particular, relies upon the power of stories which are told within the fictive world depicted on stage, but in a manner obviously differentiated from the above mentioned plays. In spite of McPherson's use of dialogue and a naturalistic set, these changes are but window dressing for another engagement with the modalities of storytelling. *The Weir* provides McPherson's clearest demonstration of various language games or, as Lyotard later

---

58 See Cummings, "Homo Fabulator," 308.

designates, "phrase-regimens" and "genres of discourse."[59] The dialogue in the play is distinctly idle and by rote, consisting of routine joking, teasing, questions about weather and the exchange of news all of which imply well-worn patterns. Consequently, conversation in the play is, for the most part, emptied of content even though the speakers are motivated to continue talking. Brendan and Jack's dialogue early in the play provides a typical example:

Brendan:	That's some wind, isn't it?
Jack:	It is.
Brendan:	Must have been against you, was it?
Jack:	It was. It was against me till I came around the Knock. It was a bit of shelter then.
Brendan:	Yeah it's a funny one. It's coming from the North.
Jack:	Mm. Ah, it's mild enough though.
Brendan:	Ah yeah. It's balmy enough. (8-9)

Stories multiply in *The Weir* propagating one another through association. Again characters are drawn in their modes of telling, although this time the boundaries of naturalism make it a more subtle process. The audience in effect are invited to eavesdrop on a night of tale telling in a rural pub. Jack, the eldest, though gruff emerges as a nostalgic and sentimental figure denoting lost pasts—lost traditions of superstition and lost love. Finbar, the prosperous businessman, speaks with bluster and regular disclaimers. Jim is a lonely bachelor who throughout the play remembers those who are absent or dead and, appropriately enough, tells a graveyard tale. Valerie though urban and young, is the most credulous of the strange tales told by the others. She continually gently supports the possibility that the inexplicable and supernatural may exist, as a means of coming to terms with the traumatic loss of her daughter. Finally Brendan, the barman who does not tell a

---

[59] These terms are introduced by Lyotard in *The Differend* (1984). The implications of this shift in terminology are discussed by Connor in *Theory and Cultural Value*, 111-12.

story, functions as mediator between the speakers and sympathetic listener, encouraging them, as he does Jack—"this is a good little story" (30)—or defending them, as he does Valerie—"she said she knew what it was" (58).

The Weir provides little of the explicit metacommentary upon narrative, perception or identity as *This Lime Tree Bower* or *St. Nicholas* yet, as Wood notes, the stories told bear an "undercurrent of self-revelation and hidden motives."[60] More interestingly perhaps, in foregrounding narrative on stage, McPherson's "hidden motive" is a challenge to the visual sensation of the contemporaneous In-Yer-Face theatre.

Incredulity Incorporated

If such narrative strategies provide a commentary on perspective and character, then another important feature is a recurrent thread of uncertainty or doubt. The stories of and within each of the plays encode the ambivalences of narrative as a means of knowing the world or oneself. Incredulity infects the plays not only from within, but also is a crucial element in the ways they interpellate an audience. Thus incredulity can be addressed at both intratextual and metatextual levels.

This Lime Tree Bower, *St. Nicholas* and *The Weir* each arguably gesture towards various metanarratives which are found inadequate. *This Lime Tree Bower* addresses questions of morality and ethical behaviour in the modern world where the principles of honesty and hard work fail to ensure success or justice. *St. Nicholas* mischievously challenges rational apprehension of the world and the rejection of superstition. While *The Weir*, similarly explores the limitations of strict boundaries between natural and supernatural.

Throughout the plays questions of fact and fiction, collusion and concealment, knowledge and ignorance repeatedly assert themselves. In *This Lime Tree Bower*, Joe is the principle voice of doubt, uncertain of what to believe in a world where no one

---

[60] Wood, *Imagining Mischief*, 47. Benedict Nightingale, "Fear, Apathy, Regret: A Happy Combination," *New York Times* 15 Mar. 1998: AR8 18.

seems to tell the truth. Faced with different versions of a story, such as why Damien has transferred to his school (137-8) or the explanation of the shipwreck in the local harbour (155), he concludes that "Lots of things could have been true, who knows?" (156) and that perhaps he should invent his own version.

Ray's story of his performance at the final Konigsberg lecture tests the limits of credulity and also refocuses the issue of multiple versions raised in Joe's monologues. Ray has fought for the opportunity to question the venerable professor in order to challenge Konigsberg's theory of language. However, when the moment comes, he is in the throes of a severe hangover:

> Everyone looked at me expectantly. Konigsberg was looking around, wondering who was going to say something. And then, absolutely beyond my control, a long stream of orange puke shot out of my mouth. [...] No one could believe what they had just seen. I stood up and cleared my throat. "Yes. Thank you, Professor Reagan," I said. "I would like to ask Professor Konigsberg if, during his long and eminent career, he has ever seen anything quite like that." (184)

The fantastically disgusting story functions as a punctuation mark in the play. Not only does it incorporate the disbelief of the spectators at the lecture, it seems designed to inspire scepticism among the play's audience or readers and finally, it also provokes the play's only lines of dialogue, which suggests the characters' questioning of the veracity of each other's narratives:

> Frank (*To Ray*): I never heard that.
> Ray: I've been saving it. (185)

This brief moment of exchange suggests the possibility that the characters have all told these stories before and that, like Joe and Frank's father's stories, each time they are ameliorated with exaggeration. Frank's reflection upon Ray's storytelling and the stage direction that the characters are aware of each other emphasise the performative dimension to all the monologues and, therefore, the blurring of distinctions between collusion, concealment, truth and falsehood. Why does Ray save this part of his story? If the characters are performing for each other then what is the status of Joe's naïvety? Is it too a performance? What is the space they occupy from which they relate their stories and how is the audience to understand their role in this space? These are dilemmas raised by the play which remain unresolved. Significantly, at the play's conclusion, Joe introduces yet another question of credulity with regard to the play's narrative structure in the shape of a coda—"So in the end it was like things started off good, and just got better. Is that cheating? I don't know. It's hard to say" (193). Joe expresses surprise at their story's happy ending, thus indirectly suggesting that they are have managed to trick their way out of the fate they deserve.

As has already been suggested, *St. Nicholas* attacks questions of credulity and theatricality head on. The Author's Note makes this clear. McPherson begins with an anecdote which highlights the contexts in which "lies" are acceptable—people do not "expect complete strangers to lie" to them in a pub for instance, but in the theatre invented stories are expected. He goes on to stress how, in a monologue, the character on stage is in fact a guide "telling us about somewhere outside the theatre, not trying to recreate it indoors. The theatre is simply where we meet him." This relationship, however, is far from "simple" and involves the audience's collusion with the actor and ultimately participation in a "type of playing."[61] As Cummings explains, "the fictive environment of the theatre invites the audience to invest belief in what on another level they know to be an artistic fabrication."[62] Yet, when McPherson encourages the audience to "[cast] judgement on the credibility of what his narrator says," it is less "because it necessitates a more general judgement of

---

[61] McPherson, *The Weir and Other Plays* 75-76.
[62] Cummings, "Homo Fabulator," 306.

his narrator's character"[63] than because it is concerned with generating a dynamic of ambiguity that undermines the boundaries between fact and fiction.

As if to highlight this matter, the speaker in *St. Nicholas* opens with a conventional orientation "once upon a time" phrase—"When I was a boy" (79). He addresses what might be the audience's immediate assumptions or associations, appealing to common knowledge of superstition and fiction and by using collective pronouns—"like all of us" or the ideas "we get in books" (79). Then he begins to challenge them with the assertion that vampires materially exist, they are "Matter of fact," "casual" and "ordinary." As such, "practical things" must be learned in order to deal with them. Later, the narrator more forcefully interrupts his own story, and appears to drop the pretence of character, to refute audience scepticism and draw them into collusion with him:

> Mm. There's always going to be a smugness about you listening to this. As we all take part in this convention. And you will say, "These vampires are not very believable, are they?" And you are entitled. This convention. These restrictions, these rules, they give us that freedom. I have the freedom to tell you this unhindered, while you can sit there assured that no one is going to get hurt. (108)

Casting convention aside, he then goes on to criticise the audience's reliance on "the lazy notions foisted upon you by others in the effort to make [them] buy more popcorn" (108). While "we" think we can apprehend the world through science, in fact we understand very little in practice. To illustrate his point he notes,

> We may know that the earth goes round the sun. And we may know that this is due to "gravity." But not one of us knows why there is gravity. So don't sit there and cast judgement on the

---

[63] Cummings, "Homo Fabulator," 307.

credibility of what I say, when you don't even know why you aren't floating off your seats." (109)

Such speculations seem to test the agreed limitations of the "well-disciplined type of playing" that McPherson suggests constitutes theatre.[64] In making disbelief the focus of attention, McPherson's play self-consciously folds back upon theatricality itself, providing an exploration of the mechanics of narrative performance.

In contrast, *The Weir* deals with questions of incredulity and belief in an internalised manner, consistent with the conventions of naturalistic drama. As Jordan argues, this gives rise to a provocative ambivalence with respect to the assumed authenticity of the pastoral mode.[65] As the characters settle down to tell stories of the supernatural in the pub, it should be obvious that no proof of their experiences is possible. The effects their stories have, however, are tangible though each is variously disclaimed or reflected upon with disbelief by the characters of the play in ways which anticipate likely audience reactions to such narratives. The first, told by Joe, relates not his own experience but that of someone now long since dead. Maura Nealon's tale of how her mother heard fairies knocking at their door is a set piece of traditional Irish storytelling. The threat of "the little people" seems far removed from modern concerns and Jack's deliberate setting of the scene and his "relish[ing] the details" (31) acknowledge its status as a "fairytale." Of course, Finbar, who has just leased the same house to Valerie is keen to deny the validity of such outmoded superstitions as "fairy roads" — "You're not bothered by that are you Valerie?" he asks, "'cause it's only old cod, you know?" (33). Fairies and fairy forts, for Finbar are merely colourful, fanciful details for tourists. Valerie, for reasons which are later revealed, is less prepared to dismiss the world of the

---

[64] McPherson, *The Weir and Other Plays*, 75.
[65] Jordan, "Narrating Authenticities in Conor McPherson's *The Weir*," 351-368.

supernatural out of hand, replying "Well. I think there's something in them. No, I do" (33).

Finbar, before relating how a neighbour's experience with a Ouija board frightened him into giving up smoking, prefaces his tale with multiple denials: "It was the … Walsh young one having us all on. It was only a cod, sure" (35). He repeatedly casts aspersions upon the reliability and sanity of the Walsh family—they are in his opinion, "a crowd of headbangers" (36). But, in spite of all his protestations, it is clear that the episode has had a deep affect on him and the story is one he has certainly told before, perhaps with less scepticism. The conflation of Niamh Walsh's hysterical terror of the spirit she believes she has summoned and can see lurking on the stairs, the "coincidental" news of their former neighbour's death (after a fall down stairs), Finbar's own isolation after his father's death and his own night of paralysing fear before the "empty fireplace" (similar to that of Bridie and Maura Nealon), designate an experience of other-worldliness Finbar cannot rationally explain. This experience not only marks the end of his smoking habit, but also, as Valerie perceptively notes, his move to the town, "down into the lights" (40) where, inevitably, the supernatural can be more easily rationalised.

Jim's story is distinct from the fairy tale and the exotic summoning of spirits, and Jim as narrator seems somewhat more inclined to believe that it actually happened. The response to the story of the deceased paedophile who wished to be buried in a child's grave, is first one of disgust and rejection of it on narrative terms by Finbar—"Jaysus, Jim. That's a terrible story, to be telling" (48) which he reiterates later in even stronger language, "Jaysus. That's some fucking story. To be telling a girl, like. Perverts out in the country. For fuck's sake" (49). The second, and predictable, reaction is one of disbelief. Both Jack and then Jim himself suggest that the encounter may be merely a poteen-induced hallucination. However, when Valerie questions Jim directly if he believes it really was an hallucination, he seems uncertain replying, "God, I don't know.

I was flying like, but it was a right fluke him showing me where he wanted to be buried and me knowing nothing about him like" (48).

Valerie's contribution is the most poignant and shocking of the stories as it is about a personal tragedy. The phone call she receives from her daughter is incredible, even to Valerie herself—"I wasn't sure whether this was a dream or her leaving us had been a dream" and even as she is on her way to collect the child she "knew she wasn't going to be there. [She] knew she was gone. […] And there was nothing [she] could do about it" (56-7). The eeriness of Valerie's experience is heightened by the suggestion that the child is threatened by a strange man even in death, just as the ghostly pervert in Jim's story desires to be buried with a recently deceased little girl. The men in horror, again attempt to explain her experience, perhaps it was just her extreme grief, or a wrong number or, as Jim rather unconvincingly suggests, "something else" (58). Valerie, nevertheless, is willing to accept that "It's something that happened" (58) which she cannot explain away. She takes comfort in her companions' stories therefore, as proof that she is not mad but Finbar insists once more on a rational explanation of their stories. Jim was "delirious with flu," Maura Nealon was an alcoholic and the Walshes were "headbangers" (58-9). Finbar, being practical and reasonable, resents being upset by such superstitions.

The men's sympathetic if bewildered response to Valerie's traumatic narrative, and Jack's story of lost love set a sentimental tone at the play's conclusion. Unsurprisingly then, most critics and reviewers have stressed the strong current of empathy in *The Weir*. The communion of storytelling is noted by both Wood and Cummings. Wood goes so far as to state that "by the end of the play, the empathy and kindness that is established among the characters in *The Weir* gain religious resonance."[66] Nevertheless, his claim seems to overstate the

---

[66] Wood, *Imagining Mischief*, 49.

comfort and assurance the characters derive from sharing their stories. In each of these plays McPherson is careful to maintain a portion of uncertainty, be it comic or tragic in timbre. Or, to return to a Lyotardian vocabulary, McPherson's storytelling dramaturgy consistently leaves space for micronarrative dissensus.

Quoting & Joking: Irony & Mischievous Citation
In current interpretations of McPherson's work considerable emphasis has been placed the moral messages it suggests. Nevertheless, if McPherson's mischief is to be found in his dubious narrators and narrative games, then it is also located in the deployment of irony and use of references, allusions and citation that characterise his work over this period.

The Weir is in some respects perhaps the least overtly mischievous of the plays under discussion.[67] Cummings remarks how the play was commissioned for the Royal Court by Stephen Daldry, and suggests that "*The Weir* is McPherson's characteristically cheeky response to the call for him to write characters who talk to each other instead of the audience."[68] In a recent interview with Carol Vander, though, McPherson denies writing *The Weir* to dispel doubts among critics about his ability to write dialogue.[69] McPherson's playfulness emerges, nevertheless, at a formal level. Dromgoole describes the play as a "clever confection of different traditions of drama," noting the shadows of Synge, O'Casey, Friel, Murphy and Billy Roche.[70] McPherson marshals an assemblage of elements that would seem to be a species of semiotic shorthand for a traditional Irish drama—a naturalistic pub setting, lonely old men, whimsical bachelors, boastful local businessmen, rural isolation, alcohol

[67] Though Jordan's reading of the play convincingly suggests otherwise. See "Narrating Authenticities in Conor McPherson's *The Weir*."
[68] Cummings, "Homo Fabulator," 308.
[69] Conor McPherson, interview with Carol Vander, *Plays: Two* (London: Nick Hern, 2004) 214.
[70] Dromgoole, *The Full Room*, 188-9.

and storytelling. Into this is blended a handful of contemporary references, and a self-conscious sense of modern-day doubt, that temper the formal echoes.

In contrast to the muted tones of *The Weir*, in *This Lime Tree Bower* engages vividly with comic irony and dubious citation. The irony that plays across the characters' self-portrayals is obvious. For instance early in the play Joe describes himself as "shrewd" (137), a characteristic clearly not demonstrated by any of his reported actions. Similarly, Ray's academic specialisation and, especially, his incomprehensible article in the journal *Ethics*, are absurdly divorced from his onstage persona. Ray claims superiority over Joe and Frank due to his "philosophical training," but his worthy and educated advice is to do "absolutely nothing" (176).

Although most of *This Lime Tree Bower*'s complexity is generated by the divergences between the narrators' perspectives, McPherson's use of citation adds a further dimension to the narrative games of the play. Samuel Taylor Coleridge's poem "This Lime Tree Bower My Prison" (1797) not only provides the play's title but is, of course, included as a preface to the play:

> A delight
> Comes sudden on my heart, and I am glad
> As I myself were there! Nor in this bower,
> This little lime tree bower, have I not marked
> Much that has soothed me.
> ... No sound is dissonant which tells of life.

McPherson's citation of Coleridge has been read as a kind of "mini-manifesto,"[71] his declaration of loyalty to the micronarrative, as it were. Yet, I would argue that in shifting attention to Coleridge's concluding line, one elides the chief element of the title, and therefore the implicit missing piece in McPherson's borrowed fragment—that is, the notion of the

---

[71] Adams, "So There's These Three Irishmen..." (online).

prison. If Coleridge finds comfort in his bower-prison in the noises of life from without, then one must ask what is the relationship of the poem's dynamic to that of the play which cites it. Is the bare stage of the play to be understood as a comparable prison? Certainly the details of life related in this space are deficient in soothing qualities. The mapping of a romantic poetics upon the starkly unpoetic modern world is indeed dissonant and at odds with the substance on the play.

More mischievous is the manner in which McPherson embeds philosophical references. One of the key thematic elements to Ray's narrative is the visit by the famous philosopher Wolfgang Konigsberg who has been, for decades, honing his theory of language as an organic thing. While the professor is a fiction, his name might be understood as a veiled, if cursory, reference to Immanuel Kant—McPherson studied moral philosophy and wrote an MA thesis on utilitarianism. Kant, sometimes known as "the sage of Königsberg," never left his place of birth, in contrast to the ancient and much travelled Professor Konigsberg of the play. Kant's three *Critiques*, of Pure Reason, Practical Reason and of Judgement, are gestured towards simply in the play, where questions of experience, judgement and morality are dramatised and the suggestion that perception is ultimately subjective is advanced. Though it would be foolhardy to claim that McPherson is attempting to create a sustained Kantian exploration of such questions, the intertext is a crucial feature of the play's structure.

As if to complicate the matter of perspective in the play still further, Professor Konigsberg's theory holds that language is now dying and that lack of sincerity is one of the signs (178). Ray's narrative might be taken as a demonstration of just such linguistic decadence or postmodern deterioration. The irony of Konigsberg's conception of language as a dying entity is further enriched by the fact that he himself prohibits communication by "insist[ing] on giving his papers with no discussion" (177), that is to say, he insists upon monologue.

In *St. Nicholas* a number of discernible allusions and citations occur. The first allusion, which is hinted at in the Author's Note prefacing the play is to Christmas. Saint Nicholas or Santa Claus suggests a time of publicly sanctioned (self)deception, illusion and indulgence. It is also a time for new beginnings and gifts. While this is never openly addressed in the play (in addition the story takes place in the summer), it provides an ironic backdrop to the cynical narrator's rebirth as storyteller.

As McPherson remarks, making the only speaker in a monologue play a theatre critic is an act of open provocation. The irony that those judging the play, first hand as it were, are represented on stage in a highly ambivalent and often distasteful manner, lingers in the narrator's self description as a bastard, a cultural arbitrator, a failed writer, an alcoholic, a potential rapist and, finally, a kind of vampire pimp. Well before the story of his encounter with the vampire household, the critic is established as a parasitical figure himself. The fact that he describes himself as "intelligent, but [having] not real thoughts on things" (80) is very close to his criticism of William later. McPherson leaves little doubt as to the target of his satire—critics who are primarily jealous because they are themselves failed writers.

The narrator's self-confessed problem is a deficit of innovation. He is plagued by what is a highly postmodern dilemma—he feels doomed to process, respond to, and recycle others' artistic products. "I had no ideas. No ideas for a story. [...] Nothing ever came. I could only write about what there was already" (81) he complains early in the play—he had unsuccessfully,

> Tried to convey the feelings I had. That I genuinely fucking had—for people. I loved people. I loved the stupid bastards. [...] I wanted to let my compassion seep out across the stage. Handicapped people in love. Queers and lesbians absolving each other. A liberal, fucking, all encompassing ... you know. (80-81)

This commentary on his narrative and imaginative crisis is richly ironic on a number of levels. The first and most conspicuous irony is that as the rest of his story amply testifies the narrator is a hardened misanthrope. Even when trying to claim compassion for humanity, his language betrays him—people are "stupid bastards" and homosexual men are "queers." Furthermore, it is evident that his interest in such emotion is only in the end it may serve in his writing. None of his reported actions might be construed as even vaguely compassionate.

More interesting is the fundamentally clichéd nature of his self-constituting narrative. The narrator boasts at the end of the play how he now has a story, but what is that story? His tale is one of self-destruction, in which the protagonist must reach a nadir in order to reevaluate his life—a familiar narrative trajectory. It is also one in which a wayward protagonist encounters vampires but manages to escape to tell the tale—again, an old favourite with multiple variations in literature and film. It might be argued, with considerable evidence, that in spite of the concluding bravado, the narrator still "only write[s] about what there was already" (81). If his story is taken as credible, then it relates a preexisting experience. If his story is taken as incredible, a fabrication, then it draws upon what preexists it through citation and allusion.

The allusions and citations playfully used throughout propagate ironic commentary on originality and true stories of conversion. The irony of the jaded theatre critic who is mesmerised by the lead actress in a production of *Salomé* is extended in her fateful name, Helen. Salomé's performance is, of course, a dance of death; the perfection of the dance is used to manipulate Herod Antipas into beheading John the Baptist (Matthew 14:1-11). Like Herod, the critic is overwhelmed by Helen's performance which he experiences as a kind of epiphany. At first he perceives her as "just one more [...] thing beyond my reach" (87), but later he refines this response. Not only is she a physically "perfect specimen" (91) but more significantly she was someone "doing what they wanted, not more and no less" (92), and both of these attributes are, it seems, far beyond the narrator's reach. Provoked by the vision of Helen as Salomé, the narrator indulges in his own "amateur dramatics," in order to catch her attention, to such an extent that he "even began to believe [his] own hype" (89) and, finally, concludes with his own stage debut.

The most extended allusions in *St. Nicholas* are clearly to Bram Stoker's archetypal vampire story, *Dracula*. The night the narrator falls under Helen's spell, he notes her cool hands—a characteristic also noted in the vampire William. That evening, like Stoker's character Lucy Westenra, he spends the night exposed—he sleeps on the sofa in his study with the windows open "and things crawled all over [him] till it got bright" (90). The change wrought by this evening encounter is the catalyst to the narrative which develops. His meeting with William at the conclusion of the first half of the play, provides an easily recognisable citation of Stoker's *Dracula*—the narrator first perceives William as a large dog and later they look down over the city contemplating "All those lives" (102-3), a direct quotation from the novel. William's warning about the female vampires who share the house and the sound of their laughter again recalls notes of Jonathan Harker's imprisonment in Dracula's castle, his encounter with the undead, his hysteria, mental breakdown and escape. These references supply further ironic testimony to the narrator's lack of ideas and his ability to recycle.

As mentioned above, the dramatic strategy of monologue coupled with a self-conscious and aggressively defensive narrator foregrounds the question of incredulity. This tension is reflected especially in the narrative's concern with superstition and truth. Belief in the power of the Bible or garlic is dismissed as mere superstition. Peculiarly, and of course ironically, the only deterrent to vampires is an overwhelming desire for empirical certainty. The Eastern European tradition of sprinkling rice on the windowsill for protection is the only guaranteed deterrent because "for some reason" "the vampire is compelled to count every grain" (107). The trap of wanting to know exactly and exhaustively is the only one that may lead the vampire to destruction, and might be considered of similar destructive potential for the narrative illusion created in the play.

Knowledge and self-knowledge are never quite what they seem. "The metaphor of the storyteller as vampire," as Cummings has observed, "suggests something about his self-consciousness and possible ambivalence about his chosen craft."[72] McPherson exploits this ambivalence by making the narrator's criticisms of the vampires equally applicable to the narrator himself who, like William, makes his faults into virtues (107-8). Although McPherson's note to the text emphasises the human quality of interpretation and the responsibility of reason, the facile nature of such a moral seems to be undermined by the play. The moment of epiphany is ostensibly about perception derived from an ability to interpret and significantly is generated by a story within the story. William's narrative takes the shape of a folk tale: A woodcutter one day rescues an old man who as a reward gives him a watch which has the power to turn back time. The woodcutter sees no use for such a device until his beloved wife dies; only then does he begin to use the watch to travel back in time to be with her. Finally, he goes back to her childhood and the watch breaks. He panics and tries to escape with her but is beaten by the villagers and left for dead. He is trapped in the past.

The story is incredulously and ironically received by the play's narrator who immediately demands an explanation of its, albeit rather obvious, meaning. The vampire responds with bewilderment, he seems unable to fix or locate the tale's moral. This episode leads to the narrator's triumphant realisation of the human capacity to reflect. Although Cummings claims that "the critic's revelation that man is the self-reflective animal, the

---

[72] Cummings, "Homo Fabulator," 307-8.

creature who looks back, judges, and regrets, may strike some as forced, simplistic or moralistic, but when seen as a direct result of a story-within-a-story, it takes on an added dimension,"[73] it could be argued that the superficiality of the revelation is precisely the point. In the words of *St. Nicholas's* narrator: "we all need a purpose in life, even if we've got to make it up ah?" (99). Despite McPherson's subsequent retreat into naturalistic forms, or monologues that are decidedly less self-reflexive or ironic, *St. Nicholas* raises issues that are pertinent to readings of all his work in this period, especially with regard to the claims made for its moral status.

Failure & Morality

As mentioned in the opening chapter, David Edgar proposes that one of the uniting concerns of British drama of the 1990s is discontented, disillusioned or disaffected masculinity.[74] It is, notably, a leitmotif that also surfaces in the work of a number of young Irish playwrights' work such as Eugene O'Brien's *Eden* (2001); Mark O'Rowe's *Howie the Rookie* (1999) and *Made in China* (2001); and is an important element to Enda Walsh's *Disco Pigs* (1996), *Sucking Dublin* (1997), *misterman* (1999) and *bedbound* (2000).[75] McPherson's falls within this ambit too, though with a good deal less of the linguistic violence of O'Rowe and Walsh. Rather, as Moroney observes:

> Generally McPherson's work is utterly male-centred, with a
> grimly philosophical tinge—quietly excoriating his characters

---

[73] Cummings, "Homo Fabulator," 307.

[74] David Edgar ed., *State of Play: Playwrights on Playwriting* (London: Faber and Faber, 1999) 26-27.

[75] Stephen Di Bendetto addresses an aspect of this leitmotif in "Shattering Images of Sex Acts and Other Obscene Staged Transgressions in Contemporary Irish Plays by Men" in *Australasian Drama Studies* 43 (2003) special issue *Performing Ireland*, eds. Brian Singleton and Anna McMullan: 46-65. See also Brian Singleton, "Am I Talking to Myself? Men, Masculinities and the Monologue in Contemporary Irish Theatre" in *Monologues: Theatre, Perfromance, Subjectivity*, for a developed exploration of the issue.

by exposing their hard-wired, anti-social desires, and offering little antidote other than black humour.[76]

If this is a prominent feature of the plays discussed above, then it has also continued to be at the centre of McPherson's subsequent work: *Port Authority* is an ensemble of monologues for three men of different ages who enumerate their lost opportunities; *Dublin Carol* features a partially reformed alcoholic who abandoned his family as a result of his addiction, his daughter, and an aimless young man who unsuccessfully attempts to break up with his girlfriend; *Come On Over* is structured principally around two monologues, one for a man and the other for a woman, yet again the male figure, a priest, is scarred by hypocrisy and doubt; *Shining City* is a naturalistic four-hander, lead by a failed priest turned counsellor and a middle-aged man who is haunted by his deceased wife to whom he was unfaithful; finally, his most recent work, *The Seafarer* gathers a now rather familiar group of beleaguered, lonely male characters around a card table at Christmas time. Female characters are narrowly defined, acting as catalysts to disruption, comforters, or figures of conscience, but above all they are survivors. Valerie in *The Weir* reconnects the men in the play with a realm of emotion; Mary in *Dublin Carol* in a messenger of death and possible reconciliation; in *Come On Over* Margaret arguably acts as Matthew's confessor, while also testifying to their past love for one another; finally, in *Shining City*, Neasa's role is as a long-suffering partner and mother, who attempts to persuade the protagonist and ex-priest, Ian, to commit to his life with them.

The thematics of failure is underpinned by McPherson's choice of form and exploration of narrative on stage. Isolation is reinforced by the absence of closure each story inevitably involves. Throughout *This Lime Tree Bower*, *St. Nicholas* and *The Weir*, McPherson investigates the potentialities of storytelling as a performative, ludic, dubious, confessional and, finally,

---

[76] Moroney, "The Twisted Mirror," 269.

communal activity. However, he consistently avoids commitment to any sort of normative ethics which is an important feature of his engagement with contemporary conditions of identity.

As noted above, it has been popular to interpret the plays as ultimately probing moral questions to some, usually undefined, ethical end. Wood, for instance, struggles to reconcile his own desire for moral closure and stability with the dissensus and provisionality these micronarratives entail. He argues that "McPherson's theatre of mischief is designed to stimulate the moral imagination of his audience, without endorsing any specific morality itself" and that the "plays invite audiences to practise compassion and, hopefully imagine their own reasonable conclusions."[77] However, this conclusion not only elides the implications of a micronarrative imperative where self is performative rather than predetermined, and where morality may prove to be just as provisional and contingent, but it also neatly shifts the "problem" of morality to the audience alone. At the same time it denies the troubled ethics of dissensus nascent in the plays.

The delicacy of McPherson's exploration of troubled masculinities, performative identities, micronarrative and ethics has arguably become his signature style. It is a style that stands in striking contrast to that of the subject of the following chapter. As a close contemporary of McPherson, Mark Ravenhill notably tackles some of these same issues but in a radically different manner.

---

[77] Wood, *Imagining Mischief*, 118, 119.

Mark Ravenhill
Plagiarism, Play or Critique?

We haven't reached perfection. But it's the closest we've come to meaning. Civilisation is money. Money is civilisation ... it's the same thing, you understand?[1]

Mark Ravenhill has been claimed by Aleks Sierz as "one of the quintessential writers of the 1990s."[2] In spite of various other provocative plays such as Anthony Neilson's *Penetrator* (1993), Judy Upton's *Ashes and Sand* (1994) or Jez Butterworth's *Mojo* (1995), it is Ravenhill's *Shopping and Fucking* (Royal Court Upstairs, 26 September 1996) that has come to exemplify In-Yer-Face theatre. Considered by some reviewers as another provocateur like Sarah Kane, Ravenhill's work has largely been defined by its use of sensation and spectacle. These have certainly also been outstanding elements in the promotion and reception of this particular play. Although not Ravenhill's first work, *Shopping and Fucking* was his first to gain widespread public recognition and notoriety. This is unsurprising given its title, which he claims is an ironic allusion to the subject matter of popular fiction novelists such as Jackie Collins.[3] As Dan Rebellato describes in his introduction to Ravenhill's first

---

[1] Mark Ravenhill, *Shopping and Fucking, Plays: 1* (London: Methuen, 2001) 87. All quotations from the plays will be taken from this edition and will be cited in-text.

[2] Aleks Sierz, *In-Yer-Face Theatre* <http://www.inyerface-theatre.com/az.html>.

[3] Sierz, *In-Yer-Face Theatre: British Drama Today* (London: Faber, 2001) 122.

collection of plays, the title could not be processed by the theatre's computers because of the risk of obscenity.[4] Similarly, Sierz notes that "under a Victorian law—the Indecent Advertisements Act 1889, amended by the Indecent Displays (Control) Act 1981—the word 'fuck' is banned from public display." The full title could not appear on any publicity material and the box office staff were unable, due to legal risk, to say the full name of the play.[5] Needless to say such sensation generated considerable free publicity and made Ravenhill something of a celebrity figure. Even the protests at performances outside London positively contributed to the Royal Court's reputation for promoting and staging cutting edge new writing.[6]

Shopping and Fucking also courted controversy with its depiction of contemporary culture in terms of graphic sex, violence and crude materialism. However, unlike the reception of Sarah Kane's *Blasted* (1995), the critical response to Ravenhill's play was generally quite positive. Journalists who had castigated Kane, found the play courageous. And although *Guardian* critic Michael Billington noted the play's unevenness and John Gross in the *Sunday Telegraph* criticised its "glib pessimism," it was soon touted as a mascot of In-Yer-Face theatre.[7] Ravenhill's popularity was further ameliorated by endorsements from the magazine media and the gay press. Rebellato describes his work as "defiantly young [and] queer,"[8] but it should also be noted that Ravenhill rejects the "gay

---

4 Dan Rebellato, Introduction, *Plays: 1*, by Mark Ravenhill (London: Methuen, 2001) ix.

5 Sierz, *In-Yer-Face Theatre*, 125-26.

6 Sierz describes the protests which took place in small cities and towns where the play was performed. For instance, in Swansea a group of Christians interrupted the performance by singing hymns. See *In-Yer-Face Theatre*, 125-126.

7 Sierz provides a popular but full account of reviewers' responses to the play, to which this survey is indebted. As he notes, Jack Tinker, the journalist who lead the outrage against Sarah Kane's *Blasted* in 1995, was among those who praised the "courage" of *Shopping and Fucking*. *In-Yer-Face Theatre*, 128.

8 Rebellato, *Mark Ravenhill Plays: 1*, ix.

writer" label.[9] Finally, the fact that the play rapidly toured in Europe and beyond served to enhance its "cult" status, at least among younger audiences.[10]

Ravenhill went on to write *Faust Is Dead* (Lyric Hammersmith Studio, September 1997,[11] revised version Zephyr Theatre Los Angeles, 23 May 1998), *Handbag* (Lyric Hammersmith Studio, 14 September 1998) and *Some Explicit Polaroids* (Theatre Royal Bury St. Edmunds, 30 September 1999; New Ambassadors, September 1999). Each of these plays is provocative, though obviously their titles are less confronting. His subsequent work includes *Mother Clap's Molly House* (National Theatre London, 2001) and *Totally Over You* (National Theatre Connections Project, 2003), *Citizenship* (National Theatre London, 2005), *The Product* (Traverse, 2005), *The Cut* (Donmar Warehouse London, 2006) and *pool (no water)* (Drum Theatre Plymouth, 2006). The focus here is on the work included in *Plays 1* which was produced in the late 1990s. Each of these plays explores similar territories of collapsed certainties, ironic intertextuality, pastiche and alienated subjectivity. Ravenhill's interest in contemporary consumer society is explicit in *Shopping and Fucking*, and as Jozef De Vos states, "contemporary uprootedness and lack of values are [...] directly and expressly put in the context of postmodernism."[12] His acknowledged influences suggest some of the literary and cultural signposts for such a context. Though Ravenhill does cite Martin Crimp's *Dealing with Clair* (1988), and the plays of David Mamet and Caryl Churchill among his inspirations, the

---

[9] See Ravenhill's contribution to *State of Play: Playwrights on Playwriting*, ed. David Edgar (London: Faber and Faber, 1999) 50-51; Andrew Smith, "Brits Riding a New Theatre Wave," *Q Online* 10 Nov. 1999; and Sierz, *In-Yer-Face Theatre*, 151.

[10] Sierz offers a detailed description of the play's travels and of some of its productions in London and overseas. See *In-Yer-Face Theatre*, 127-28 and 133-34.

[11] No specific premiere date is given in the *Plays 1* edition.

[12] Jozef De Vos, "Ravenhill's Wilde Game," *Crucible of Cultures: Anglophone Drama at the Dawn of a New Millenium*, eds. Marc Maufort and Franca Bellarsi (Brussels: Peter Lang, 2002) 48.

majority are significantly from American fiction rather than theatre—"Douglas Coupland's *Generation X*, Bret Easton Ellis's *Less than Zero*, Tama Janowitz's *Slaves of New York* and Jay McInerney's *Bright Lights, Big City*." For Ravenhill these texts "managed to capture the essence of what a generation had experienced, a sense of materialism and a kind of moral vacuum" and they "reflected [his] sense of the world better than any British fiction or drama."[13] Perhaps more immediately important as will be discussed below, is the shadowy presence of cultural theorists and philosophers like Michel Foucault, Jean François Lyotard and Jean Baudrillard, whose ideas percolate through the plays.

Two aspects of Ravenhill's drama might be remarked at the outset: the formal qualities of its engagement with postmodernity and the political implications of that engagement. Key features of the plays from *Shopping and Fucking* to *Some Explicit Polaroids* are citation and reference woven into dialogue and social observation. Bits and pieces of pop culture elements are mixed with allusions to and borrowings of ideas from critical texts on postmodernism, highlighting identity as arbitrary and performative, and delineating a pervasive sense of alienation. In contrast to Conor McPherson's relatively static stage spaces, Ravenhill's drama is characterised by rapid sequences of scenes and visceral images. Yet, as will be illustrated below Ravenhill's visceral theatricality is distinguished from that of the other major 1990s playwright of provocation, Sarah Kane, in its dramatic precedents, form and intention. Rather than extended and, ultimately, literary narrative devices, his work usually unfolds in multiple interrelated short scenes that seem more indebted to television or cinema. Nevertheless, the extent of such parallels should not be overstated. Although *Faust Is Dead* incorporates the use of various technological devices—the internet, a video camera, projections (depending on directorial preference)—and *Handbag*

---

[13] Sierz, *In-Yer-Face Theatre*, 124.

involves the splicing of action in the nineteenth and twentieth centuries, rather than being formally innovative, Ravenhill returns to fairly conventional dramaturgical techniques. The worlds of these plays are violent and materialistic in the extreme, yet they are also peppered with disconcertingly familiar elements of contemporary urban life. For the most part they follow, as De Vos comments, a "slice of life" realist mode.[14] For Ravenhill the question of responsibility inheres in these contexts, and his work explicitly depicts postmodern culture in order to explore issues of contemporary selfhood and responsibility. The way in which his plays amalgamate the appropriation and assimilation of postmodern superficiality or depthlessness, with a critique of these same features and values is arguably their most interesting and problematic quality. In particular I will explore how these issues are focused through a varied thematics of consumption and commodification, the ambivalence of father figures, the formal implications of citation and, finally, through questions of politics and responsibility.

Surface Tension

The perception of Ravenhill among some critics as a purveyor of "sexually explicit, sensationalist, shock-loaded drama"[15] has given rise to a number of interpretations of his work that are worth unravelling. Grouping Ravenhill with other writers like Sarah Kane, Jim Cartwright, Irvine Welsh and Enda Walsh, Merle Tönnies juxtaposes their work with the "extreme forms of 'sensation drama'" of the 1890s which "aim[ed] at the strongest possible effect through uncommonness and extremity [often leading to a focus] more on excess of incident than on the overall cohesion of the plot."[16] Tönnies points out how in

---

[14] De Vos, "Ravenhill's Wilde Game," 47.

[15] Rebellato, *Mark Ravenhill Plays: 1*, x.

[16] Merle Tönnies, "The 'Sensationalist Theatre of Cruelty' in 1990s Britain, its 1960s Forebears and the Beginning of the 21st Century," *(Dis)Continuities: Trends and Traditions in Contemporary Theatre and Drama in English*, CDE 9, eds.

comparison with both 1890s theatre and the provocative drama of the 1960s, the twentieth century fin de siècle theatre amplified "both the shock effects and the obviousness with which a 'message' suggested itself."[17] While this assertion is questionable with regard to Kane, it may be verified in Ravenhill's work. Certainly the surface tension of the message is remarked upon briefly by Dominic Dromgoole who praises Ravenhill's visual and verbal wit, but worries that "it's perilously close to soap, where everyone knows and describes what they're feeling."[18] Sierz too has noted the way in which "characters openly proclaim their worldview.[19] Similarly, reviewers complained of the "occasional explicitness of intent" or the way in which Ravenhill seemed to "bludgeon" spectators "with his overriding point."[20] The political element of Ravenhill's work, Dromgoole claims, can be traced back to the dramatic concerns of George Bernard Shaw. Indeed, when the pyrotechnics of shock and provocation are set aside, this is one of the most tenable genealogies to be identified. The "verbal wit [...] resistance to the morality of the preceding generation, [...] a keen sense of sociology" and the intellectual energy of Shaw, as Dromgoole says, are also much in evidence in Ravenhill.[21] The currents of the sociological, the anthropological and the political that run through the plays are openly acknowledged by Ravenhill himself, who claims that he is a materialist committed to social observation and compelled to write about the present. More precisely, he goes on to declare:

Margarete Rubik and Elke Mettinger-Schartmann (Trier: Wissenschaftlicher Verlag Trier, 2002) 57-72. 59, 60.

[17] Tönnies, "The 'Sensationalist Theatre of Cruelty' in 1990s Britain," 65.

[18] Dominic Dromgoole, *The Full Room: An A-Z of Contemporary Playwriting* (London: Methuen, 2002) 236.

[19] Sierz, *In-Yer-Face Theatre*, 148.

[20] Paul Taylor, *"Shopping and Fucking,"* *Independent* 3 Oct. 1996: 7 and Benedict Nightingale, "Bargain Debasement," *Times* 18 June 1997: 21.

[21] Dromgoole, *The Full Room*, 235.

I want to write about globalisation or, to give it a more honest name, Americanisation. To capture the truth of this new world we live in [...]. To write about the virtual markets of images and information spinning around us and threatening to drag us into perpetual postmodern giddiness. To write about the hypocrisy of our calls for universal freedom and democracy as we destroy the world for profit.[22]

Here again, before turning to his specific contemporary subject matter, Ravenhill might be considered in the light of Shaw's iconoclastic legacy. Shaw's attempts through his drama to provide "a means of public thinking on the ideological conflicts of his time"[23] have had a profound impact on modern Anglophone drama that is traceable in the work of playwrights like John Osborne, David Edgar, Howard Brenton and, perhaps Ravenhill's most immediate predecessor, David Hare.[24] As Christopher Innes describes, Shaw's interpretation of Henrik Ibsen's work in his lecture "The Quintessence of Ibsenism" (1890) and in his own plays "became [a] decisive factor." Whereas,

> elsewhere in Europe symbolic or psychological themes predominated. By contrast, the mainstream of serious English

---

[22] Mark Ravenhill, "A Touch of Evil," *Guardian* 22 Mar. 2003 (online).

[23] R.J. Kaufman, Introduction, *G.B. Shaw: A Collection of Critical Essays* (Englewood Cliffs NJ: Prentice-Hall, 1965) 7.

[24] Hare has established himself a kind of middle-class voice of social conscience at the National Theatre and as such might seem an unlikely forerunner for Ravenhill. However, with his critical portrayals of modern British society, attention to history and documentary, left wing politics, often coolly articulate characters, Hare has laid a solid, if less fashionably provocative, foundation for Ravenhill's political questioning. See for instance Peter Ansorge chapter 2 on Hare and the National Theatre in *From Liverpool to Los Angeles: On Writing for Theatre, Film and Television*, 22-61; Christopher Innes, *Modern British* Drama, 218-233; on early Hare and political theatre see Ronald Hayman, *British Theatre since 1955: A Reassessment* chapter 3; and Klaus-Peter Müller "Political Plays in England in the 1990s," in *British Drama of the 1990s*, 15-36.

drama has continued to reflect the realistic treatment of social questions that Shaw promoted.[25]

The Shavian commitment to the debate and critique of values with an emphasis, as Innes puts it, on discussion rather than on denouement, can be identified in modified and updated form in Ravenhill's drama.[26] Like Shaw, Ravenhill provokes with a view to generating an awareness, in his audience/readers, of "imperative historical realities."[27] Ravenhill's work though is tinged with a sense of despair in relation to the society he depicts. By the end of the twentieth century an early Shavian "confidence in the force of progressive intellectual enlightenment,"[28] seems misplaced in a world defined by a "sense of materialism and [...] moral vacuum."[29] Compared with Shaw's bold assertions, the political convictions of Ravenhill's plays may seem somewhat weak and superficial. Yet, criticism of Ravenhill on the basis of superficiality must be qualified and tested against the contexts and value systems he explores and dramatises, in particular those of contemporary consumerism and postmodernity where a play of surfaces is a prime substantive quality.

From Spectacle to Simulacrum

Apart from what Linda Hutcheon calls "a grand flourish of negativised rhetoric,"[30] there seems little consensus as to the exact nature, the implications of or appropriate response to the much vaunted "crisis of representation" in the postindustrial world. Ravenhill's plays from *Shopping and Fucking* to *Some Explicit Polaroids* reflect upon society in the thrall of

---

[25] Innes, *Modern British Drama*, 14.

[26] For detailed discussion of Shaw's development of discursive dramaturgy see Innes, *Modern British Drama*, 19 and following.

[27] Kaufman, *G.B. Shaw: A Collection of Critical Essays*, 3.

[28] Innes, *Modern British Drama*, 20.

[29] Sierz, *In-Yer-Face Theatre*, 124.

[30] Linda Hutcheon, *A Poetics of Postmodernism: History, Theory, Fiction* (New York and London: Routledge, 1988) 3.

consumerism, globalisation and a profound sense of instability. Given that a strong tendency in theorising the postmodern is towards fragmentation and excessive claims,[31] Ravenhill employs some of these theories in a manner which is, significantly, fragmented, superficial and exaggerated. In other words, the plays wear their references on their sleeves in a display of knowingness. While Ravenhill is clearly acquainted with the main landmarks of a particular discursive terrain, what emerges in the plays is a bricolage, a readily consumable "beginner's guide" version[32] to perspectives on a society of commodity, the micronarrative and the death of the subject. As Rebellato states, these are "all recognisable postmodern slogans" and Ravenhill employs them with a deliberate scepticism.[33] Nevertheless, even in his scepticism, Ravenhill rarely goes beyond the face values of the issues he raises. Though it has regularly been noted that he explicitly refers to and pastiches both Lyotard and Baudrillard, not to mention the Foucault-Baudrillard hybrid character, Alain, in *Faust Is Dead*,[34] the discourses of spectacle, commodity and ultimately, postmodernity assumed in Ravenhill's work might be considered in more detail than they have been to date, as means of both avoiding and explaining the casual amnesia his characters so often seem subject to or struggle with.

In exploring this terrain a number of coordinates need to be taken into account. Ravenhill's prime concerns are arguably "times like these"[35]—the contemporary—and responses to the

---

31 See Hans Bertens, *The Idea of the Postmodern: A History* (London and New York: Routledge, 1995) chapter 11 for a review of some postmodern theory's excesses.

32 See Sierz, *In-Yer-Face Theatre*, 135. Ravenhill describes how he studied Foucault and Baudrillard, beginning with *Baudrillard for Beginners*, but felt that these writers were "being quite chic, having these dangerous thoughts about violence and sexuality, but they lacked any responsibility."

33 Rebellato, *Mark Ravenhill Plays: 1*, xiv.

34 For example, Sierz, *In-Yer-Face Theatre*, 135; De Vos, "Ravenhill's Wilde Game," 46-47; Johan Callens, "Sorting Out Ontologies in Mark Ravenhill's *Faust (Faust is Dead)*," *Mediated Drama Dramatized Media*, CDE 7, ed. Eckart Voigts-Virchow (Trier: Wissenschaftlicher Verlag Trier, 2000)167-177.

35 Ravenhill, "A Touch of Evil" (online).

contemporary—ways of living, understanding and acting. And these interests serve to locate his work within a tradition of political (and leftist) theatre in Britain. As a starting point to a mapping of the postmodernism which obtains in Ravenhill's theatre, Guy Debord's *The Society of the Spectacle* (1967) is perhaps one of the more invisible predecessors to Baudrillard's oft-cited ideas regarding society and simulacra, and also to Fredric Jameson's discussion of the crisis in representation that allegedly characterises postmodernity. Debord argues that

> The whole life of those societies in which modern conditions of production prevail presents itself as an immense accumulation of *spectacles*. All that once was directly lived has become mere representation.[36]

Though Debord does not overtly concern himself with postmodernity—his focus is the formation and operation of a consumer society—the conditions he explores bear upon the debate, in particular the way in which this turn to spectacle involves surfaces and a transformation of the perception and experience of time. The spectacle is omnipresent; it is neither a decoration nor a supplement to the real world, instead

> it is the very heart of society's real unreality. In all its specific manifestations—news or propaganda, advertising or the actual consumption of entertainment—the spectacle epitomises the prevailing model of social life.[37]

Rather than an assemblage of images, spectacle for Debord is "a social relationship between people that is mediated by images"[38] in which the spectacle implies the commodity,

---

[36] Guy Debord, *The Society of the Spectacle*, trans. Donald Nicholson-Smith (1967; New York: Zone, 1995) 12.

[37] Debord, *The Society of the Spectacle*, 13.

[38] Debord, *The Society of the Spectacle*, 12.

transforming the earlier economic dominant of "being into having" to "a generalised shift from *having* to appearing." [39]

The five aspects of "integrated" spectacle, which Debord subsequently enumerates in the *Commentary on the Society of the Spectacle* (1988), resurface in modified form in the major critiques of postmodernity and postmodernism, by Lyotard, Jameson and Baudrillard, among others; these include, "incessant technological renewal, integration of state and economy, generalised secrecy, unanswerable lies, and an eternal present." [40] The other point of contiguity is a sustained interest in production and consumption. Both Lyotard's and Baudrillard's early work has a strong neo-Marxist strain, abandoned later; while Jameson's arguably continues in that direction. As Hans Bertens states, Jameson and Baudrillard (one might also add Lyotard) assume "a causal relationship between the new developments in western capitalism and the rise of the postmodern" [41] — a causality that is likewise implicit in Ravenhill's drama. Also prominent is an ongoing concern for the spectacular and surface quality of the postmodern, as well as its distortion of time. However, whereas the former two envision this situation in apocalyptic terms, Lyotard finds in the changing conditions of knowledge, what he calls the "crisis of legitimation," the possibility for ethical "dissensus" (as discussed in relation to McPherson's micronarratives) in place of totalising "grand narratives" of legitimation such as "the life of the spirit" or "the emancipation of humanity." [42] In contrast, Jameson predicts an end to the possibility of emancipatory politics, a view which Ravenhill appears to adopt. In concordance with Baudrillard, Jameson describes postmodernism as "the transformation of reality into images,

---

[39] Debord, *The Society of the Spectacle*, 16.

[40] Qtd. in Len Bracken, *Guy Debord: Revolutionary* (Venice CA: Feral House, 1997) 198.

[41] Bertens, *The Idea of the Postmodern*, 162.

[42] Jean-François Lyotard, *The Postmodern Condition: A Report on Knowledge*, trans. Geoff Bennington and Brian Massumi (1979; Manchester: Manchester University Press, 1986) 46.

the fragmentation of time into a series of perpetual presents."[43] His 1984 essay, "Postmodernism, or the Cultural Logic of Late Capitalism," proposes an interpretation of postmodernism as "a cultural dominant" which is also a social phenomenon, and offers "a periodising hypothesis." For Jameson what is at stake is political:

> every position on postmodernism in culture—whether apologia or stigmatisation—is also at one and the same time, and *necessarily*, an implicitly or explicitly political stance on the nature of multinational capitalism today.[44]

Consumer society is structured by patterns of consumption which, with their focus on speed and obsolescence, lead to a pervasive sense of depthlessness and the erosion of history. Depthlessness is evidenced in postmodernism's "fascinat[ion] precisely by this whole 'degraded' landscape of schlock and kitsch [...] materials they no longer simply 'quote,' as a Joyce or a Mahler might have done, but incorporate into their very substance," as exemplified by the "commodity fetishism" of Andy Warhol's images of soup cans and cola bottles.[45] Two recurrent characteristics of postmodernist art and writing, then, are pastiche and fragmented discontinuity. For Jameson pastiche is but the empty shell of parody.[46] The second feature is a schizophrenic sense of time, of the perpetual present, "an experience of isolated, disconnected, discontinuous material signifiers which fail to link up into a coherent sequence."[47] As a

---

[43] Fredric Jameson, "Postmodernism, or the Cultural Logic of Late Capitalism," *Postmodernism: A Reader*, ed. Thomas Docherty (New York: Harvester Wheatsheaf, 1993) 85.

[44] Jameson, "Postmodernism, or the Cultural Logic of Late Capitalism," 64.

[45] Jameson, "Postmodernism, or the Cultural Logic of Late Capitalism," 63, 68.

[46] Jameson, "Postmodernism, or the Cultural Logic of Late Capitalism," 73.

[47] Fredric Jameson, "Postmodernism and Consumer Society," *The Anti-Aesthetic: Essays on Postmodern Culture*, ed. Hal Foster (1983; New York: The New Press, 1998) 137.

result of these features culture becomes ingrown, reviewing, remaking and simulating pasts in a nostalgic reflex.

In his discussion of contemporary nostalgic modes Jameson's attitude is comparable to Baudrillard's in *La Société de consommation* (1970), which in turn not only closely echoes Debord's text in title, but approaches fundamentally the same issue. While Debord speaks of spectacle, Baudrillard argues "that consumption, as 'a system of meaning' is not organised along lines of needs, pleasure, etc."[48] As a system of signs rather than of concrete realities, like Debord, Baudrillard contests that the "the process of signification is, at bottom, nothing but a gigantic simulation model of meaning."[49] Baudrillard later extends this notion as "the precession of simulacra," where epoch of the spectacle becomes an age of simulation in which the hyperreal has replaced the real, and where even alienation disappears in the plethora of simulacra and the disappearance of the individual.[50] Postmodernism likewise, according to Jameson, names "a new kind of superficiality in the most literal sense"[51] in which the absence of depth or authenticity and the "waning of affect" must be "seen in terms of the so-called death of the individual subject, a death that does not mean the end of all feeling but of the modernist feelings of alienation."[52]

Jameson's pessimistic diagnosis and, as Hutcheon has remarked, rather nostalgic desire for "genuine historicity,"[53] Lyotard's shattered grand narratives and Baudrillard's hyperbolic hypotheses regarding "a technological determinism that through its unassailable code serves the interests of a

---

48 Bertens, *The Idea of the Postmodern*, 147.
49 Jean Baudrillard, *For a Critique of the Political Economy of the Sign* (1972; St. Louis: Telos, 1981) 91. Qtd. in Bertens, *The Idea of the Postmodern*, 148.
50 Jean Baudrillard, *Simulacra and Simulation*, trans. Sheila Faria Glaser (1981; Michigan: University of Michigan Press, 1994).
51 Jameson, "Postmodernism, or the Cultural Logic of Late Capitalism," 68.
52 Bertens, *The Idea of the Postmodern*, 166.
53 Linda Hutcheon, "Irony, Nostalgia, and the Postmodern," University of Toronto <www.utlink.utoronto.ca/www.utel/criticism/hutchINP.html>.

hyperreal, meaningless capitalist system"[54] resonate throughout Ravenhill's plays. He nevertheless clings to some sense of possible action or agency. Repeatedly the plays address the social and ontological effects of postmodernity. These effects are broached in the plays' content—thematically expressed through the interaction of consumerism, identity and communication, and via the leitmotif of paternity threaded through them. Clearly, Ravenhill's dramaturgy is primarily mimetic, representing and questioning the values (or lack of values) of postmodern consumer society. More ambiguously the work formally engages with postmodernism (as an aesthetic mode) through citation, its use of performative micronarratives and, to a lesser extent through the fragmentation of multiple short scenes. While it might be argued that Ravenhill diverges from Jameson's dismissal of pastiche to reinstitute parody as a political strategy, his work hangs in the balance between appropriation and assimilation.

Consumption & Commodity

In many respects Ravenhill's work considers a world no longer inhabited by citizens or even individuals, but by consumers. *Shopping and Fucking, Faust Is Dead, Handbag* and *Some Explicit Polaroids* each reflect what Johannes Birringer describes as the "image-ridden and hysterical world of postmodern consumer capitalism."[55] It is a world that reverberates with the spectacular unrealism noted by Debord where social relations have shifted into commodity relations. Consumption conditions all aspects of life, apparently offering an ever increasing freedom of choice and power to the consumer. Selfhood is translated into a question of not only what one consumes, but also what one can sell in this self-perpetuating system.

Consumption is therefore unavoidably at the centre of each of the plays. As Sierz describes, Ravenhill's starting point for

---

[54] Bertens, *The Idea of the Postmodern*, 156.

[55] Johannes Birringer, *Theatre, Theory, Postmodernism* (Bloomington and Indiana: Indiana University Press, 1991) xi.

Shopping and Fucking was a group of "characters whose whole vocabulary had been defined by the market, who had been brought up in a decade when all that mattered was buying and selling."[56] The characters, Mark, Robbie, Lulu, Brian and Gary, are sketched with the minimum detail. Their identities are delineated primarily by their roles in a system of commodities and commodification with little or no reference to the past. Unlike McPherson's characters, they are, as Ravenhill has stated, "the sum of their actions"[57] and, it might be added, only the sum of their actions in the present moment. This sense of presentness and transience chimes with the playful references of their names—as Ravenhill confesses, the characters were named after the members of the now defunct, but erstwhile phenomenally successful boy band Take That.[58] The fact that Take That were an entirely synthetic group assembled as a product to be marketed to youth consumers of generically produced pop music, and have vanished practically without trace (with the exception of Robbie Williams), provides another ironic gloss on the ephemerality of consumer culture in the play.

In *Shopping and Fucking* the language of consumption is used to express everything—most strikingly the group relationships around which the play is structured. These relationships might be classified as familial, business and sexual, though notably the categories are often indistinct and overlap in a variety of patterns throughout the play's fourteen scenes. The central group consists of Lulu, Mark and Robbie who live together in an ill-defined ménage à trois or alternative family unit. This relationship explained only by means of a "shopping story"

---

56 Sierz, *In-Yer-Face Theatre*, 123.

57 Ravenhill qtd. in Sierz, *In-Yer-Face Theatre*, 131.

58 Formed in 1992, Take That marked the beginning of a trend in the UK of pop music tailor-made for a teenage market that continues today. The group of five teenagers (only one of whom played a musical instrument) was assembled by a music producer after interviews on the basis of appearance, singing and dancing ability. Sierz also traces the reference made in the use of Lulu as a character name. See *In-Yer-Face Theatre*, 130-31.

that frames the play, in which Mark is the narrating protagonist:

> It's summer. I'm in a supermarket. It's hot and I'm sweaty. Damp. And I'm watching this couple shopping. I'm watching you. And you're both smiling. You see me and you know sort of straight away that I'm going to have you. You know you don't have a choice. No control. Now this guy comes up to me. He's a fat man. Fat and hair and lycra and he says: See the pair by the yoghurt?
> Well, says fat guy, they're both mine. I own them. I own them but I don't want them—because you know something?—they're trash. Trash and I hate them. Wanna buy them?
> How much?
> Piece of trash like them. Let's say … twenty. Yeah, yours for twenty.
> So I do the deal. I hand it over. And I fetch you. I don't have to say anything because you know. You've seen the transaction. And I take you both away and I take you to my house. And you see the house and when you see the house you know it. You understand? You know this place. And I've been keeping a room for you and I take you into this room. And there's food. And it's warm. And we live out our days fat and content and happy. (5)

The story is a clear example of what Marie MacLean refers to as an "embedded narrative."[59] This embedded narrative functions as a précis of all relationships in the play, and sounds a note of self-conscious performativity at the outset. As will reoccur in *Some Explicit Polaroids*, identity is considered in terms of ownership of oneself or others. In this pseudo family Mark, apparently the dominant partner, is the customer or consumer. Yet Lulu and Robbie are more than quiescent in this imagined transaction, as is illustrated by their demand at the beginning of the play that Mark reiterate the story. Like children they require that Mark tell it in a particular manner—he must "start at the beginning" (4) and use the appropriate language, "it starts with

---

[59] See Marie MacLean, *Narrative as Performance* (New York: Routledge, 1988) 12-13.

'summer'" insists Robbie (5). The narrative is significant in that it gives shape to their experience in a world which is apparently shapeless. It has a clear linear development of beginning, middle, end, and is fundamentally performative. J. Hillis Miller's assertion that, "a story is a way of doing things with words. It makes something happen in the real world: for example, it can propose modes of selfhood or ways of behaving that are then imitated"[60] has a clear resonance here. The fiction to which the central characters subscribe is indicative of both the culture of which they are a part, and the identities they perform in relation to it. The shopping story functions on a number of levels entangled with commodification. First, it is easily recognisable as a somewhat warped love-at-first-sight narrative that exaggerates a vocabulary of possession commonly and popularly applied to love. But it also is based on a notion of consumer choice. In this case the prospective lovers are rather unromantically chosen as products in a supermarket, thus setting the tone for the ensuing relationships in the play. While the shopping story expresses a fantasy of objectification, it is significantly the means by which Lulu, Robbie and Mark negotiate and perform identities in the alternative family unit as is emphasised by its revision and retelling at the end of the play as a coda.

Mark's drug consumption threatens to destroy his "purchased" household. His departure for a clinic serves as a plot catalyst, obliging Robbie and Lulu to assert their independence and self-sufficiency—as Lulu declares, "You don't own us. We exist. We're people. We can get by" (7). After the rupture of the family unit, the play follows its former members' attempts to "get by" in a sequence of enacted encounters and narrated incidents. Lulu and Robbie's efforts to succeed in the marketplace bear ambivalent results and tend to perpetuate their objectification. In participating in the

---

[60] J. Hillis Miller, "Narrative," *Critical Terms for Literary Study*, eds. Frank Lentricchia and Thomas McLaughlin (Chicago: University of Chicago Press, 1990) 69.

circulation of commodities—notably trash commodities—they are forced to sell themselves in increasingly degrading ways spiralling from the fast food service sector to drug dealing. The latter assignment proves disastrous when Robbie, rather than selling the Ecstasy, under the influence distributes it for free; he ecstatically rejects the system: "Fuck Money. Fuck it. This selling. This buying. [...] let's be beautiful [...] and happy" (39). Yet, if Robbie's epiphanic denunciation of the economic rat race is hilarious, it is also short lived. Not only is he beaten up by clubbers who want more free drugs (his confessional story is told in the hospital), but is threatened with torture by Brian, owner of the Ecstasy, who requires payment. Ironically, Lulu and Robbie are most financially successful when, in desperation, they diversify into the sale of ephemeral rather than material goods by setting up a phone sex line.

A parallel plot line is developed following Mark who, having been thrown out of the clinic for indulging in a sexual encounter with another patient, hires a rent boy as a means of breaking his perceived addiction to personal relationships. Gary identifies himself openly as a commodity, and offers Mark a selection of sexual experiences according to his tastes. Yet in spite of his intentions, Mark becomes emotionally involved with Gary. The latter's gesture of friendship is to take Mark shopping with his collection of stolen credit cards, thus reversing the power positions in their relationship, but also commenting wryly on the nature of friendship in an age of consumption.

These two plot trajectories coincide when Mark brings Gary home. To diffuse the tension the characters play a truth or dare storytelling game that results in a violent sexual confrontation. Gary contracts the others to fulfil his darkest fantasy, however when it transpires that this involves risk of death, Robbie and Lulu renege on the agreement. Eventually Mark offers to complete the job on his own, though the act is not carried out on stage, and the result of his promise is not revealed.

Closure is brought about when Brian returns to collect the money owed to him, but in the end refuses to accept it. He declares that they are now civilised since they understand its absolute value. The play concludes with the original family unit reunited. A revised version of the "slave" story from scene one is told in which the slave is liberated against his will, and then Lulu, Mark and Robbie feed each other ready-meals.

As should be clear from this synopsis, the language and logic of commodity infects all aspects of communication. The most obvious is the translation of sex into transaction and the attendant preference of being bought over being freely loved. Sex as a service for exchange is constantly replayed be it in terms of fantasies of being bought and sold; the so-called "Lick and Go" (19) or emotion-free sex Mark desires; Gary's query as to whether Mark is "looking for regular?" (24); or the impersonal orgasmic fulfilment offered over the phone by Robbie and Lulu. However, the jargon of consumerism and its values are deployed in several other ways. Brian is the principle spokesperson for a kind of cutthroat consumerism and the marketing of illusions. As he emphasises to Lulu, it is not a question of the product itself, in other words, not its use value but its symbolic value. Customers "have to believe that what we hold up to them is special. For the right sum—life is easier, richer and more fulfilling" (10). Robbie's drug induced moment of generosity which descends into a chaotic and uncivilised punch up is juxtaposed with an order imposed by Brian's bald assertion that "money is civilisation" (87).

The privilege of consumer choice, arguably one of the cardinal values of a developed consumer society, surfaces in anecdotes and exchanges throughout the play and is repeatedly problematised. One early anecdote is humorous—when an indecisive customer is so provoked by Robbie telling him, "For once in your life you have a choice so for fuck's sake make the most of it" (14), that he leaps over the counter and attacks Robbie with the restaurant cutlery. Though Robbie escapes without injury since the fork is plastic, he immediately loses his job. The episode is repeated later with more serious consequences—Lulu relates how when momentarily dazed by the wide selection of chocolate in the Seven Eleven shop, she witnesses a customer brutally stabbing the sales assistant and, rather than intervening, steals a bar of chocolate. Finally, at the play's climax, the right to choose and obtain what one pays for is brought to a critical point when Gary, as customer, demands that the others fulfil a thinly veiled death fantasy. When Robbie and Lulu refuse, Gary reminds them: "When someone's paying, someone wants something and they're paying, then you do it. Nothing right. Nothing wrong. It's a deal. So then you do it" (85). By means of these exchanges Ravenhill hones in on the individualistic moral paralysis that underwrites an ideology of consumerism.

Perhaps the most poignant evidence of the characters' isolation from one another is their perpetual consumption of pre-prepared, individually wrapped meals in the form of takeaways or microwave dinners. This convenience food serves as yet another ambivalent example of consumer choice. As Lulu says when she encourages Robbie to eat: "you've got the world here. You've got all the tastes in the world. You've got an empire under cellophane. [...] In the past you'd have to invade, you'd have to occupy just to get one of these things" (61). The main characteristic of these meals is not, however, their exotic flavour, but the fact that they cannot be shared. This seems symptomatic not only of the characters' apparent inability to "form any kind of connection with one another,"[61] but of the fundamentally isolating quality of the consumer system. According to Baudrillard,

> whereas the directed *acquisition* of objects and commodities is individualising, atomising, and dehistoricising. [...] As a consumer, humans become again solitary, cellular, and at best *gregarious* (for example in a family viewing TV [...]).[62]

---

[61] Rebellato, *Mark Ravenhill Plays: 1*, xi.

[62] Jean Baudrillard, *Selected Writings*, ed. Mark Poster (Cambridge: Polity, 1988) 54.

The characters' communal feeding of each other at the end of the play obviously suggests an attempt to overcome this condition in some small way, nevertheless, the gesture is mitigated by the fact the they are still eating individualised portions of convenience food.

A similar sense of disconnection, desensitisation and moral vacancy is revisited in *Faust Is Dead*, though from a bleaker and more complex perspective. Ravenhill transposes the sixteenth century European legend of Faust to the home of postmodern consumer society—North America. In this context the traditional roles of Faust and Mephistopheles, though still perceptible, are considerably destabilised. The play is structured around two protagonists Alain (the European) and Pete (the American) and a fateful encounter of two world views. The former, is a jaded French intellectual who refusing to pander to institutional political correctness or potential sponsors of the university, has left his academic job and come to America to "live a little" (99). "Only in America, am I truly at home. For me, and for so many children of this twentieth century, it is only in America that we really believe that we are alive, that we are living within in [sic] our own century. In Europe, we are ghosts, trapped in a museum, with the lights out and the last visitor gone" (101) Alain drunkenly proclaims early in the play in a speech which is clearly memorised and quoted, presumably from his own work. Throughout the play the irony of this bombastic statement is repeatedly highlighted, not only by the characters' inability to feel and their attempts to "really" live (or indeed die), but the persistent lack of any sense of home. As argued by Zygmunt Bauman, postmodern society is characterised precisely by the impossibility of being or feeling at home:

> we are all—to one extent or another […] on the move; none of us can be certain that he or she has gained any right to any place once for all and no one thinks that his or her staying in

one place is a likely prospect; wherever we happen to stop, we are at least in part displaced or out of place.[63]

This being the case, "tourists and vagabonds are the *metaphors* of contemporary life," they are the "heroes and victims of postmodernity."[64] The characters of *Faust Is Dead*, with varying degrees of success, are all explicitly drawn as peripatetic citizens of postmodernity.

The form of *Faust Is Dead* pays ample tribute to sense of displacement brought by a globalised ahistorical unreality where the "abstract vision of the world is shaped by a massive mediation of products/commodities."[65] The Faustian pursuit and consumption of experience in the play is most strikingly an experience of mediation and hyperreality. This is underscored by Ravenhill's use of television, screens and projections and, most importantly, the layering of a video chorus with the onstage action.[66] The chorus sporadically interjects with confessions and anecdotes which reflect upon the sense of disjunction in contemporary society. Throughout the play Alain's thought proceeds according to a couple of repeated and deliberately obscure "examples." (One concerns a woman who cuts out her eyes and sends them to her lover; the other concerns a man who kills a poet and declares his love for her while he consumes her body.) The chorus counterpoints these with a number of clearer parables of the postmodern society about which Alain theorises, foregrounding processes of "simulation, depersonalisation and dehistoricisation."[67] The most revealing of the choric speeches, from the point of view of

---

[63] Zygmunt Bauman, *Postmodernity and its Discontents* (Cambridge: Polity, 1997) 93.

[64] Bauman, *Postmodernity and its Discontents*, 83.

[65] Birringer, *Theatre, Theory, Postmodernism*, 4.

[66] Sierz notes how in the first production the chorus was recorded on video, as was Donny's meeting with Alain and Pete. In the US production, Donny became an onstage character and the chorus was performed by actors live. *In-Yer-Face Theatre*, 136-7.

[67] Callens, "Sorting Out Ontologies in Mark Ravenhill's *Faust (Faust is Dead)*," 170.

consumption and the overturning of a system of basic needs, is an anecdote about looting during the LA riots in 1992. A young looter steals a state of the art VCR during the melee but is reprimanded by his mother for not stealing food instead as they have nothing to eat. His response is to ask, "what is the point of having food in the house when you have nothing to watch while you're eating it?" (107).

Significantly, Alain first appears not in person but on television. As Johan Callens observes,

> Ravenhill's multimedia *Faust* somehow posits Baudrillard's "precession of simulacra" as a departure point. Hence the symbolic relevance of introducing the drama proper with a television show as an illustration of theatre's inevitable imbrication into the televisual, of the real's tension with the symbolic.[68]

Alain enters the society of spectacle as an image, a transient, exotic celebrity talking about his latest book, *The Death of Man*, on the David Letterman show, where his co-guest is Madonna. The distinctions between reality and fiction are, quite obviously, blurred by the inclusion of two real figures in the same lineup as a fictional one. The interview is typically a sound bite: Letterman finds the title of the book preposterous as he feels "pretty much alive" (98) and Madonna has only read one of Alain's earlier works the "book about sexuality" (98)—an obvious nod to Michel Foucault. The death of man is, as Alain tells his sceptical host, "a complex thing to explain in a few minutes" (97) and as such is reduced to trivia by the talk show format.

Later, on the west coast around the time of the LA riots, Alain encounters Pete, the son of an American computer magnate known only as Bill (presumably Gates). Under the impression that he is a record producer, Pete takes Alain back to his apartment to persuade him (sexually) to give his friend's

---

68 Callens, "Sorting Out Ontologies in Mark Ravenhill's *Faust (Faust is Dead),*" 174.

band a contract. The lyrics of the "great" song Pete sings for Alain are blatantly inane, but the main talent of the band's lead singer, Stevie, is his ability to perform in an emotionally convincing manner; he sings as though "he really totally means it"; a valuable asset which as Pete says, "is [...] totally marketable" (100). Later, the issue of the performance of authentic feeling is reintroduced by the chorus. In a barely concealed comment on ubiquitous commodification of emotion, the chorus notes how the death of Donny, a boy Alain and Pete meet via the internet, not only was discussed on "every TV show, every talk show" (134), but also instantly became the subject of one of Stevie's songs, "which he has performed unplugged and is now showing three times an hour on MTV" (135).

Pete, like the characters of *Shopping and Fucking*, is a citizen of the present. He is the realisation of Bauman's figure of the tourist—someone who travels light, whose interests wander, who controls uncertainty by controlling the spaces in which he travels, and consumes the world around him in manageable portions.[69] His identity is flexible according to his circumstances. Although apparently not homosexual, he is willing to seduce Alain to aid his friends' success, just as by the end of the play despite his hatred of his father he is willing to work as his second in command. Contracts and deals are frequently referred to throughout the play—Alain's broken contract with the university, Stevie's music contract, Pete and Alain's neo-Faustian bargain, Pete's negotiation of a settlement with his father. In this manner, reference to Faust is rendered ever-present but is exaggerated and extended in a contemporary context.

Similar to Mark in *Shopping and Fucking*, Pete is happy only when experience can be mediated and consumed under restricted conditions, and preferably filtered through convenient commodities. In the world of consumer

---

[69] Bauman, *Postmodernity and its Discontents*, 89-92.

hyperreality, the word "real" ceases to signify. For instance, Pete fantasises, without apparent irony, about all the "totally real experiences" he will buy when he sells the "chaos" programme back to his father:

> I'm gonna keep the peace in Bosnia. I'm gonna take Saddam Hussein out for a pizza. I'm gonna shoot pool with the Pope and have Boris Yeltsin show me his collection of baseball stickers. (112)

Perhaps unsurprisingly, Pete's closest relationships are with objects, namely his camcorder and computer. Arguably this dependence on the camcorder demonstrates succinctly Debord's hypothesis that spectacle now constitutes social relations.[70] The recorder is as Callens notes, his "best friend, a roving mechanical eye"[71] and functions in a complex manner, both in mediating reality and by creating it. It enables Pete not only to record and remember, but also to frame and therefore limit experiences which are too threatening or confronting. Thus the vast expanse of the desert—a space without cultural interference—is better when seen on TV, and his immediate homophobic reaction to Alain fellating him can be deadened by keeping "it all within the frame" (114).

When the camcorder will no longer suffice, chemical mediation and creation of reality is preferred. Pete wishes to navigate their path through "the Nature thing" and "the Sex thing" with the aid of drugs. Again, the language used to describe nature and sex is noteworthy. Modified by the word "thing" they are designated as objects to be consumed. Having arranged a magic circle of pills around them, Pete puts forward his attitude towards experience. Experience, he tells Alain,

> is fine. But just by themselves, on their own, okay, experiences don't have a shape. They don't have a shape and they don't

---

70 Debord, *The Society of the Spectacle*, 12.
71 Callens, "Sorting Out Ontologies in Mark Ravenhill's *Faust (Faust is Dead)*," 170.

have a rhythm. And without shape, without rhythm, the experience can be too much. It can be too painful. So we shape the experience. (116)

Alain, while accepting the pills, refuses to "decide the shape […] in advance" (116) thus forcing Pete to temporarily abandon his limits and "embrace […] chaos" (121). Pete nonetheless never strays too far from the logic of commodity. If, as Debord suggests, "time-as-commodity is an infinite accumulation of equivalent intervals,"[72] then Pete's response to Alain after their trip is illustrative of the equivalence of experience for him:

> Okay, we had an experience. Fine. That's cool. Thank you. There, see. I'm grateful. We shared an experience. I did a lot of new stuff. I was scared but we got through it … when we were there … great. But that's over … I'm bored. (118)

Finally, Pete introduces Alain to the internet which proves to be the ultimate commodity to facilitate, simulate and control experience. On one hand, as Pete contradictorily maintains the internet allows "you to get to know people […] really, really well but they don't know who you are" (122). On the other, it is most obviously a domain in which reality caves into simulation most fully and knowing someone in cyberspace any conventional sense is impossible. Again, Pete wants to maintain some boundaries—"Just because it's virtual, doesn't mean you can lie […]. Just because no one can reach out and touch it doesn't mean you can fake it" (125), he tells Alain. Yet contrary to his claims, this is precisely the most salient quality of virtual reality.

In cyberspace Pete meets with people who are self-scarring. Pete reveals that he also cuts himself, as a means of feeling some sort of reality amid the imitation, or rather, simulated world in which he lives. Yet, even this revelation seems phoney. According to Alain's theory, to "live in this new age of chaos"

---

[72] Debord, *The Society of the Spectacle*, 110.

(121) demands an espousal of cruelty and suffering, so he is fascinated by this postmodern ritual and forces a meeting with one of the subscribers to Pete's homepage. Donny arrives and is filmed by Alain while he tells a story about his childhood which is dominated by his excessive consumption of a cherry flavoured iced soft drink. As a consequence of his slushie intake his mouth and teeth were dyed red, so as a child he was known as "Red Mouth Donny" or "Red" (129). The removal of the slushie machine precipitated an identity crisis for Donny which coincided with his pubescent delinquency, the break up of his family and his mother's cancer. Although it is not explicitly stated, it is clear that Donny has invested in a new identity which references the "colour" of his childhood and mitigates the trauma he has experienced through the infliction of pain on his own body. As in *Shopping and Fucking*, the anguish of the past is transposed onto a masochistic desire to consume pain. Donny trumps Pete's efforts to compete with him by cutting his jugular. Alain's response to Donny's suicide is to withdraw into a ponderous speech about the death of reality, while it is Pete who disposes of the body. If Donny is regarded as a symbol of the tragic dysfunctionality of contemporary consumer society, then the in responses of the other characters to his demise (both of which "bury" the problem in different ways) Ravenhill's attitude must be read as not merely satirical, but intensely critical.

Alain's verbose European philosophising ultimately proves no match for Pete's postmodern American pragmatism. Alain, having been shot by Pete in an altercation over the precious computer disk, must listen to Pete's plagiaristic adaptation of his work. With brutal inevitability, Pete leaves Alain in a critical condition both physically and intellectually as he sets out on a career in technological problem solving.

Consumption and the notion of commodity also shape Ravenhill's next play, *Handbag*. The play's action revolves around two sets of characters. The first group are contemporary, urban and mostly middle class. Mauretta and

Suzanne, David and Tom are two homosexual couples who assist each other in conceiving a child. Suzanne and David work together in an advertising firm. As the play proceeds their plans to be ideal alternative parents are complicated and, ultimately, destroyed by David's relationship with Phil, a homeless junkie, and Suzanne's entanglement with one of the working class subjects of their ad survey, Lorraine. This contemporary story of sex and parenting is intercut with a prequel to Oscar Wilde's *The Importance of Being Earnest* (1895). Set twenty eight years before the action of Wilde's play, this strand of the plot follows the characters Cardew, Prism, Constance, Augusta and Moncrieff around the time of the birth of Jack (Ernest) and concludes with Prism's giving of baby Jack to the overly attentive former director of a home for foundling boys and suspected paedophile, Cardew.

By splicing scenes from contemporary and Victorian periods, Ravenhill produces an intertextual structure which enables him to develop a set of concerns from different perspectives. Although the values which predominate in the contemporary strand are largely those of consumerism, in placing them alongside those of his fictional upper class Victorians, Ravenhill makes oblique connections between them. This is underscored by the fact that with the exception of Phil, the same actors play roles in both time periods, so Tom doubles as Cardew, Lorraine as Prism, Suzanne as Constance, Mauretta as Augusta and David as Moncrieff. De Vos argues,

> the formality and politeness of Victorian society is juxtaposed with contemporary frankness and directness, especially in sexual matters, but both sets of attitudes are shown to be just a veneer covering the characters' cynicism and lack of emotions.[73]

However, while this may be true of the somewhat farcical Victorian figures, the contemporary characters are not necessarily lacking emotion. Instead, Ravenhill claims, they

---

[73] De Vos, "Ravenhill's Wilde Game," *Crucible of Cultures*, 49.

have been "infantilised" by the society in which they live: "They live in a greedy society in which the emphasis is on each individual's needs. They've become completely self-centred. [...] they're selfish people trying to do something selfless, having a child."[74] Their attempts to be parents and those individual needs are portrayed as coming into a direct conflict that cancels out their future hopes; the victim of the conflict being the child they produce.

If there is a unifying symbol in the play, then it is that of the handbag. Ravenhill is, of course, making reference to Lady Bracknell's exclamation of horror at the prospect of Jack's being "born, or at any rate bred, in a hand-bag."[75] The handbag provides not only the bridge between past and present, it is an important, if veiled signifier of the economies of commodification and consumption in the play. Once again the reduction of sex to transaction and the mingling of commodities with identity are features of the territory. As De Vos remarks, the "commodification and commercialisation of love and sex" in the contemporary strand of the play find a clear echo in "the frankly mercenary approach to love and marriage" of Augusta, the future Lady Bracknell in the Victorian strand,[76] but in the contemporary component this tendency is divorced from the stabilising structures of marriage or class identity.

David and Suzanne's work in advertising foregrounds consumption and connections between identities and products. Their market research strategy involves living with "consumers" for a week and videoing all their choices (156). Their investigation into how consumers spend their money is prefaced upon a pseudo-scientific policy of not "getting

---

74 Ravenhill qtd. in Sierz, *In-Yer-Face Theatre*, 142-3.
75 Oscar Wilde, *The Importance of Being Earnest* Act I Scene I (1895; London: Penguin, 1986) 268. Sierz also notes that Handbag is a form of house music, which was used extensively in the production of the play he attended. See *In-Yer-Face Theatre*, 141.
76 De Vos, "Ravenhill's Wilde Game," 50.

involved" (160). Nonetheless entanglements occur and cruel consequences ensue.

Both Phil and Lorraine refuse to be discarded after they have been used. Phil establishes a violent and parasitical relationship with David to the detriment of his partnership with Tom, while Lorraine through a hysterical and self-abusive performance, obliges Suzanne to assist her and is hired as a live-in nanny. David and Suzanne's respective attempts to dispose of people after they have been of use tragically backfire when Phil begins a relationship with Lorraine and they steal the baby which dies in their care. The image in the final scene of Lorraine holding the body of the dead baby in the bin-bag juxtaposed with Cardew lovingly cradling the living baby lifted from the handbag, is a harsh indictment of a contemporary society dedicated to individual needs and, as De Vos suggests, presents "the rather unsettling conclusion that Cardew's treatment remains the more humane one."[77]

With *Some Explicit Polaroids*, Ravenhill reconsiders the terrain of *Shopping and Fucking*. As Sierz states, although the play takes

> once again a sceptical look at contemporary consumer society [it is also] based on Ernst Toller's 1927 play, *Hoppla, wir leben! (Hurrah, We Live!)*—which tells the story of a revolutionary who returns home after eight years in an asylum to find that his old comrades have become corrupt conformists—Ravenhill's version combines a seventies state-of-the-nation play with an acerbic critique of both nineties youth culture and traditionalist leftist militancy.[78]

Set in contemporary London, *Some Explicit Polaroids* follows Nick, who has just been released from prison after fifteen years, and his adjustment to postmodern society. He finds this society practically unrecognisable and the social geography he knew

---

[77] De Vos, "Ravenhill's Wilde Game," 52.
[78] Sierz, *In-Yer-Face Theatre*, 144.

has been replaced with rampant individualism, consumerism and as Michael Billington memorably puts it "a scorched-earth attitude to the day before yesterday."[79] A former socialist activist, Nick was imprisoned for the kidnap and torture of Jonathan, a wealthy businessman and asset stripper. When he is released he seeks Helen, who was also a militant activist and the friend who encouraged him to carry out the attack. Helen is now a respectable city councillor and is hoping to become an MP. His first encounters with the minutiae of everyday life set the tone for this sense of disorientation in a realm of overturned values and commodification. His attempts to telephone Helen are thwarted by the fact that public pay phones no longer take money only cards—a system he has never heard of. Then, on his way to Helen's flat he meets a child selling smack. When he tells the child "you shouldn't be selling drugs at your age," the child responds "how else am I gonna buy a PlayStation?" Once again Nick has no idea what the product is. Helen refuses to be his guide in this new age, all she advises him to do is to "start with the little stuff [...]. Bit by bit, you do what you can and you don't look for the bigger picture, you don't generalise" (236). When Helen finally tells him precisely what she does, Nick is incredulous that, as a councillor, she should dedicate herself to ensuring the buses run so people can go shopping.

As in *Shopping and Fucking*, relationships are framed in terms of ownership of others, or the self and consumer choice. Nick wanders through the city and finds the attitudes of the younger people he meets infuriatingly incomprehensible. He rescues a young woman, Nadia, who is being beaten up by her "friend" Simon on the street. Nadia works as a lap dancer and articulates her identity in terms of new age, pop-psychology style platitudes about being her "own person," a phrase oft-repeated throughout the play. As her own person, Nadia protects herself emotionally by denial and selective memory. All negative events are purposely erased, "filed away" or put in

---

the past tense while, in a gesture of auto-therapy, she reassures her reflection in the mirror that she is "a nice person" who "attract[s] nice people" (251-252). Nick's understanding of identity being fixed or accumulative is seemingly irrelevant to a generation accustomed to disposability and obsolescence.

Nadia's friends introduce Nick to the new world of postmodern "trash" culture of consumption at its most self-indulgent. Their celebration of the inauthentic, the kitsch and the frivolous, clashes with Nick's apparently hopelessly outdated values and politics. Tim, a young man with AIDS has bought and "downloaded" his Russian boyfriend, Victor, from the internet. While Tim controls his illness by the consumption of medication—more "chemical [trash] to fill [his] body with" (245)—Victor identifies himself primarily as a consumable object, a "fantastic body" (240). Victor not only wants to be consumed, as a consumer he loves trash, "trash music, trash food, trash people" and London, a city which "gave up on that meaning bullshit years ago," (241) is, in his view, ideal.

Like the portions of food in *Shopping and Fucking* which cannot be shared, Tim warns Nick that responsibility is now a matter for individuals only (269). They mock his concern with politics and justice which Tim describes as outmoded, very "nineteen eighty-four" (267). When criticised by Nick for not being "connected with anything," for "not fighting anything," they tell him they are happy. When asked what happiness means they define it as follows:

> Tim: It means we're content with what we've got.
> Nadia: And we're at peace with ourselves.
> Tim: And we take responsibility for ourselves.
> Nadia: And we're our own people.
> Tim: And we're not letting the world get to us. (273)

"Happy world" (268) is politics-free and one of momentary commodity induced pleasure. As Rebellato notes, Tim and Nadia's speech about the nature of happiness is an "avalanche of triteness [...] hilariously well-observed. In particular the phrase 'we're our own people' hangs around in [all Ravenhill's] plays and subtly suggests that economic ownership has come to characterise even the way we view ourselves."[80]

Later, the cracks in "happy world" begin to show when Tim refuses to take his medication. However, even Tim's refusal is bound up with consumer choice—he feels the pills have deprived him of the predictable course of his illness and his right to die. Although his friends temporarily persuade him to live on, he soon reasserts his rights to: "My hospital room. My illness. My body. My death. My choice" (287).

When Nadia is once more rescued from Simon, this time by Nick's old adversary Jonathan, he forces her to acknowledge some home truths—namely that she is alone and helpless in a world she does not understand. Significantly, her first response to Jonathan is to offer herself as an object to him. By the end of the play, though, Nadia rejects the comfort of amnesia, "I want to remember" (308) she tells Victor as she takes a farewell photograph of him. Ironically, of course, the object she has "to remember [him] by" (308) is only a Polaroid snapshot, suggesting that despite her good intentions, there is little likelihood of Nadia freeing herself from the vagaries of the consumerist culture that have shaped her.

By contrast, Jonathan is the spokesperson for an alternative to the shallow individualism espoused by the younger generation and to the exhausted oppositional politics of Nick. In an echo of Alain's theory in *Faust Is Dead*, Jonathan presents his perspective on survival in a world driven by consumption:

> you embrace the chaos…you see the beauty of…the way money flows, the way it moves around the world faster and faster. Every second a new opportunity, every second a new disaster. The endless beginnings, the infinite endings. And each of us swept along by the great tides and winds of the markets. (293)

---

[80] Rebellato, *Mark Ravenhill Plays: 1*, xii.

This is, evidently, the apotheosis of posthumanist, postmodern capitalism. When Nick and Jonathan finally meet, they acknowledge a nostalgia for the old left, right political dichotomy they once identified with; both express their sense of disorientation. For Nick life was easier when he hated Jonathan, he "knew where he stood" (311). Similarly Jonathan remarks, "you know the territory and then suddenly…" (311). Jonathan has, in as much as is possible, found new bearings in a territory that has been transformed by what is, basically, globalisation. Although it is possible to "rush around, regulate a bit. Soften the blow for a few of the losers," Jonathan argues that it is better to accept that "this is the way things are" and "ultimately the market is the only thing sensitive enough, flexible enough to actually respond to the way we tick" (311).

In *Some Explicit Polaroids* Ravenhill returns full circle to some of the questions provocatively posed about the nature of contemporary urban life in *Shopping and Fucking*, though with greater political clarity. Throughout Ravenhill's 1990s work a vision of consumerism and postmodernity is developed that, while often sardonically humorous, is at root sceptical and suspicious. Ravenhill depicts a generation that is morally and politically adrift "with no values but economic ones, media-fixated and self-obsessed."[81] Nick's question to Jonathan "There's nothing better?" (311) seems to sum up Ravenhill's sense of ambivalence about "times like these."[82] The moderate optimism of *Shopping and Fucking*'s final scene dwindles in each of the plays discussed above. Although *Some Explicit Polaroids* ends with would be MP Helen declaring that she "want[s] to make [Nick] into what [he] used to be" (314), that is activist and angry, it is Jonathan's speech (cited above) that fatefully resonates to the play's conclusion. Rebellato situates Ravenhill's pessimism in the context of the transformation of British society since 1979, arguing that the dismissal the welfare state and other elements of civic society by Conservative governments as

---

81 Rebellato, *Mark Ravenhill Plays: 1*, xiii.
82 Ravenhill, "A Touch of Evil" (online).

"wrong-headed 'paternalism'" surfaces in Ravenhill's work especially in the troubled roles of fathers in the plays.[83]

Parental Guidance—Ambivalent Father Figures
As already discussed with regard to McPherson's drama, "masculinity and its discontents"[84] is a recurrent topos in mid 1990s theatre, where masculinity, homosexuality, male bonding and "laddism" are frequently in focus. If the subject of 1960s drama was class, and that of 1970s drama the "failures of social democracy," then David Edgar claims, drama at the end of the twentieth century reflects

> the unintended consequences of huge social changes [...] the great tectonic shifts in the political, cultural and economic geology of the times. The decline of the dominant role of men—in the workplace and in the family—is probably the biggest single story of the last thirty years in western countries.[85]

Nevertheless, the crisis of masculinity Edgar highlights has to be seen as contiguous with a more general crisis of authority in postmodernity, in which the metanarratives of masculinity and masculine authority have been destabilised. As Elinor Fuchs argues, the last decades of the twentieth century are marked by the erosion of assumed certainties and boundaries to such an extent that from "global crisis of political authority" to institutions as basic as the family, all "seemed to be entering a 'legitimation crisis.'"[86] The consequent eruption of doubt about ontological grounding has given rise to the notion of the self and identity as performative rather than substantive. Rather

---

[83] Rebellato, *Mark Ravenhill Plays: 1*, xiii.

[84] David Edgar, *State of Play: Playwrights on Playwriting* (London: Faber and Faber, 1999) 27.

[85] Edgar, *State of Play*, 28.

[86] Elinor Fuchs, *The Death of Character: Perspectives on Theater after Modernism* (Bloomington and Indianapolis: Indiana University Press, 1997) 3. In referring to legitimation Fuchs is, of course, drawing on Lyotard's terminology in *The Postmodern Condition*.

than treating any generalised crisis of masculinity, Ravenhill's theatre hones in on father figures both thematically and intertextually. Ravenhill describes the characters in *Shopping and Fucking* as "kids without parental guidance."[87] The lack or ambivalence of parental figures, but in particular father figures, is a pivotal element in each of the plays' commentary on postmodernity and its attendant sense of ontological rootlessness. For Rebellato "Ravenhill's work has a complex and difficult relationship with fathers, who are variously abusing, absent, sugar daddies, roles adopted for daddy/son sexual role play."[88] The father as symbol of continuity, heredity, responsibility, authority and security contrasts starkly with the father figures of the plays, falling into two main categories, as abusive or inept, and as ambivalent guides.

Abusive or inept fathers are employed by Ravenhill both in the background and foreground of the plays discussed above. Most strikingly, sexual abuse appears in three of the plays. *Handbag* offers the most chilling incidents of brutal fathering where the victims are too young to defend themselves. The character Phil confesses rather elliptically to Prism how, in the grip of heroin addiction, he allowed his dealer to abuse his five year old daughter in order to supply his habit. When Phil takes on the role of father again at the end of the play, his inability to function as a protector is revealed in a shocking onstage spectacle when he attempts to revive the stolen baby by burning it with a cigarette butt to encourage it to breathe. This scene cannot but recall Edward Bond's 1964 play, *Saved*, and the fate of the baby therein, and produces a similar effect. In *Shopping and Fucking* a history of paternal abuse shapes the character Gary who longs for a father to look after him in a brutally sexual fashion. More subtly abuse surfaces in *Some Explicit Polaroids*, when Nadia questions Nick about the reason he was in prison. Nick reacts with horror to the suggestion that he might be a paedophile, to which Nadia replies, "I've never

---

87 Sierz, *In-Yer-Face Theatre*, 130.
88 Rebellato, *Mark Ravenhill Plays: 1*, xiii.

met a paedophile. Well, only my father. But I don't count him" (257).

The other fathers and father figures in the plays variously exemplify ineptitude or insufficiency. Mauretta's memory of her father is as someone who abandoned his family. Moncrieff, the unfeeling the Victorian father wishes to maintain a role as a distant patriarch. Cardew, the overly attentive and likely homosexual philanthropist, dreams of a bygone mythical age of "the Ancients" (196) which prized the rituals of masculinity above the cloying atmosphere of the family. David, a self-centred pseudo-father in a pseudo-family, would prefer to be called uncle. Tom, the biological father to the ill-fated Jack, though well-intentioned is weak-willed and is reduced to a mere donator of sperm.

As guides father figures are also a recurring motif in the plays, but their credentials are always ambivalent or deliberately undermined. In *Shopping and Fucking* Ravenhill affords considerable stage presence to Brian, the self-appointed humorous and sinister voice of fatherhood and streetwise authority. What is notable about Brian is his lack of culture or education, and the shallowness of both his paternal teary-eyed emotion and his bludgeoning lessons on the way "civilisation" works. There is an inescapably derivative quality to the way in which Brian casts himself as a godfather style guide not only to his own son, but to his employees or potential employees. This menacing paternal authority is performed using various techniques both verbal and physical which are deployed to convince the latter of his superior knowledge or experience. Mostly, he conveys his "lessons" to Lulu and Robbie by bullying them into submission verbally using question and answer games, and addressing Robbie overbearingly as "son." The values Brian wishes to impress upon Lulu and Robbie invariably pertain to the social order of capitalism or consumerism rather than morality. Ironically, these are the values his own father has allegedly handed down to him and those he intends to transmit to his own son. When Brian shows

Lulu and Robbie a video of his son playing the cello, it is not so they can appreciate the talent and effort of the boy or the importance of paternal support. When he asks Robbie to tell him what exists "at the end of the day, at the final reckoning, behind beauty, behind God, behind paradise," the answer he is seeking is not "a father" or "a sort of a dad" as Robbie suggests, but money (48). Similarly, at the end of the play, Brian harks back to a lesson his own father taught him. Again it takes the form of a question and answer game, he asks "Son, what are the first few words in the Bible?" to which Robbie correctly answers "In the beginning." Brian tells him he is wrong—according to his father "the first few words of the Bible are ... get the money first. Get. The Money. First" (86-87). Brian as paternal guide offers an openly flawed narrative to give meaning to the chaotic world—by rewriting the Bible's opening phrase he overturns traditional patriarchal structures to replace them with the sanctification of monetarism.

Brian's character and world view are without doubt overtly and cartoonishly one-dimensional; in his later plays Ravenhill explores the role of father-guides in a more nuanced fashion. In *Faust is Dead*, the slacker Pete is presented with a choice of paths and beliefs both of which lead figuratively to different versions of chaos. Initially he is seduced by the discourse of the exotic foreign academic, Alain. The character Alain functions to point out the extremes of a particular intellectual construction of postmodernity. He guides Pete through a mishmash of ideas and provocative statements about the death of man and the end of history. Alain advocates the acceptance of chaos and an almost Artaudian notion of the necessity of cruelty in this new age in which reality has died. Pete's student or filial relationship with Alain concludes when Pete learns to plagiarise Alain's ideas, to which he adds "examples of 'original thought'" (130).

In contrast, Pete's father is a much more sinister figure, perhaps because he is never seen on stage. Overtly compared to God, Bill's goal is ubiquity, to be achieved through his computer programme, Chaos. To extend the analogy further, Pete fears his father's godlike vengeance for stealing the programme but is also the recipient of his forgiveness at the play's conclusion. While Alain's thought leads to a heterogeneously chaotic future, paralysis when faced with the absoluteness of actual death, and a proliferating sense of ambivalence, Bill is described as a problem solver. As Pete remarks, "in my father's house, his vision of the future, of perfection, is realised" (139). Chaos is but a brand name for a product that will defeat competitors and achieve homogeneous universality. Bill's progress is wrought through a transcendence of reality; in his house perfection is attained by simulating environments to suit his mood. Despite the fact he hates him, Pete chooses to join forces with his father because he offers an alternative to Alain's postmodern despair, however illusory his perfect solutions may be.

The character Jonathan in *Some Explicit Polaroids* stands as a more sophisticated version of the ambivalent paternal businessman figure represented by Brian, and unlike to the rather nebulous figure of Bill, he appears on stage. Jonathan's panegyric to the flows of the market is yet another means of imposing meaning in a system where traditional oppositions no longer apply. As the eloquent voice of globalisation, Jonathan is seductively persuasive and magnanimously forgiving towards his former torturer, Nick, inviting him on a charity excursion to Eastern Europe. He is also perceptive enough to catch the "little flash of hatred" in Nick and in the recipients of his bounty (312), though unlike Nick they do not reject his favour.

Ravenhill spares none of these figures of authority or paternal responsibility from criticism; significantly, few seem in any way redeemable. Worryingly it is a critique that seems trapped, in a very similar manner to Alain's theorising, in a realm of hermetic despair. The choice offered by Ravenhill between brutal monetarism, seductive dehumanised globalisation and bombastic, apocalyptic abstraction, or wilful political blindness presents a grim picture of the contemporary society leavened only by a playful intertextuality.

Citational Strategies: From Lyotard to Lion King
Intertextuality is a pivotal aspect to Ravenhill's work in the late 1990s; it is also one of its most problematic. His appropriation of various cultural references and citations focus the question of fathers and by implication origins and guidance meta-textually and return to the issue of surface and depth in postmodernity. Ravenhill only thinly disguises the texts and ideologies he incorporates with a number of salient consequences: first, such a practice renders the terms of debate accessible allowing a broad band of the audience the knowing satisfaction of recognition; second, these sound bites and slogans are at times so well polished and self-consciously parodic that their abrasive complexity and variety arguably vanishes.

Citations and references, then, serve less as legitimating gestures or integral parts of an aesthetic project, than as signposts Ravenhill erects to guide his audience/readers to or through the problems or social scenarios he wishes to examine. These are both trivial and significant, both overt and, occasionally, covert. Ravenhill is not only an able pasticheur, he excels in generating humorous dissonance through juxtaposition and displacement.

As suggested by the naming of the characters of *Shopping and Fucking* after the members of a pop group, Ravenhill employs an eclectic mixture of references and styles which are blended irrespective of whether they are, in traditional terms, popular or academic, absurd or serious. In *Shopping and Fucking* the most humorous paternal allusion is Brian's love of one of Walt Disney's most successful recent products, the hugely popular animated film and musical, *The Lion King*. Predictably enough, the film was surrounded by considerable merchandising of the order of the illustrated plastic plates which Brian is aiming to sell on television. Brian's enthusiastic description of the film's plot to Lulu while he interviews her is comically undermined as she can easily guess the course of the action. This is not surprising as it is a poorly camouflaged and sanitised, zoomorphic, version of *Hamlet*. Whereas Lulu recognises the recycled nature of this father-son mythic narrative, Brian does not, thus casting his authority as a paternalistic guide in an ambivalent light, as well as suggesting the erosion of shared cultural reference. Furthermore, it might also be noted that what Brian and his son appreciate most about this narrative is not so much the poignancy or loyalty of the father-son relationship, but the moment when violence is required and the son lion realises that to take his place in the "Cycle of Being" he must kill his uncle (9).

The overly explicit reference to a Disney film and its merchandising paraphernalia is counterpointed with Lulu's audition piece. She recites Irina's speech from the end of Chekhov's *Three Sisters*: "One day people will know what all this was for. All this suffering. There'll be no more mysteries. But until then we have to carry on living. We must work. That's all we can do" (13). As Rebellato remarks, "the speech tears a stylistic hole in the fabric of the play"[89] and unlike *The Lion King* the source is not made readily available to the reader or spectator, it is merely something Lulu has learnt "from a book" (13). There is no stage directional indication as to whether Lulu comprehends the text she performs. Certainly, Brian fails to discern its origin, but one would imagine that a large proportion of Ravenhill's youth audience might also. It remains a discrete literary appropriation that accrues significance because it is all but obliterated by the pop culture Disney production. As Rebellato argues, "the hundred year old speech is making a prediction which Ravenhill's play itself rebuts."[90] If anything the world is less explicable, less comprehensible than it was in the past.

Similarly, other literary texts are embedded in the plays to serve transformed or debased ends. *Romeo and Juliet* surfaces

---

[89] Rebellato, *Mark Ravenhill Plays: 1*, xix.
[90] Rebellato, *Mark Ravenhill Plays: 1*, xix.

later when Lulu recites part of Juliet's soliloquy, "Gallop apace, you fiery-footed steeds" (Act III Scene II), for a phone sex customer. *Faust Is Dead* gestures towards its textual heritage in its title, though as this title suggests this, along with various other western myths and ideas, may well have joined the ranks of other poststructuralist deaths.[91] Callens notes how the "ATC [Actors Touring Company], which commissioned [the play], as a matter of artistic policy is intent on radical recreations of classic tales, exploiting current multimedia resources."[92] The play attempts to bring Faust up to date more through its deployment of contemporary references "to Bill Gates and Kurt Cobain, Saddam Hussein and Boris Yeltsin, CNN and MTV, Prozac and the Internet, chaos theory and the millennium,"[93] than through recourse to previous literary or theatrical versions. For Callens, "Pete and Alain are clearly alter-egos in the Faustian psychodramatic tradition, forming food for the Manichean conviction that good and evil are inextricably entwined within the human being itself."[94] Ultimately, in its recycling of the Faust story, *Faust Is Dead* achieves a considerable distortion and transformation the legend, the most prescient of which is the destabilisation of the distinctions between good and evil, real and simulated. Meanwhile, *Handbag* blatantly appropriates the characters from Oscar Wilde's *The Importance of Being Earnest* to act as rather schematic counterpoints to the characters of the present. In addition, Ravenhill, as if to bolster the play's ambivalent message, plants a much noted allusion to Bertolt Brecht's *The Caucasian Chalk Circle*—when Prism arranges to leave the baby for Cardew in the final scene she quotes Brecht: "To he who needs the child, the child will be given" (226). Yet despite its provocative

---

91 Sierz describes how Ravenhill changed the play's title from *Faust* to *Faust is Dead* after the first production in 1996. See *In-Yer-Face Theatre*, 137.
92 Callens, "Sorting Out Ontologies in Mark Ravenhill's *Faust (Faust is Dead)*," 167.
93 Sierz, *In-Yer-Face Theatre*, 136.
94 Callens, "Sorting Out Ontologies in Mark Ravenhill's *Faust (Faust is Dead)*," 168.

themes and images, *Handbag* fails to transcend its own citational cleverness.

More notorious are Ravenhill's borrowings from and pastiche of postmodern theory and some of its propagators. Both *Shopping and Fucking* and *Some Explicit Polaroids* allude to Lyotard's theory of micronarrative as a means of broaching the postmodern debate around meaning and reality. Again Ravenhill barely conceals his sources—in *Shopping and Fucking* Robbie tells Gary:

> I think we all need stories so that we can get by. And I think that a long time ago there were big stories. Stories so big you could live your whole life in them. The Powerful Hands of the Gods and Fate. The Journey to Enlightenment. The March of Socialism. But they all died or the world grew up or grew senile or forgot them, so now we're all making up our own stories. Little stories. It comes out in different ways. But we've each got one. (66)

As discussed above, the play is framed by versions of a performative story through which the three housemates affirm their relationship. In addition, in at least ten of the play's fourteen scenes characters relate stories to one another. The above speech also "tears a stylistic hole" in the play, seeming to overstate its purpose. Robbie, who just moments before has been trying to strangle his rival, suddenly delivers a potted Lyotardian theory of micronarratives, in order to sell Gary an erotic fantasy. In *Some Explicit Polaroids*, the younger generation deliberately ignores anything that might develop into a larger explanation of their lives. Tim comforts Nadia with the pointedly hollow assurance that "nothing's a pattern unless you make it a pattern. Patterns are only there for people who see patterns, and people who see patterns repeat patterns. So we don't look for that" (278). The inability or refusal of the characters in these plays to join up the stories that constitute their existence into a bigger picture entails a levelling of reality and unreality and a profound disempowerment that is the target of Ravenhill's scepticism.

Faust Is Dead the figure of Alain is a perhaps all too obvious a reanimated version of Michel Foucault, using ideas adapted, primarily, from Jean Baudrillard's work. As Sierz among others notes, the play is partly based on the story of Foucault's trip to the US. Ravenhill's recourse to historical and contemporary personages involves a collapsing of their ideas into a single and popular amalgam. Rebellato warns:

> we should not let ourselves be dazzled by self-congratulation for spotting these references to the doyens of postmodernist thought, if in doing so we blind ourselves to the fact that Ravenhill's use of their ideas is fiercely sceptical. [...] The breathtaking abdication of responsibility that these ideas entail is pointed up sharply in *Faust is Dead*, when Alain discourses with the utmost seriousness about the death of reality, while Donny lies at his feet, really dying.[95]

Yet here Rebellato perpetuates the problem of over-simplification and superficiality that haunts the play itself. Ravenhill's "Foucaudrillard" functions as a sensationalist straw man who propounds the end of history (suggesting Francis Fukuyama's *The End of History and the Last Man*) and the death of reality (suggesting Baudrillard's *Simulacra and Simulation*), and who is mesmerised by Donny's self-mutilation, describing it as an art, "a testament of suffering upon the body [...] A moment of power, of control over the self [...] An initiation rite for the end of the twentieth century" (124). This is not to suggest that much postmodern theorising is unproblematic, but that the citational practices inherent to Ravenhill's critique are subject to some of the same questions of responsibility and representation.

Responsibility & Politics?

---

[95] Rebellato, *Mark Ravenhill Plays: 1*, xiv-xv.

Ravenhill's theatrical vision is a political one ambivalently realised. These plays in various ways struggle to account for and critique a mode of existence that is detached, unreal or simulacral. For some critics, he fails in this objective because his work seems too entangled with the very processes it attacks. Vera Gottlieb, for instance, dismisses *Shopping and Fucking* on the grounds that,

> the politics are *implicit* and the values seem to represented by sexual obsession on the one hand—and consumerism on the other: both are "neat" points about today, but it loses itself and a sense of direction by providing little challenge, debate or provocation on the level of serious analysis.[96]

In contrast, both Sierz and Rebellato stress Ravenhill's committed leftist politics. For Sierz, "Ravenhill is not an angry young man, but a more paradoxical figure: his plays may explore contemporary life, using gadgets, pop culture icons and poststructuralist ideas, but his values are traditional."[97] Rebellato goes further arguing that he "is profoundly moral in his portraiture of contemporary society. His vision is elliptically, but recognisably social, even socialist. He addresses not the fragments but the whole, offering us not just some explicit polaroids but the bigger picture."[98] While this overstates the playwright's achievements, it does appropriately align him with the genealogy of political theatre discussed earlier in this chapter. The plays critique, but also are prone to, a sense of postmodern superficiality and fragmentation. As Sierz admits, "his chosen territory […] lies uneasily between postmodern irony and engaged criticism, remains problematic."[99] Ravenhill's irony does have a target, and the intertextuality of his work tends towards a pursuit of meaning

---

96 Vera Gottlieb, "Lukewarm Britannia," *Theatre in a Cool Climate*, eds. Vera Gottlieb and Colin Chambers (Oxford: Amber Lane, 1999) 211.
97 Sierz, *In-Yer-Face Theatre*, 151.
98 Rebellato, *Mark Ravenhill Plays: 1*, x.
99 Sierz, *In-Yer-Face Theatre*, 152.

rather than flatness and sheer play. However, the reception of the play reveals that this is not always the message that audiences (especially the youth audiences the play has attracted) choose to take as Sierz documents.[100]

A central and unresolved difficulty is that, like Baudrillard's apocalyptic closed system, Ravenhill never presents any convincing alternative, while his satire is weakened by either reliance on sentiment, or on unlikely or hasty character transformation. In *Shopping and Fucking*, Brian's return of the money to Robbie and Lulu is in the realm of soap opera fantasy. The play's conclusion, in which the reunited flatmates feed each other ready meals, is overshadowed only marginally by the suggestion that Mark may well have killed Gary (as hinted by the splash of blood on his face that Robbie points out in the play's closing moments). In *Faust Is Dead* the harsh finale of Alain's journey is modulated by Donny's return as a nurturing ghost. Nadia in *Some Explicit Polaroids* for all her previous self-delusion only requires a brief conversation with Jonathan to set her on a path to a more honest and realistic self-awareness. While it might be argued that it is not the playwright's responsibility to provide such solutions, his implicit avocation of responsibility and memory is weakened by this ambivalence.

"A global culture," states Birringer, "would be a culture without perspective. We would be trapped in a perpetual present, in the same space, circulating the same cultural products over and over."[101] Ravenhill succeeds in capturing this disquieting prospect. His particular commitment to this project is one that distinguishes him from most of his contemporaries, most notably Martin McDonagh, master of postmodern ironic recycling and for many of his critics an irresponsible cultural vandal.

---

[100] "Ravenhill also points out in dismay that some young people reacted as if the whole play was meant to be 'ironic, cool, unfeeling'." Sierz, *In-Yer-Face Theatre*, 129.

[101] Birringer, *Theatre, Theory, Postmodernism*, 4.

Martin McDonagh
"Pastiche Soup," Bad Taste, Biting Irony

I suppose I walk a fine line between comedy and cruelty because I think one illuminates the other. [...] I tend to push things as far as I can because I think you can see things more clearly through exaggeration than through reality [...] how else are can you react to all that has happened through writing or art [...] if not through absurdity?[1]

Comedy, cruelty and absurd exaggeration have been the tradmarks of the work of Martin McDonagh, perhaps the most commercially successful of the new playwrights to have appeared in the 1990s. On more than one occasion the London Irish playwright has been likened to Johnny Rotten, the front man of the 1970s British Punk band the Sex Pistols.[2] His much vaunted objective has been to disrupt the "cycle of boredom" of British drama[3] and to create a theatre that is "some kind of punk destruction of what's gone before."[4] All of which may

---

[1] Sean O'Hagan interview with Martin McDonagh, "The Wild West," *Guardian* 24 Mar. 2001 (online).

[2] See O'Hagan, "The Wild West" and also Peter Lenz, "'Anything new in the feckin' west?' Martin McDonagh's *Leenane Trilogy* and the Juggling with Irish Literary Stereotypes," *(Dis)Continuities: Trends and Traditions in Contemporary Theatre and Drama in English*, CDE 9, eds. Margarete Rubik and Elke Mettinger-Schartmann (Trier: Wissenschaflicher Verlag Trier, 2002) 25-38.

[3] Martin McDonagh qtd. in Richard Zoglin, "When O'Casey Met Scorsese," *Time.com* 13 Apr. 1998 (online).

[4] McDonagh qtd. in Matt Wolf, "Martin McDonagh on a Tear," *American Theatre* 15:1 (1998): 48-50. 48.

seem somewhat peculiar when juxtaposed with the fact that each of McDonagh's "radical" and "challenging" plays from this period is set in the rural west of Ireland. McDonagh's cult status did not develop from a drama based in contemporary urban experience, but rather, as Karen Vandevelde claims, has grown from a drama that focuses instead on "members of a rural community who are victims of loneliness, depression and economic progress."[5] Vandevelde's statement, however, in common with so much said and written of McDonagh and his work is already somewhat misleading. It can equally be contended that McDonagh's success has not been due to the plays' interest in the unfortunate situation of the "victims" of progress, but rather because of their raucously grim humour and carefully calibrated plots combined with McDonagh's incendiary dealings with the press. If for some McDonagh is "one of the most skilled and brilliant creators of theatrical potboilers,"[6] then for others he is but a disseminator of "fifth-rate bad Synge" and reprehensible stage oirishry.[7] Both perspectives point towards a debate which will be explored more fully in the course of what follows.

McDonagh's debut was a co-production by the Druid Theatre Company in Galway and the Royal Court Theatre in London of *The Beauty Queen of Leenane*. The play premiered in Galway's Town Hall Theatre on the 1 February 1996, followed by a London opening at the Royal Court Theatre Upstairs on the 5 March 1996. By 1998, McDonagh had won the George Devine Award for Most Promising Playwright, the Evening Standard Award for Most Promising Newcomer, and the Writers' Guild Award for Best New Fringe Play, not to mention the four Tony Awards won by the Druid Theatre and Garry

---

[5] Karen Vandevelde, "The Gothic Soap of Martin McDonagh," *Theatre Stuff: Critical Essays on Contemporary Irish Theatre*, ed. Eamonn Jordan (Dublin: Carysfort, 2000) 292-302. 292.

[6] Dominic Dromgoole, *The Full Room: An A-Z of Contemporary Playwriting* (London: Methuen, 2000) 198.

[7] Emer O'Kelly of the *Sunday Independent* qtd. in Vandevelde, "The Gothic Soap of Martin McDonagh," 293.

Hynes for their production of the Leenane Trilogy.[8] Further work appeared in rapid succession: *The Cripple of Inishmaan* (Royal National Theatre Cottesloe Auditorium, 12 December 1996), and the remaining plays of the trilogy, *A Skull in Connemara* (Town Hall Theatre Galway, 3 June 1997; Royal Court, 17 July 1997) and *The Lonesome West* (Town Hall Theatre Galway, 10 June 1997; Royal Court, 19 July 1997). The full Leenane Trilogy was presented as a combined matinée and evening performance on the 21 June in Galway and the 26 July in London and then transferred to the 1997 Dublin Theatre Festival. McDonagh's success with this relatively narrow portfolio of work has been phenomenal. According to Sean O'Hagan, McDonagh at the age of twenty-seven was the first playwright since Shakespeare to have four plays running simultaneously in London[9]—a catch phrase much circulated but fallacious. There followed a good deal of media attention generated by the very successful New York productions of the plays, subsequent productions throughout Europe and in Australia and, most notably, the playwright's own showmanship.[10] As Werner Huber describes,

> McDonagh fashioned for himself the image of a loud mouth, genius, and punk artist [...]. If we take his word for it then [he] would have left school at the age of sixteen and spent the next ten years like a recluse living on dole money and odd jobs,

8   This list of awards is to be found in Werner Huber, "The Plays of Martin McDonagh," *Twentieth-Century Theatre and Drama in English: Festschrift for Heinz Kosok on the Occasion of his 65th Birthday*, ed. Jürgen Kamm (Trier: Wissenschaflicher Verlag Trier, 1999) 555 and in Vandevelde, "The Gothic Soap of Martin McDonagh," 292.

9   O'Hagan's article, "The Wild West," includes this claim which has been often recycled in various popular media and academic work on McDonagh. Patrick Lonergan at the Irish Theatre Magazine Critics Conference in October 2003 highlighted the inaccuracy of this information.

10   Aleks Sierz, *In-Yer-Face Theatre: British Drama Today* (London: Faber, 2001) 220, notes that by the year 2000, *The Beauty Queen of Leenane* had been translated into 28 languages.

watching films and TV soaps and doing his own writing in between.[11]

Typically provocative, McDonagh has on numerous occasions denied both an interest in theatre and any deep knowledge of the Irish literary sources his work makes use of.[12] Finally, after a hiatus of four years and an unsuccessful incursion into scriptwriting, the second play in the Aran Trilogy, begun with *The Cripple of Inishmaan*, was produced. Controversy surrounded *The Lieutenant of Inishmore* which premiered at the RSC The Other Place, Stratford-on-Avon on the 11 April 2001.[13] Apparently due to its inflammatory and ambivalent satire on Irish Republican terrorism, both the Royal Court and the National Theatre had refused the play hence the delay in its production and its displacement to Stratford-on-Avon. Reputedly a third play, entitled *The Banshees of Inisheer*, is to complete the trilogy although no news of a production has been forthcoming. Meanwhile, McDonagh's latest play, *The Pillowman* (National Theatre, 2003) sets a precedent in departing from Irish subject matter entirely to focus upon the interrogation of a writer in an unnamed totalitarian state.[14]

---

[11] Huber, "The Plays of Martin McDonagh," 556. Huber surveys various newspaper articles which demonstrate McDonagh's alleged arrogance.

[12] McDonagh has claimed "I'm coming to the theatre with a disrespect for it. I'm coming from a film fan's perspective on the theatre […] Theatre bored the socks off me." Qtd. in Joseph Feeney, "Martin McDonagh: Dramatist of the West," *Studies* 87.345 (1998): 28. Also in interview with Sean O'Hagan, he says "the whole theatre thing makes me intensely uncomfortable to the point where I react just like my parents […], 'Theatre's not for the likes of us.'" Qtd. in "The Wild West," *Guardian* 24 Mar. 2001 (online). Similar comments are to be found in Penelope Dening's *Irish Times* article, "The Scribe of Kilburn" 18 Apr. 2001. The article is incidentally a rehash of a piece written by Dening under the title "The Wordsmith of Camberwell" for the *Irish Times* 8 July 1997.

[13] The play was purportedly written in 1994, but took five years to find a theatre to produce it. See Penelope Dening, "The Scribe of Kilburn" (online).

[14] Significantly, McDonagh has revealed that his latest play was written around the same time as his Irish plays, thus disrupting any claims to his "progress" as a writer.

Finally, his short Oscar winning film *Six Shooter* (2005) returns to an Irish setting and gory humour.

Although criticism on McDonagh frequently claims his work to be either postmodern or indicative of postmodernity in some way, few have delved into what this might involve in any detail, beyond that of its illustrative potential. Rather than continuing the debate as to whether McDonagh's work provides an accurate or inaccurate representation of Ireland, I want to trace how the work recycles particular forms in its approach to narrative and plot. Then with a view to situating McDonagh's citational practices, I will map two principle approaches to pastiche and parody in postmodernity—as an effacement of history or, conversely, as critical intertextuality— before turning to the historical discourse of authentic Irish identity the plays interpellate. McDonagh's narratives are excessive in their devotion to action, the diminution of character and the arch nature of their language. These features, however, only gain edge because of their parody of stereotypes and pastiche of discourses ranging from the literary and theatrical to the popular to the political. The plays demonstrate postmodern tendencies in their combinations of recycling, ironic detachment and "bad" taste or kitsch that ultimately constitute a spectacular arrangement, in that what is circulated are representations of representations with no guaranteed recourse to an original. As such they might be viewed as "sites of the disappearance of meaning and representation."[15] Simultaneously, however, they have also facilitated a debate as to the political potential of parodic practice in contemporary theatre.

"Punk Destruction," Absurdity & Exaggeration
Although McDonagh is included by Aleks Sierz among the writers of In-Yer-Face theatre, he sits uneasily with the majority

---

[15] Jean Baudrillard, "The Evil Demon of Images and the Precession of Simulacra," *Postmodernism: A Reader*, ed. Thomas Docherty (New York: Harvester Wheatsheaf, 1993) 194.

of the selected playwrights who, with the exception of Sarah Kane, write with varying degrees of seriousness about contemporary urban experience. McDonagh's work also differs in its exploitation of destructive absurdity and exaggerated often cruel, comedy. Both, as will be discussed below, have given rise to considerable disagreement over the nature and value of his drama. Critics notwithstanding, McDonagh has met with much admiration of his use of black humour, which emerges through the brutality of his rural misfit characters, as well as more obliquely through generic, literary and cultural references. With regard to the issue of comedy and its perimeters, it is worth returning to Christopher Innes's observation that "as the most socially dependent of all dramatic forms, the definition of comedy shifts continually; and in the modern era the change has been particularly extreme." He illustrates his point with an assertion from an eighteenth century writer that nothing "horrific or unnatural could ever be a theme for comedy."[16] It is not difficult to see how such an attitude has been impressively and provocatively overturned in various ways and at different periods throughout the twentieth century, but especially in its concluding decades. However, despite the significant role of humour in McDonagh's plays it would be erroneous to claim that all his work is adequately served by the term comedy alone. In his strongest plays the humour is balanced with dark undercurrents and destructive ambivalence. As one member of the audience at the Galway premiere of *The Beauty Queen of Leenane* put it, "I have a funny feeling that I shouldn't be laughing so hard,"[17] a comment which gestures towards much of what seems to be at stake in so much of McDonagh's work to date.

[16] Christopher Innes, *Modern British Drama: The Twentieth Century* (1992; Cambridge: Cambridge University Press, 2002) 251. Innes refers specifically to Henry Fielding's assertion that horrific or unnatural incidents could never be matter for comedy—the example he uses to demonstrate this incongruity and repeated by Innes is that of "Nero, ripping out his mother's belly."

[17] O'Hagan, "The Wild West" (online).

The provocation of a volatile mixture of humour and horror, in addition to a widely publicised dismissal of tradition, has lead to the popular labelling of McDonagh as punk. Indeed the word "punk" crops up repeatedly in interviews with McDonagh and responses to his work. It remains, nevertheless, of limited use as an heuristic device, not least because punk as an anti-social, anarchic rejection of the values and authority in 1970s Britain has arguably become in contemporary consumer society merely another style to be adopted complete with safety pins, designed dishevelment and ready-made attitude. While it is wise to reflect on McDonagh's stated ambitions with a modicum of scepticism, a closer inspection of this alleged "destruction of what went before" leads in a number of directions, not only in terms of what traditions his writing may be dismantling, but also those it preserves. The conventions upon which he explicitly draws are hybrid (just as McDonagh is himself) and eclectic, ranging from American gangster film to the classics of Irish drama, elements of which are simulated and parodied. Perhaps inevitably, much attention has been devoted to this engagement with Irish dramatic tradition and literary stereotypes.[18] Because from the very beginning, the plays have been publicised as breaking up and recasting the work of now canonical Irish dramatists like John Millington Synge, little serious attention has been paid to the other formal traditions imprinted on his work and his non-Irish theatrical predecessors which, significantly, remain untouched by so-called "punk destruction."

Firstly, it is noteworthy that McDonagh preserves most of the elements of melodrama—suspense, sensational episodes and romance—though unambiguously happy endings are in short supply. As in the melodramatic comedy of manners, the unities of time, place and character are observed. The plays are, for the most part, set in the familiar, realistically presented,

---

[18] A particularly useful essay on this subject is Lenz, "'Anything new in the feckin' west?' Martin McDonagh's *Leenane Trilogy* and the Juggling with Irish Literary Stereotypes." See also Huber, "The Plays of Martin McDonagh."

spaces of cottage and farmhouse kitchens. The action comprises primarily of dialogue (usually highly mundane or practically meaningless) and sporadic violence, both of which have so far been the core of McDonagh's theatrical practices. He has particular fondness for the device of the letter—(lost, found, forged, destroyed or read aloud) in *The Cripple of Inishmann, The Beauty Queen of Leenane, The Lonesome West*—or the confession (written and then destroyed) in *A Skull in Connemara*. These are used to heighten tension, drive the plot or to reveal secrets in a manner that again strongly links his work with the narrative traditions of melodrama. As Dromgoole notes in this regard, McDonagh has "great narrative skill, and a strong imaginative grasp of theatrical plasticity."[19] Other points of contiguity are the schematic quality of his characters, some of whom function merely as mouthpieces for cycles of banter, and the episodic, though ultimately linear, development of plot.

Furthermore, though it has been fashionable to compare what McDonagh is doing on stage with the films of Quentin Tarantino or Martin Scorsese (for which the playwright has undeniable and much publicised enthusiasm), rather than turning too hastily to contemporary Hollywood film as an easy model of suspense and violent action, McDonagh's drama might be juxtaposed with older models of violent sensationalist melodrama (which are the underlay of more recent cinematic versions) such as that of the Théâtre du Grand Guignol. In operation in Paris from 1897 to 1962, Grand Guignol constituted a particular mutation of melodrama for the masses. The term is derived from the French version of the child's puppet Punch and Judy show, Petit Guignol. The adult version was remarkable for its grotesque and visceral performances that exploited suspense and fear, but also humour. Violence was integral to the spectacle. Torture and dismemberment were among the most infamous features of the repertoire, which became progressively more absurd and histrionic in the course

---

[19] Dromgoole, *The Full Room*, 199.

of its existence.[20] As a theatrical forerunner of the gruesomely graphic violence of so much recent Hollywood cinema,

> aided by trick lighting, fearsome props and make-up, the Guignolers [went] happily, if homicidally, about their business of gouging out one another's eyes, cooking villains in vats of sulphuric acid, hurling vitriol and cutting throats, all to the accompaniment of hysterical laughter and hideous shrieks.[21]

While obviously McDonagh's work has not sunk to quite such sensationalist depths, the violent Punch and Judy qualities of *A Skull in Connemara*, *The Lonesome West* and, above all, *The Lieutenant of Inishmore*, which infamously features onstage torture and dismemberment, serve to place his work on a continuum with it. Both McDonagh's plays and those of the Grand Guignol share a concept of, as John Callahan comically describes, "la douche écossaise" or "the hot and cold shower,"[22] jarring audiences with doses of comic absurdity and terror. Significantly, both have suffered a similar exhaustion of effect in part due to the increasing superficiality of character and plot.

In addition to the brutality of some of the plays, there is also a keenly observed absurdity in the quotidian exchanges between characters. McDonagh on many occasions has cited the work of Harold Pinter and David Mamet (specifically *American Buffalo* [1975]) as being among his literary influences. Leaving aside the use of exaggerated Hiberno-English syntax and vocabulary, echoes of the mundane menace and uncomfortable humour of Pinter's early work and Mamet's *American Buffalo* can be identified. As Martin Esslin writes of Pinter in *The*

---

[20] For detailed discussions of the history of the Théâtre du Grand Guignol see Victor Emeljanow, "Grand Guignol and the Orchestration of Violence" and John M. Callahan, "The Ultimate in Theatre Violence" both in *Violence in Drama*, ed. James Redmond, *Themes in Drama* Vol. 13 (Cambridge: Cambridge University Press, 1991) 151-163 and 165-175 respectively.

[21] "Speaking in Pictures," *Life* 22 (28 Apr. 1947): 15. Qtd. in Callahan, "The Ultimate in Theatre Violence," 165.

[22] Callahan, "The Ultimate in Theatre Violence," 166.

Theatre of the Absurd (1961), the among the basic components of his work are "the uncannily cruel accuracy of his reproduction of the inflections and rambling irrelevancy of everyday speech [and] the commonplace situation that is gradually invested with menace, dread, and mystery."[23] Comparable qualities are distinguishable in *American Buffalo,* especially in Teach's attempts to assert his macho authority. Furthermore, the tones of Mamet's halting exchanges and streetwise obscenities can be heard throughout McDonagh's work. McDonagh, though no dramatist of the absurd in Esslin's sense, adapts the vernacular tone of circular dialogue and spiralling misunderstandings from Pinter and Mamet, exaggerating and extending them through his use of dialect.

Exaggeration is evidently an element in all McDonagh's plays, however *A Skull in Connemara, The Lonesome West* and, especially, *The Lieutenant of Inishmore* are increasingly farcical. The simplification of character, the broadside humour, improbable twists of plot and an increasing reliance upon violent action serve to align him also with a particular history of farce in British theatre. Innes outlines the split in the comic genre in this context as follows:

> The lines were already set right at the beginning of the century. On the one hand conscious artifice becomes a dominating aesthetic principle [...] on the other stands an essentially realistic approach, where actuality is the touchstone against which illusory ideals are measured (epitomised by the Irish dramatist J.M. Synge's 1907 classic, *The Playboy of the Western World*).[24]

Though the ghost of Synge will reappear later, I would argue that the self-consciousness of McDonagh's work places him in the former category. Another unavoidable purveyor of conscious artifice in modern British theatre is, of course, Joe

---

[23] Martin Esslin, "Harold Pinter: Certainties and Uncertainties," *The Theatre of the Absurd* (1961; London: Pelican, 1980) 235.

[24] Innes, *Modern British Drama,* 252.

Orton, a playwright to whom McDonagh has been, in passing, likened.[25] Parallels between Orton's brief career and work and that of McDonagh are indeed more extensive than is usually acknowledged. Orton's exaggeration of lust and cruelty served up relentlessly to 1960s audiences in *Entertaining Mr Sloane* (1964), *Loot* (1965) and *What the Butler Saw* (1969), flaunted characters without psychological depth, stock clichés and action which though callous and often shockingly cruel, mixed these elements freely with melodramatic gags. Echoes of these techniques are plentiful in McDonagh's later plays. Both trivialise accepted morality or codes of seriousness. The sinister police inspector, Truscott, in *Loot* finds a counterpoint in the equivocal Garda Thomas Hanlon in *A Skull in Connemara*; the irreverence of Orton exemplified by the manhandling of a mother's corpse in *Loot* and the callous murder of the helpless old father in *Entertaining Mr Sloane* is mirrored by the treatment of Johnnypateenmike's aged mother and the politically incorrect jibes at Cripple Billy's expense in *The Cripple of Inishmaan*, the attitude of Coleman and Valene Connor to the murder of their father in *The Lonesome West*, the gleeful smashing up of disinterred human skulls and bones in *A Skull in Connemara*, and finally in the brutality of *The Lieutenant of Inishmore*. Unsurprisingly, both playwrights have been criticised for their lack of compassion and bad taste. However, for Orton the glue holding his notion of farce together is sexual perversity and in this McDonagh clearly differs. Nevertheless, Innes's synopsis of Orton's dramaturgy with a few minor adjustments uncannily foreshadows a good deal of what McDonagh has practiced:

[25] See for example Fintan O'Toole's introduction to *Plays 1* (London: Methuen, 1999). Also Mária Kurdi, "Gender, Sexuality and Violence in the Work of Martin McDonagh," *The Theatre of Martin McDonagh: A World of Savage Stories*, eds. Lilian Chambers and Eamonn Jordan (Dublin: Carysfort, 2006) 96-115 mentions correspondences with Orton's work.

His dramatic figures have no characteristics other than egoism, and all moral standards have been inverted. Sexual deviation is seen as the norm, killing acceptable, and "a bang on the nose … human contact." Any innocence is presented as stupidity, all authority is revealed as the source of chaos; and egalitarian principles only mean that everyone is equally corrupt. The whole society is "a madhouse. Unusual behaviour is the order of the day … It's democratic lunacy we practice."[26]

Finally, one might remark that not only do Orton and McDonagh have a lot in common as farceurs, their rapid rise to fame also shares some characteristics. Orton, of course, adopted a histrionic persona and stoked up controversy by writing outraged letters about his work to the press under the pseudonym Edna Welthorpe. McDonagh has similarly provoked outrage by comparing himself to Muhammad Ali and Orson Welles, and by very publicly insulting Sean Connery at an award ceremony.

These are some of the less conspicuous ingredients in what Dromgoole colourfully calls McDonagh's "pastiche soup."[27] The dominant flavour is undoubtedly that of Irish drama, but it is important to recognise these other elements before making claims as to the innovation of his work or its disruption of tradition. McDonagh's Irish predecessors can be traced from the nineteenth century master of melodrama, sensational effects and overt stage Irishry, Dion Boucicault, through to the thematic focus of George Bernard Shaw's tongue-in-cheek *John Bull's Other Island* (1904) to, inevitably, the language and plot of John Millington Synge's *Playboy of the Western World* (1907) and latterly to the work of playwrights like Brian Friel and Tom Murphy. It is this aspect of McDonagh's work and the ways in which he (mis)represents the Irish that have lead to most heated debate.

---

[26] Innes, *Modern British Drama*, 298. In this excerpt he cites Orton's *Complete Plays*, 329 and 412.

[27] Dromgoole, *The Full Room*, 199.

Broadly, two opposing approaches have dominated critical analysis of McDonagh's work. The first addresses the plays in terms of their mimetic validity. As Ondřej Pilný notes "the overall approach in Irish drama criticism tends to be determined by the notion of Irish drama essentially holding a 'mirror up to nature/nation,'" as the title of Christopher Murray's theatre history *Twentieth-Century Irish Drama: Mirror up to Nation* (1997) likewise indicates.[28] Predictably, this motive has been the basis of a number of responses to McDonagh's work, though they are split as to whether the perceived dramatic representations of Ireland are true or false. The latter camp maintains that his drama lacks moral responsibility and circulates negative and facile stereotypes of Ireland and the Irish. The former suggests that, in contrast, it is subversive of stereotypes concerning Ireland in a postmodern, playful manner and as such is perhaps a more truthful perspective. However, both are imbricated with an implicit (though sometimes explicit) debate over authenticity.

The second approach is marked by attempts to move beyond issues of specific representation to the textual and thematic devices of the plays and their implications. Werner Huber, for instance, has analysed certain features of McDonagh's drama, unpicking its "polarised structures, positions, and movements, e.g. centrifugal vs. centripetal, diastole vs. systole, exile vs. home, or synthetically as unresolved juxtapositions, clashes, jarring sounds and emotions, dramatic twists of fate and the overturning of expectations."[29] Significantly, Huber points out the difficulty of interpreting McDonagh's "art of 'codding'" as straightforward satire, since "value system" within the plays is perpetually unstable. Huber concludes that "considering McDonagh's action-orientation and the plethora of dramatic development

---

[28] Ondřej Pilný, "Martin McDonagh: Parody? Satire? Complacency?" *Irish Studies Review* 12.2 (2004) 225-232. 225
[29] Huber, "The Plays of Martin McDonagh," 563-4.

[...] [it] is tempt[ing] to suggest that McDonagh is restoring an original dimension to the meaning of drama as 'action.'"[30]

Both Peter Lenz and Ondřej Pilný have explored the use of literary stereotypes in the plays as a strategy for satirising or critiquing tradition. Both tease out aspects of the web of intertextual reference in the plays, but conclude that McDonagh's humorous deconstruction of tradition has reached a point of exhaustion.[31] Following Huber's warning with regard to the satiric dimensions to the plays, Pilný argues that "there is another sense in which McDonagh operates as a satirist: his plays in fact ironise the very notion of Irish dramatic realism."[32]

Michal Lachman treats the ways in which McDonagh dissolves boundaries and hierarchies to arrive at an equalisation of elements in the plays. In particular, he looks at the way that the notion of exile, and exile as a theme in Irish drama, is affected by this equalisation. Lachman contends that "the logic which operates [in the plays] is not that of irreducible extremes but that of enumeration: an endless acceptance of the flow. It is a logic of consumerism in the realm of myth, identity, nationhood and entertainment."[33]

Both of these approaches will be explored further here, but in particular I wish to follow the implications of reading McDonagh in relation to a postmodern crisis of representation.[34] In concordance with Lachman and Pilný, I argue that McDonagh's work ironises the notion of authenticity, rather than wantonly deprecating the Irish. This

---

[30] Huber, "The Plays of Martin McDonagh," 568, 570.

[31] See Lenz, "'Anything new in the feckin' west?'" and Pilný, "Martin McDonagh: Parody? Satire? Complacency?"

[32] Pilný, "Martin McDonagh: Parody? Satire? Complacency?" 228.

[33] Michal Lachman, "Happy and in Exile? Martin McDonagh's 'Leenane Trilogy,'" *Engaging Modernity*, eds. Michael Böss and Eamonn Maher (Dublin: Veritas, 2003) 204.

[34] See also José Lanters, "Playwrights of the Western World: Synge, Murphy, McDonagh," *A Century of Irish Drama: Widening the Stage*, eds. Stephen Watt, Eileen Morgan and Shakir Mustafa (Bloomington and Indiana: Indiana University Press, 2000) 204-22.

does not mean that the plays are unproblematic—their citations, ludic recycling, coupled with farcical superficiality and casual brutality, makes any simple reading on the basis of satiric parody difficult, but not necessarily, as some critics of McDonagh have asserted, impossible.

Irony, Parody & Pastiche

Before turning to the Irish-English cultural and political co-ordinates of the debate McDonagh has ignited, several terms regularly applied to his work deserve closer attention. These gesture to a wider context of the contemporary culture of which he is a part. More precisely, what does it mean to claim that McDonagh's drama is ironic, parodic or a pastiche in a "postmodern" sense?

Although as noted earlier there are precious few points of uncomplicated consensus with regard to *post*modernism and *post*modernity, one widely accepted perspective is that modernism and postmodernism share many of the same ideas even as their *attitude* to those ideas differs. Thus, a concern for the process of composition, the erosion of the supposed objectivity of, for instance, an omniscient third person narrator, the blurring of genres, fragmented forms, self-reflexivity and citational strategies are to be found among both modernist and postmodernist literary or artistic practices.[35] Irony is arguably the most crucial element of this attitude shift. More generally, much of what has marked off postmodernism and postmodernity is the disintegration of shared values or assumptions, or what Jean-François Lyotard terms metanarratives. In cultural terms the devalued currency of

---

[35] Lists of similarities or differences between modernism and postmodernism are now very common, even if they are intended primarily to be tentative rather than concrete. Among the more informative of such approaches is Ihab Hassan's "Toward a Concept of Postmodernism" in *Postmodernism: A Reader* 146-156, cited above in which he offers a list of "schematic differences." Hassan is, nevertheless, quick to remind readers that "the dichotomies [of his opposing lists] remain insecure, equivocal." 152.

metanarratives has lead to stylistic profusion and the confusion of former hierarchies of taste and aesthetic privilege or value.

Perhaps the first issue to address, therefore, is that of style. To some degree one might read McDonagh's plays and their popularity as a testimony to the stylistic eclecticism of late twentieth century postmodern society. As suggested above, McDonagh draws upon multiple styles and genres without distinguishing between high or popular cultural references in an apparently gratuitous display of manic intertexuality. Such a profusion/confusion of styles is one of the prime characteristics of postmodernity according to Lyotard:

> Eclecticism is the zero degree of contemporary general culture: one listens to reggae, watches a western, eats McDonald's food for lunch and local cuisine for dinner, wears Paris perfume in Tokyo and "retro" clothes in Hong Kong: knowledge is a matter for TV games. It is easy to find a public for eclectic works. By becoming kitsch, art panders to the confusion which reigns in the "taste" of patrons. Artists, gallery owners, critics, and public wallow together in "anything goes," and the epoch is one of slackening.[36]

Postmodernity, then, is marked by the pastiche and parody of multiple heterogeneous styles—old forms of content become mere traits leading to the circulation and recirculation of surface effects. The features of such so-called postmodern styles are familiar—the proliferation of nostalgic or retro modes; the recycling of earlier genres and styles in new contexts; the recasting of history as style or the rewriting of history according to fantasy and nostalgia; an apparently ever increasing acceleration of stylistic changes. In the light of such observations one might argue that what McDonagh has done is to exploit Irishness as a style—one that in particular has many resonances in the theatre.

---

[36] Jean-François Lyotard, *The Postmodern Condition: A Report on Knowledge*, trans. Geoff Bennington and Brian Massumi (1979; Manchester: Manchester University Press, 1986) 76.

The instability and disposability of styles evidently bears implications for the possibility and functioning of parody and irony, and a number of recent theoretical positions on the status of these terms are, I would suggest, of immediate relevance to reading McDonagh. The first of these is posed by Fredric Jameson. In attempting to define postmodernism, Jameson identifies two common features: "first, most [...] postmodernisms [...] emerge as specific reactions against the established forms of high modernism" and second, these postmodernisms involve "the effacement of some key boundaries or separations, most notably the erosion of the older distinction between high culture and so-called mass or popular culture."[37] For Jameson, because of the erosion of the subject and diffusion of political metanarratives in "late capitalism," which he aligns with postmodernity, "parody finds itself without a vocation it has lived, and that strange new thing, pastiche, slowly comes to take its place."[38] Although

> both pastiche and parody involve the imitation or, better still, the mimicry of other styles and particularly of the mannerisms and stylistic twitches of other styles [...] parody capitalises on the uniqueness of these styles and seizes on their idiosyncrasies and eccentricities to produce an imitation which mocks the original.[39]

The key to this process is not only that the parodist must be able to identify with "the original" but, more significantly, the assumption of some normative basis or "linguistic norm" against which this "original" is critiqued. However, for Jameson because postmodernism is constituted by an

---

[37] Fredric Jameson, "Postmodernism and Consumer Society," *The Anti-Aesthetic: Essays on Postmodern Culture*, ed. Hal Foster (1983; New York: The New Press, 1998) 128.

[38] Fredric Jameson, "Postmodernism, or the Cultural Logic of Late Capitalism," *Postmodernism: A Reader*, ed. Thomas Docherty (New York: Harvester Wheatsheaf, 1993) 62-92. 73.

[39] Jameson, "Postmodernism and Consumer Society," 130.

obliteration of norms and boundaries, parody can no longer gain any footing since only "stylistic diversity and heterogeneity" remains.[40]

While parody and irony conventionally serve political ends—subversion, social commentary, provocation—in postmodernity, it is frequently argued that they have lost their potency because of the dissolution of common values or political beliefs. In place of parody and irony, the strategy of pastiche appears. As already discussed in relation to Mark Ravenhill's drama, Jameson remarks upon postmodernism's captivation by a "degraded" cultural landscape, which is not only quoted but incorporated.[41] Pastiche, for Jameson, then is only imitation of "dead styles" in "a world in which stylistic innovation is no longer possible" and art refers only to itself.[42]

Clearly, parody and pastiche are set up here as antithetical, although pastiche also frequently encompasses satire or ironic intent. But Jameson must establish them as discrete entities if his critique of the recycling practices of the postmodern is to be sustained. Consequently, pastiche as defined by Jameson is merely,

> a neutral practice of [...] mimicry, without any of parody's ulterior motives, amputated of satiric impulse [...]. Pastiche is thus blank parody, a statue with blind eyeballs.[43]

Jameson connects the "omnipresence of pastiche" with spectacle and simulacrum and goes on to discuss the simulacral histories generated by American "nostalgia film."[44] It is at this point that Jameson's argument seems to converge with the terminology of Jean Baudrillard, in particular in "The Precession of Simulacra" (1981). And as previously outlined, the crisis of representation discussed by Jameson is carried to a

---

40 Jameson, "Postmodernism and Consumer Society," 130-31.
41 Jameson, "Postmodernism, or the Cultural Logic of Late Capitalism," 63.
42 Jameson, "Postmodernism and Consumer Society," 132.
43 Jameson, "Postmodernism, or the Cultural Logic of Late Capitalism," 74.
44 Jameson, "Postmodernism, or the Cultural Logic of Late Capitalism," 74-5.

radical and apocalyptic conclusion in which simulation
dominates and recourse to the authentic, original or, indeed,
reality is impossible. As a result, Baudrillard claims nostalgia
comes into its own and authenticity becomes a matter of mere
spectacle.[45]

In opposition to Jameson's proposition that postmodernism
is defined by reactionary nostalgia and superficiality, or
Baudrillard's closed system of hyperreality and simulation,
Linda Hutcheon argues for a re-evaluation and recuperation of
postmodernism's aesthetic practices. Central to her attitude is
the thesis that postmodernism co-joins nostalgia and irony
through what she calls "double coding," to enable a critical
consideration of modernity.[46] The process, though, is far from
straightforward since,

> postmodernism is a fundamentally contradictory enterprise: its
> art forms (and its theory) at once use and abuse, install and then
> destabilise convention in parodic ways, self-consciously
> pointing both to their own inherent paradoxes and
> provisionality and, of course, to their critical or ironic re-
> reading of the art of the past.[47]

Hutcheon deploys "ironic parody" to contend that "the
paradox of postmodernist parody is that it is *not* essentially
depthless, trivial kitsch, [...] but rather that it can and does lead
to a vision of interconnectedness" illustrating both the
"aesthetic conceptualisation" and the "social situation" of the
work. In doing so, ironic parody enacts a reality which is
openly acknowledged as "discursive" and lays bare the
Jamesonian fiction of "genuine historicity."[48] What is more,
"parody sets up a dialogical relation between identification and

[45] Jean Baudrillard, *Simulacra and Simulations*, trans. Sheila Faria Glaser (1981; Michigan: University of Michigan Press, 1994) 6-7.

[46] Linda Hutcheon, *A Poetics of Postmodernity: History, Theory, Literature* (London and New York: Routledge, 1988).

[47] Hutcheon, *A Poetics of Postmodernity*, 23.

[48] Hutcheon, *A Poetics of Postmodernity*, 24.

distance. Like Brecht's *Verfremdungseffekt*, parody works to distance and, at the same time, to involve both artist and audience in a participatory hermeneutic activity."[49]

Contrary to Jameson's negation of the potentialities of pastiche, Hutcheon stresses the status of pastiche as intertextuality, pointing out how

> intertextuality replaces the challenged author-text relationship with one between reader and text, one that situates the locus of textual meaning within the history of discourse itself. A literary work can actually no longer be considered original; if it were, it could have no meaning for its reader. It is only as part of prior discourses that any text derives meaning and significance.[50]

Such intertextuality for Hutcheon is valuable because it "challenges [...] both closure and single centralised meaning. It willed and wilful provisionality rests largely upon its acceptance of the inevitable textual infiltration of prior discursive practices." So it foregrounds context and yet also undermines it.[51]

Parody fused with pastiche for Hutcheon, therefore, is far from extinct or without contemporary function, rather it has

> come to be a privileged mode of postmodern formal self-reflexivity because of its paradoxical incorporation of the past into its very structures often points to these ideological contexts somewhat more obviously, more didactically, than other forms. Parody seems to offer a perspective on the present and on the past which allows an artist to speak *to* a discourse from *within* it, but without being totally recuperated by it.[52]

If Jameson errs on the side of negativity, then it could be argued that Hutcheon's claims for postmodernist parody err on the

---

[49] Hutcheon, *A Poetics of Postmodernity*, 35.
[50] Hutcheon, *A Poetics of Postmodernity*, 126
[51] Hutcheon, *A Poetics of Postmodernity*, 127.
[52] Hutcheon, *A Poetics of Postmodernity*, 35.

side of positivity. While such forms of parody may not be depthless, there seems little guarantee that they *per se* draw artist and spectator into a meaningful or communal exegetics. Nevertheless, it is precisely the question of the position of the artist and the nature of the discourse with which he engages that presents itself in McDonagh's work and surfaces in interpretations of his drama.

"Do you want to play 'England versus Ireland'?"[53]
In *The Cripple of Inishmaan*, Helen forces her brother to play a game "England versus Ireland." The game is a short one, Helen tells Bartley to "be Ireland" and close his eyes, she then smashes raw eggs on his forehead (50). Perhaps the most tantalising suggestion of this brief episode is the performative space of national identity, gesturing towards one of the longest running debates in Irish-English cultural relations. "If Ireland had never existed, the English would have invented it," writes Declan Kiberd in the opening chapter of *Inventing Ireland* (1995).[54] Ireland as England's Other, he argues, has long served as "a foil to set off English virtues, as a laboratory in which to conduct experiments, and as a fantasy-land in which to meet fairies and monsters."[55] Kiberd goes back to the sixteenth century to begin his study of the stereotypes of the Irish adopted by the English planters, suggesting that Ireland has functioned as "England's unconscious."[56] However, it was not until the nineteenth century that the perception of the Celts as a racial category with distinct and essential characteristics was formalised through the work of Ernest Renan (writing of Brittany) and Matthew Arnold (writing primarily of Wales and Ireland), who adapted many of Renan's assertions to an Irish context. The Celts were

---

[53] Martin McDonagh, *The Cripple of Inishmaan* (London: Methuen, 1996) 50. All subsequent quotations will be cited in-text.
[54] Declan Kiberd, *Inventing Ireland: The Literature of the Modern Nation* (London: Jonathan Cape, 1995) 9.
[55] Kiberd, *Inventing Ireland*, 1.
[56] Kiberd, *Inventing Ireland*, 29-32.

defined as an innately emotional, spiritual and creative people preserving ancient qualities of "piety and nobility" in the face of philistine advancements of "more mundanely successful races."[57] More dubious still is Renan's averment that,

> if it be permitted us to assign sex to nations as to individuals, we should have to say without hesitance that the Celtic race ... is an essentially feminine race. No other has conceived with more delicacy the ideal of woman, or been more fully dominated by it. It is a sort of intoxication, a madness, a vertigo.[58]

The underside of such qualities, in the context of Irish-English relations during the Victorian period, was a good deal less complimentary. As Stephen Regan notes in an essay on the Celtic spirit in literature, "the most intriguing shift in representation of the Irish national character occurred, however, because of the unusual convergence of Fenianism with the heated debate over *The Origin of the Species* in the 1860s."[59] As a result the caricatures of simian Celts in the British press (in *Punch* especially) promoted a stereotype which conflated a purportedly Irish capacity for violence with primitive animality. Ireland being cast as the antithesis of England, it was self-evident for Arnold that the Irish Celt needed the strong-handed, masculine guidance and governance of the practical Saxon.

Put simply, the many national revivalists at the turn of the century (among whom one must count W.B. Yeats, Lady Gregory, and their predecessor, Standish O'Grady) worked to overturn these representations of the Irish, which had been

---

[57] W.J. McCormack, *From Burke to Beckett: Ascendancy, Tradition and Betrayal in Literary History* (1985; Cork: Cork University Press, 1994) 227.

[58] Ernest Renan, *Poetry of the Celtic Races and Other Essays*, trans. W.G. Hutchinson (London 1896) 1-2. Qtd. in McCormack, *From Burke to Beckett*, 227.

[59] Stephen Regan, "The Celtic Spirit in Literature: Renan, Arnold, Wilde and Yeats," *Irish Encounters: Poetry, Politics and Prose*, eds. Alan Marshall and Neil Sammells (Bath: Sulis, 1998) 28-29.

used to justify English colonial rule. Attempting to transform
negative stereotypes through a return to indigenous language
and culture, revivalists and political activists aimed to foster
national pride and self-respect. Or, as Lady Gregory famously
stated with regard to the objectives of the Irish Literary Theatre,
"we will show that Ireland is not the home of buffoonery and of
easy sentiment, as it has been represented, but the home of
ancient idealism."[60] Considering the discourse of Irish national
identity from the vantage point of the late twentieth century,
Colin Graham perceptively clarifies what was at stake as
follows, "the history of the nineteenth-century Irish cultural
nationalism can be seen as [...] a process of reclamation,
restaking the grounds for Irishness, "proving" Irish
authenticities."[61]

One clear, albeit ambivalent, example of an attempt to
parody essentialist national or racial identities is George
Bernard Shaw's 1904 play, *John Bull's Other Island*.[62] In it Shaw
satirically takes up the above described stereotypes of the
Englishman and the Irishman and shuffles their allegedly
racially determined characteristics. In the opening scene
romantically impractical and bombastic Englishman, Tom
Broadbent, is swindled by "Irishman" Tim Haffigan. Haffigan
charms him with all manner of Irish clichés from top-o-the-
mornin' greeting to enthusiastic whiskey consumption. When
Broadbent's colleague, Larry Doyle, returns he soon unmasks
Haffigan as a Glaswegian swindler and impostor. Doyle, a real
and rather cynical Irishman, chastises Broadbent for believing
in such music hall antics. Throughout the play, by means of
strategies of inversion, displacement and humour, Shaw
emphasises the mutual self-deception of the English and Irish in

---

[60] Lady Augusta Gregory, *Our Irish Theatre: A Chapter of Autobiography* (Gerrards
Cross: Colin Smythe, 1972) 20.

[61] Colin Graham, *Deconstructing Ireland: Identity, Theory, Culture* (Edinburgh:
Edinburgh University Press, 2001) 141.

[62] Alexandra Poulain also explores this association in "In-Yer-Face, Irish Style: *The
Leenane Trilogy* ou l'Irlande simulée" (unpublished essay).

their performances of identity for one another's benefit, and undermines the claims to authenticity of both postures. Interestingly, Shaw's play was a great success among the English (which perhaps suggests that its critique was taken merely as humour). Nevertheless, the strongly negative reactions to J.M. Synge's *In the Shadow of the Glen* and *Playboy of the Western World* revealed that contemporaneous with Shaw's humorous performative identities was serious dispute over representation and authenticity.

As has been well documented, the conflicted site of Irish authenticity was the mythologised figure of the peasant, and more specifically the peasant of the Western seaboard, who was perceived as unsullied by modernity and untainted by Englishness (or, later in the century, by the corrupting influence of American culture). Notably, this is precisely the location and population McDonagh takes as his principle setting and dramatis personae. The qualities of a chaste and aspirational version of authentic Irish identity are testified to most remarkably perhaps by Irish Taoiseach, Eamonn de Valera's oft quoted St. Patrick's Day broadcast of 1943:

> The Ireland that we dreamed of would be the home of a people who valued material wealth only as the basis of a right living, of a people who were satisfied with frugal comfort and devoted their leisure to the things of the spirit; a land whose countryside would be bright with cosy homesteads, whose fields and villages would be joyous with the sounds of industry, with the romping of sturdy children the contests of athletic youths, the laughter of comely maidens; whose firesides would be forums for the wisdom of old age. It would, in a word, be the home of a people living the life that God desires men should live.[63]

McDonagh it seems has taken each element of this vision and distorted it through the lens of a perversely ironic postmodernist style. However, well before McDonagh, this

---

[63] Eamonn de Valera qtd. in *Irish Writing in the Twentieth Century: A Reader*, ed. David Pierce (Cork: Cork University Press, 2000), 487.

vision of national purity and spirituality so finely articulated by de Valera in the 1940s, met with criticism and dissent because of the way it was deployed to justify puritanical cultural and social practices, and to underwrite isolationist economic and political policies.

Lachman discusses the nature of such dissenting attitudes to issues of identity in Irish drama from the 1950s to the 1980s. Referring to how Tom Kilroy claims that playwrights of his generation are marked by a "self-consciousness" with regard to national identity. Lachman explores the ways in which this drama "show[s] the moment when a unified universe of authoritarian and dominating language collapsed into a multitude of discourses each representing its own insular logic."[64] He then notes how "the characters in the plays of Friel, Murphy, Parker, and so on, could be suspended between two extremes precisely because extreme notions existed, could be recognised, were impossible to ignore, and had to be identified with."[65] The 1990s seem to mark an end to this era. The erosion of Church authority, the halting development of the Peace Process, and perhaps most significant the ushering in of a fully fledged consumer society with the Celtic Tiger has signalled the breakdown of such belief systems and strongly felt oppositions. Arguably McDonagh's plays, with their excess of postmodern knowingness, rake over the embers of a discourse of authentic identity once again, while problematically offering a new dynamic of circular citation-driven spectacle, rather than the tension of dichotomy.

Melodramatic Narratives & Ludic Excess
The claims made for and responses to McDonagh's work often threaten to obscure the plays themselves and the distinctions between them. They are, nevertheless, strongly linked by their

---

[64] Tom Kilroy, "A Generation of Playwrights," *Irish University Review* 22.1 (1992) discussed in Lachman, "Happy and in Exile? Martin McDonagh's 'Leenane Trilogy,'" 197.

[65] Lachman, "Happy and in Exile? Martin McDonagh's 'Leenane Trilogy,'" 198.

use of setting and language—all McDonagh's work produced up to the year 2001 takes the West of Ireland as its setting. The Leenane Trilogy concerns the activities of members of the eponymous Connemara locale; the uncompleted Aran Trilogy is set on the islands. Moreover, apart from *The Cripple of Inishmaan*, the action takes place in the 1990s, as specified in *The Lieutenant of Inishmore* and somewhat less precisely by cultural references in the remaining plays. Commenting on McDonagh's dramaturgy, Huber describes some of the salient advantages of the time/place unity with regard to the Leenane Trilogy;

> not only does it provide a great degree of thematic coherence in the sense that a microcosm is created by the life stories of the three different families living in contact, however tenuous, with each other. It is also a felicitous dramatic device facilitating exposition and the introduction of characters.[66]

Huber goes on to point out how in the Leenane Trilogy these dramatic devices and thematic threads enable various levels of allusion and cross-reference where *"dramatis personae* of the Trilogy [are] mentioned or prefigured" in the plays in which they do not appear. They also facilitate the "running gag" of the mispronunciation of Father Welsh/Walsh's name across all three plays.[67] Such connections are clearly much less relevant to the two extant plays of the Aran Trilogy, though the observant might note the repetition of the surnames Osbourne (Eileen and Kate in *The Cripple*, Donny and Padraic in *The Lieutenant*) and Claven (Cripple Billy, and Mairead and Davey) in both.

The other aspect unifying McDonagh's West of Ireland microcosm, and functioning across both trilogies is the quality of language used. Undoubtedly there is more than a pinch of Synge's poeticised peasant speech in McDonagh's drama. However, the end product is far from poetic. Perhaps the most bizarre aspect of his work is the way in which he deliberately

66   Huber, "The Plays of Martin McDonagh," 564.
67   Huber, "The Plays of Martin McDonagh," 564.

and farcically simulates the syntax of a pseudo Hiberno-English. Packed with the swear word "feck" and its variants, McDonagh's language is described by one reviewer as "a hybrid of the Irish-English that Synge invented for his own Aran Island characters, and a street-wise Dublin-London 1990s argot."[68] McDonagh mimics and exaggerates various idiomatic ticks: for instance by adding the suffix "-een" — "biteen" "bitcheen" "tadeen"; or by imitating the syntactic differences of Hiberno-English — "I'll have to be taking another look for meself so" (*The Cripple of Inishmaan*, 11), "Me mother does love this oul song" (*The Beauty Queen of Leenane*, 23), or "Be bringing your bag of skulleens, now" (*A Skull in Connemara*, 51). This has certainly also contributed to the raised hackles of critics and commentators who claim the plays are terminally contaminated by colonial stereotyping.[69] But it is notable that the characters themselves draw attention to their own vocabulary and pronunciation. For instance, in *The Lonesome West*, Father Welsh, Coleman and Valene get caught up in a discussion of the validity of some words and the merits of others:

Valene:	Never unbare are your cupboards.
Coleman:	I suppose they're not now, but isn't that life?
Welsh:	And there's no such word as unbare.
Coleman:	He's right! (5)

Welsh:	It seems like God has no jurisdiction in this town. No jurisdiction at all.
Coleman:	That's a great word, I think.
Valene:	What word?
Coleman:	Jurisdiction. I like J-words.
Valene:	Jurisdiction's too Yankee-sounding for me. They never stop saying it on *Hill Street Blues*. (6)

---

[68] C.L. Dallat, "From the Outside," *TLS* 17 Jan. 1997: 14. Qtd. in Huber, "The Plays of Martin McDonagh," 567.

[69] See for instance Victor Merriman's "Settling for More: Success & Excess in Contemporary Irish Drama," *Druids, Dudes and Beauty Queens*, 55-71 and "Decolonisation Postponed: The Theatre of Tiger Trash," *Irish University Review* 29.2 (1999): 305-307.

Similarly, Valene's mispronunciation of reservoir as "russaway" (*The Lonesome West* 24), or Thomas's pronunciation of the word ghoul so it sounds like whore (*A Skull in Connemara* 6) are highlighted. In both cases other characters question the mistake drawing the audience into a joke that extends beyond the fictional world of the play.[70] Ultimately this language makes no pretence to documentary accuracy, in contrast somewhat to that invented by Synge. Rather it is a self-conscious simulation, created from fragments, copied phrases and exaggerations of various "Irish" dialects, both real and literary/theatrical, that functions to comic effect, because it pastiches "Synge-song" and then grafts on contemporary vocabulary and expression. The nature of the reference, though, has divided critics as to whether this strategy functions as an "updating," or as pastiche in a Jamesonian sense.[71] Unlike Synge, McDonagh's language, as the above examples illustrate, is marked by self-consciousness; he carries the process of syntactical jumbling to such excess that, in effect, he creates his own language and a style that is recognisably Irish, but also underscores its own artificiality.

While the plots of the plays differ, structurally they depend on comparable melodramatic strategies of reversal, concealment and revelation. *The Beauty Queen of Leenane* is perhaps McDonagh's best made play in the conventional sense. While like all McDonagh's work, plot and dramatic tension are of central importance, what distinguishes *The Beauty Queen of Leenane* is a depth of character development unparalleled in any of the subsequent work. The play weaves the lonely, humorous and, ultimately, tragic story of middle aged Maureen Folan who lives alone with her mother, Mag, in an isolated farmhouse. Like Mary and Mommo of Tom Murphy's

---

[70] Huber remarks upon this "stylisation" and the way in which it permits McDonagh to introduce "playful elements of meta-communication." "The Plays of Martin McDonagh," 568.

[71] For the former perspective see Huber, "The Plays of Martin McDonagh," 567 and following, for the latter see Merriman, "The Theatre of Tiger Trash," 316.

Bailegangaire (1985) it is clearly a relationship of longstanding attrition. Also like Mommo, Mag appears to be fully dependent on Maureen for day to day care, provoking the latter with her recalcitrance. In contrast to Murphy's aged matriarch who may be interpreted as a complex symbol of Mother Ireland, Mag is by turns callous, slow-witted and vindictively devious. As such she remains an ambivalent echo of Murphy's Mommo. Mag repeatedly complains about the physical ailments (a urine infection and a bad hand) that apparently prevent her from doing anything, and Maureen's frustration seems justified by her constant demands. The couple's conversations revolve on what seem to be well-worn tracks. The irritations of making tea, porridge, cod in butter sauce and the choice of brands of biscuits are the territory of disputes, petty victories and defeats. The insults they trade are vicious yet familiar: Mag calls the virginal Maureen a whore (15), Maureen retaliates with her day-dream of happily attending Mag's funeral with "a fella beside me there, comforting me" (16). Yet, while cruel, their exchanges are ultimately more pitiful than ominous.

McDonagh further builds sympathy for Maureen's predicament when a young neighbour, Ray Dooley, arrives with an invitation to a farewell party hosted by his "Yankee uncle" (10) who is returning to the States. Mag promises to pass on the message however, as soon as he leaves, she burns the note thus revealing a more actively malicious dimension to her character. Maureen, nevertheless, receives news of the party and the middle-aged Cinderella returns from the ball with her prince charming, Pato Dooley, Ray's older brother who works in England. Hopes of romance are soured by a bitter argument between Maureen and Mag the following morning in which Maureen accuses Mag of emptying her chamber pot of urine in the kitchen sink every morning (a practice confirmed at the beginning of the scene), while Mag claims that it was Maureen who hurt her hand and reveals that her daughter had a nervous breakdown years previously when she was working in England.

Pato returns to England but writes to Maureen inviting her to go to America with him to start a new life. Again McDonagh deploys the letter as a pivotal element to the plot; artfully building a sense of tense inevitability as finally, at the end of his patience, Ray leaves the letter with Mag who again solemnly promises to give it to Maureen. On this occasion Mag succeeds in destroying the missive. When Maureen guesses what might have happened she starts to heat a pan of oil on the stove, as she questions her mother. With a sudden dramatic twist it becomes evident that not all Mag's claims to abuse are false. Maureen brutally forces Mag to confess by pouring hot oil over her already shrivelled hand, and then rushes off to meet Pato before he leaves. In the following scene in the darkened kitchen, Maureen toys with a poker while telling Mag of how she caught Pato just before his train left. As she finishes speaking, Mag gradually topples out of her chair, her head split open with a blow from a poker. On the day of the funeral, Maureen is busy packing her belongings in preparation for departure to America, when Ray calls in with a message from Pato. In another dramatic plot twist it is revealed that Maureen's interception of Pato was but a figment of her imagination, and he is already engaged to another. Maureen is, finally, left confused and alone, looking, as Ray says, just like her mother.

The second play in the trilogy, *A Skull in Connemara*, takes up a different and, indeed, more playful frame of reference. The title, as Sierz, Huber and others have remarked, refers to a phrase in Lucky's "Think" speech in *Waiting for Godot*. The play opens in the cottage of Mick O'Dowd, a man in his fifties. He has a visitor, Mary Rafferty, an elderly woman who often pops in to drink poteen with him. Mick and Mary chat and then argue with each other over her cheating at bingo and her insinuations about Mick's late wife, Oona, who died under mysterious circumstances.

Mick is employed each year to make space in the graveyard by clearing graves that are more than seven years old. This year Mairtin, Mary's grandson, has been paid by Father Welsh to assist him. Mary is disapproving of the practice of exhuming and disposing of bodies. Mick teases her by telling her that he smashes up the bones and throws them in with the slurry, though he is deflated by the news that they will be starting on the part of the cemetery where Oona is buried.

In the next scene Mairtin and Mick are working in the graveyard and bickering. Mick finally begins on his wife's grave under supervision of Garda Thomas Hanlon, Mairtin's elder brother. Thomas fancies himself as a Hollywood style detective but has little to occupy him in rural Galway. Mick digs up the grave but, in another McDonagh *coup de théâtre*, the coffin is empty. Later, as Mick and Mairtin are drunkenly dealing with the bones and skulls they have exhumed, and which are to be dumped in the lake, Mairtin accidentally reveals that he was involved in stealing Oona's bones.

In scene four Mick is at home, his shirt smeared with blood, when Mary comes to have a free drink. Then Thomas arrives with Oona's skull in a bag demanding that Mick write a confession. The skull has a pronounced crack in the forehead. Mick agrees with surprising alacrity and sets to looking for a pen (a matter that involves humorous stage business), and then to writing the confession (a matter that involves asking Thomas for synonyms so he does not repeat himself). The confession turns out to be not to Oona's murder but to Mairtin's. Thomas is incredulous. Mairtin, he contends, is at the disco. To which Mick colourfully retorts: "But sure, if down the disco Mairtin was, how would I have ended up with his bastard brains dripping down the front of me?" (58) Thomas is in the midst of attempting to strangle Mick when Mairtin stumbles in with "a bloody crack" on his forehead. Thomas wants to arrest Mick, but Mairtin maintains he was injured while drink driving. Discretely, Mick burns the confession. Mairtin reveals that it was Thomas who stole Oona's remains and Thomas, insane with rage, attacks Mairtin with the mallet. Mick and Mary must prevent him from killing his brother and Thomas exits in a daze. The play finishes with Mick cradling Oona's skull, leaving the audience/reader none the wiser as to the real cause of her death.

The Lonesome West, again, makes use of a reference in the title, this time a direct quotation from *The Playboy of the Western World* ("Oh, there's sainted glory this day in the lonesome west; and by the will of God I've got you a decent man Pegeen"). The protagonists, Coleman and Valene Connor, are a pair of middle-aged bachelor brothers who have just lost their father. The play begins after the funeral when Father Welsh comes back to the house with Coleman for a drink. Their kitchen is lined with religious figurines all carefully marked with his brother's initial. Father Welsh is in a state of despair as his congregation includes Maureen Folan, who murdered her mother, and Mick O'Dowd, who reputedly killed his wife with an axe, neither of whom he has persuaded to confess. Coleman offers a show of support which is really cold comfort, gesturing towards the waves of revelations of Church abuse of power that broke in the 1980s and 1990s:

> Ah there be a lot worse priests than you, Father, I'm sure. The only thing with you is you're a bit too weedy and you're a terror for the drink and you have doubts about Catholicism. Apart from that you're a fine priest. Number one you don't go abusing poor gasurs, so, sure, doesn't that give you a head-start over half the priests in Ireland? (7)

Meanwhile, the tone of the play as a whole is set by Coleman's and Valene's constant squabbling over poteen, Tayto crisps and women's magazines. Seventeen-year-old Girleen visits to see if the brothers wish to buy more poteen and jokes with Coleman in front of Father Welsh about prostituting herself to make a bit of extra money, traumatising him still further. Valene, who has inherited their father's money, invests in a new stove, more figurines, magazines and crisps.

In the midst of yet another argument, Father Welsh returns with news of Tom Hanlon's suicide. While Valene assists with dragging the body from the lake, Coleman takes the opportunity of destroying the figurines by baking them in the new stove. Inevitably this gives rise to further violent confrontation, ineffectually moderated by the priest, who learns by the way that Coleman is guilty of murdering their father. Father Welsh, duly horrified, halts the fighting by desperately plunging his hands into the bowl of molten plastic—the remains of the religious figurines. Utterly depressed by the spiritual and moral poverty of his parish, he gives Girleen a letter for the Connor brothers and then drowns himself in the lake.

The following scene is after Father Welsh's funeral. The letter is pinned up above the stove and the brothers attempt to get along for the dead priest's sake. Their efforts do not last very long as their gestures of forgiveness are soon transformed into a vindictive game of one-upmanship. Their new-found forgiveness degenerates into yet another violent stand-off: Coleman armed with a perhaps loaded shotgun and Valene with a knife. Finally, when the new figurines have once again been destroyed and the new stove blasted with shot from the gun, they relent, but more trouble is brewing as Coleman exits to the pub having told Valene that he spent the house insurance money on drink. The play concludes with Valene, who was about to burn Father Welsh's letter blowing out the flames and pinning it once more above the wrecked stove before heading off to join Coleman in the pub.

It is manifest from the plots of the plays in the trilogy that, as McDonagh privileges action over contemplation, his characters grow increasingly schematic and his destabilisation of traditional notions of value becomes progressively more farcical. In its exploitation of a fine division between horror and empathy, *The Beauty Queen of Leenane* achieves a suspense and depth unequalled in the other plays. This play's poignancy lies in McDonagh's portrayal of Maureen as a hopelessly trapped character. As Lenz points out, Maureen's predicament as unmarried carer of an ageing parent is a recurrent theme in "traditional realist Irish literature."[72] The loneliness of this role is treated not without feeling, as befits the play's melodramatic structure, serving to heighten the shock of the revelation of her psychosis.

Reversal and unexpected denouement, however, are the central dramatic strategies. For Sierz *The Beauty Queen of Leenane* can be summed up as follows:

> McDonagh also takes a stock theatrical form—the country melodrama—and turns it upside-down: the wise old woman becomes an ignorant toad, the spinster daughter a psychopath; in this grim fairy tale, the spinster daughter is transformed not into a princess but into her own ugly mother. A mythical place—the West of Ireland—is deconstructed with meticulous attention to detail. Scenic beauty becomes constant rain, folksy charm is really inbred ignorance, the old-fashioned village is isolated and full of hatred, and the family a nest of vipers.[73]

Vandevelde similarly, though in considerably milder terms, notes how McDonagh distances the setting of the play from any stereotypical exoticism.[74] As has been frequently mentioned, the play seems to be built around parodic references to well-worn themes in Irish drama of identity, exile and community. As Lachman comments, the logic of extremes which traditionally anchored such themes is collapsed;

> what once preserved mythological or ritualistic value, be it unifying or dividing, now remains obsolete. [...] Family, neighbourhood, church, language as well as places like the country kitchen, village pub, farm, land and so forth stand merely as one dimensional iconography.[75]

---

[72] Lenz, "'Anything new in the feckin' west?'" 29.

[73] Sierz, *In-Yer-Face Theatre*, 224.

[74] Vandevelde, "The Gothic Soap of Martin McDonagh," 294.

[75] Lachman, "Happy and in Exile? Martin McDonagh's 'Leenane Trilogy,'" *Engaging Modernity*, 198.

What remains is a play of familiar surfaces, slightly distorted by globalisation. In this manner, McDonagh seems to draw on the ironic parody Hutcheon describes as formally self-reflexive, incorporating "the past into its very structures" and gesturing towards their ideological contexts, to instigate a new dialogue about the familiar through the establishment of distance from it.[76]

Ireland is a place characterised, as Maureen puts it, by someone always leaving. There is, however, no easy dichotomy between a positive locale and the threatening world outside, or vice versa. Neither the home space nor the world beyond is cast as simply preferable—pain, violence and loneliness are in abundance in both. The emigrant's dilemma is articulated by Pato as follows:

> I do ask meself, if there was good work in Leenane, would I stay in Leenane. I mean, there never will be good work, but hypothetically, I'm saying, Or even bad work. Any work. And when I'm over there in London and working in rain and it's more or less cattle I am, [...] when it's there I am, it's here I wish I was, of course. Who wouldn't? But when it's here I am…it isn't *there* I want to be, of course not. But I know it isn't here I want to be either. (21-22)

But if home is reduced to a cliché of provincial obsessiveness— a place where "everybody knows everybody else's business [… and where] you can't kick a cow [...] without some bastard holding a grudge twenty year" (22)—then elsewhere is subject to the same reduction. The virtues of America shrink to the apparently more appealing climate, "in America it does be more sunny anyways. Or is that just something they say, that the weather is more sunny, Maureen? Or is that a lie, now?" (5), says Mag in scene one. Whereas for Pato, England might just be preferable to Leenane, because "they don't care if you live or die, and it's funny but that isn't altogether a bad thing" (22).

---

[76] Hutcheon, *A Poetics of Postmodernity*, 35.

McDonagh's rural Ireland is also a place overtly permeated with cultural influences from elsewhere. References to Australian soap operas on television and bickering over brands of biscuits and mingle freely with traditional allusions. In each of the plays in the trilogy, these references serve to heighten the ironic humour. In *The Lonesome West* the quarrelling that takes place in *The Beauty Queen* over biscuits is rerun as wrangling over brands of crisps and women's magazines. In *A Skull in Connemara*, Maryjohnny holds Eamonn Andrews (the television presenter) up as a model of someone who never cursed, before she settles on Jesus as perhaps a better candidate (5), while Mick castigates her for swindling American tourists by telling them her "Liam's place was where *The Quiet Man* was filmed" and selling fake John Wayne photos and Maureen O'Hara mugs (7). Thomas O'Hanlon's dreams are built on American detective and police television shows—*Hill Street Blues*, *Quincy* and *Starsky and Hutch*. Mairtin drunkenly confesses his affection for Dana (Scanlon, winner of the 1970 Eurovision Song Contest with the song "All kinds of everything," and who later gained a reputation as a highly conservative politician and campaigner). When Mairtin concedes that "she's a born-again Christian now," Mick's wry response is "Honestly, Mairtin, I'd avoid her" (48). Mairtin rues the day when he lost his *Star Wars* models (49), while Valene's collection of Virgin Mary figurines in *The Lonesome West* seem of the same order of importance as Luke Skywalker, Han Solo and Princess Leia. In *The Beauty Queen*, the juxtaposition of the photo of John and Robert Kennedy with the "touristy-looking embroidered tea-towel" with the ominous adage "may you be half an hour in Heaven afore the Devil knows you're dead" (1) does not, in this context, so much point out the contrast between modernity and tradition, foreign icons and proverbial folk mottos, as their similarity as accreted clichés and exhausted "kitsch." The fact that Ray reads the motif on the tea-towel out loud twice, the second time in a "funny voice," assures that the message will not be missed.

When the issue of national identity is thematically raised it is treated with a similar parodic accent. If Mag bears some of the symbolic residues of a Mother Ireland figure then it is all the more significant that it is she, rather than the younger generation, who rejects the Irish language. It is the elderly Mag who, when hearing an Irish song on the radio, wants the "nonsense" switched off:

> Maureen: It isn't nonsense anyways. Isn't it Irish?
> Mag: It sounds like nonsense to me. Why can't they just speak English like everybody?
> Maureen: Why should they speak English?
> Mag: To know what they're saying. (4)

The debate degenerates into a clash of clichés. Mag with comic pragmatism reminds Maureen that Irish would not be much use to get a job in England, or America for that matter. Maureen retaliates with the conventional nationalist rejoinder: "If it wasn't for the English stealing our language, and our land, and our God-knows-what, wouldn't it be we wouldn't need to go over there begging for jobs and for handouts?" (5). The discussion is soon short circuited by Maureen's retort: "You're oul and you're stupid and you don't know what you're talking about. Now shut up and eat your oul porridge" (6). As Vandevelde points out, "this becomes an interesting feature of the trilogy: whenever characters come too close to major questions of Irish history or identity, they dismiss the topic and change the subject." She goes on to query "whether this apparent apathy and the fragmentation of identity are typical representations of contemporary Ireland, or whether McDonagh is questioning the magnitude of significance assigned to these issues in Irish drama."[77] The fact the plays are progressively unrealistic and farcical suggests the latter option is the more plausible.

---

[77] Vandevelde, "The Gothic Soap of Martin McDonagh," *Theatre Stuff*, 295.

Interestingly, although many critics remark upon the themes of exile or emigration and identity, the remaining plays in the Leenane Trilogy make few allusions to either in quite the explicitly parodic manner of *The Beauty Queen of Leenane*. Beyond a linguistic and locational unity, what links the plays is an enduring sense of "ironic distance towards every aspect of life, be it religion, history, land or language."[78] This irony is constituted in the practice of pastiche that juxtaposes reference to, and fragments from, an eclectic range of materials. If *The Beauty Queen of Leenane* echoes *Bailegangaire*, then *A Skull in Connemara* goes further in its citational strategies. As noted above, the title of the play is a quotation from a frenzied, memorised speech made by Lucky in *Waiting for Godot*:

> I resume but not so fast I resume the skull to shrink and waste and concurrently simultaneously what is more for reasons unknown in spite of the tennis on on the beard the flames the tears the stones so blue so calm alas alas on on the skull the skull the skull the skull in Connemara in spite of the tennis the labours abandoned left unfinished graver still abode of stones in a word I resume alas alas abandoned unfinished the skull the skull in Connemara.[79]

The citation resonates in the play covertly as both a bizarre analogy and a bridge between the previous play in the trilogy and this one. In *The Beauty Queen of Leenane* one of Ray's grudges against Maureen is that a decade previously she confiscated his Swingball game and refused to return it. At the play's conclusion Ray spots "a faded tennis ball with a spring sticking out of it" (58) on the window ledge and his hard feelings are reactivated. He promises in the end, nevertheless, to pass on Maureen's last message to Pato, "The beauty queen of Leenane says goodbye" (59), in spite, as it were, of the tennis. The narrative of the following play is, of course, comically

---

78 Lachman, "Happy and in Exile? Martin McDonagh's 'Leenane Trilogy,'" 199.
79 Samuel Beckett, *Waiting for Godot* (London: Faber and Faber, 1956) 44-45.

orientated, quite literally, around skulls in Connemara—their destruction, their loss, their recovery and their status as evidence. Like Lucky's speech, the end result is violence. More significantly, also like the "Think" speech, these narratives seem doomed to repeat themselves without progress in a play of manic revelations that lead nowhere.

This suggestion interlocks with the other principal literary allusion in the play—that of *The Playboy of the Western World*. McDonagh freely exploits this intertext throughout on the level of visual echoes. Mairtin's return to the stage with a cracked head and subsequent brush with death at the hands of his own brother, is all too reminiscent of Old Mahon's reappearance "coming to be killed a third time" at the conclusion of Act three of *The Playboy*. But if in Synge's play a father-son power struggle emerges as the motivation for a murder that turns out to be a fiction, then in McDonagh's the motivation may well be poorly cooked scrambled eggs (54) and the cause of Oona's death is never clarified. If Old Mahon has been replaced by the feckless and juvenile Mairtin Hanlon, then young Christy's boastfulness is supplanted by old Mick's denial, while the feisty Pegeen Mike is transformed into the irritable and nosey, poteen swilling Maryjohnny.

Besides these more extended analogies the play also solicits reference to *Hamlet*, with its grimly comical midnight graveyard scene. In *Hamlet* the owner of the skull is identified by the playful gravedigger,

Hamlet:	Whose was it?
Gravedigger:	A whorseson mad fellow's it was. Whose do you think it was?
Hamlet:	Nay, I know not.
Gravedigger:	[...] This same skull sir, was Yorrick's skull, the King's jester.
Hamlet:	This?
Gravedigger:	E'en that. (V.i.169-77)

The revelation gives rise to a more general discussion of memory and mortality. In contrast, in *A Skull in Connemara* this recognition is recycled farcically:

<pre>
Mairtin: Who is he? (*glances behind.* [at the headstone])
              Daniel Faragher. Never heard of him.
Mick: I knew him to say hello to.
Mairtin: Would you recognise him?
Mick looks at Mairtin as if he's stupid.
Mairtin: Not from his bare skull, no, of course. Although
              he still has a lock of hair there, now. (24)
</pre>

The improbability of recognising someone from their skull alone problematises the play's climactic antics concerning Oona's skull and Mick's final attempt to remember the truth of what happened to her. The play deconstructs the fantasy, inherent to the detective series Thomas O'Hanlon romanticises, of returning to a single self-evident point of origin—the primal scene, as it were. Despite the surfeit of evidence (guaranteed by Thomas's intervention), a singular truth fails to emerge.

Moreover, the characters demonstrably fail, as Alexandra Poulain observes, to attain any degree of abstract thought on the topic of memory or death, even when faced with the macabre evidence of mortality that surrounds them.[80] Mairtin's preoccupations remain utterly prosaic and naïve—he quizzes Mick, "where does your thing go? When you die, I mean. None of them have their things at all. And I've looked" (26). In response, Mick explains with deadpan irony that the penises are snipped off and sold to the tinkers as dog food, but during the famine the tinkers began to consume them themselves. If Hamlet and Horatio's dialogue concludes with the chastening inference that the dust of "Imperious Caesar" may be found plugging a beer barrel, then Mick dryly chastises Mairtin for his ignorance: "That's the trouble with young people today, is they

---

[80] Alexandra Poulain, "'Bodies flying everywhere': *A Skull in Connemara* ou l'exhumation impossible," 5 (unpublished essay).

don't know the first thing about Irish history" (27). Here again McDonagh's work engages in what might be seen as a meta-commentary on its own parodic narratives. The character explicitly engages in the invention of an utterly ludicrous falsification of history, which overtly seems to follow Jameson's claim that pastiche involves a denial, or rather an effacement, of history. Yet, in this instance, the play incorporates its own critique of Mairtin's inability to distinguish real from false history, and in doing so prevents a complete "disappearance of the historical referent"[81] from the space of the performance.

The Lonesome West is the most farcical play of the trilogy, and as such is the most one dimensional. Despite the Syngean allusion of its title, the play has been described by Sierz as "a macabre rerun of [Sam] Shepard's *True West* [1980]."[82] It is also close to the general tone of much of Joe Orton's drama. Certainly more of the order of Punch and Judy than Vladimir and Estragon, or Shepard's Austin and Lee, *The Lonesome West* is a triumph of action over character or plot. In contrast to *True West*, in which Austin is rational and responsible and Lee anarchic and irrational, the brothers in *The Lonesome West* are barely distinguishable, and there is certainly no West to which they plan to escape. As one reviewer critically observes, "there is a lot less to it than meets the eye, and it frequently amounts to little more than what it appears to be: cartoonish mayhem about two gibbering idiots, trading on shock."[83] The play seems best to confirm Lachman's assertion that "the trilogy narrates not only the demise of Irish myths but indirectly sketches the impossibility of any traditional form of myth in a world of postmodern sensibility."[84]

---

[81] Jameson, "Postmodernism, or the Cultural Logic of Late Capitalism," 79.
[82] Sierz, *In-Yer-Face Theatre*, 225. See also Huber, "The Plays of Martin McDonagh," 560.
[83] Harvey O'Brien, rev of *The Lonesome West*, by Martin McDonagh, *CultureVulture.net* 6 Aug. 2001 (online).
[84] Lachman, "Happy and in Exile? Martin McDonagh's 'Leenane Trilogy,'" 200.

The plays in McDonagh's second trilogy suffer from a comparable ludic excess and reliance upon violent action, though they too are propelled by stylistic pastiche, parody of stereotypes and, in the case of *The Lieutenant of Inishmore*, bad taste. Set in 1934 on the island of Inishmaan, *The Cripple of Inishmaan* follows the protagonist, a teenager known as Cripple Billy, who lives with his ageing "aunts" Eileen and Kate. Billy, a disabled orphan, has been in their care since he was an infant. Eileen and Kate own a small shop, which seems to stock little more than cans of peas, sweets and, sometimes, eggs. They are visited by the local gossipmonger and self-proclaimed newsman Johnnypateenmike who, like Brian Friel's schoolmaster Hugh in *Translations*, always has three items of information to impart. Johnnypateenmike informs them that the American film director Robert J. Flaherty is making a film on Inishmore about life on the Aran Islands. Helen and her younger brother Bartley arrange to go to with a neighbour, Babbybobby, to see and perhaps participate in the filming. Billy persuades Babbybobby to take him along by showing him a letter allegedly from the doctor. The letter indicates that Billy has tuberculosis and has only three months to live, and as Babbybobby's wife died of T.B. recently, he agrees to help Billy out of sympathy. Helen and Bartley return from Inishmore but not Billy, he has apparently gone to Hollywood for a screen test. Months pass and there is no news of Billy. Apart from Eileen and Kate, the rest of the community are convinced that Billy has probably died of T.B. already. Scene seven in which Billy is shown alone and dying, albeit in rather melodramatic fashion, bolsters this view. Later, Flaherty's film is shown and is poorly received by its native audience. As the screening concludes, Billy appears. While his aunts welcome him home, Babbybobby revenges himself by beating him viciously with a lead pipe. After he has been bandaged up by the doctor, Billy begs Johnnypateenmike to tell what really happened to his parents. Johnnypateenmike assures him that they drowned themselves in order to raise the insurance money to pay for his treatment. Billy finally summons the courage to ask Helen out, but unsurprisingly she laughs in his face. Later Eileen and Kate discuss the true story of Billy's parents' demise—they were in fact trying to drown their crippled son. It was Johnnypateen who saved him and provided the money to pay the hospital fees. Unbeknowst to them Billy overhears. He fetches the old sack hanging on the wall, fills it with cans of peas and is about to set off to drown himself when Helen comes back and agrees to go out with him. The play ends with Billy delighted but coughing up blood. It turns out he has T.B. after all.

The Lieutenant of Inishmore, McDonagh's final play, contrasts in the way it departs from the literary allusions of his former work, and in the way it takes on overtly political subject matter. It does so, however, in a manner that precludes serious consideration of that subject matter. Padraic Osbourne is a young and psychopathically violent INLA man from Inishmore. The play opens in what is now McDonagh's standard set, a cottage kitchen, with Donny, Padraic's father and a teenage neighbour, Davey, and a dead cat on the table. The cat, Wee Thomas, belongs to Padraic and is his "best friend in the world" (15). The next scene graphically shows Padraic at work gruesomely torturing a drug dealer, James, in Northern Ireland. Further torture is mercifully interrupted when Padraic's mobile phone rings. It is Donny with the news that Wee Thomas is "poorly" (14). Back on Inishmore, Davey is being cross examined at gun point by his sister Mairead about his involvement in Wee Thomas's death. Mairead, who bears a strong resemblance to the character Helen in *The Cripple of Inishmaan*, has a history of blinding cows with her air rifle. Davey secretly substitutes Mairead's cat, Sir Roger for Wee Thomas but since he is ginger not black, Donny and Davey blacken him with shoe polish. Meanwhile, Padraic's former INLA colleagues lie in wait for him, having killed the cat in order to lure him home so they can assassinate him. Mairead overhears their plans and goes off to meet Padraic on his way.

Donny and Davey awaken from a drunken sleep to find Padraic has arrived. In rage he shoots the shoe polished cat in its basket, flings the corpse into the bathroom and is about to shoot Donny and Davey too when his INLA friends arrive. Christie, Brendan and Joey take Padraic outside to execute him, but in one of the play's many reversals, Mairead blinds the three with her sharp shooting and they dive for cover back into the house. There follows a shootout in which Padraic kills Brendan and Joey, and then sets to work torturing Christy for murdering Wee Thomas. Afterwards Donny and Davey are seen hard at work in "the blood soaked living room [now] strewn with body parts" (55) cutting up the corpses while Padraic strokes what is left of Wee Thomas. Mairead is set to join forces with Padraic, but all is overturned when she accidentally discovers the mangled Sir Roger. She dispatches Padraic, instructs Donny and Davey to get on with dismembering him as well and promises soon to begin an investigation into the circumstances of Sir Roger's murder. While the unfortunate survivors hold their heads in dismay, a black cat enters the kitchen—it is the real Wee Thomas. Realising that all the "terror has been for absolutely nothing" (68) they turn on the cat with Padraic's guns, but cannot bear to kill him. The play concludes with Danny and Davey feeding Wee Thomas breakfast cereal surrounded by the day's carnage.

Perhaps more so than the Leenane plays, much of the parodic humour of *The Cripple of Inishmaan* is generated by its references to a single text and its history—Robert Flaherty's famous "documentary" film, *Man of Aran*.[85] The play seems to demonstrate Jameson's contention that "we are now [...] in 'intertextuality' as a deliberate, built in feature of the aesthetic effect, and as the operator of a new connotation of 'pastness' and pseudo-historical depth, in which the history of aesthetic styles displaces 'real' history."[86] Yet it also disrupts this

---

[85] See also Werner Huber, "Contemporary Drama as Meta-Cinema: Martin McDonagh and Marie Jones," 13-23.

[86] Jameson, "Postmodernism, or the Cultural Logic of Late Capitalism," 76.

contention by highlighting the slippery modalities of "real" history suggested by the referent text. If a note of satiric parody is to be found in the play (which is otherwise primarily a provincial comedy) then it is in the inferences regarding representation that the citation of the film elicits. As Lance Pettitt describes, Flaherty's

> ideas and practice emphasised different aspects of a realist tradition in documentary. "Realist" here refers to the desire through film to reveal truths about the condition of the social and historical world, to show "how life is."[87]

Despite the now obvious fact that *Man of Aran* is a romantic homage to "ahistorical ethnicity," at the time of its release in 1934, it was received warmly in Ireland as a much needed accurate representation that conveniently coincided with "the dominant State ideology of self-reliance and ascetic frugality."[88] As one reviewer enthused:

> We have become almost resigned to being traduced in literature, whether under the guise of the comic "Paddy" of Victorian music halls, or the drunken swindler of some Irish farces or the "gunman" of more sombre writers to-day. Not three generations of protesting could do as much to rehabilitate the Irish people in the imagination of the peoples of other countries as this faithful and beautiful motion picture will do.[89]

Luke Gibbons in *Cinema and Ireland* (1987), analyses the film as illustrating a "hard primitivist ideal at its most powerful elemental level"[90]—the noble savage in a mortal struggle with nature. Yet the constructedness of this narrative is highlighted,

---

[87] Lance Pettitt, *Screening Ireland: Film and Television Representation* (Manchester: Manchester University Press, 2000) 72.

[88] Pettitt, *Screening Ireland*, 72, 80.

[89] Dorothy Macardle, *Irish Press*, 7 May 1934. Qtd. in Kevin Rockett, Luke Gibbons and John Hill, *Cinema and Ireland* (London: Routledge, 1987) 195.

[90] Luke Gibbons, "Romanticism, Realism and Irish Cinema," *Cinema and Ireland* 201.

as Pettitt notes, by Flaherty's selection of appropriate material and the aestheticisation of that material in order to create an "authentic" documentary. Flaherty combed the local population for "the most attractive and appealing characters […] to represent a family and through them tell [the] story," commenting that "it is always a long and difficult process […] for it is surprising how few faces stand the test of the camera."[91] McDonagh's characters ironically reflect on Flaherty's casting choices: "if Colman King can play a role in a film anybody can play a role in a film, for Colman King is as ugly as a brick of baked shite" says Johnnypateenmike (7). The play similarly alludes to some of the liberties Flaherty took with historical accuracy in order to produce a heroic narrative, namely that shark hunting was already an abandoned practice among the islanders. When Kate does not know what a shark is, Bartley remarks that "it's rare that off Ireland you get sharks. This is the first shark I've ever seen off Ireland (55). The play's open engagement with *Man of Aran* and its history enables it to indulge in intertextual jokes, but also implicitly opens the question of representation, and once again access to "genuine historicity." This is extended in scene seven in which Cripple Billy's performance of a dying Irish immigrant, is played out in fully fledged parodic kitsch style. But the play also is complicated by the improbability of its own historical references as Pilný has remarked.[92] The selection of sweets at Kate and Eileen's shop, Johnypateenmike's omelettes and beetroot paella, and the quality of the rapid fire dialogue, deconstruct the authenticity of the play's own representation, which is ultimately just as simulated as *Man of Aran* ever was.

The Lieutenant of Inishmore attracted more media attention than any of McDonagh's plays on account of its graphic and humorous satire on paramilitary violence. McDonagh has claimed that the play expresses "pacifist rage," and is, despite

---

[91] Pettitt, *Screening Ireland*, 78.
[92] Pilný, "Martin McDonagh: Parody? Satire? Complacency?" 228.

its violence "wholeheartedly anti-violence."[93] Nevertheless, the play turns upon the cartoonish spectacle of a mixture of visceral brutality and black humour, and relies heavily on the "douche écossaise" technique of the Grand Guignol mentioned above. The stereotype of the Irish gunman is exaggerated fiercely and relentlessly. Padraic, the "brave son of Erin," is as Davey avers, "as thick as a mongo fecking halfwit" (19). The republican struggle is reduced to a collection of jingoistic clichés and blatantly cynical absurdities. Padraic is determined to "rid[…] Erin of them jackboot hirelings of England's foul monarchy" (33). His INLA colleagues more "democratically" maintain

> isn't it for everybody we're out freeing Ireland? That's what Padraic doesn't understand, is it isn't only for the schoolkids and the oul fellas and the babes unborn we're out freeing Ireland. No. It's for the junkies, the thieves and the drug pushers too. (29)

The traumatic and tragic history of Northern Ireland is transposed onto a massacre of felines. The brutal deaths of cats, as reviewer Mark Lawson commented, "deliberately set a trap for […] audiences and reviewers, which is to make [them] worry more about the cats than the humans killed."[94] The play is problematically torn between the way in which it displaces heroism and justification of violence and yet, at the same time, seems to revel in dehumanisation and melodramatic gore. Perhaps the primary postmodern characteristic of *The Lieutenant of Inishmore* is that everything is equally levelled by irony and nothing, not even murderous INLA terrorists, can be elevated to seriousness. Authenticity, reality, depth in the McDonagh play-world are never to be found where they ought to be.

Authenticity: Debates and Debacles

---

[93] McDonagh, qtd. in Sean O'Hagan, "The Wild West," *Guardian* 24 Mar. 2001 (online).

[94] Mark Lawson, "Sick-Buckets Needed in the Stalls," *Guardian* 28 Apr. 2001 (online).

Many of the responses to these plays have been governed by the dynamics of a discourse of authenticity. This relates to the content of the work as well as to perceptions of McDonagh himself.[95] If for some, McDonagh's dramaturgy is founded on the ironic emptying out of stereotypes, then for others he is guilty of propagating damaging misrepresentations. As Graham states, "authenticity is claimed and disclaimed in Irish culture, functioning as a standard of worth and a cultural core value" which significantly "overlaps with nationalism's self-projections in crucial ways."[96] This is particularly pronounced in the history of Irish theatre and informs some critics' arguments about McDonagh and his work. The notion that theatre has a duty not only to represent the nation in some respect, but also should have some discernable moral core, shadows claims like those of Kevin Barry, who argues that "when it travels, [the work] taken at face value [...] McDonagh has no imaginative empathy with the characters or their language. It's a relationship of distance."[97]

Barry's criticism is obviously laden with value judgements that demand some unpacking. While McDonagh's drama is, undeniably, not one of great hidden depths, the assumption of a stable "face value" regardless of the audience, language or location of performance is rather naïve to say the least. As both John Waters and Ondřej Pilný maintain, this seriously underestimates the capacities of audiences.[98] In addition, it seems to suggest that audiences experience plays in a bubble, without the interference of the media, or even, more mundanely, the mediation provided by a theatre programme. If this were the case then plays like Brian Friel's *Translations* or

---

[95] See Lenz for a synopsis of opinions on McDonagh's status as an Irish playwright, "'Anything new in the feckin' west?'" 26-27.

[96] Graham, *Deconstructing Ireland*, 134-5, 136.

[97] Kevin Barry, qtd. in Nadine O'Regan, "Theatre Queen," *Sunday Business Post* 22 July 2001 (online).

[98] Pilný, "Martin McDonagh: Parody? Satire? Complacency?" 225 and John Waters, "The Irish Mummy: The Plays and the Purpose of Martin McDonagh," *Druids Dudes and Beauty Queens*, 30-54. 38.

Marina Carr's *On Raftery's Hill* might similarly be in danger of being understood at "face value." Barry's comments also suggest that there may be a singular value, yet as Sierz maintains "[McDonagh] offers a method of attacking nostalgia that applies not just to Ireland but to any nation's culture."[99]

In asserting that McDonagh's relationship with his material is one of distance, Barry alludes to the playwright's qualifications to write Irish plays. Garry Hynes, the director who discovered McDonagh, energetically rejects the criticism that his vision is somehow inauthentic: "I have always had a huge problem with authenticity," she states, "Why do you validate theatre? If you want authentic, then just don't go there. Why have it mediated through a writer? Is it a world which compels the attention and the imagination of an audience in the theatre for a particular time? If it is, then in itself, it is valid."[100] As is well-known, although he has been adopted as an Irish playwright, McDonagh has never lived there and this fact is repeatedly mentioned as a preface to an analysis or dismissal of the plays. McDonagh's relationship to the discourses his drama interpellates is, it seems, perpetually problematic. McDonagh has defended himself by claiming: "I've always felt half-Irish, half-English. The suggestion seems to be that I'm not allowed to write about where my parents are from. I hate that idea of authenticity that you must be tied down only to what you know first-hand."[101] McDonagh himself has stressed how he is both English and Irish, but critical response to his work has almost totally eclipsed his status as an English playwright.[102] This may well lie in the sense that while American and Irish

---

99 Sierz, *In-Yer-Face Theatre*, 225.
100 Garry Hynes, qtd. in Nadine O'Regan, "Theatre Queen," *Sunday Business Post* 22 July 2001 (online).
101 Martin McDonagh, qtd. in Dominic Cavendish, "He's Back, and Only Half as Arrogant," *Telegraph* 6 Apr. 2001 (online).
102 See O'Hagan, "The Wild West." Notably, discussion of McDonagh's appeal to English audiences is critically treated by Mark Luckhurst, "Martin McDonagh's *Lieutenant of Inishmore*: Selling (-Out) to the English," *The Theatre of Martin McDonagh*, 116-129.

identities may co-exist, Irish and English still bear an antonymic resonance, and McDonagh is perhaps an irksome reminder of an identity that is difficult to countenance. Interestingly, McDonagh claims that he has not written about London because "that's too close to home,"[103] adding another problematic layer to the question of his work and distance.

The polar opposite of Hynes's view is perhaps most powerfully voiced by Victor Merriman, who contends that these plays are morally abject "forms of communal self-loathing."[104] Merriman sees in the plays only "gross caricature with no purchase on the experiences of today's audiences, their appeal to the new consumer-Irish consensus lies in their appearance as ludicrous Manichean opposites—the colonised simian reborn."[105] He considers both Marina Carr's and McDonagh's work as symptomatic of a harmful neo-colonialism that seeks to disown the past. Furthermore, he questions the view that the work is,

> in some postmodern sense metatheatrical, that the whole project is a wonderful jape in which the jaded repertoire of Boucicault, Synge, and the "lesser" Abbey playwrights has been plundered as an antique hoard of quirky, dated images. Such theatrical freaks have no currency in an urbane present, so to parade them in all their benightedness is a big joke, in which the laugh is on the naïve drama of the past which really must be left behind.[106]

Yet, very popular recent revivals of precisely these playwrights' work belie Merriman's argument. Moreover, as Shaun Richards has pointed out, while Merriman casts Synge as a hero, as is well documented Synge was demonised by early nationalist

---

[103] Sierz, *In-Yer-Face Theatre*, 223.
[104] Merriman, "Settling for More," 60.
[105] Merriman, "Decolonisation Postponed," 313.
[106] Merriman, "Decolonisation Postponed," 315.

critics.[107] Like Merriman, Barry argues that "the work is posited on the idea of the cultural poverty of the people on stage. The relationship of the playwright to his material is most easily explained by a relationship of easy and lazy hatred. Contemptuous hatred."[108] One can only wonder how these critics would deal with the "cultural poverty" of the dramatis personae of a play by Harold Pinter or David Mamet.

In direct contrast to such responses are those of Fintan O'Toole and Vandevelde. O'Toole sees McDonagh's work

> at one level, [mapping] a very real and immediate Ireland. However grotesque the exaggerations, they inflate a recognisable truth so that it can be seen more clearly. But at another level, the world that is imagined in this way is also a version of one of the great mythic landscapes—the world before morality.[109]

Taking a somewhat different tack, Vandevelde claims that "the imitations and echoes of literary precursors are so apparent throughout the trilogy that the playwright's self-reflexivity becomes ironical, if not subversive. As such this double edge makes it perfectly possible to read the trilogy as either a canonical or a radical text." Vandevelde sees McDonagh interrogating the canon of Irish drama and thus prompting "spectators to question their expectations and definitions of Irish drama." Vandevelde, however, like McDonagh's detractors still returns to the plays' mimetic capacities. She asks "if [the] plays present rural Ireland at the end of the twentieth century in a form that is at once fictional and real, is his 'new

---

107 Shaun Richards, "'The Outpouring of a Morbid Unhealthy Mind': The Critical Condition of J.M. Synge and Martin McDonagh," Department of English and American Studies, Charles University, Prague 29 Nov. 2002. Published in *The Theatre of Martin McDonagh*, 246-263.

108 Kevin Barry qtd. in Waters, "The Irish Mummy," 33.

109 O'Toole, rev. of *The Leenane Trilogy* by Martin McDonagh, *Irish Times* 24 June 1997. Also in *Critical Moments: Fintan O'Toole on Modern Irish Theatre*, eds. Julia Furay and Redmond O'Hanlon (Dublin: Carysfort, 2003) 180.

voice' powerful enough to stage the devastating effects of the modernisation of Irish life?"[110] This quite obviously reinscribes the question of authentic representation and the playwright's duties to it.

John Waters has perceptively described the debate surrounding McDonagh as "another opportunity for a re-enactment of the collective neurosis of modern Ireland." Waters finds the celebrations and rejections of the plays on the basis of their engagement with Ireland of the past or present to be irrelevant. McDonagh's work deploys that which it purports to attack—the reduction of Ireland to a selection of kitsch signs.[111] If, as Graham asserts, kitsch is "the cultural form which most clearly challenges authenticity's hold on cultural identity, then at the same time "finding meaning in kitsch is troublingly paradoxical."[112] The difficulty of connecting McDonagh's work with a notion of kitsch lies in just how seriously one is to consider it. Waters admits that McDonagh "exploit[s] the gap between the pre-modern and the postmodern," however, he also maintains that the main goal of the playwright is not to represent reality, but to produce work that engages an audience. Nevertheless, Waters too concludes with a reaffirmation of the concerns he critiques: "challenging impenetrably cosy delusions and flawless feats of landscaping, our best playwrights continue to present us with unsettlingly truthful versions of ourselves."[113] It remains to be seen how extensively McDonagh's most recent play, *The Pillowman*, will ultimately disrupt the interpretation of McDonagh's work within this frame.

[110] Vandevelde, "The Gothic Soap of Martin McDonagh," 293, 294.
[111] Waters, "The Irish Mummy," 34, 48.
[112] Graham, *Deconstructing Ireland*, 170, 171.
[113] Waters, "The Irish Mummy," 51, 53-4.

In a sense Barry is correct in identifying a relationship of distance in McDonagh's dramaturgy, but not in the sense he intends. Instead, distance inheres in the constructs and construction of McDonagh's ironic parody and pastiche, and the focal point of parody in the work from this period is genre and the notion of representation itself. McDonagh's parodies, to paraphrase Hutcheon, seem to speak to a discourse of Irish drama and its genres from within, but also at a distance that enables him to make a spectacle of this intertextuality.[114] The question of responsibility, however, remains problematic; as Douglas Crimp observes,

> appropriation, pastiche, quotation [are] methods [that] can now be seen to extend to virtually every aspect of our culture, from the most cynically calculated products of the fashion and entertainment industries to the most committed critical activities of artists, from the most clearly retrograde works […] to the most seemingly progressive practices.[115]

McDonagh's work is dogged by precisely this issue; while the plays discussed continually draw attention to the genres, themes and stereotypes they quote, formally they are highly conservative dramas. In spite of the playful and unruly energy of the work, the traditional unities of time, place and character remain firmly in place. He can, as he says, "do dialogue and storytelling,"[116] but his use of stage space does not stray far from the borders of naturalism. Certainly, McDonagh's plays exceed Jameson's "neutral practice of […] mimicry"[117] yet, they also fall short of the postmodern pastiche that Hutcheon claims as a form of radical provisionality and intertextuality. Old

---

[114] Hutcheon, *A Poetics of Postmodernity*, 35.

[115] Douglas Crimp, "Appropriating Appropriation," *Image Scavengers: Photography*, ed. Paula Marincola (Philadelphia: Institute of Contemporary Art/ University of Pennsylvania Press, 1982) 27-34. 27.

[116] O'Hagan, "The Wild West" (online).

[117] Jameson, "Postmodernism, or the Cultural Logic of Late Capitalism," 74.

forms are filled with new content and a display of attitude. By contrast, the work of Sarah Kane is founded on an attempt to fuse form and content that takes the risks McDonagh's ultimately avoids.

Sarah Kane
Radical Alterity & Staging Trauma

There's only the same danger of overdose in the theatre as there is in life. The choice is either to represent it, or not to represent it. I've chosen to represent it because sometimes we have to descend into hell imaginatively in order to avoid going there in reality.[1]

Sarah Kane is renowned as one of the most contentious of the new playwrights in 1990s British theatre. For some, Kane's drama is gratuitously brutal and naïve, the product of a precocious but immature writer, while for others, especially beyond Britain, she among the most significant and innovative voices in British drama of the late twentieth century. The debate surrounding her work is poignantly accentuated, but also complicated, by the author's suicide in 1999 at the age of twenty-eight. Kane is the subject of an extensive website which serves as a locus of much information on the plays and their production histories, as well as a forum for discussion and commemoration.[2] In addition, since 2000 her plays have been frequently and widely performed outside the UK—at least one hundred productions are listed on the website—recently attracting interpretations by such actors as Isabelle Huppert (BAM-Harvey Theater, October 2006). Similarly, academic

---

[1] Sarah Kane, interview, *Rage and Reason: Women Playwrights on Playwriting*, eds. Heidi Stephenson and Natasha Langridge (London: Methuen, 1997) 132-3.

[2] The Sarah Kane website is hosted at <www.ianfisher.com/kane.html>.

commentary has rapidly accumulated. Besides a dedicated interest in Kane's work in Europe, Aleks Sierz's chapter on Kane in *In-Yer-Face Theatre*, Christopher Innes's updated *Modern British Drama* and numerous other short publications,[3] the first monograph by Graham Saunders, *"Love Me or Kill Me": Sarah Kane and the Theatre of Extremes*, appeared in 2002.[4] In contrast to some of the more culturally specific new writing for theatre of the period, the ways in which Kane's drama depicts extreme physical and psychological states has been compelling to audiences who are, culturally and linguistically, vastly diverse.

The story of Kane's debut is by now familiar. Her first play, *Blasted*, premiered in January 1995 in the Royal Court Theatre Upstairs but was little publicised by the theatre. Nevertheless, as Sierz describes, this "play by an unknown twenty-three-year-old [...] not only became the focus of some of the most aggressive reviews of the decade, but also the centre of the biggest scandal to hit theatre since Mrs Whitehouse tried to close Howard Brenton's *The Romans in Britain* in 1981."[5] The

---

[3] See Eckart Voigts-Virchow, "Sarah Kane, a Late Modernist: Intertextuality and Montage in the Broken Images of Crave," *What Revels are in Hand? Assessments of Contemporary Drama in English in Honour of Wolfgang Lippke*, CDE Studies 8, eds. Bernhard Reitz and Heiko Stahl (Trier: Wissenschaftlicher Verlag Trier, 2001) 205-220; Merle Tönnies, "The 'Sensationalist Theatre of Cruelty' in 1990s Britain, its 1960s Forebears and the Beginning of the 21st Century," *(Dis)Continuities: Trends and Traditions in Contemporary Theatre and Drama in English*, CDE 9, eds. Margarete Rubik and Elke Mettinger-Schartmann (Trier: Wissenschaftlicher Verlag Trier, 2002) 57-72; Peter Buse, "Sarah Kane In and On Media," *Nach Dem Film* 2 (Dec. 2000) <http://www.nachdemfilm.de>; Peter Buse, *Drama + Theory: Critical Approaches to Modern British Drama* (Manchester: Manchester University Press, 2001); Kenneth Urban, "An Ethics of Catastrophe: The Theatre of Sarah Kane," *PAJ: A Journal of Performance and Art* 69 (Sept. 2002): 36-46.

[4] Graham Saunders, *"Love Me or Kill Me": Sarah Kane and the Theatre of Extremes* (Manchester: Manchester University Press, 2002).

[5] Aleks Sierz, *In-Yer-Face Theatre: British Drama Today* (London: Faber, 2001) 91. Graham Saunders associates Kane's debut to that of John Osborne, as did Stephen Daldry the artistic director of the Royal Court at the time. Like Aleks Sierz, Saunders however also views the mythologising of *Blasted* as a planned

production was infamously condemned by *Daily Mail* journalist, Jack Tinker, as a "disgusting feast of filth,"[6] while more measured reviews questioned the play's problematic relation to realism. *Blasted*, however, did receive strong support from other quarters, most notably from seasoned playwrights Edward Bond and Harold Pinter.[7] Kane went on to write four other plays—*Phaedra's Love* (Gate Theatre, 15 May 1996), *Cleansed* (Royal Court Theatre, 30 April 1998), *Crave* (Traverse, 13 August 1998) and *4.48 Psychosis*—as well as a ten minute film script entitled *Skin*.[8] Each of the plays has drawn divergent and often extreme responses, though admittedly none as vehement as those to *Blasted*. These have been adequately documented by both Sierz and Saunders and shall not be repeated here, however, as Saunders describes, *Crave* with its shift away from visceral spectacle marks "a significant breakthrough in an appreciation and understanding of [her] work."[9] Finally, *4.48 Psychosis* premiered on 23 June 2000 at the Royal Court Jerwood Theatre Upstairs, generating some debate as to whether it constituted, as Michael Billington wrote, "a 75-minute suicide note."[10]

Kane adamantly denied that she was at the cutting edge of any movement, an accurate statement if her work is viewed in the context of European avant garde theatre. In particular, she

---

launch of a "new writing" movement in British theatre sceptically, because the Royal Court did little to promote the play. He also attributes at least some of the journalistic scandal around the play to "mock-outrage" and press "mischief-making." See page 3 and following.

6 Saunders, *Sarah Kane and the Theatre of Extremes*, 37.

7 Bond claimed *Blasted* to be "the most important play on in London" and defended it on the grounds that "the images [...] are ancient. They are seen in all great ages of art—in Greek and Jacobean theatre, Noh and Kabuki." Edward Bond, *Guardian* 28 Jan. 1995 (online).

8 All quotations from are from Sarah Kane, *Complete Plays* (London: Methuen, 2001) and will be cited in-text. *Skin* was first broadcast by Channel 4 on 17 June 1997.

9 Saunders, *Sarah Kane and the Theatre of Extremes*, 102.

10 Michael Billington, "How do You Judge a 75-minute Suicide Note?" *Guardian* 30 June 2000 (online).

directly rebuffed the claim that she was a "New Brutalist"[11] and rejected other more traditional identity labels, insisting that her work be judged "on its quality, not on the basis of [her] age, gender, class, sexuality or race."[12] Rather than identity in this sense, the complex issue of subjectivity is predominant in all her plays, and one of the central accomplishments of her work may be found in her deeply disturbing, if at times rather obsessive, negotiations of subjectivity on stage. This view echoes that of David Greig in his introduction to the *Complete Plays*; he regards "each play [as] a step on an artistic journey in which Kane mapped the darkest and most unforgiving internal landscapes: landscapes of violation, of loneliness, of power, of mental collapse and, most consistently, the landscape of love."[13]

Greig's description seems an appropriate point of departure for an extended exploration of Kane's journey. This chapter while acknowledging the aptness Saunders's thesis which positions Kane in relation to what he refers to as "the theatre of extremes," sets out to examine in greater depth some of the ways in which Kane works with extremes in a different frame. Specifically, I wish to approach the plays through a notion of radical alterity to analyse how Kane's theatre tests and pursues the extreme boundaries of her subjects. The term radical alterity I use to facilitate an analysis of Kane's experiments with the outer limits of the tolerable, the stageable, as well as with the, at times absurd, torments of the unbearable or abject self. What all the "landscapes" enumerated by Greig above have in common is arguably a missed encounter with some form of radical alterity—something which cannot be fully accessed, comprehended or assimilated, and thus remains fundamentally shocking or disturbing. What is apprehended are the masks of the Other, which appear in Kane's theatre as an engagement with the (quasi) taboo subjects of torture, sexualised violence,

---

11 Kane qtd in Saunders, *Sarah Kane and the Theatre of Extremes*, 7, 8.
12 Kane, *Rage and Reason*, 134.
13 David Greig, Introduction, *Complete Plays* by Sarah Kane (London: Methuen, 2001) ix.

death, absolute or abusive love and psychosis. The experiential impact of the thematics of desire and obsession, alienation and the performance of traumatic narratives and actions in the plays hinges upon this primary and primal relation to alterity.

In an age of apparently unprecedented ontological uncertainty, Kane proclaims herself responsible, as a writer, only to "the truth, however difficult that truth happens to be."[14] As is evident in all her plays, this pursuit of truth, where truth and trauma map onto one another, involves a double coding in the sense that her pursuit of "truth" incorporates a mixture of modernist, expressionist and postmodern strategies. My analysis is structured around four significant elements in Kane's drama—her use of violent or visceral spectacle, the erosion of character and dispersed selves, the role of textuality and intertextuality, and finally absolutes and instability in her work.

Experiential Theatre & Radical Alterity
The notion that that bulk of new writing in British theatre, especially from 1995 onwards, has been structured by an experiential, rather than a speculative, aesthetic is one which has been widely circulated, not least by Sierz's seminal book on the topic. Central to this notion is the tendency towards provocation, towards the staging and generation of intense experience (often privileging "gut-reaction" over intellectual response), and this tendency is acknowledged as one of the hallmarks of much of the new playwriting of the era. As Sierz notes, provocation and theatre share a long history. But while his "brief history of provocation"[15] is primarily concerned with British theatre in concordance with the perimeters of his project, Kane's work solicits reference to the histories of the European avant garde and expressionism in its concerns.

European theatre history of the twentieth century reveals how pivotal provocation and the discourse of intense and

---

[14] Kane, *Rage and Reason*, 134.
[15] Sierz, *In-Yer-Face Theatre*, 10.

alternate realms of experience have been in shaping contemporary theatre and, especially, to avant gardes past and present. Recognition of this matter is partially evident in the attempts that have been made to connect Kane's work with that of Antonin Artaud. Mal Smith's "Sarah Kane: A Nineties Take on Cruelty" (part of a Theatre Museum Education Pack entitled *Antonin Artaud and His Legacy*) or James Hansford's piece on Kane, which associates her work also with Howard Barker's Theatre of Catastrophe are cases in point.[16] Saunders, while identifying some nodes of contingence between the violence and extremity of Kane's, Artaud's and Barker's drama, however cautions against any fixed analogising. While he suggests that "many of the features of *Cleansed*—the diminution of language, the extraordinary set and theatrical imagery, the ritualised cruelty, its extremes of love and pain" seem to invite comparison with Artaud's Theatre of Cruelty, he draws attention to Nils Tabert's interview with Kane in February 1998, in which she expresses a great enthusiasm for Artaud's writings, but also claims only to have started reading his work.[17] There is, moreover, some disagreement on this point even among Saunders's sources. Jannette Smith, assistant director to Royal Court production, sees *Cleansed* as approximating Artaud's notion of total theatre, while the director, James McDonald, disassociates the first production from this objective claiming that they "were just trying to translate that extraordinary imagery into a consistent theatrical language."[18] This does not, of course, preclude the possibility of analysing Kane's theatre in relation to her continental predecessors. Nevertheless, it is perhaps judicious to note that such correlations can only be made in a partial sense and are

[16] Mal Smith, *Antonin Artaud and his Legacy* (London: Theatre Museum Education Pack, 1999); James Hansford, "Sarah Kane," *Contemporary Dramatists*, ed. Thomas Riggs, 6th ed. (Detroit: St. James, 1999) 348-9.

[17] Nils Tabert, "Gespräch mit Sarah Kane," *Playspotting: Die Londoner Theaterszene der 90er*, ed. Nils Tabert (Reinbeck: Rowohlt, 1998) 8-21. See Saunders, *Sarah Kane and the Theatre of Extremes*, 91, 16.

[18] Saunders, *Sarah Kane and the Theatre of Extremes*, 91, 123.

more informative if placed within the wider context from which Artaud himself emerged and of which he is a part.

Many of the agreed characteristics and objectives of expressionist theatre are not only crucial to Artaud's concept of theatre but also, are latently in evidence in Kane's work. For instance in *Avant Garde Theatre 1892-1992* (1993), Christopher Innes lists the techniques of expressionist drama as including: "the free associations of images [which] replaced logical organisations of mimetic shapes;" the use of "discontinuous scenes;" the erosion of "time and space [...] as categories for organising experience;" the use of montage; the diminution of character to the "status of figures as archetypes;" the reduction of speech and dialogue in "an attempt to reflect uncontrolled emotional depths of subconscious;" and finally, anti-mimetic effects which were "artificial, exaggerated and rhetorical." The aim of all these techniques is a fundamental rejection of realism and an attempt to express a world on stage which is interior and not subject to the rules of naturalistic representation. Perhaps of most interest and relevance here is the significance attributed to experience, to the total involvement of both the performers and the audience. Through the techniques cited above, the "absolute emotional truth" of subjective experience is to be conveyed at a pitch of intensity which is intended to radically challenge the world views and comfort zones of the spectators.[19]

Richard Murphy (*Theorizing the Avant-Garde* [1999]), attentive to the ambivalences of the expressionist project, notes one of the principle problems that haunt expressionist theatre, and is also an issue in Kane's experiential theatre, that is:

> [the] inherent danger within expressionism [is that] the seemingly liberating impulse towards expression turns into mere excess, into an hysterical "sound and fury" which

---

[19] Christopher Innes, *Avant Garde Theatre 1892-1992* (London and New York: Routledge, 1993) 39-43.

exhausts itself at the level of its extravagant and desperate
gestures and fails to carry any further meaning along with it.[20]

The excesses of expressionism are familiar: "bombast, the
unashamed opening of the soul, its 'sentimental' claims to
privileged insight into a transcendental world beyond."
Nevertheless, ultimately Murphy defends expressionism's turn
to excessive methods as a tactic used "only in order to reach
beyond dominant representational systems, codes and
conventions, and beyond the epistemological and discursive
restrictions associated with them."[21] Here too a strong
connection might be made with Kane's work.

Artaud inherits many of these aims and qualities, in
particular in his attitudes towards character, dialogue and
staging, a fact often obscured by his currency as a theatre
innovator. As a result interpretive openness of his writings, his
interpreters have defined his work and its message diversely.[22]
Artaud's concept of total theatre, which closely echoes the
preoccupations of many expressionist dramatists in its appeal
to an intense all-encompassing experience of theatre,
foreshadows the renewed focus upon the experiential in
dramatists like Kane. "Everything that acts is cruelty. Theatre
must rebuild itself on a concept of this drastic action pushed to
the limit" and "if theatre wants to find itself needed once more,
it must present everything in love, crime, war and madness"[23]

20 Richard Murphy, *Theorizing the Avant-Garde: Modernism, Expressionism, and the
Problem of Postmodernity* (Cambridge: Cambridge University Press, 1999) 142.
21 Murphy, *Theorizing the Avant-Garde*, 143. Murphy wishes to reclaim melodrama
of the expressionist period (1910-1920) as "a mode of counter-discourse"
drawing attention to what is normally repressed of disallowed by the
conventions of naturalism or realism.
22 For examples and discussion of Artaud inspired experimental theatre see Innes,
Avant Garde Theatre 1892-1992 and Theodore Shank, "Framing Actuality: Thirty
Years of Experimental Theater, 1959-89," in *Around the Absurd: Essays on Modern
and Postmodern Drama*, eds. Enoch Brater and Ruby Cohn (Ann Arbor:
University of Michigan Press, 1990) 239-272.
23 Antonin Artaud, *Theatre and its Double*, trans. Victor Corti (1964; London:
Calder, 1993) 65. First French edition 1938.

are among Artaud's most cited statements on the necessity of
cruelty expressed in *Theatre and its Double* (1938). If these claims
seem to literally describe Kane's drama, then simultaneously, as
Innes cautions, it must be remembered that there is
considerable disparity between Artaud's assertions on cruelty
and its role in his work:

> In Artaud's actual stage work the "cruelty," which appears as a
> definition of existence in his metaphysical writings, is no more
> than an agent to heighten response by magnification [...]. It is
> in fact the dynamics that are primary, not any intrinsic violence:
> "the spectator [...] will be shaken and set on edge by the
> *internal dynamism* of the spectacle."[24]

Cruelty as such is primarily a tool, utilised to affect the
audience to achieve an "experiential" goal. Correspondingly,
while staging visceral and violent action, Kane denies any
interest in glamorising violence.

Beyond their interest in expressing extreme states of being, it
is more difficult to find commonalities between Artaud and
Kane, however. Artaud's interest in ritual, in rigid archetypal
movement, in breaking down the barrier between stage and
audience find no powerful counterpoints in Kane's work chiefly
because the notion of the sacred is absent. What is shared is a
vocabulary of disruption, extremity, excess, truth, and alternate
worlds of interiority that can be traced from expressionist
theatre through Artaud via Howard Barker's Theatre of
Catastrophe to Kane. If one is to accept Murphy's assertion that
expressionism emerges in response to radical historical change
and crisis (modernity, war, industrialisation) then the echoes of
expressionism to be found in Kane's work can be said to
emerge from a comparable, but contemporary, crisis. Both
expressionism and Artaud have a pronounced interest in the
status of the self and the unconscious, what is purged from this

---

[24] Artaud, *Œuvres Complètes*, vol. 2, 27. Qtd. in Innes, *Avant Garde Theatre 1892-1992*, 65.

concern in Kane's work is any pretence to the recovery of the sacred. The world of Kane's drama is one in which transcendental values are short circuited from the outset. In this she is closer to the heritage of Samuel Beckett than to Artaud, and it is noteworthy that Kane echoes one of her favourite lines from Beckett—Hamm's spleenful exclamation concerning God, "The bastard! He doesn't exist," from *Endgame*—in *Blasted*.[25]

These legacies are significant to an understanding of Kane's work, but her staging of extreme emotional states (and her absolutism) also require a critical apparatus that accounts for a crucial shift, itself a product of the changed quality of crisis—that of the destabilised self in a world of spectacle and simulacra. As Thomas Docherty asserts "the avant garde used to legitimise itself precisely by being untimely and incomprehensible: a challenge to history and to reason." In opposition to the attempts in conventional aesthetic practice to present the world "as it is, *tel quel* […] the avant-garde presents the world as it is not; more precisely, it has to present a world which is, strictly speaking, unrepresentable." He goes on to argue that the avant garde therefore "shocks its audience or spectator out of the forms of Identity and into the anxieties of alterity and heterogeneity, into the perception of a world and a Subject of consciousness which is always radically Other." This shift from a "philosophy of Identity" to a "philosophy of alterity" is articulated in various forms, not least in the psychoanalytic theories of Jacques Lacan, some of which are especially pertinent to Kane's drama.[26]

In his well-known revision of Freud, Lacan redraws the map of the subject in terms of the real, the symbolic and the imaginary, claiming that the unconscious is structured like a

---

[25] Samuel Beckett, *The Complete Dramatic Works* (London: Faber, 1990) 119. When Cate tells Ian God has prevented him from shooting himself, the blind Ian responds, "the cunt" (57). For further discussion of this connection see Saunders 22-23.

[26] Cf. Thomas Docherty, Introduction, *Postmodernism: A Reader* (New York: Harvester Wheatsheaf, 1993) 16-17.

language.[27] The mechanisms of the unconscious described by Freud in terms of condensation and displacement are extended by Lacan in terms of metaphor and metonymy. The symbolic order is "the determining order of the subject," that of "signifiers, speech [and] language."[28] In the imaginary order the effects of the unconscious are not acknowledged and in which the subject misrecognises the nature of the symbolic. Finally, the real "stands for what is neither symbolic nor imaginary" and, therefore, is inaccessible to the subject as it is autonomous of language. As such it is "the ineliminable residue of all articulation, the foreclosed element, which may be approached, but never grasped." For Lacan "the function [...] of the real as [...] essentially the missed encounter—first present[s] itself in [the] form [...] of the trauma."[29] It is at this point a connection might be made with the plays and their exploration of the dimensions of traumatic radical alterity.

Kane's drama falls into two stages in which she explores extremes in very different ways. Consequently, it is important to acknowledge that the shift from a visual to verbal aesthetic moderates the negotiation of alterity considerably. If *Blasted*, *Phaedra's Love* and *Cleansed* communicate traumatic encounters with alterity in a physical and often visually explicit manner; in *Crave* and *4.48 Psychosis* they are textually, or linguistically, generated. However, in both cases as the embedded response to radical alterity ((mis)recognised in death, violence, desire, mental breakdown), trauma emerges in coded form—in displacements, fragments, condensations and repetitions.

Blasted, *Phaedra's Love* and *Cleansed* rely strongly upon the force of visceral spectacle. *Crave* and *4.48 Psychosis* shift entirely to a linguistic focus where ultimately, as Kane says, "all there is

---

[27] Jacques Lacan, "Of Structure as an Inmixing of Otherness Prerequisite to any Subject Whatever," *The Languages of Criticism and the Sciences of Man: The Structuralist Controversy*, eds. R. Macksey and E. Donato (Baltimore MD: John Hopkins University Press, 1970) 188.

[28] Lacan, *The Four Fundamental Concepts of Psychoanalysis*, trans. Alan Sheridan (1973; London: Vintage, 1998) 279, 280.

[29] Lacan, *The Four Fundamental Concepts*, 280, 55.

are language and images. But all the images are within language rather than visualised."[30] One might read these stages as loosely corresponding to different facets of the question of alterity in postmodernity and a crisis of representation. As Merle Tönnies points out, much of the action of the "sensationalist" theatre of the 1990s seems arranged primarily "according to visual criteria."[31] The visual overload or excess of the earlier plays engages with the logic of postmodern spectacle, where spectacle structures what is communicated and spectacle is self-perpetuating.

The second stage in Kane's work abandons viscerality in favour of disparate, polyvocal micronarratives and fragments. The isolated and indeterminant voices of *Crave* and *4.48 Psychosis* suggest a correlation with the crisis of identity originating in the erosion of an Enlightenment notion of a stable, knowable self. In these plays "the autonomous subject of modernity, objectively rational and self-determined [...] gives way to a postmodern subject which is largely other-determined, that is, determined within and constituted by language."[32] If in all the plays "fixed" identity is questioned, then the alienated and negated vision of the self grows particularly acute from *Cleansed* onwards. In a manner similar to that remarked upon by Elinor Fuchs in *The Death of Character*, Kane's later work explicitly interrogates the viability of the pretence of unified character in an age typified by "a dispersed idea of self."[33]

Violent Spectacles

Thanks in part to the initial outraged reaction to her first play, *Blasted*, one of the most remarked upon features of Kane's first three plays is their extreme, and what was perceived as unbearable, violence on stage. The anguished early responses to

---

[30] Saunders, *Sarah Kane and the Theatre of Extremes*, 111.

[31] Tönnies, "The 'Sensationalist Theatre of Cruelty,'" 62.

[32] Hans Bertens, *The Idea of the Postmodern: A History* (London: Routledge, 1995) 6.

[33] Elinor Fuchs, *The Death of Character: Perspectives on Theatre after Modernism* (Bloomington and Indiana: Indiana University Press, 1996) 9.

Blasted, and later, to a lesser extent, *Phaedra's Love* and *Cleansed*, found the visceral imagery of Kane's work excessive. What was apparently most objectionable was the fact that the violent spectacles were severed from a context or moral interpretation that would sufficiently explain or alleviate them. They were not just unpalatable but unrealistic, or in the words of Billington, "the reason the play falls apart is that there is no sense of external reality."[34] In a society conditioned by what Herbert Blau terms "a warp of specularity,"[35] in which spectators are habitually exposed and largely desensitised to violent and sexual spectacles via other media, such a reaction might be a little surprising. It remains a glaring irony, that unlike the mass appeal and consumption of gratuitously violent Hollywood cinema, Kane's shocking debut was as the director James MacDonald describes "perhaps the least seen and most talked about play in recent history."[36]

Again, context is required in order to appreciate the dimensions of Kane's theatre in its spectacular phase. On one level, Kane's work may be read in terms of its experiential provocation. As Tönnies notes, critics and reviewers of the new drama of the 1990s baulked at the intensity of the visceral spectacle apparently so frequently offered by numerous new playwrights. Measuring the era against "seminal 1960s works, it thus seems that the 1990s dramatists consciously piled up and exaggerated taboo breaks" and that this drama can "be taken to have sought out excess deliberately and exploited all possible means to achieve the most intense effect on its audience."[37]

<hr>

34 Michael Billington, *Guardian* 20 Jan. 1995: 22. Qtd. in Sierz, *In-Yer-Face Theatre*, 96.

35 Herbert Blau, "The Oversight of Ceaseless Eyes," *Around the Absurd: Essays on Modern and Postmodern Drama*, eds. Enoch Brater and Ruby Cohn (Ann Arbour: University of Michigan Press, 1990) 281.

36 James MacDonald, "They Never Got Her," *Observer Review* 28. Feb. 1999 (online).

37 Tönnies, "The 'Sensationalist Theatre of Cruelty,'" 58, 59.

Kane's first three plays are undeniably structured "according to visual criteria,"[38] but in a manner which is both complex and calibrated to various dramatic and literary precedents, as well as to contemporary cultural phenomena. In addition the influences of expressionist theatre, Artaud's Theatre of Cruelty, Edward Bond's *Saved* and references to *King Lear*,[39] one might also consider the traces of early modernism's engagement with violence and aesthetics, as does Eckart Voigts-Virchow. He aligns *Blasted* with Wyndham Lewis's Vorticist manifesto *Blast*, which was committed to providing "the avenue for all those vivid and violent ideas that could not reach the Public in any other way."[40] Associating the plays with a modernist fascination with creative destruction, Voigts-Virchow positions *Blasted* within this tradition reading *Crave* as a modernist retreat from violence, to an involvement with a poetic methodology of semi-Beckettian "verbal despair."[41]

While this intricate web of connections can be traced, it must also be recognised that the conditions of representation at the end of the twentieth century differ in certain important respects, in particular, with regard to mediation. The notion that war and atrocity as seen on television and in other media, have been represented and simulated to such an extent that they become empty spectacles, is one which Kane powerfully responded to when speaking about *Blasted*. She speaks of the horror of this loss of any sense of reality as follows:

---

[38] Tönnies, "The 'Sensationalist Theatre of Cruelty,'" 62.

[39] Saunders, *Sarah Kane and the Theatre of Extremes*, 24, 54-70. See also Saunders's "'Out Vile Jelly': Sarah Kane's *Blasted* and Shakespeare's *King Lear*," *New Theatre Quarterly* 20:1 (2004).

[40] Wyndham Lewis, *BLAST. The Review of the Great English Vortex* 1 (1914). repr. in *A Modernist Reader: Modernism in England 1910-1930*, ed. Peter Faulkner (London: Batsford, 1986) 42-46. Qtd. in Voigts-Virchow, "Sarah Kane, a Late Modernist," 209.

[41] Jeanette Malkin, *Verbal Violence in Contemporary Drama* (Cambridge: Cambridge University Press, 1992) 5. Qtd. in Voigts-Virchow, "Sarah Kane, a Late Modernist," 209.

There's a famous photograph of a woman in Bosnia hanging by her neck from a tree. That's lack of hope. That's shocking. My play is only a shadowy representation of a reality that's far harder to stomach. It's easier to get upset about that representation than about the reality because it's easier to do something about a play—ban it, censor it, take away the theatre's subsidy. But what can you do about that woman in the woods?[42]

It is noteworthy here that while Kane wishes to preserve a clear distinction between representation and reality, the appalling reality of the Yugoslav war to which she refers is available to her primarily as representation, in the form of photographic evidence. In fact, the division she wants to maintain might, in the context of her own work, be said to fail since the plays themselves not only represent but are experienced as violent events. As Harold Pinter says with reference to *Phaedra's Love*:

> [The violence] jumped right out of the page. The page itself was violent. The act of turning the page was violent [...]. What frightened me was the depth of her horror and anguish.[43]

Kane's use of violence, then, in *Blasted*, *Phaedra's Love* and *Cleansed* goes beyond the adjectival relation of violence to spectacle and gestures towards the way in which violence inheres in spectacle as it is experienced in postmodernity. On a theoretical level, this work, rather than titillating specular desire, thwarts the pleasure of seeing by rendering everything too visible and too close, by translating desire too literally. As Innes comments,

> all these images are not only presented as irrational—motivated by sexual desires or perversions—but also *in full view*. Masturbation, oral and anal sex, incestuous copulation and rape

---

[42] Sierz, *In-Yer-Face Theatre*, 106.

[43] Harold Pinter qtd. in Simon Hattenstone, "A Sad Hurrah," *Guardian* 1 July 2000 Weekend: 26-33. 31.

are performed *front stage* and [in the case of *Cleansed* often] in the nude.[44]

In addition as Sierz has emphasised on various occasions the issue of proximity is essential—theatres in which her work was first staged were small, so audiences had difficulty distancing themselves not just psychologically but also physically.[45]

Analysing Kane's drama in terms of the trauma theory of Shoshana Felman and Dori Laub, Peter Buse (*Drama + Theory* [2001]) focuses upon the audience's experience, remarking how the early plays especially are characterised by the administration of "heavy doses" of "brutalising shock" to the audience.[46] According to Buse, "*Blasted* [...] could be said to bring its audience to face the 'traumatic kernel of the Real.'"[47] The term trauma generally designates a psychological and, above all, an entirely subjective response to an experience or event. The event may be an emotional experience which cannot be processed, or it may be a time when the subject has felt radically threatened—a threat to life, bodily integrity, or sanity.[48] This sense of being physically, cognitively or emotionally overwhelmed seems to be a salient feature of Kane's dramaturgy, not only of the plays, but also, as Buse argues, in their relation to the audience. The effect is perceived as a physical assault, as reviewers' opinions testify. Paul Taylor of *The Independent* memorably responded as follows:

---

[44] Innes, *Modern British Drama: The Twentieth Century*, 532. My italics.

[45] The exception here is *Cleansed* which opened in the larger space of the Royal Court Theatre Downstairs.

[46] See Shoshana Felman and Dori Laub's *Testimony: Crises of Witnessing in Literature, Psychoanalysis, and History* (London and New York: Routledge, 1992). The article quoted here is "Sarah Kane In and On Media," (online), though Buse develops the reading further in *Drama + Theory: Critical Approaches to Modern British Drama.*

[47] Buse, "Sarah Kane In and On Media."

[48] Laurie Ann Pearman and Karen W. Saakvitne, *Trauma and the Therapist* (New York: Norton, 1995) 60.

sitting through *Blasted* is a little like having your face rammed
into an overflowing ash tray, just for starters, and then having
your whole head held down in a bucket of offal. As a theatrical
experience, there's nothing wrong in principle with either of
these ordeals. Provided, that is, you can feel something
happening to your heart and mind as well as to your nervous
system as a result.[49]

With regard to *Phaedra's Love*, Charles Spencer of the *Telegraph*
claimed "it's not a theatre critic that's required here, it's a
psychiatrist."[50] While John Peter of the *Sunday Times* felt,

> *Cleansed* is a nightmare of a play, it unreels somewhere between
> the back of your eyes and the centre of your brain with an
> unpredictable but remorseless logic. As with a nightmare, you
> cannot shut it out because nightmares are experienced with the
> whole of your body.[51]

Such comments seem to indicate Kane's attempts at experiential
theatre were indeed successful in aggravating and even
overwhelming their first spectators.

Set in an expensive but anonymous hotel room in Leeds,
Blasted includes three characters all of whom are
simultaneously unsympathetic and vulnerable. The play opens
with Ian and Cate entering the room. Ian is an ailing, middle-
aged journalist. He carries a gun, is vociferously racist and later
in the play claims that he is a hit man. In the first two scenes he
is depicted as a repulsive figure, manipulative and coercive.
Cate is young, overtly naïve and apparently not very
intelligent. She and Ian have had a sexual relationship which
finished some time ago. The fact that she is twenty-one and he
is forty-five suggests that this previous relationship was also
rather unusual, if not somewhat abusive. Cate is unemployed
and still lives with her parents and her mentally handicapped

---

49 Paul Taylor, "Courting Disaster," *Independent* 20 Jan. 1995: 27.
50 Charles Spencer qtd. in Sierz, *In-Yer-Face Theatre*, 108.
51 John Peter, "Short Stark Shock," *Sunday Times* 10 May 1998: 28.

brother, who is repeatedly referred to by Ian as a "joey" and a "spaz" (5). She is prone to what seem to be fainting "fits" or vaguely epileptic seizures when under stress. The third character is a soldier, an anonymous perpetrator and victim of the horrors of war.[52]

The action of the play is deceptively simple. During the first scene Ian attempts to seduce Cate. She rejects his advances and, when he pressures her too actively, faints. Nevertheless she stays the night with him and in the morning it is clear he has raped her. Although Cate wishes to leave immediately, Ian attempts to persuade her to stay. A physical struggle ensues in which Cate threatens Ian with his gun. She faints a second time during which Ian holds the gun to her head while he rubs himself between her legs. Later, she persuades him to confess why carries a gun by fellating him. At the point of his orgasm she bites his penis. Cate then retreats to the bathroom and escapes. Meanwhile, a soldier appears at the door and forces his way into the room. An unspecified war has started and the soldier is part of the invading army. Suddenly the hotel room is blown asunder. Both Ian and the soldier survive. The soldier describes the atrocities of killing and war. He then rapes and mutilates Ian before shooting himself. The now blinded and helpless Ian waits in the wrecked room. Cate returns with an abandoned baby. Ian begs her for his gun so he can kill himself; she finally gives it to him, unloaded. The baby dies. Cate buries it under the floorboards and leaves to scavenge for food. The deserted Ian is seen in various states—crying, masturbating, attempting to strangle himself, defecating and, finally, eating the dead baby. He then crawls into its grave and dies. Cate returns with food and alcohol; Ian wakes up. The final gruesome image of the play has also an ambivalent quality of hope. As Innes vividly puts it, "*Blasted* ends with the girl,

---

[52] As is noted in Saunders, Sierz and other texts, Kane was struck by the horror of the war in Yugoslavia and the sense of indifference in Britain to the victims of the atrocities taking place there. The stories told by the soldier, and the torture of Carl in *Cleansed* are drawn from reports of real events in Bosnia.

bleeding from between her legs—the sign of violent rape—
feeding and mothering the eyeless man in the hole."[53]

Her next play *Phaedra's Love*, which Kane wryly referred to
as "my comedy,"[54] is a provocative version of Seneca's play on
the Phaedra myth. Kane's intention was that "the play could be
at one moment intimate and personal, at the next epic and
public."[55] Unlike Seneca's, Euripides's or Racine's versions of
the story, Kane realigns the focus of the play to Hippolytus
rather than the lovesick Phaedra. Hippolytus, the central figure,
is a character in despair at the hypocrisy and superficiality of
the world around him. His downfall is a result, not of his purity
as is stressed in the other well-known versions of the Phaedra
myth, but rather his pursuit of absolute honesty. The Phaedra
myth is, of course, rooted in violence however, as has been
noted by various critics, Kane also reverses the acts
traditionally occurring on stage and those reported. The
outcome of this strategy is a heightened spectacle of traumatic
viscerality. Phaedra's suicide takes place offstage while a host
of other brutal actions—including the mutilation and
disembowelment of Hippolytus, the rape and murder of
Strophe, and Theseus's suicide—take place in full view.

The play consists of eight relatively short scenes. Hippolytus
is introduced in the opening scene as decadent, overweight and
bored, lethargically watching television, eating junk food and
masturbating into his discarded socks. Phaedra, his obsessively
concerned stepmother, is first seen consulting with the royal
doctor about her stepson's condition. They talk at cross-
purposes—the doctor's diagnosis is "he's just very unpleasant.
And therefore incurable" (68). Phaedra's daughter, Strophe,
similarly attempts to disillusion her mother about Hippolytus.
Although he cruelly taunts her, Phaedra makes an idealistically
absolute declaration of her love for Hippolytus and insists on

---

53 Innes, *Modern British Drama: The Twentieth Century*, 533.
54 Sarah Kane, interview with Nils Tabert qtd. in Saunders, *Sarah Kane and the Theatre of Extremes*, 78.
55 Kane qtd. in Sierz, *In-Yer-Face Theatre*, 108.

fellating him as a "birthday present." Hippolytus continues, with brutal honesty, to reject her romantic notions, finally rupturing her tolerance with a double revelation: both he and Theseus have had sex with Strophe, and he has gonorrhoea, so she ought to see a doctor. Following the traditional narrative, Phaedra accuses Hippolytus of rape and commits suicide. Strophe attempts to save Hippolytus, but he refuses to confirm or deny the charge, and seems content with his new identity. Upon hearing of Phaedra's suicide, Hippolytus delighted that real life seems to be happening at last, turns himself in to the authorities. In prison he refuses the hypocritical option of an "eleventh hour confession" (94), to recognise any duty to his family or country or to, ultimately, forgive himself. Theseus returns for Phaedra's funeral and swears revenge. During the final scene, which descends into spectacular carnage, the public gather in anticipation outside the court. Theseus and Strophe are in the crowd disguised. Hippolytus throws himself into the violent mob who beat him. When Strophe attempts to intervene, Theseus rapes her before the cheering crowd and cuts her throat. The people mutilate Hippolytus by cutting off his genitals, which are thrown by the hysterical crowd into the auditorium—an action that drew one sceptical reviewer to comment that the play was more "in-yer-lap" than "in-yer-face."[56] Then Theseus disembowels him and his body is kicked and spat upon. Theseus finally recognises Strophe with horror. Police disperse the crowd and spit on the motionless Hippolytus. In remorse at Strophe's murder, Theseus cuts his own throat and dies. Finally, as the vultures descend, Hippolytus now an uncannily literal body without organs, smiles and exclaims: "If there could have been more moments like this" (103).

Cleansed is Kane's most ambitious and visually experimental piece. Intended to be a play that "could never be turned into a film, that could never be shot for television, that could never be

---

56   David Nathan qtd. in Sierz, *In-Yer-Face Theatre*, 108.

turned into a novel,"[57] it remains her most sexually explicit and violent work, and her most difficult to stage. As Sierz puts it, *Cleansed* is "a parable about love in a time of madness [and is] full of metaphors of addiction, need, loss and suffering."[58] The title may well be read as a reference to the supposedly cathartic function of tragedy, but it also plays upon the ways in which its characters are cleansed of both their illusions and of their identities. *Cleansed* is composed of twenty short scenes set in what stage directions call a university, but what is in effect an asylum or prison-like clinic. It is structured around various couples and couplings of characters: Tinker, a drug dealer and self-styled doctor; Graham, an addict; Grace, his sister; Carl and Rod a gay couple; Robin a young inmate of the "university," and an unnamed woman who is an erotic dancer. Although the scenes are ostensibly non-sequential, several interconnected stories can be identified. These are shuffled through each other in the play. For clarity I have separated them below, however it must be acknowledged that doing so detracts from the self-contained nature of each individual scene and the sense of tension and dislocation achieved by their interspersal.

The first is that of Graham, Grace and Tinker. In the opening scene Graham meets Tinker. The latter is heating a spoonful of heroin. Graham wants to die. Tinker assists him by injecting a lethal quantity of the drug into the corner of his eye. Some time later, Grace comes to the institution for Graham's clothes. When they are produced, she puts them on and breaks down in hysteria. Tinker handcuffs her to a bed and sedates her. Grace declares that she wants to stay in the institution. Robin, a young inmate who has been wearing Graham's clothes, is then forced to wear Grace's. Grace meets Graham's ghost and begins to take on his identity. As they dance together, she mimics his movements. They make love, after which a sunflower sprouts through the stage. Meanwhile, Grace begins to teach Robin how to write. Grace tells Robin of her desire not only to feel like

---

[57] Kane qtd. in Sierz, *In-Yer-Face Theatre*, 115.
[58] Sierz, *In-Yer-Face Theatre*, 114.

Graham but to look like him. Robin tells Grace that he is in love with her. Tinker vindictively destroys what Robin has been drawing—a flower for Grace. Later, Grace is beaten and raped by invisible torturers. Graham supports her while the torture climaxes. Stage directions indicate their stigmatic bond: "Graham presses his hands onto Grace and her clothes turn red where he touches, blood seeping through. Simultaneously, his own body begins to bleed in the same places" (132). Afterward daffodils burst through the stage. Tinker declares that he will "save" Grace, and she undergoes violent electro-shock therapy. He then makes Grace's "wish" come true by amputating her breasts and transplanting Carl's genitals on her body.

The second principle narrative is that of homosexual lovers, Rod and Carl. Carl wants a declaration of eternal love, Rod wants realistic honesty. Carl obliges Rod to swap rings as a symbol of their commitment to and love for one another. Tinker, the manipulating voyeur of the play, watches them. Tinker tortures Carl, first by having him beaten (again by invisible torturers), then by threatening to impale him. In a scene reminiscent of the torture of Winston in George Orwell's *Nineteen Eighty-Four*, Carl betrays Rod: "Not me please not me don't kill me Rod not me don't kill me ROD NOT ME ROD NOT ME" (117). Though Carl attempts to apologise, Tinker cuts out his tongue and makes him swallow the ring he had given to Rod. Carl and Rod sit in the mud near the university. Carl, now dumb, asks Rod's forgiveness by writing in the mud. Tinker watches and then cuts off Carl's hands. When Carl attempts to express his love for Rod by dancing, Tinker cuts off his feet, which are then taken by rats. Carl and Rod make love. Rod promises to always love Carl and never to betray him. Carl swallows Rod's ring. Tinker enters and forces Rod to choose between his own life and Carl's. Rod chooses to defend Carl. Tinker cuts his throat and he dies. Tinker then amputates Carl's genitals and gives them to Grace.

In another part of the institution Tinker masturbates as he watches a woman dancing from a peep-show booth. He calls her Grace, though the woman does not affirm or deny that this is her name. Grace and the woman are played by different actresses. Later, back in the peep-show booth the woman asks Tinker to save her. Robin watches the woman dancing from the booth and cries in despair. Tinker verbally abuses the woman, who now seems reliant on him. Robin has bought a box of chocolates for Grace but Tinker cruelly forces him to eat them all. Robin urinates involuntarily and Tinker rubs his face in it. Tinker forces Robin to burn the books which he has been studying. Grace watches, completely tranquillised. Robin learns to count and realises how long he will have to stay in the institution. He hangs himself with help from Tinker and Graham. Grace is oblivious. Tinker watches the woman from the booth. Finally she "opens the partition and comes through to Tinker's side" (147) and they make love. The woman finally tells him her name really is Grace.

Finally, Grace/Graham and Carl appear on stage swathed in bloodied bandages, physically transformed by their desires. In the final scene, Carl is dressed in Grace's clothes while Grace wears Graham's. They sit in the mud with the rats. The sun comes out and the play concludes in blinding light.

Form, Content & the Logic of Nightmare
The catalogue of brutal images and events from *Blasted*, *Phaedra's Love* and *Cleansed* are, as the above descriptions illustrate, impossible to ignore, critically circumnavigate or omit. These are images which are deliberately searing in concordance with Kane's declared aesthetic project.[59] Experiential in the extreme, the plays draw heavily on a storehouse of taboos: incest, cannibalism, sexual violence, dismemberment, mutilation, suicide and murder. Moreover, the

---

[59] See Kane's views on theatre from "The Only Thing I Remember is…," *Guardian* 13 Aug. 1999: 12, "Theatre has no memory, which makes it the most existential of the arts. No doubt that is why I keep coming back, in the hope that someone in a dark room somewhere will show me an image that burns itself into my mind, leaving a mark more permanent than the moment itself."

discomfort of the plays' content is exacerbated by their perceived lack of moral legibility, and their alienating formal properties.

Critics of Kane's work have repeatedly complained of the pointlessness and arbitrariness of visceral incidents in the plays, while among those who support Kane diverse efforts have been made to resolve their ambiguity into a clearer moral, more acceptable, stance. These explanatory, defensive strategies attempt to rationalise the forms of uncompromising, intolerable alterity seeping through the plays and to map a more recognisable signification onto them. Edward Bond, defending *Blasted* focused on its "humanity," he goes on to distinguish between Tarantino's work and Kane's claiming that although "both deal with chaos [o]ne says chaos is dangerous for us but we have to go into chaos to find ourselves. The other says chaos is a gimmick, a new device—it's a trick." [60] Billington, too, subsequently came to view *Blasted* as "a serious play, driven by *moral ferocity*."[61] Kane, ever reluctant to interpret her own work or do the audience/reader's work for them, complicates the matter further:

> A lot of people who have defended me over *Blasted* have said that it's a deeply moral play [...]. I don't think *Blasted* is a moral play—I think it's amoral, and I think that is one of the reasons people got terribly upset because there isn't a defined moral framework within which to place yourself and assess your morality and therefore distance yourself from the material.[62]

This statement, however, is itself belied to some extent by the plays themselves and the absolute values they stage.

One means of managing the problem of the ambivalence of morality in Kane's drama is to exchange the term morality for ethics. Ken Urban's article, "An Ethics of Catastrophe: The

---

[60] Edward Bond, *Guardian* 28 Jan. 1995.

[61] *Nightwaves*, BBC Radio 3, broadcast 23 June 2000, qtd. in Saunders, *Sarah Kane and the Theatre of Extremes*, 9.

[62] Kane qtd. in Saunders *Sarah Kane and the Theatre of Extremes*, 27.

Theatre of Sarah Kane," seeks to understand Kane's work as a "quest for ethics."[63] Referring to Gilles Deleuze's distinction between morality as a system of "constraining rules" structured by "transcendent values," Urban reads *Blasted* terms of an ethical rather than moral approach, where ethics are not fixed, but "emerg[e] from specific moments and certain modes of being." From this angle, *Blasted* demonstrates "the possibility that an ethics can exist between wounded bodies, that after devastation, good becomes possible."[64] Arguably, this moment occurs at the end of the play in which Cate feeds the now helpless man who raped her, and he simply expresses his thanks. In *Phaedra's Love*, the protagonist uninterested in good or evil seeks some means of ethical, if immoral, existence in a world saturated with dishonesty and self-delusion. In *Cleansed*, for Urban, the question is of "[h]ow to live in the midst [of the madness of love] is the ethical problem at the heart [of the play]."[65] Urban's ethical interpretation seems best fitted to *Blasted*; the overwhelming sense of decimation and negation of *Phaedra's Love* and *Cleansed*, and the traumatic disintegration of *Crave* and *4.48 Psychosis* makes a reading based on good becoming possible somewhat difficult to sustain. In addition, such an analysis of Kane's work, although it responds to the thematics of catastrophe, avoids the central issue of Kane's engagement with form as not only means but message.

Kane's attempts to unify form and content are of central importance to interpretations of the plays and to the ways in which extreme interior states are staged. Her interest in innovation in form was ongoing and explicitly stated; "As soon as I've used one theatrical form, it becomes redundant. So each time I've tried to do something different."[66] Saunders is representative in his claims that, "it is this rejection, or at least

---

[63] Ken Urban, "An Ethics of Catastrophe: The Theatre of Sarah Kane," *Performing Arts Journal* 23.3 (2001): 36-46. 37.

[64] Urban, "An Ethics of Catastrophe," 37.

[65] Urban, "An Ethics of Catastrophe," 43.

[66] Claire Armistead, "No Pain, No Kane," *Guardian* 29 Apr. 1998 (online).

manipulation, of the conventions of realism that is perhaps the key distinguishing feature of the dramatic strategy employed in [her] work."[67] Ultimately she asserts that,

> All good art is subversive, either in form or content. And the best art is subversive in form *and* content. And often, the element that most outrages those who seek to impose censorship is form. Beckett, Barker, Pinter, Bond—they have all been criticised not so much for the content of their work, but because they use non-naturalistic forms that elude simplistic interpretation.[68]

As suggested above, in the first stage of her work, violent spectacle is integral. Like Artaud, she exploits the "internal dynamism of the spectacle"[69] to explore extreme states through a constellation of images and metaphors of seeing, the self and desire.

In *Blasted* Kane's shift from "socio-realism to surrealism, to expressionism"[70] allows her to explore the nature of power in a domestic shape which is then suddenly displaced and magnified to grotesque proportions. Kane argues that the shock of *Blasted* is chiefly because of the play's "odd theatrical form, apparently broken-backed and schizophrenic, which presented material without comment and asked the audience to craft their own response."[71] She stresses:

> The tension of the first half of the play, this appalling social, psychological and sexual tension, is almost a premonition of the disaster to come. […] The play collapses into one of Cate's fits. The form is a direct parallel to the truth of the war it portrays— a traditional form is suddenly and violently disrupted by the

---

67 Saunders, *Sarah Kane and the Theatre of Extremes*, 9.

68 Kane, *Rage and Reason*, 130.

69 See Innes *Avant Garde Theatre 1882-1992*, 65.

70 Mel Keynon, *Nightwaves*, BBC Radio 3, broadcast 23 June 2000, qtd. in Saunders 40.

71 Kane, *Rage and Reason*, 131.

entrance of an unexpected element that drags the characters
[…] into a chaotic pit without logical explanation.[72]

Nevertheless, in its structure *Blasted* is in many respects recognisably traditional. Despite the stark quality of language and dialogue, the play's three characters are surprisingly rounded and self-consistent, a practice abandoned in the later work. They remain the compass points of the action, however arbitrary or symbolic the changes in time, the world outside or that on stage. This relative stability of character in *Blasted*, conditions its staging of traumatic alterity which takes place in several principle ways in the play: through the abandonment of realism, through the performance of identity, through metaphors and images of sight and through the role of the body as site of trauma.

The idea of collapse, in particular, facilitates a reading of the structure of the play as psychotic episode in an alternate reality where meaning is organised according to the apparent illogicalities of the unconscious. As Kane admits, in earlier drafts of play the soldier was Ian's hallucination, in the final version he becomes real, but anonymous.[73] Buse follows this possibility to some extent in an article entitled, "Sarah Kane In and On Media." He proposes that given the traumatic nature of the play's story and that trauma is generally communicated in a fragmentary, illogical and non-linear manner, the second part of the play might also interpreted as alternate order of experience, perhaps a figment of Ian's imagination.[74] While directors have tended to interpret the second half of the play metaphorically as a dream or nightmare, Kane suggests that "by the end, we should be wondering if the first half was a dream."[75] Thus, while the play is "about" manipulation,

---

[72] Kane, *Rage and Reason*, 130.

[73] Sierz, *In-Yer-Face Theatre*, 102. See Saunders, *Sarah Kane and the Theatre of Extremes*, 46-47 on the development of the character of the soldier.

[74] Buse, "Sarah Kane In and On Media."

[75] Sierz, *In-Yer-Face Theatre*, 106.

violation and war, it simultaneously deals with an interior terrain, which is structured by the logic of dream and association.

Certainly a logic of Freudian dream-work of condensation and displacement, or in Lacanian terms metonymy and metaphor, is suggested by the mirroring effects and repetitions in the play. In the figure of the soldier, Ian encounters a character like himself, whose actions to some extent reflect, but also exaggerate, his own behaviour in the first part of the play. Ian's racism is mirrored in the soldier's engagement in brutal ethnic cleansing. Ian is forced to listen to tales of real atrocities and is mocked for his naïvety:

Soldier:	You never killed anyone.
Ian:	Fucking have.
	[...]
Soldier:	Couldn't talk like this. You'd know.
Ian:	Know what?
Soldier:	Exactly. You don't know.
Ian:	Know fucking what? (46)

Ian's rape of Cate is juxtaposed with the soldier's description of raping and torturing enemy women and girls. Though Cate is in the first scene dependent and childlike, in the altered territory of the remaining scenes she mothers a dying baby and then finally cares for Ian by feeding him. The logic of nightmare is not only articulated through the arbitrariness of transformation brought by the blast, where rationality and causality seem to break down and in the symmetry of the soldier's violation of Ian, but also in the way he is, literally, blinded by violence to which earlier he seems morally blind.[76] While Ian reports on the murder of a young British woman in New Zealand as a tabloid spectacle (the lurid details of how the victim "had been stabbed more than twenty times" are coupled

---

[76] Buse compares Ian's callous report on a murder with his later inability to tell or to bear witness to the soldier's horrific stories of war and relates this to Felman's notion of witnessing and trauma.

with a vaguely titillating description of her as a "bubbly
nineteen year old" and "a beautiful redhead with dreams of
becoming a model" [12]), he is unwilling to report and record
the soldier's experience:

> I do other stuff. Shootings and rapes and kids getting fiddled by
> queer priests and schoolteachers. Not soldiers screwing each
> other for a patch of land. It has to be…personal. You're
> girlfriend, she's a story. Soft and clean. Not you […]. Why bring
> you to light? (48)

In the altered logic of the second half of the play Ian
misrecognises himself as other, becoming a victim of his own
prejudices and desires embodied in the extreme figure of the
soldier whose experiences are, in effect, unspeakable for him.
Extending the dreamlike displacement still further, it is perhaps
a form of perverse wish-fulfilment that Cate, initially a
vulnerable, simple-minded victim, becomes a calculating
survivor who prolongs Ian's suffering by thwarting his attempt
to commit suicide. Cate's repetition of the phrase "You're a
nightmare" (33, 51) though at first understood as a metaphoric
displacement, seems, when repeated, to describe him literally.
Innes also notes "the purely associative connections in the
action, characteristic of the subconscious," the way in which the
idea of abandoned babies is introduced and soon afterward
Cate returns with a baby, the connection between the starving
baby and the starving Ian and how the grave Cate makes for
the dead baby also serves for Ian who buries himself there.[77]

Time is similarly treated in an overtly non-realistic manner.
In the warp of dream logic "events [tend] to unroll according to
a logic of their own like the abrupt changes of season and of the
weather in *Blasted* and *Cleansed*, which [aim] at emotional (or
symbolical) rather than meteorological accuracy."[78] It is
noteworthy that the symbolic use of seasons pertains

---

77 Innes, *Modern British Drama*, 531
78 Tönnies, "The 'Sensationalist Theatre of Cruelty,'" 63.

throughout the play, even the part which is "realistic," though the expressionist contraction of time becomes most significant at the end of the play in which Ian is shown in various states: masturbating, attempting suicide, defecating, laughing, dreaming, in despair and hungry. Not only does each state express a need or drive, but the spiralling of scenes through seven stages ending in death reverses of the seven "days" of creation. Ian's terror at the prospect of total negation, of "not being" is contrasted with Cate's childish notion of death: "You fall asleep and then you wake up" (10). Rather than release into non-existence, Ian's fears are surreally realised in his death and apparent resurrection at the conclusion of the play—as stage directions indicate:

> *He dies with relief.*
> *It starts to rain on him, coming through the roof.*
> *Eventually.*
> Ian: Shit. (60)

If *Blasted* is structured by the enigmatic qualities of dream where particular orders of logic are suspended and alternate co-ordinates of images come into play, the topology of subjectivity is a central feature of the play's exploration of extremes. In the latter part of the play Ian's self-perception and therefore, identity are radically interrogated. The role of the dream and the unconscious are of significance here. Writing of the position of the subject in dreams, Lacan emphasises how "our position in the dream is profoundly that of someone who does not see. The subject does not see where it is leading, he follows."[79] Ian, in the hallucinatory order of scenes two to five, is shown by the soldier the extremities of his own desires and, literally, becomes the subject who does not see. This starkly contrasts with the self assured identity claimed by Ian in scene one, in which he repeatedly sees himself in opposition to others. This is clear in the simple dichotomies of self-other evident in his attitudes to

[79] Lacan, *The Four Fundamental Concepts*, 75.

race, sex and even football. Non-whites are "wogs," "Pakis," "conkers" and "whodat[s];" homosexuals are "dyke[s]," "lesbos," "cocksuckers" and "scum." Ian's attitude to death is similarly stark, while his assertion of his masculinity in scenes one and two is extreme to the point of cliché. The status of the gun as phallic symbol is subtly introduced in scene one and gradually heightened as the play continues. In the first scene after he strips for Cate and she laughs, he retreats in embarrassment to the bathroom to dress, returns and quite unnecessarily *"picks up his gun, unloads it and reloads it"* (8). He then begins to verbally revenge himself on her.

In effect, Ian's identity is structured by an aggressive relation to others, an overstated masculinity and a desire for control exacerbated by his failing health and imminent physical demise. All these values are called into question by the soldier's appearance on stage. The soldier takes the gun without difficulty. Later Ian's homophobia is rendered meaningless when confronted with the soldier's experience of torture. Ian's feminisation is insinuated as the soldier compares him to his girlfriend: "You smell like her. Same cigarettes" (49). Ultimately he is forced to literally take her place when he is raped and then brutally threatened with the gun. Finally, the symbolism of the gun is once more evident in Ian's impotent attempt to shoot himself, unlike in scenes one and two the gun (and by implication Ian's masculine agency) is out of ammunition.

Similarly his macho nationalism in the early scenes is eroded as the play proceeds. In spite of the vicious talk about kidnapping and killing, the possibility of eradicating homosexuals and bombing football grounds, he cannot stomach the soldier's stories of mutilation, torture and violent death. In this other order of experience Ian does not "know what the sides are here" (40). His nationalist identification is also ironically undermined by the soldier:

Ian: I'm Welsh.
          [...]
Soldier: Foreigner?

Ian: English and Welsh is the same. British. I'm not an
          import.
Soldier: What's fucking Welsh, never heard of it. (41)

Later the soldier asks him to imagine killing a woman, "in the line of duty. For your country. Wales" (45), he humorously undercuts Ian's confident and exclusionist national identity.

Questions of self perception are further investigated throughout the play via the symbolism of eyes and seeing. For Lacan, a crucial formative stage (the Mirror stage) in the development of the subject is associated with the act of seeing. Further, in his discussion of the role the gaze as structuring aspect to subjectivity, Lacan notes the fundamental significance of the metaphorical relation of the subject (I) with the organ of sight (the eye).[80] These concerns are pertinent to the ways in which acts of seeing in *Blasted* signify at different levels of reality and association. Ian perceives himself as worldly wise; he has seen everything, even his own cancer rotten lung, while Cate seems explicitly "in the dark" about many things, including Ian's intentions. During Ian's traumatic encounter with the soldier, perspective is altered in a play of metaphorical light and darkness which recalls Lacan's assertion that dreams are characterised by not seeing or not understanding. Significantly, though Ian claims to be a killer, the soldier highlights his ignorance of real brutality, advising Ian to "Stay in the dark." (46). The relation of light and darkness is then reversed when the soldier demands that Ian testify to his existence. In this instance it is the soldier who is "in the dark," and not configured in the gaze he fears his own disappearance. As the ellipsis in his request suggests, all the soldier can ask is a record that he has been seen, "Tell them you saw me. Tell them … you saw me" (48), while Ian asks "Why bring you to light?" (48) Finally this debate culminates gruesomely when the soldier eats Ian's eyes.

---

[80] Lacan, *Écrits: A Selection*, trans. Alan Sheridan (1966; New York and London: Norton, 1977) 91.

The erotic symbolism of the eye in the work of Freud through Lacan to George Bataille might be noted here. For Freud, and later Lacan, the symbolism of blinding in dreams is connected with castration anxiety, and it is possible to see such anxiety at work in *Blasted* at a number of key points. Ian is threatened with castration—when Cate points his loaded gun at his crotch—and then is blinded by the soldier. Although Saunders has discussed the play in terms of its echoes of *King Lear*, Kane also claims the psychoanalytic symbolism of Ian's mutilation, referring to it explicitly as a "metaphorical castration." [81]

Although the eye-gouging episode gives rise to a web of literary, symbolic and psychoanalytic connotations, more generally the play presents bodies as sites of trauma: as terminally ill, dysfunctional, abused or mutilated. Ian's fear of death is coupled with his abject self-destructive consumption of alcohol and nicotine. His body is already decaying as repeated references to his odour and frequent coughing suggest. The lung he has had removed is described as a stinking "lump of rotting pork" (11). At the play's beginning Ian is a body on the point of collapse, in scene two he collapses in agony but survives, and by the play's conclusion he has become an uncanny body—mutilated and dead. Cate's body too is dysfunctional, stuttering and subject to seizures under stress. Her hysterical laughter and crying during these fits give vent to the anxiety felt but inarticulable. Lastly, the soldier is most obviously reduced to the status of "just" a body—a mutilation and murder machine expert in physical torment.

While *Blasted* explores the territory of power and violation by juxtaposing micro and macro levels of violence, *Phaedra's Love* and *Cleansed* are thematically linked in their dramatisation of the extremes of desire and love. In both plays points of crisis are reached when the relationship between subject and object of desire is carried to absolute extremes and this extremism is

---

[81] Saunders, *Sarah Kane and the Theatre of Extremes*, 54. For discussion of Lear see 58-63.

expressed in the plays' formal qualities. *Phaedra's Love*, though formally less complex than *Blasted* or *Cleansed* works with the conventions of Classical tragedy.

Kane's version of the Phaedra myth, has two principle points of interest. First, as noted above, in the description of the play, Kane's decision to stage violent acts which in Greek and Roman theatre would traditionally have been reported rather than performed, results in a spectacle of traumatic viscerality. Second, Kane's rewriting of Hippolytus adds a new dimension to the mythic narrative of obsession and desire usually centred on Phaedra. As Kane intended to retain "the classical concerns of Greek theatre"—"love, hate, death, revenge, suicide"[82]—notably all violent, the question of tragedy's supposed cathartic function inevitably arises.

Both these modifications to the formal and thematic elements of the Phaedra myth seem to undo an Aristotelian description of tragedy as the performance of deeds of seriousness and magnitude with the intention of "arousing fear and pity" in order "to accomplish [...] catharsis of such emotions."[83] The emotions stirred up by the play are largely the result of the concluding spectacle. However, *Phaedra's Love* deliberately pursues visual excess to terrible and absurd lengths, with a view to trauma rather than a safe cathecting of unhealthy or intense emotion.

The thematics of desire and emotion also comment ironically upon the role of feeling and catharsis. Through the characters Kane explores extreme emotions and their release in a manner which departs from traditional treatments of the myth. In Seneca's *Phaedra* Kane found Hippolytus "unattractive for someone supposed to be so pure and puritanical" and decided that "the way to make him attractive is to make him unattractive but with the puritanism inverted."[84] Hippolytus's

---

[82] Sierz, *In-Yer-Face Theatre*, 109.

[83] Aristotle, *Poetics* trans. Ingram Bywater (New York: Random House, 1954) 230.

[84] Kane, interview with Nils Tabert qtd. Saunders, *Sarah Kane and the Theatre of Extremes*, 73

absolutism is recast as a depressive's uncompromising, and at times bleakly humorous, pursuit of honesty and true feeling.

Self destructive desire, states of despair, and the symmetry of Phaedra and Hippolytus's plights, structure the play. It is not a little ironic that while Phaedra feels too much, she is in the grip of an emotion she "[c]an't switch [...] off. Can't crush" (71), Hippolytus feels too little. In his cosseted world of privilege, Hippolytus may have anything he wants, but can identify nothing for which he might feel desire. Phaedra's inexorable pursuit of her misanthropic stepson results predictably in her abject self-annihilation. Phaedra repeatedly describes her desire for Hippolytus as burning—"You burn me" (84) she tells him. This emotional experience is, after her suicide, translated into a physical one when her body is burnt on a pyre. Phaedra's surfeit of illogical, clichéd, feeling for her stepson haemorrhages into suicidal numbness when she is rejected.

In contrast, Hippolytus only begins to feel in relation to the prospect of his own destruction. In his depressive state he indulges in excessive consumption—of junk food and of sex— with neither pleasure nor satisfaction. The ultimate experience of his life is paradoxically his own mutilation and death. The very organs he has overused and abused with indifference (his genitals and stomach), are those which are violently taken from him. Whereas Ian in *Blasted* is metaphorically castrated, Hippolytus is literally castrated in another of Kane's outrageously impossible scenes. As Hippolytus is emptied out physically, he is conversely filled with ecstatic feeling—as an uncanny body and negated self, he is ironically most fulfilled.

Similarly in *Cleansed*, Kane refines the staging of excessive states in a manner which extends what she had begun in *Blasted*. The desire to possess another permanently or to identify completely with another—fundamentally self-deceptive and self-destructive obsessions—is translated into vivid spectacles of torture. Alluding to the influence of Roland Barthes's *A Lover's Discourse* on her variations on the theme of love in *Cleansed*, Kane describes love without boundaries as "a kind of madness."[85] Specifically, she refers on a number of occasions to how she was particularly struck by Barthes's analogy between the position of a rejected lover and a concentration camp prisoner:

> When you love obsessively, you do lose yourself. [...] It can completely destroy you. And very obviously concentration camps are about dehumanising people before they are killed. I wanted to raise some questions about these two extremes and apparently different situations.[86]

Cleansed also formally and thematically cites Georg Büchner's *Woyzeck*, George Orwell's *Nineteen Eighty-Four* and, to a lesser extent, August Strindberg's *The Ghost Sonata*. Kane was interested in the way Büchner's scenes might be organised in various patterns. *Cleansed* is composed of scenes which are, to a considerable degree, independent units arranged according to a loose sequential pattern. Echoes of *The Ghost Sonata* might be discovered in the colour-coding of interior spaces each with a specific meaning. For instance, in addition to the round room or library and the muddy outdoor spaces, the room in which torture occurs is red, the space of sexual voyeurism is black, and the room where operations take place is white. As Saunders notes, Strindberg's "use of rooms as places of discovery and revelation for characters constitutes a form of ongoing journey or pilgrimage [... and is] an important motif in later expressionist theatre."[87]

Arguably *Cleansed* is Kane's most expressionist work, utilising many of the techniques described by Innes cited above including associative imagery, discontinuous scenes, the stripping back of conventional characterisation, and in

---

85 Kane, interview with Nils Tabert qtd. in Saunders, *Sarah Kane and the Theatre of Extremes*, 93.

86 Kate Stratton, "Extreme Measures," *Time Out* 25 Mar.-1 Apr. 1998, qtd. in Saunders, *Sarah Kane and the Theatre of Extremes*, 93, Sierz, *In-Yer-Face Theatre*, 116

87 Saunders, *Sarah Kane and the Theatre of Extremes*, 94-95.

particular the use of anti-mimetic strategies which tend towards the "artificial, exaggerated and rhetorical."[88] Like *Blasted*, the play is driven formally by the surreal logic of a traumatic dream. The adoption of expressionist strategies of representation which determine characterisation and dramatic structure, however, is clearly more pronounced in *Cleansed*. Here, Kane hones a non-linear form, comprised of numerous visually intense short tableau-like scenes which deliberately prevent the audience from "calm[ing] down."[89] Dialogue is minimal, while the oscillation between peculiarly sentimental and tender love scenes and graphic physical torture promotes a keen sense of representational instability. As a result of this strategy, Kane empties out conventional characterisation or development, and to borrow from Murphy, "the individual figures frequently become a [mere] montage of separate characteristics or an amalgam of roles, rather than a complete individual with whom the audience might identify."[90] As director of the first production of *Cleansed*, James McDonald, observes, it "removes the psychological signposts and social geography that you get in the Great British Play."[91] What remains is a play of synthetic fragments which as one reviewer remarked "accumulate" rather than "unfold."[92]

Cleansed explores love as madness by translating the figurative into the literal and making the body the site of trauma. The theme of self loss is played out from different perspectives. The imbalance between the first couple, Rod and Carl is clear from the beginning. While Carl's desire is for possession, to fix (even institutionalise) the relationship through the symbolic exchange of rings and vows, Rod will

---

88 Innes, *Avant Garde Theatre 1892-1992*, 43.

89 Dan Rebellato, "Brief Encounter Platform," interview with Sarah Kane, Royal Holloway College, London 3 Nov. 1998 qtd. in Saunders, *Sarah Kane and the Theatre of Extremes*, 88.

90 Murphy, *Theorizing the Avant-Garde*, 18-19.

91 James Christopher, "Rat with Hand Exits Stage Left," *Independent* 4 May 1998: 6-7.

92 Susannah Clapp, *Observer*, 10 May 1998: 13.

only make promises for the present: "I love you *now*. I'm with you *now*. I'll do my best, moment to moment, not to betray you. Now. That's it. No more. Don't make me lie to you" (111). In the surreal space of Tinker's "institution," Carl's absolute vow of loyalty is tested through grotesque physical torture and effectively leads to his mutilation and Rod's self-sacrifice. Following his betrayal of Rod, Carl is forced to "eat his words" by swallowing the rings and each time he attempts to express his love he loses the part of his body he has used.

Similarly with the Grace Graham couple, loss of self is mapped on the body. In a vivid play of negation, Graham the absent object of Grace's desire is rendered present through imitation and self annihilation. Grace wishes her body "look[ed] like it feels. Graham outside like Graham inside" (126). Grace "becomes one" with her brother/lover only by becoming other to her self, through the erasure of her identity, first by wearing his clothes, then by undergoing a lobotomy and rudimentary sex change. Ironically, Tinker's "saving" of Grace in fact is the destroying of her—her memory and her sex. The emotional pain of love is rendered physical, and though acts of physical torture in the play require stylisation (and indeed were heavily stylised in the original production), they retain their shocking effect.

In each of the plays discussed, sensory excess and radical negation of self in desire is distant from an Artaudian interest in ritual or magic; rather they seem a good deal more proximate to a poetics of negation to be found in the work of contemporary authors like Kathy Acker. The fetishised spectacle of self-mutilation, critiqued by Ravenhill in *Faust is Dead*, surfaces in Kane's work as a problematic metaphor for an experience of traumatic alterity that is extended in her last plays.

The Erosion of Character

It is hardly astonishing that the formal shift in her later work was greeted with relief among critics, given the unrelenting intensity of what went before. *Crave* marks a move away from the physicality of the earlier plays towards explicitly interior, psychological spaces. The linguistic aesthetic of *Crave* in particular and, to a lesser extent, *4.48 Psychosis* was welcomed for its poetic qualities. Voigts-Virchow notes how critics complained of the failure of Kane's first three plays to make their violent spectacles meaningful, to provide recognisable context and characters or to make her intentions clear, yet he emphasises "*Crave* might be rejected on similar grounds—world not recognisable, pointless, no social observation or real people."[93] Nevertheless, the difference in reception was marked. While *Crave* and *4.48 Psychosis* are ambiguous and deal with harrowing psychic states, they also share recognisable aspects of modernist literature, and some familiar elements of contemporary confessional monologue. There is a disintegrative quality to these plays evoked in their key formal techniques: the erosion of character and citation of other texts. Consistent with Kane's interest in form and content correlations, both elements are significant in relation to subjectivity and alterity.

Kane's progressive questioning and dismantling of modern conventions of character, contrasts with the vast majority of playwrights working in the UK or Ireland today. In this respect her work again bears the influences of earlier experimental dramatists—notably Samuel Beckett, to name but the most obvious of her admired dramatists. Simultaneously, this tendency in her work may also be connected with the performance of ontological uncertainty which marks postmodern theatre. As Kane was not only a playwright who was astutely theatre-literate but also highly articulate with regard to what she believed her project as a writer was, it is perhaps inevitable that among her attacks on dramatic convention, unified character is one of her principle targets. This is not to say that the subject vanishes as character is eroded in the plays, rather Kane advances towards a painfully

---

[93] Voigts-Virchow, "Sarah Kane, a Late Modernist," 210.

obsessive focus upon subjects in crisis, making and unmaking multiple and contradictory selves through language. While each of the plays might be read as steps towards the full erosion of character, not merely in the sense of dramatic figures but also in ontological terms where meaning seems on the verge of collapse, it is in *Crave* and *4.48 Psychosis* that collapse predominates.

The extent to which character is significant and the ways in which it signifies are heavily dependent on historical and cultural context. As Fuchs writes:

> each epoch of character representation—that is, each substantial change in the way character is represented on the stage and major shift in the relationship of character to other elements of dramatic construction or theatrical presentation—constitutes at the same time the manifestation of a change in the larger culture concerning the perception of self and the relations of self and world. "Character" is a word that stands in for the entire human chain of representation and reception that theatre links together.[94]

She goes on to explore the ways in which alternative theatre in the latter half of the twentieth century has questioned the viability of the pretence of unified character in an age typified by heterogenous, nonunified views of self,[95] and concludes that "in the modern period, demonstrating that character no longer offers the spectator ontological assurance, but embodies and unsolvable ontological problem."[96]

Fuchs's contextualising of the notion of character is useful in that it is revelatory of what is at stake in Kane's last plays. Certainly her work has an affinity with this final state of instability. Her emptying out of character results in subject positions which are increasingly in flux or in states of psychic disintegration, and also increasingly difficult to discuss in terms

[94] Fuchs, *The Death of Character*, 8.
[95] Fuchs, *The Death of Character*, 9.
[96] Fuchs, *The Death of Character*, 34.

of character at all. In addition, the turn from the subject as physical spectacle to the subject as textual or linguistic spectacle tends in a complex manner towards fragmentation and, especially in *Crave*, extensive citation.

Apart from Beckett, an important contemporary influence upon Kane's work was Martin Crimp's *Attempts on Her Life* (1997). Both Sierz and Saunders connect Kane's later plays with the formal innovation of this work. Structured around seventeen various scenarios, Crimp's play is essentially a performance text which designates neither fixed speakers nor a particular number of actors. Heiner Zimmermann analyses the play using Hans-Thies Lehmann's term "postdramatic theatre,"[97] and indeed a number of the characteristics of "postdramatic theatre" are in evidence in *Crave* and *4.48 Psychosis*. These include the erosion of the conventions of character, the preference for monologue or blocks of speech in place of dialogue, the jettisoning of causally structured narrative, self-referentiality and so on.[98]

Like Crimp's *Attempts on Her Life*, *Crave* is described as "more as a text for performance than as a play;"[99] in both *Crave* and *4.48 Psychosis*, the conventions of character are dismantled through the play of rhythmic, at times poetic, speech. Any pretence of external reality vanishes, giving way to structurally open and polysemic performance texts which incorporate a variety of citations. *Crave*'s four speakers, designated merely by letters, return compulsively to dislocated memories, fragments of stories and volleys of conversation which may or may not concern the other speakers. With regard to the letter designations for the speakers Kane states:

---

[97] Heiner Zimmermann, "Martin Crimp, *Attempts on Her Life*: Postdramatic, Postmodern, Satiric?" *(Dis)Continuities: Trends and Traditions in Contemporary Theatre and Drama in English*, CDE 9, eds. Margarete Rubik and Elke Mettinger-Schartmann, 106.

[98] See Hans-Thies Lehmann, *Postdramatic Theatre*, trans. Karen Jürs-Munby (1999; London and New York: Routledge, 2006).

[99] Kane qtd. in Saunders, *Sarah Kane and the Theatre of Extremes*, 17.

To me A was always an older man. M was always an older woman. B was always a younger man and C was always a young woman [...]. A, B, C and M do have specific meanings [...]. A is many things which is The Author, Abuser (because they're the same thing Author and Abuser); Aleister—as in Aleister Crowley who wrote some interesting books [...] and Antichrist. [...] It was also the actor who I originally wrote it for who's called Andrew. M was simply Mother, B was Boy and C was Child, but I didn't want to write those things down because then I thought they'd get fixed in these things forever and nothing would ever change.[100]

Certainly any sustained reading of *Crave* in terms of these more specific meanings becomes either overly simplistic or remains fragmented. The figures A, B, C and M tell various and increasingly fragmented and inconsistent stories which are then denied or cast into doubt with the result that subject positions are destabilised. In striking contrast to the earlier plays, traumatic or painful events are suggested (child abuse, rape, betrayal, broken relationships) but are always approached tangentially and recede again amid the layers of voices. As reviewer Christine Evans observes,

the mode of speech alternates between reverie and dialogue, which is written as a rhythmic interplay on certain speech motifs rather than conventional dramatic interaction. There are suggested pathways of exchange but relationships are hinted at rather than developed: dialogue functions as collision, which spins the solitary balls back into their own orbits.[101]

The first production of the play in which the actors sat in a row facing the audience, front lit on a bare stage, visually reinforced this sense, as well as the play's debt to Beckett. However, it

---

[100] Kane, interview with Dan Rebellato qtd. in Saunders, *Sarah Kane and the Theatre of Extremes*, 104.

[101] Christine Evans, "Surface Tension in New York Theatre," *Real Time Arts* 41 (2000) <http://www.realtimearts.net/rt41/evans.html>.

must be noted that the absence of stage directions leaves the arrangement of the stage up to the director.

The play opens with C's line "You're dead to me" (155). Throughout, C appears to be on the verge of a breakdown provoked by some traumatic event in her past. She claims, "I am here to remember. I need to […] remember. I have this grief and I don't know why" (171). At various points she presents herself as deserted lover (158), sexually abused child (158), rape victim (178), child who has witnessed domestic violence (179), a mother who has lost her children (178). This plethora of possible traumas is accompanied by a similarly excessive list of symptoms (that effectually cancel each other) ranging from a terror of death, a longing to die, self disgust, anorexia, bulimia, extreme emotional neediness and anger. Though less overtly, the other voices are similarly marked by lack and desire. M claims to be "the kind of woman about whom people say Who *was* that woman?" (165). She longs for love—"If love would come" (160, 166) is repeated twice—but by the end of the play seems to reject the prospect—"Couldn't love you less" (194). B is the most flippant, but the most confused, speaker as the line "okay, I was, okay, I was, okay okay. I was, okay, two people, right?" (163) suggests. B appears to be careless and faithless, rejecting M's advances and her wish to have a child (167, 171, 172), though by the play's conclusion the locus of power between M and B has shifted and finally B too admits to self disgust (173), asking to be raped (199) and later killed (200). A's status seems determined by his striking claim at the beginning of the play—"I'm not a rapist […] I'm a paedophile" (156)—yet it is A who delivers the longest, most romantic, and vulnerable declaration of love (169-170). All four figures, as the play's title suggests, are shaped by unfulfilled cravings.

A number of thematic clusters are scattered through *Crave*, yet these are deliberately disassociated from fixed character positions and are played out from different perspectives in a number of fragmented reported scenarios. These include: that of an older woman who wants to conceive; the sexual assault of a child; a man who is serially unfaithful; a ruptured relationship; someone who is suicidally depressed; and someone in search of their mother. In particular, the mother references threaded through the play demonstrate the ambiguity and instability of perspective. C introduces this chain of associations:

> C: Somewhere outside the city, I told my mother, You're dead to me. […]
> C: Three summers ago I was bereaved. No one died but I lost my mother. (155)

The thread is reintroduced repeatedly in the course of the play:

> B: You could be my mother.
> M: I'm not your mother. (168)
>
> C: You could be my mother.
> M: I'm not your mother. (173)
> M: I could be your mother.
> B: You're not my mother. (182)
>
> C: You killed my mother.
> A: She was already dead. (184)
>
> M: Grow up and stop blaming mother. (191)
>
> C: You're not my mother. (196)

The quest for mother, or mothering, and the recovery of a place of origin inscribed in the maternal, as these lines demonstrate, is continuously denied.

The play also punctuated by stories that suggest particular lines of flight or significations for the exchanges that surround them. A introduces most of these beginning with the disturbing fragment about "a small dark girl" in a parked car with her grandfather and father, who is about to be sexually abused (157-8). C responds violently to this story as if she were the little girl. She interjects: "I feel nothing, nothing," and it seems she is the one who "has been hurtling away from that moment ever since (158). Nevertheless, both these responses are recycled in the play in different contexts—before this episode B similarly chants "I feel nothing, nothing" (156) and, much later, A likewise describes hurtling away from a moment of grief (177). A goes on to tell stories about a bus driver who has a mental breakdown (158), an American woman and a Spanish man who misunderstand one another (160), a little boy with an imaginary friend (163), a little girl terrified by her parents' violent arguments (185). Significantly, these fragments, unlike the first shocking story, are not taken to refer to the experiences or histories of the other figures.

The dubious quality of such narratives, memories or reminiscences is illustrated also in the stories told by M, C and B. M remembers how she "ran through the poppy field at the back of [her] grandfather's farm" and interrupted her grandparents kissing, only to indicate that this happened to her mother not to her (159). C remembers being raped by "a handsome blond fourteen year old" at the age of six (176). B tells of how although he has never broken it, his nose looks broken because his body remembers his father's smashed nose, even though this is "genetically impossible (162). When M relates how "a psychic predicted that [she] would not get on this flight but that [her] lover would. The plane would crash and he would be killed." Her dilemma—whether abandon her lover to his fate or to break the prophecy by boarding the apparently doomed plane—is short circuited. A asks "what did you do?" and M replies "begin again" (176). This equivocal response subverts a sense of narrative closure, there is no answer to the dilemma or attempt to authenticate the experience. It may refer to M's course of action, or equally may be an instruction to the other figures to begin a new narrative— which is precisely what C does.

Lurking behind *Crave*'s poetic repetitions, clipped exchanges and fragmented narratives is the suggestion that these four figures may also be, as Voigts-Vichow puts it, "splintered voices of a single consciousness. As M comments in typical autoreflexive fashion: 'You stop thinking of yourself as I, you think of we'."[102] This is reinforced by C's claim: "I am an emotional plagiarist, stealing other people's pain, subsuming it into my own" (195). Like Freud's hysterics, Kane's figure(s) then "suffer mainly from reminiscences."[103] The latent hysteria of each of the voices radically challenges efforts to establish the truth of experience histrionically presented. Various possible scenes of primal trauma or disturbance are offered but, as the above description reveals, they are consistently undermined. As Elisabeth Bronfen maintains, "hysteric symptoms are overdetermined, excessive, exaggerated precisely because they weld together several syntactically unconnected, psychic moments."[104] In this sense *Crave* might be seen to stage the hysterical split subject whose inherently theatrical symptoms are "not determined by a mysterious trauma then, but by an inarticulable desire continuously displaced."[105]

This sense of inarticulable, impossible desire is also of feature of *4.48 Psychosis* which dispenses with fixed speakers entirely. Saunders notes the structural similarity the play bears to Crimp's *Attempts on Her Life*, "bringing together a myriad of unidentified and unnumbered voices."[106] Kane claimed that she wished the play to approximate,

> what happens to a person's mind when the barriers which distinguish between reality and different forms of imagination completely disappear, so that you no longer know the difference between your waking life and your dream life. And

[102] Voigts-Virchow, "Sarah Kane, a Late Modernist," 212.

[103] Sigmund Freud, and Joseph Breuer, *Studies on Hysteria 1893-95, Project for a Scientific Psychology*, standard edition, vol. 1 (London: Hogarth 1966) 7.

[104] Elisabeth Bronfen, *The Knotted Subject: Hysteria and its Discontents* (Princeton NJ: Princeton University Press, 1998) 33.

[105] Paul Verhaeghe, *Does the Woman Exist? From Freud's Hysteric to Lacan's Feminine*, trans. Marc du Ry (London: Robus, 1997) 15.

[106] Saunders, *Sarah Kane and the Theatre of Extremes*, 111.

you no longer know where you stop, and where the world
starts.[107]

This abject state, dramatised in her final work in a play of
voices of despair, perhaps best expresses a form of radical
alterity where the subject effectively cannot distinguish
between self and other. The text is an assemblage of possible
doctor patient dialogues, diary monologues, strings of
numbers, lists of medications and their effects, lists of verbs and
questions. Like C in *Crave*, the voice bemoans the fact that s/he
"love[s] a person who does not exist" (215). The convolutions of
a desire to be loved and self hatred conclude in projection: "I
think that you think of me the way I'd have you think of me"
(243). Such statements suggest an affinity with Lacan's
description of love,

> as a specular mirage [… as] essentially deception. It is situated
> in the field established at the level of the pleasure reference, of
> that sole signifier necessary to introduce a perspective centred
> on the Ideal point, capital I, placed somewhere in the Other,
> from which the Other sees me, in the form I like to be seen.[108]

Ironically "4.48 the happy hour when clarity visits" (242) is the
moment of self-annihilation, the vanishing point of the self,
which the voice invites one to watch (244).

Both *Crave* and *4.48 Psychosis* turn upon the experiential
qualities of mental, rather than physical, anguish. Though the
formal contrast to the earlier plays is clear, the later work shares
an engagement with the notion of spectacle but it is a theatrics
turned inward. Deploying a "versatile histrionics" these plays
sustain a public performance of private traumas,[109] which aligns
them with tendencies in postmodern performance, though this
affiliation is questioned by some of Kane's interpreters.

---

[107] Kane, interview with Dan Rebellato qtd. in Saunders, *Sarah Kane and the Theatre of Extremes*, 111-112.

[108] Lacan, *The Four Fundamental Concepts*, 268.

[109] Bronfen, *The Knotted Subject*, xii.

Lost in Citation?

In addition to its spectacular and experiential dimensions, Kane's theatre also depends upon strategies of appropriation. The plays are formally highly self-aware and often playful: *Blasted*'s naturalism is literally blown up mid-play; in *Phaedra's Love* classical tragedy inverted as a gory spectacle of excess; *Cleansed* is a collage of expressionist and Artaudian scenarios; *Crave* and *4.48 Psychosis* pay tribute to Beckettian drama.[110]

Crave most obviously and extensively is structured by textual reference that is significant to the notion of radical alterity in her work. Both Saunders and Voigts-Virchow explore Kane's use of allusion and in particular her use of the text that dominates *Crave*—T.S. Eliot's *The Waste Land*. As has often been noted, certain lines of the poem such as "Hurry up please its time" and "Give, sympathise, control" are directly quoted and "In the mountains, there you feel free" is translated back into German.[111] If as Saunders states "*The Waste Land* is [...] very much the precursor for the twentieth century preoccupation with intertextuality"[112] then Kane incorporates this core modernist poem, along with references to the work of Beckett, the Bible, and other texts into a dense jumble of semi-identifiable allusions in which every statement made by the four voices seems to suggest an antecedent text. These are sometimes humorously adopted as for example:

    C: You've fallen in love with someone who doesn't exist.
    A: Tragedy.
    B: Really.
    M: Oh yes.
    A: What do you want?

---

[110] See Voigts-Virchow, who notes that the "reduced individualities" of *Crave* may be traced back to Beckett's *Act Without Words*. "Sarah Kane, a Late Modernist," 210-11.

[111] See Saunders, *Sarah Kane and the Theatre of Extremes*, 103-105. Voigts-Virchow also provides a detailed discussion of these references and includes a list of the allusions in *Crave* at the end of his essay.

[112] Saunders, *Sarah Kane and the Theatre of Extremes*, 103.

C: To die.
B: To sleep.
M: No more. (158)

Though *Hamlet* is never mentioned, the ghostly presence at the beginning of the segment and, as Voigts-Vichow points out, "the keyword 'tragedy' triggers off a tragic literary cliché."[113] Simultaneously, though, the reference is comic—tracing in miniature Hamlet's destiny and concluding with a double meaning. "No more" is both a fragment of the original text, but also an interruption, forcefully calling a halt to the "literary cliché." Other references such as the Biblical one: "But God has blessed me with the mark of Cain" (195), are ironically metatextual. For Voigts-Virchow the literariness of *Crave* distinguishes it as a late modernist rather than postmodernist text, primarily because of its "foregrounding language in the best tradition of modernism and the modernist equivalents in academia, formalism and New Criticism"[114] made explicit by A: "don't forget that poetry is language for its own sake. Don't forget when different words are sanctioned, other attitudes required" (199). Yet *Crave* is, I would argue, more that just a homage to *The Waste Land* or *Act Without Words*. Kane's recycling of texts stages a crisis of representation and identity that has a signification distinct from the modernism of Eliot or Beckett. Voigts-Vichow is right to describe *Crave* as "a forceful statement on behalf of an 'adversary culture' against stale cynicist posturing as well as against insularity, ephemerality, and anti-intellectualism."[115] But it is a statement that is both a product of these conditions and a rejection of them. Taking Kane's work as a whole (with its techniques of montage, fragmentation and citation), like its expressionist forebears, "takes up [the] experiential complex of alienation and decentring not as an abstraction, a literary topos or describable

---

[113] Voigts-Virchow, "Sarah Kane, a Late Modernist," 211.
[114] Voigts-Virchow, "Sarah Kane, a Late Modernist," 212.
[115] Voigts-Virchow, "Sarah Kane, a Late Modernist," 216.

'content'—such as the way that the 'theme' of 'dehumanisation' is frequently treated in modernism—but as an unavoidable *effect* of the [...] text which the reader is made to experience at first hand."[116]

Absolutes & Instabilities

While the instability of contemporary subjectivity is at the heart of Kane's work, it is shadowed by a recurrent and challenging absolutism. This lies in the structures of metaphor and metonymy inherent to the plays. For example, despite her claim, cited above, that *Blasted* is amoral, on the contrary it follows a very clear, if problematic, logic, reminiscent of the preachiness of Edward Bond in the sixties. Kane herself has described this as follows: "The logical conclusion of the attitude that produces an isolated rape in England is the rape camps in Bosnia, and the logical conclusion to the way society expects men to behave is war."[117] In *Phaedra's Love*, Hippolytus's traditional purity is translated into a commitment to an absolute honesty that is brutally destructive of all the play's characters. In *Cleansed*, as Sierz describes,

> Grace and Graham represent the fantasy of incestuous identity-sharing twins [a configuration also used, interestingly, by Marina Carr in *Portia Coughlan*]; Carl and Rod are the classic couple, one member of which is idealistic, the other realistic; Tinker and the dancer represent domination and alienated love; Grace and Robin experience a teacher and pupil, mother and child rapport.[118]

The limits of honesty, faithfulness and love are metonymically presented as madness, torture and mutilation. While the analogy made by Barthes and retrieved by Kane between the experience of a concentration camp and that of a rejected lover is provocative in the extreme and, however figurative, is not a

---

[116] Murphy, *Theorizing the Avant-Garde*, 17-18.
[117] Kane qtd. in Sierz, *In-Yer-Face Theatre*, 104.
[118] Sierz, *In-Yer-Face Theatre*, 114.

little objectionable. Her claims that the play is basically a positive message about love must be balanced against the overarching sense that absolute truth is to be found only in trauma. This truth is reiterated with a greater despair in *Crave* and *4.49 Psychosis*, both of which conclude in what seems to be, within the playwright's world view, a necessary and inexorable free fall into abnegation.

If Kane's commitment is to the cathartic function of art, then the unifying characteristic of her drama is an engagement with radical alterity, and an attempt to encode these experiences in "truthful" forms. A species of absolutist fatalism differentiates her work from the tentative ethics of Conor McPherson, or the moralist tendencies of Mark Ravenhill, but arguably surfaces, albeit in a different costume, in the tragedies of Marina Carr.

Marina Carr
Nostalgia for Destiny

> We repeah an' we repeah, th'orchestration may be different but
> the tune is allas tha same.[1]

If Irish literature has laid claim to a substantial list of world
renowned playwrights then it is a list that boasts few, and more
often no, women's names. In the 1990s Marina Carr stepped
into this breach to become perhaps the most widely known and
most successful female dramatist to emerge in Ireland in
decades. So far her work has fallen into a number of stages. The
earlier plays—*Low in the Dark* (1989), *The Deer's Surrender* (1990),
This Love Thing (1991) and *Ullaloo* (1991)—are strongly
influenced by avant garde experimentalism, the absurd and
feminism. Of this group only *Low in the Dark* exists in print.
Carr has distanced herself from these plays and in critical terms
they seem fated to be regarded principally as juvenilia, youthful
experiments on the road to a more mature dramatic oeuvre.
Carr's subsequent work includes *The Mai* (Abbey/Peacock, 5
October 1994), *Portia Coughlan* (Abbey/Peacock, 27 March 1996;
Royal Court 1996), *By the Bog of Cats...* (Abbey, 7 October 1998),
On Raftery's Hill (Town Hall Theatre Galway, 9 May 2000; Royal
Court 4 July 2000), *Ariel* (Abbey, 2002) and *Woman and Scarecrow*
(Royal Court, 2006).[2] The plays from *The Mai* to *By the Bog of*

---

[1] Marina Carr, *The Mai* (Meath: Gallery, 1995) 23.
[2] Marina Carr, *The Mai* (Meath: Gallery, 1995), *Portia Coughlan* (Meath: Gallery,
1996), *By the Bog of Cats...* (Meath: Gallery, 1998), *On Raftery's Hill* (Meath:

Cats... constitute a second stage in Carr's drama, marking a radical departure from the kind of experimental abstraction and feminism of her earlier work, and are formally largely a return to familiar well-worn dramatic modes. The staging of this more recent work has often been impressively imaginative, while the plays themselves draw upon more conservative, traditional theatre genres and regularly allude to Classical and Shakespearean sources. The references to Beckettian theatre of the earlier work have been almost entirely purged, as has the overtly satirical feminism and gender destabilisation of plays like *Low in the Dark* or *Ullaloo*. Finally, *On Raftery's Hill*, *Ariel* and *Woman and Scarecrow* while maintaining tragic themes and structures, depart from the pattern of self destructive heroines, and open onto an unevenly non-naturalistic treatment of broader questions of incest, corruption, human failing and death.

Like Sarah Kane, Carr has been championed by older, well-established playwrights—Frank McGuinness and Tom Mac Intyre, in particular. In contrast to Kane however, her work has never provoked such savage critical responses. Even if they share a good deal of subject matter, formally Carr remains firmly within the bounds of dramatic theatre. While a few dissenting opinions have been voiced, they are markedly few. Indeed, generally, Carr has won acclaim for her dramatic representations of female figures "most of whose aspirations do not sit easily in the context of Irish cultural norms,"[3] and this, to a great extent, has been popularly interpreted as an effort to "unsilence" women's voices on the stage. More importantly, her attention to narrative, her rich use of language and dialect, and her choice of rural settings arguably to situate her as the contemporary heir to a Syngean legacy. Beyond this, her commitment to tragedy, myth, the supernatural and the exploration of extreme emotions are identifiable as central

Gallery, 2000), *Ariel* (Meath: Gallery, 2002). All quotations from the plays will be taken from these editions and will be cited in-text.

3   David Nowlan, *Irish Times* 6 Oct. 1994: 12.

characteristics of her plays since *The Mai*. Although Michael Billington found *Ariel* to be "thematically overloaded," significantly he argued that the play "confirms Carr's status as a writer who, in an age of ironic detachment, believes in the possibility of tragedy."[4] These elements obviously set her work apart from the In-Yer-Face cohort and yet it might fairly be claimed that Carr, on her own terms, also pursues the notion of an experiential theatre of shocking images and powerful emotions. Like Kane, she seems dedicated to accessing truth via an extreme and often non-naturalistic theatre, although there the similarity between their work ends.

In comparison to the majority of new playwrights of the same period, Carr's work has attracted substantial critical attention. A number of routes have been taken by commentators. Early studies focused upon Carr's first plays and their absurdist, feminist tendencies. Some have examined the plays in terms of Irish theatre and its preoccupations with memory and storytelling (shaping the past into a narrative). Others have approached her work in a social context as an expression of post-colonial anxieties in contemporary Ireland. Furthermore, the publication in 2003 of the first collection of critical essays on Carr, *The Theatre of Marina Carr: "Before Rules was Made,"* consequently broadened the scope of available interpretations considerably.[5]

Among the earliest discussions of Carr is that of Anthony Roche, who discusses *The Mai* in conjunction with J.M. Synge's *The Shadow of the Glen* and Teresa Deevy's *Katie Roche* and has likens the role of Grandma Fraochlán in Carr's play to that of the tramp in Synge's. For him, "Marina Carr is among those who have restored the storyteller's perspective to the drama," [6]

---

4 Michael Billington, rev. of *Ariel*, by Marina Carr, *Guardian* 5 Oct. 2002 (online).
5 Cathy Leeney and Anna McMullan, eds., *The Theatre of Marina Carr: "Before Rules was Made"* (Dublin: Carysfort, 2003).
6 Anthony Roche, "Women on the Threshold: J.M. Synge's *The Shadow of the Glen*, Teresa Deevy's *Katie Roche* and Marina Carr's *The Mai*," *Irish University Review* 25.1 (1995): 160.

a mantle since taken on by Conor McPherson. Concentrating on the matter of narrative perspective in *The Mai*, Donald Morse explores the staging of memory and the ambivalence of the narrator, Millie.[7] Both essays interpret the play in relation to enduring concerns in the context of Irish theatre—the familiar territory of storytelling and the deceptive nature of memory. Frank McGuinness, a great patron of Carr, is not far from this traditional approach in his introduction to *The Dazzling Dark: New Irish Plays* (1996) when he writes, of her being "haunted by memories," although significantly he remarks upon Carr's use of tragic destiny.[8] Indeed her subsequent plays have revealed an increasing mythologising of these narratives.

Both Anna McMullan and Christopher Murray refer to absurdist and avant garde tendencies in Carr's earlier work.[9] Although this line of investigation has dwindled given the direction Carr's work has since taken, arguably *Woman and Scarecrow* marks a return to some of the more experimental dimensions of her first plays. In contrast, several more politicised interpretations have also emerged. Bruce Stewart describes *By the Bog of Cats...* as a triumph of Irish cultural atavism. He reads the play not as tragedy of an individual, but as a political statement viewing the play's principal figure, Hester, as:

> a proxy for the political violence upon which the Irish state was founded and which is now in process of being jettisoned as we move from rurally-based Catholic nationalism towards civic

---

7 Donald E. Morse, "Sleepwalkers Along a Precipice: Staging Memory in Marina Carr's *The Mai,*" *Hungarian Journal of English and American Studies* 2.2 (1996): 111-22.

8 Frank McGuinness ed., *The Dazzling Dark: New Irish Plays* (London: Faber and Faber, 1996) ix.

9 Anna McMullan, "Irish Women Playwrights since 1958," *British and Irish Women Dramatists since 1958: A Critical Handbook*, eds. Trevor R. Griffiths and Margaret Llewellyn-Jones (London and New York: Open University Press, 1993) 118. Christopher Murray, *Twentieth Century Irish Drama: Mirror up to Nation* (Manchester: Manchester University Press, 1997) 235-38.

ways of feeling more appropriate to the cosmopolitan attainments of the Celtic Tiger.[10]

Stewart's observations on the political implications and background of Carr's play resonate with those expressed in more detail by Victor Merriman who also interprets the protagonist of this play as illustrative of aspects of Irishness which must be purged in order to attain a new formulation of cultural identity.[11] He concludes that Carr's *By the Bog of Cats...* and McDonagh's "Leenane Trilogy" celebrate a "spurious post-coloniality" which counter productively serves to "negate the interrogation of conditions in which such images are produced and have their points of reference."[12] The post-colonial implications of Stewart's piece are rendered explicit in Merriman's, where theory seems to be brandished to chastise these playwrights for their regressive portrayals of Ireland. Merriman modifies his tone in a later article on Carr in *The Theatre of Marina Carr* and devotes greater space to analysis of some of the plays, however, he maintains a critical stance towards *Portia Coughlan* and *By the Bog of Cats...* on the basis that they function merely as spectacle, an idea that will be pursued further below. Returning to the political, he emphasises the necessity of questioning "the meaning of these representations as constitutive events in the evolution of civil society."[13]

Mária Kurdi also has taken post-colonial theory into account in her approach to Carr, but her focus is primarily upon female subjectivity and the role of gender in the plays. She concludes that Carr's "achievement can best be called a kind of re-

[10] Bruce Stewart, "'A Fatal Excess' at the Heart of Irish Atavism," *IASIL Newsletter* 5.1 (1999): 1.

[11] Victor Merriman "Decolonisation Postponed: The Theatre of Tiger Trash," *Irish University Review* 29.2 (1999): 305-307.

[12] Merriman, "Decolonisation Postponed," 305, 317.

[13] Merriman, "'Poetry Shite': A Postcolonial Reading of Portia Coughlan and Hester Swayne [sic]," *The Theatre of Marina Carr*, 152.

familiarisation with the needs and concerns haunting the Irish female sensibility on its way to a fuller self-recognition."[14]

Meanwhile Melissa Sihra returns the critical focus to the shared territory between Carr and Synge—"the restlessness, the darkness of the vision and the carnivalesque, almost absurd consciousness that slowly accumulates."[15] She reads *By the Bog of Cats...* in terms of its mythic dimensions and "within the rich legacy of a century of Irish theatre. The works of Synge, Yeats, Beckett, Friel and McGuinness continue to hold dialogue, and Carr adds a new voice to their conversation on the human condition."[16]

Evidently, the tendency for Carr's work to be interpreted rather narrowly in relation to Ireland, or as representative of Irish social concerns can be problematic and often reductive. Contributions to *The Theatre of Marina Carr* begin to remedy this bias with pieces by directors and observations on Carr's work from alternative perspectives. Commenting on the nature of Carr's drama, Dominic Dromgoole remarks that having been nurtured by the Abbey, she is perhaps too influenced by a particular Abbey style which he ironically sums up as "high, literary, sorrowful, washed by water and weeping women."[17] Dromgoole's perspective may sacrifice accuracy on the altar of provocation, but still raises a valid point with regard to the boundaries she appears to have set herself. It is this issue and the aesthetic and theoretical positions that inform it I find most worthy of further investigation.

If the weaknesses of Carr's drama as debated by critics and academics have been largely attributed to a failure to accurately represent current Irish society, its strengths are ascribed

---

14 Mária Kurdi, *Codes and Masks: Aspects of Identity in Contemporary Irish Plays in an Intercultural Context* (Frankfurt: Peter Lang, 2000) 71.

15 Eamonn Jordan, Introduction, *Theatre Stuff: Critical Essays on Contemporary Irish Theatre* (Dublin: Carysfort, 2000) xxxii.

16 Melissa Sihra, "A Cautionary Tale: Marina Carr's *By the Bog of Cats...*," *Theatre Stuff*, 267.

17 Dominic Dromgoole, *The Full Room An A-Z of Contemporary Playwriting* (London: Methuen, 2002) 48.

primarily to its engagement with eternal and essential dilemmas through tragic forms. The notion of destiny, allusion to myth and folktale and a harsh version of midland speech permeate Carr's writing to such a degree that in many respects it hardly seems of the contemporary world at all. But her drama is still a product of the late twentieth century and, despite appearances to the contrary, is informed by that context. This chapter examines how Carr's work in the 1990s can be seen to problematically recall a discourse of authenticity in a postmodern context. In particular, I will focus on the modalities of citation, destiny and desire, to argue that the tensions between these elements can to a large extent be read as the tensions between nostalgia and a desire for authenticity.

Nostalgic Frames of Reference

The significance attributed to the "Irishness" of Carr's work may be seen as symptomatic of wider concerns regarding theatre in and from Ireland, some of which have been discussed and questioned in previous chapters in relation to the work of Martin McDonagh and Conor McPherson. Nevertheless, Ireland's realities (and unrealities) have radically changed since the mid-1990s to the extent that now the nation's post-coloniality appears to be overlaid, or at least interwoven, with a kind of postmodernity that has destabilised notions of national identity. The narratives of progress, success and inflation which have been apparently structuring a "New Ireland" are powerful, but equivocal. If globalisation has brought to Ireland the inescapability of information technology and consumer culture accompanied by the disintegration of the familiar narratives of identity, then the question remains of how contemporary theatre is responding to these realities. Jordan poses some salient questions about today's drama—asking "what are our playwrights peddling? […] what is the standing of contemporary writing practice?" and concludes with a pertinent, if unanswerable, question—"How do you write about the present?"[18]

Each of these enquiries has provocative implications; playwrights as part of consumer culture must have something to sell and products are marketed. If, on one hand, a kind of "Buy Irish" spin is put on some of the work competing for attention in London and elsewhere, on the other, these products are often (over)interpreted as being representative of dilemmas of Irish identity. This dynamic can been seen in responses to plays by writers like McPherson; it is also a dynamic that has been very fruitfully exploited by McDonagh.

Moreover, the work is also being evaluated by audiences and readers who, given the contradictory fragmentation and homogenisation of postmodern culture in the developed world, may well understand the product or, indeed, the "us" Jordan's enquiries assume, in an unforeseen manner. Kevin Barry's anxieties regarding McDonagh's work might be interpreted in this environment. The familiar elements of "real" Irish theatre—the sovereignty of language, storytelling, frequent recourse to myth and folklore—have brought considerable international success to a number of Irish playwrights, but also generate some frustration. Playwright and director Declan Hughes voices this forcefully:

> Too often when I go to the theatre, I feel like I've stepped into a time capsule: even plays supposed to be set in the present seem burdened by the compulsion to … well, in the narrowest sense, be Irish […]. Irish drama needs to show more guts: the guts to stop flaunting its ancestry, to understand that the relentless dependence on tradition collapses inevitably into cannibalism. The village will eat itself.[19]

What Hughes decries, to some degree, is Irish theatre's tendency towards self-citation and a kind of nostalgia, which he

---

[18] Jordan, Introduction, *Theatre Stuff*, xiii-xiv, xlviii.

[19] Declan Hughes, "Who The Hell Do We Think We Still Are? Reflections on Irish Theatre and Identity," *Theatre Stuff*, 13.

envisions as, ultimately, cannibalistic. This is not necessarily a "new" response—see for example Tom Murphy's memories of how Noel O'Donoghue and he collaborated on their first play, *On The Outside*, in 1962.[20] The issue, for Hughes among others, is not

> that people don't live in the country any more, or that rural life isn't "valuable"; it's that culturally, it's played out [...] culturally we persist in defining ourselves by the ethnic, the pastoral (and that qualified form, the tragic pastoral).[21]

The tendency to privilege certain cultural definitions and formal reliance upon particular dramatic traditions is ongoing and is in striking contrast not only with the changes in Irish society in the last thirty years, but also with many of the experiments, innovations and trends in theatre and performance in the last sixty. In order to explore why this is the case and by implication, what role Carr might play in this scene, one first needs to interrogate how concepts of "Irishness" can be entangled with notions of value and authenticity.

In *Deconstructing Ireland*, Colin Graham traces some of the dynamics of concepts of authenticity both in general and as they pertain to Ireland. He remarks how, in many respects, as colonial domination was displaced, the definition of the authentically Irish became central to claims for value.[22] "Irishness" is still, in multiple sometimes contradictory ways, conceived of as what might be called a "marketable sign of

---

[20] Murphy recalls a now famous exchange with O'Donoghue, the tone of which is replicated in Hughes and others: "'O'Donoghue said to me, 'Why don't you write a play?' I said, 'What would we write about?' And he said, 'one thing is fucking sure, it's not going to be set in a kitchen.' That was the most progressive thing anybody had ever said to me." In David Murphy, ed., *Education and the Arts: A Research Report* (Dublin: Department of Higher Education and Educational Research Trinity College, 1987) 173.

[21] Hughes, "Who The Hell Do We Think We Still Are?" 12.

[22] Colin Graham, *Deconstructing Ireland: Identity, Theory, Culture* (Edinburgh: Edinburgh University Press, 2001) 132.

value," but one which also needs supplementary commentary.[23] Unlike Martin McDonagh's "Leenane Trilogy" which deploys "Irishness" in an ironic, comic fashion, the "Irishness" of Carr's work is essentially serious. Nevertheless, both the stereotypes that tend to be satirised by McDonagh, and those commented upon in Carr's plays have solicited critical attention along the axis of authentic and inauthentic identities and representations.

The language of authenticity, as has often been noted, inevitably involves the privileging certain qualities and, explicitly or implicitly, excluding others.[24] One of the primary modes of asserting and authorising authenticity is the citation of origins, although, as Graham observes, this relationship is ambiguous since it relies upon antiquity to guarantee its value but at the same time mystifies or mythologies that history.[25] These "origins" can never be definitively located or dissected; in the same manner as authenticity itself necessarily eludes absolute definition. This coupling of the drive towards self-legitimating referentiality with the mystification of sources is integral to the machinations of authenticity and is evident in much of Carr's drama and in her published comments on playwriting.

The modalities of authenticity and nostalgia in postmodernity have obviously been subject to extended debate; most readily one might note Fredric Jameson's anxieties about what he refers to as "the waning of affect" and the effacement of history,[26] or Jean Baudrillard's speculations on the loss of reality in a postmodern order of simulacra, as have been discussed elsewhere in this work. In the midst of postmodern

---

[23] For further discussion of the need for essence and the authentic to be explicated see Graham, *Deconstructing Ireland*, 133.

[24] One might refer here to Theodor Adorno's conceptualisation of authenticity as a jargonised system, see Theodor Adorno, *The Jargon of Authenticity* (1964; London: Routledge, 1986) 5.

[25] Graham, *Deconstructing Ireland*, 137.

[26] Fredric Jameson, "Postmodernism, or the Cultural Logic of Late Capitalism," *Postmodernism A Reader*, ed. Thomas Docherty (New York: Harvester Wheatsheaf, 1993) 69-78.

insecurity, proliferation of information and apparent amnesia, authenticity may no longer be the measure of value, but reveals a need for value, which it then fulfils. As Baudrillard argues, authenticity might be thought to simulate what is lacking or lay claim to legitimacy through "retro." It (re)produces origins and in a circular movement (re)produces itself so that:

> When the real is no longer what it used to be, nostalgia assumes its full meaning. There is a proliferation of myths of origin and signs of reality; of second-hand truth, objectivity and authenticity.[27]

Nostalgic modes, then, proliferate at all levels of contemporary culture to the extent that it seems that oxymoronically, nostalgia is the future. Evidently, this transforms cultural practices and products—one striking example being the popularity of the remake, in which a cultural entity is made again, often in more convincingly authentic style than the original which then, in a further gesture of doubling, is judged by the standards of the reproduction.[28]

Theatre in Ireland has adopted the remake, more respectfully referred to as the adaptation, with gusto. Brian Friel's "translations" of plays by Anton Chekhov, for instance, illustrate a particularly complex mesh of relations between authenticity and simulation. In fact, Friel's "translations" are worked from the existing English translations of the plays, which are then transposed to an Irish cultural context and idiom generally deemed (among many Irish theatre critics at least) a more authentic version of Chekhov than had existed previously (the old versions being in a standard English considered colonial and non-Irish). Perhaps more striking and more specifically of relevance to reading Carr is contemporary

---

[27] Jean Baudrillard, *Simulations*, trans. Paul Foss, Paul Patton and Philip Beitchman (New York: Semiotext(e), 1983) 12-13.

[28] Jameson devotes considerable attention to the significance of the remake to reading/viewing practices. See "Postmodernism, or the Cultural Logic of Late Capitalism," *Postmodernism A Reader*, 76.

Irish theatre's penchant for classical theatre. Marianne McDonald offers an impressive list of over thirty adaptations of Greek tragedy since 1984 produced by some of Ireland's best known writers.[29] While McDonald argues that this phenomenon is a result of colonial oppression and that Greek tragedy being the "epitome of civilisation" is a suitable vehicle for a "literature of protest,"[30] such a diagnosis fails to engage with the aesthetic implications of such referencing practices.

Indeed, this may be another dimension to Hughes's provocative indictment. The "time capsule" of Irish drama is (re)produced through the citation of signs of "ancestry" and these are not restricted to Irish traditions alone. Nostalgia and simulacra interact to produce a kind of neo-primitivist reflex action which gives weight and meaning to their products. Undoubtedly, Hughes's comments are not applicable to all theatre in Ireland; certainly he has his own agenda which involves producing a more "real" and contemporary theatre. Nonetheless, the criticism and the agenda still lead back to the core issue of authenticity and its operations in a postmodern context.

Performing Authenticity

In the following sections some of these theoretical issues will be unpacked in relation to Carr and her work. As the role played by commodification in the making of Carr's image is quite marked, space will be afforded not only to analysis of the plays but also how Carr's public persona has developed through interviews and speeches.

Accessible, printed interviews with Carr are few. However, her statements on writing, on theatre and on her beliefs are revealing. In a lecture given at the Peacock Theatre in 1997

---

29 Marianne McDonald, "Classics as Celtic Firebrand: Greek Tragedy, Irish Playwrights and Colonialism," *Theatre Stuff*, 16.
30 McDonald, "Classics as Celtic Firebrand," 17, 16.

entitled "Dealing with the Dead,"[31] subsequently printed in *Irish University Review*, Carr relates some of her attitudes about creativity, in the form of reverent speculations on "great dead writers." In this piece Carr's approach relies quite explicitly upon strategies of glorification and mystification of "genius." The writers she discusses (Homer, Keats, Dickenson, Ibsen, and Shakespeare) take on an heroically untouchable status; "They are the poet god's children, Apollo's favourites, Apollo's golden offspring," "Apollo's darlings," "Apollo's royals."[32] She asserts that,

> there are the royal writers and then the rest of us who write. The royal writers—their ink is supplied from the blue veins of God, from the lyre strings of Orpheus, from the well spring of another world. The rest of us are not aware of that inkwell or are dimly aware or are struggling very hard to hear those sounds.[33]

Predictably Shakespeare tops the bill: "Apollo gave him so much that I think he grew jealous and decided never to do that again and ever since has fed the rest of us on scraps."[34] What is in evidence in these statements is peculiarly anachronistic; an almost Kantian notion of genius, that is the genius as "no product of history [but] a gift of nature."[35] There is a double movement in the logic of creativity here, which on one hand attempts (however hesitantly or humbly) to claim a literary heritage—the writer struggles hard to hear the "lyre stings of Orpheus"—while on the other, depicts it as unattainable—the "well spring of another world" is one which most writers may not draw from, or in the wake of Shakespeare's genius, may only pick through the leftovers. As an aesthetic stance, Carr

---

[31] Marina Carr, "Dealing With the Dead," *Irish University Review* 28.1 (1998): 190-196.

[32] Carr, "Dealing With the Dead," 190, 194.

[33] Carr, "Dealing With the Dead," 190.

[34] Carr, "Dealing With the Dead," 195-6.

[35] David Cook, "The Last Days of Liberalism," *Postmodernism: A Reader*, 124.

distances herself from most of the twentieth century, and expresses a desire "to return to an old and simple division, that of prose and poetry."[36] Interestingly coming from a dramatist, this reversion erases theatre writing from the equation entirely.

In an essay on *By the Bog of Cats…*, Melissa Sihra cites how, "as information technology, global systems and genetic manipulation rapidly transform contemporary reality Carr ponders over 'this anti-heroic age [where] the all consuming intellectual pursuit seems to be that of de-mystification'."[37] The contradiction inherent in the stress upon "old and simple" and the desire for the complexity of mystification stands as a nostalgic sleight of hand which refuses resolution, and is part of the structure of the concept of the authentic at work here. The repeated invocation of Apollo suggests a compulsion, if not to return to a point origin—the myth cradle of Western civilisation—to reproduce and thus repossess it. If Apollo, as an authentic source, authorises genuine creative talent to his "favourites," then, according to the exclusionary logic which sustains authenticity, those not in favour must be labouring under a delusive and inauthentic creativity.

When speaking specifically on theatre Carr emphasises her belief that plays are primarily texts, and should be read and treated as texts.[38] Her favoured dramatists are those whom she locates on Apollo's side of the "old and simple division":

> In the theatre too there are poets […] and there are prose writers […]. The ones who interest me are the poets of the theatre: Chekhov, Ibsen, Tennessee Williams, Wilde, Beckett and of course the king himself—Mr Shakespeare.[39]

She regretfully remarks how "theatre seems to have been demoted […]. Plays are not read anymore and hardly ever

---

36 Carr, "Dealing With the Dead," 194-5.
37 Melissa Sihra, "A Cautionary Tale," 265.
38 See Eileen Battersby interview with and article on Carr, "Marina of the Midlands," *Irish Times* 4 May 2000 and "Dealing with the Dead."
39 Carr, "Dealing With the Dead," 194-5.

reviewed. Performances are, of course, but that is an entirely different discipline to that of the art of playwriting."[40] Carr's avocation of plays as text hence diminishes the role of performance in play making; a gesture which it may be argued, is a foundational element of what defines theatre as theatre. More recently in an interview with Mike Murphy in the RTÉ series *Reading the Future*, she speaks of theatre with continuing pessimism:

> People don't believe in things anymore. They go to the theatre and they want two episodes of a soap opera. They don't want to be told about a ghost. They don't want anything that isn't like a Kodak instamatic photograph, and that's one of the things that infuriates me about the theatre. The worst thing they can say about you is that it's not believable. But the yardstick is frighteningly limited, and to work within those parameters is impossible for any writer who is on a journey, or who is trying to figure out what we're here for.[41]

Here theatre, drama and playwright are conflated and viewed nostalgically as a single dying art which is being suffocated, in part, by technology. Carr's stress upon a textual base is not surprising however. As Anna McMullan has noted, Irish theatre of the last century is usually understood as a history of dramatic texts.[42] Similarly, Caoimhe McAvinchey points out the incongruence between the "high level of visceral stimulation"[43] that audiences expect from other media such as the internet, television and film, and the techniques and structures of most contemporary theatre produced in Ireland, which have remained largely static. McAvinchey notes "directors like Peter Brook, Robert Wilson and Elizabeth le Compte have shattered

---

[40] Carr, "Dealing With the Dead," 194.

[41] Marina Carr, "Reading the Future: Irish Writers in Conversation with Mike Murphy" <www.rte.ie/radio/readingthefuture/carr.html>.

[42] Anna McMullan, "Reclaiming Performance: The Contemporary Irish Independent Theatre Sector," *The State of Play: Irish Theatre in the 'Nineties*, ed. Eberhard Bort (Trier: Wissenschaftlicher Verlag Trier, 1996) 30.

[43] Caoimhe McAvinchey, "Theatre—Act or Place?" 85.

the mould of audience expectations," but in Ireland their methods are "rarely seen [...] as a possible alternative, exciting and successful approach."[44] Although Carr opposes what she seems to posit as an audience demand for realism—soap opera and photography—to the fantastical—"They don't want to be told about a ghost," the opposition elides a multitude of other variants explored by theatre practitioners in the twentieth century.

The other issue which emerges with clarity is how Carr sees her role as a writer. In a statement ripe with (one hopes unintended) ambivalence, Frank McGuinness has described Carr as "a writer haunted by memories she could not possibly possess."[45] Eminent in her statements in the various pieces quoted here, is her belief in the supernatural and to some extent the inevitable—creativity and inspiration are other-worldly, theatre has been in her blood since she was a child and she claims to believe, in some sense, in angels, ghosts and banshees. Ghosts and banshees, like the art of playwriting, are remnants of a cultural heritage which is waning:

> The culture believes in ghosts, certainly in the country. The banshee was a huge thing [...]. In the city everything is forgotten now, everything is homogenised, and all of this seems so remote, but to me it's not remote it's entirely natural. I'm a great believer in the whole angel thing, I don't know what I believe in, but I do believe in something.[46]

The author's role in "trying to figure out what we're here for" introduces an important ontological dimension. Ghosts, banshees, angels are seen to be part of a culture of belief that is non-urban, non-modern and, above all, natural to the writer. These beliefs, which have largely been dismissed or forgotten in the modern age, are reinstated by Carr as valuable to an

---

[44] McAvinchey, "Theatre—Act or Place?" 85.

[45] McGuinness, *The Dazzling Dark*, ix.

[46] Marina Carr, "Reading the Future: Irish Writers in Conversation with Mike Murphy" <www.rte.ie/radio/readingthefuture/carr.html>.

understanding of identity and furnish the severe alternative world of her drama.

The combined force of Carr's explicit and implicit appeals to tradition the supernatural, and the natural, are evidently enmeshed in a web of connotation. Stereotype is an important aspect of this. Tom Kilroy notes the persistence of stereotypes of the Irish writer—usually as outspoken, alcoholic, male, inspired rather than intelligent, a cliché, incidentally, performed in full by Martin McDonagh and, in part, by Conor McPherson. Carr's public image is most recognisable in the last characteristic quality he mentions—the writer as "un-tutored, natural genius and Irish writing as a pure natural flow of words."[47] Carr herself is partly responsible for the doggedness of such stereotypes. A striking illustration is, for instance, to be found in her descriptions of poetic or lyrical writing as typically Irish:

> How we tell a story is so important. It is not the facts we are looking for, it is the details, the embellishments. I think that most Irish people know how to tell a story instinctively and to tell it well.[48]

"Writing in Greek": Tragedy, Destiny & Uncertainty

Carr's drama is notable for the ways in which she draws upon certain sources. If in her earlier plays the influence of Beckett, the absurd and feminism dominated, then from *The Mai, Portia Coughlan* and *By the Bog of Cats…*, she turns to a different set of references with differing significations. The propensity to citation as a means of authentication in her drama has far reaching implications. As she says herself with respect to Shakespeare,

> He took from everywhere, but what he did with his plunder! And this points up something else about all these great dead writers. It seems that you are allowed to steal what you need

---

[47] Tom Kilroy, "A Generation of Playwrights," *Theatre Stuff*, 7.
[48] Marina Carr, interview, *Rage and Reason: Women Playwrights on Playwriting*, eds. Heidi Stephenson and Natasha Langridge (London: Methuen, 1997) 149.

while learning the craft and that there is no crime in that. The crime would be to diminish or desecrate what you have stolen.[49]

Citation creeps in here as inevitable, but it is also a duplicitous process which fails to preserve pristine original signs. Rather, as Jacques Derrida has observed, "the possibility of extraction and citational grafting [...] belongs to the structure of every mark spoken or written" and that every sign may function "cut off, at a certain point, from its 'original' meaning and from its belonging to a saturable and constraining context."[50] Though Carr's ideas on "great dead writers" and genius/genesis, seem to fit poorly with the notion of the floating signifier, in her writing the slippery nature of origins is constantly present.

Citations surface in Carr's drama in a number of ways, in particular how she inflects of generic aspects of tragedy in *The Mai, Portia Coughlan* and *By the Bog of Cats…*will be explored in detail. In an effusive programme note to *By the Bog of Cats…* Frank McGuinness ponders Carr's approach to tragedy: "I wonder what Marina Carr believes? I think it might be the Greek gods—Zeus and Hera, Pallas Athena. She knows what the Greeks know."[51] In reality, her interest in "the Greek idea of destiny and fate and little escape"[52] has taken shape in these plays through a much less mystical than complexly intertextual process.

The term tragedy can only be understood as both hybrid and heterogeneous. Definitions have given rise to as many dilemmas as they propose to resolve. The foundational Aristotelian prescription is perhaps the most appropriate point of departure:

---

[49] Carr, "Dealing With the Dead," 196.

[50] Jacques Derrida, "Signature Event Context," *Margins of Philosophy*, trans. Alan Bass (Chicago: University of Chicago Press, 1982) 320.

[51] McGuinness, "Writing in Greek: *By the Bog of Cats…*," Programme Note: Abbey Theatre, 1998, in *The Theatre of Marina Carr: "Before Rules was Made,"* 87.

[52] James F. Clarity, "A Playwright's Post-Beckett Period," *New York Times* 3 Nov 1994: C23.

> A tragedy, then, is the imitation of an action that is serious and also, as having magnitude, complete in itself; in language with pleasurable accessories, each kind brought in separately in parts of the work; in a dramatic, not in a narrative form; with incidents arousing fear and pity, wherewith to accomplish its catharsis of such emotions.[53]

Subsequent definitions have usually reiterated, reinterpreted or recycled some aspects of this early one, while tailoring it to fit the drama of other periods or, modifying it to focus upon the desired effect upon the audience rather than the formal constituents. Walter Kaufmann's description is illustrative of this tendency; he describes tragedy as:

> a form of literature that presents a symbolic action as performed by actors and moves into the centre immense human suffering in such a way that it brings to our minds our own forgotten and repressed sorrows as well as those of our kin and humanity, releasing us with some sense that suffering is universal—not a mere accident in our experience, that courage and endurance in suffering or nobility in despair are admirable—not ridiculous—and usually also that fates worse than our own can be experienced as exhilarating.[54]

Carr's plays do not adhere to any single definition nor do they replicate Classical or Elizabethan tragic drama. Rather her recent work incorporates fragments of different formulations and (mis)understandings of tragedy and the tragic, assembled from various sources. Her use of tragedy, therefore, is complex, simultaneously drawing upon retrospective elements as well as highly contemporary ones. The principle elements in the three plays that will be explored here include strong character development in particular in terms of the figure of tragic heroine in each play; a thematics driven by heightened emotion

---

[53] Aristotle, *Poetics*, trans. Ingram Bywater (New York: Random House, 1954) 230.
[54] Walter Kaufmann, *Tragedy and Philosophy* (New York: Doubleday/Anchor, 1969) 98.

and extreme situations; narratives reinforced through repetition; a persistent emphasis on heredity as destiny; fables and stories which serve to provide a meta-commentary on the theme of destiny in each play; and finally heightened significance achieved through a mythologised sense of place and stigmatic naming of characters. But before turning to a close reading of the plays, some theories of tragedy of relevance to Carr's work will be briefly discussed in an attempt to clarify what "writing in Greek" as McGuinness puts it, could possibly imply.

McGuinness's and Carr's references to Greek and Shakespearean dramatic forms appear to assume a stable meaning for tragedy as form and in content, yet as already mentioned it is clearly a term with intensely cohesive *and* divisive potential. One might ask if tragedy can still be written in a post-sacral age. If so, what are the elements of this contemporary incarnation of tragedy and what are some of its significations? These questions, debated by Friedrich Nietzsche, George Steiner and Raymond Williams, continue to be negotiated, as recent texts by John Orr, Richard Kuhns and William Storm indicate.[55] If the question of tragedy is broached from the relative perspectives of Nietzsche and Steiner, the diagnosis for its contemporary viability, is bleak. For Nietzsche, Attic tragedy was the product of a duality, the tension between Apollo and Dionysus:

> Apollo embodies the transcendent genius of the *principium individuationis*, through him alone it is possible to achieve redemption in illusion. The mystical jubilation of Dionysos, on

---

55 John Orr, *Tragic Drama and Modern Society: Studies in Social and Literary Theory of Drama from 1870 to the Present* (London: Macmillan, 1981); Richard Kuhns, *Tragedy: Contradiction and Repression* (Chicago: University of Chicago Press, 1991); William Storm, *After Dionysus: A Theory of the Tragic* (Ithaca: Cornell University Press, 1998).

the other hand, breaks the spell of individuation and opens a
path to the maternal womb of being.[56]

However, the spirit of tragedy has been eroded by the
emergence of Platonic rationalism which has denigrated the
mythic world and deceptive arts.[57] The centrality of the
individual and the individualism at the root of the idea of the
tragic hero, have for Nietzsche overwhelmed Dionysiac ritual
which enables a "mystical experience of the collective."[58]
Similarly, for Steiner, "the decline of tragedy is inseparably
related to the decline of the organic world view and its
attendant context of mythological, symbolic, and ritual
reference."[59] Yet, while these death knells have been sounded,
neither theory can adequately account for tragedy's continued
force and sporadic regeneration.

Indeed, Raymond Williams has attempted to deal with this
regeneration in *Modern Tragedy* (1966), and many of his remarks
are highly relevant to the work of Marina Carr. Williams notes
that discourse concerning tragedy tends to assume a tradition
which is conceived of as continuous, but has, in fact, been
continuously chameleonic. Twentieth century readings of
Greek tragedy tend to psychologise a form, although an
individualised "tragic hero" did not clearly exist in Attic drama.
However, the desire to unify tradition has lead to "the
assumption of a common Graeco-Christian tradition which has
shaped Western civilisation."[60] The powerful illusion of cultural
continuity, of "Hellenes and Christians, in a common activity"[61]
is, therefore, particularly attractive, as has been evidenced
perhaps most strikingly in contemporary Irish theatre by Brian

---

[56] Friedrich Nietzsche, *The Birth of Tragedy*, trans. Francis Golffing (New York:
Doubleday/Anchor, 1956) 97.

[57] Nietzsche, *The Birth of Tragedy*, 86.

[58] Nietzsche, *The Birth of Tragedy*, 22.

[59] George Steiner, *The Death of Tragedy* (Oxford: Oxford University Press, 1961)
292.

[60] Raymond Williams, *Modern Tragedy* (London: Chatto and Windus, 1966) 16.

[61] Williams, *Modern Tragedy*, 15-16.

Friel's *Translations*. To a degree it would appear that this is the "illusion" on which Carr's engagement with tragedy is founded. "The Greek idea of destiny and fate and little escape" she has remarked upon is fascinating not because of a shared Greek sense of the meaning of Fate, but because of the evocation of origin. The spectre of *Medea* haunting *By the Bog of Cats…* bears witness to what Stewart refers to as an atavistic urge. But this urge is directed, not primarily towards a narrowly defined Irish cultural or historical past, but towards a legitimising connection with moral values and dilemmas understood as part of a tradition of tragic drama.

For Williams, at the very core of modern tragedy is an experience of "irreparable loss" which supersedes an adherence to any set of Aristotelian edicts, themselves far from consistent. In the development of this tragedy the conceptualisation of the tragic hero and notions of fate or destiny are of key significance along with a lessening concern for dramatic formalism. The figure of the tragic hero is one which has, of course, mutated considerably over the centuries. According to Williams, in modern drama, this figure is characteristically marked by social isolation rather than by social rank or nobility, a creature who ultimately "desires and eats and fights alone." Life is a matter of "tense and cruel struggles" ending, predictably, in death. Society is of arbitrary significance, love and destruction are inevitably fused. Fate is blind, detached from either divinity or mythology. Inheritance is naturally tainted. Tragedy from this perspective is, as Williams puts it, "in the bloodstream" and inevitable. [62] It is important to recognise that this tragic mode is not a return to antiquity—ritual, order and destiny are clearly reconfigured and signify differently. It is this modern version of tragedy, which comes filtered through playwrights such as August Strindberg and, more importantly, Eugene O'Neill, and stands at quite a remove from Greek ideas of fate or destiny that has had most influence over Carr's work. One might

---

[62] Williams, *Modern Tragedy*, 106, 107, 114.

especially remark upon her adoption of this isolated, alienated hero(ine) and the idea of tainted or poisoned heredity as central features of her latest plays.

However, in *Tragic Drama and Modern Society* (1981), John Orr takes issue with Williams's assertion of a historical movement from social to personal drama in modern tragedy. Rather he asserts there are "changes in theme where new forms of social mediation replace older ones as a means of expressing that alienation in theatrical performance."[63] Orr's reconsideration of Williams's model for the development of modern tragedy introduces a more complex notion of the figure of the contemporary tragic hero. Alienation and irreparable loss take on a multidimensional character. In this frame we might consider Carr's heroines as estranged from the predominant values of their societies and differentiated on the basis of gender, but their experiences of irreparable loss must be understood in the context of a conflict involving the self and desire. Moreover, the female tragic figure is an eminently twentieth century mediation of the experience of alienation as are the questions of selfhood raised in the plays. Thus, Carr's drama while being formally conservative brings to that form a psychological and social dimension which, to some extent, must reinterpret this form for the present context.

William Storm's *After Dionysus: A Theory of the Tragic* (1998) further clarifies and links notions of tragedy as dramatic form and as subject. He emphasises the necessity of differentiating between tragedy as genre, the tragic as an ahistorical ontological condition and tragic vision which refers to the extent to which this condition is felt or how it is expressed at a particular time and in a particular culture.[64] In doing so, *After Dionysus* returns to both Williams's focus on irreparable loss and to the Nietzschean concern with Dionysus. The assertion is that selfhood is fundamentally tragic. This condition of identity

---

63 Orr, *Tragic Drama and Modern Society*, xvi.
64 Storm, *After Dionysus*, 29.

is timeless although the mode in which it might be expressed may change. Storm suggests,

> what is represented in tragic drama is an experience of pure selfhood—and moreover, that the depicted self is the primary site of a Dionysian pattern of rift and separation that is the signature event in such representations.[65]

This is of direct relevance to the work in question. Carr's plays explore the territory of identity which can be regarded as twofold. The protagonists struggle to achieve a narrative unified self which is inevitably impossible. This conflict also involves a split between the individual and the society which has contributed to the formation of that individual. Storm sums up the tension determining tragic destiny (so evident in Carr's work) as follows:

> The dramatic character who aspires towards cohesive selfhood is, in tragic drama, directly connected to a field matrix of characters and action that will inevitably defeat that purpose. [...] At the same time as the field connotes an overall fabric of connection and unification, it produces an effect of rending and fragmentation. It is in this paradox, with its own Dionysiac character, that we find the clearest and most indelible stamp of the tragic field—and also the source for one of tragedy's more potent dialectics.[66]

If one compares *The Mai*, *Portia Coughlan* and *By the Bog of Cats…* with attention to the characterisation of the heroines and the notions of fate and destiny implied or stated in the plays, Carr's blending these multiple notions of tragedy and the tragic may be observed. Each of the plays gestures towards well-known models of the form. They incorporate the Aristotelian elements of *hamartia* and *catharsis*, draw upon the heritage of Shakespearean tragic heroes, as well as sharing a family

---

65 Storm, *After Dionysus*, 5.
66 Storm, *After Dionysus*, 116-17.

resemblance, to works by Ibsen, Strindberg and O'Neill. Carr's drama might be said to juxtapose Williams's tragedy "in the bloodstream," Orr's points on alienation and the psychological aspects of Storm's theory. In her assemblage of references and influences Carr produces a problematic contemporary tragedy and her heroines are subject to the paradox of a unified narrative or destiny which returns to and is founded upon fragmentation and lack.

In *The Mai*, the story of the eponymous heroine is narrated by her daughter Millie. At the play's opening, the Mai's husband, Robert, returns after a five year absence. Robert's absence in *The Mai* sets up a tantalising structural parallel, as a reversal of the Odysseus legend viewed from the perspective of Penelope. Robert/Odysseus's wanderings in the outside world are elided, what is of consequence is the life of anticipation and waiting experienced by the Mai/Penelope. As Penelope repeatedly weaves and unweaves her father's shroud in an effort to forestall suitors in the absence of her husband, so too the Mai's attempt to secure her identity as a wife involves a sewing metaphor. "[She] set about looking for that magic thread that would stitch us together again" says Millie, "and she found it at Owl Lake"(14). The house she has built, overlooking the lake, is a testament to her enduring belief that her errant spouse would return. Close on Robert's heels come various members of the Mai's family including her two sisters, her two maternal aunts and her maternal grandmother, all of whom provide commentary and "wisdom" on the nature of relationships between the sexes. Act two of the play, set a year later, repeats the encounters of act one with variations. Robert although still physically present in the family home, he has already embarked upon an affair with a local woman much to the Mai's dismay. Her family rallies round and attempt to console her, but the inevitable showdown and rupture take place. The Mai's suicide is dramatically revealed in a tableau scene at the end of the first act. The entire narrative is overlaid with Millie's memories concerning her parents and her own scarred life.[67] The two act structure of *The Mai* plays upon repetition which is further underscored by narrative devices such as Millie's recounting of the events of the two summers, of the legend of Owl Lake and Grandma Fraochlán's reminiscences which serve to produce an echo effect of the past in the present.

Portia Coughlan is also structured by echoes and return. Portia is haunted by memories of her twin brother, Gabriel, who drowned in the local river fifteen years previously. Carr, like Kane, uses the trope of "incestuous identity-sharing twins"[68] who have been tragically separated and cannot exist without one another. Act one opens on Portia's thirtieth birthday and follows the course of her day which unfolds as a series of encounters. She is visited by various members of her family, meets her lover Damus by the Belmont river, has a drink with her friend Stacia in the pub, meets the local barman Fintan on the riverbank and finishes the day with a vicious verbal attack on her well-meaning, but misguided, husband. However, more significant than Portia's disjointed series of actions is the sense that she is constantly conscious of Gabriel's ghostly presence and she fixates upon repetitious memories of him. Carr's shift here from the predominantly naturalistic mode of *The Mai* is signalled by the presence of the ghost on stage. This physical embodiment of the dead past is reinstated in *By the Bog of Cats…* and is congruent with the movement of these plays towards what might be tentatively referred to as mythical narratives. As in *The Mai*, the audience is made aware of the heroine's suicide mid-play, which lends the play a similar symmetry. Act two opens with Portia's drowned body being hoisted from the river and proceeds to depict an embittered post-funeral family scene. Act three returns to the day after Portia's birthday where Portia meets with the characters of act

---

67 See "'Sleepwalkers along a precipice' Staging Memory in Marina Carr's *The Mai*"; Morse discusses in detail the role of memory and Millie as narrator.
68 Aleks Sierz, *In-Yer-Face Theatre: British Theatre Today* (London: Faber and Faber, 2001) 114.

one again in a slightly different order and it is revealed by her aunt Maggie to Stacia that Portia's parents, Marianne and Sly are "also twins," or more precisely, half-brother and sister. The play concludes with another thwarted exchange between Portia and Raphael shadowed as ever by the oppressive memory of Gabriel.

By the Bog of Cats… differs in its adherence to linear chronology, but repetition is still a significant aspect of its structuring devices. The play traces the events of the last day in the life of Hester Swane, a tinker or traveller, who lives by the Bog of Cats. Carthage Kilbride, her former lover and father of her seven year old daughter, Josie, has abandoned her and is about to marry Caroline Cassidy, the daughter of a wealthy local farmer. Evidently, *By the Bog of Cats…* is already an echo, a reiteration of the Medea legend. In addition, as in *Portia Coughlan*, haunting plays a central role in Hester's tragedy. She is "haunted" by her own mother's unexplained departure from the bog, and implores a number of the other characters to remember and retell stories of her mother (also named Josie) to revive her fading and indeterminate memories. She insists on remaining by the bog to await her return. Moreover, Hester is literally haunted by the ghost of the brother whom she has murdered years previously. She unsuccessfully attempts to persuade Carthage to come back and resume their relationship. In act one Hester is warned repeatedly that she must leave or face dire consequences. These warnings take on the status of prophecy when delivered by her sibylline neighbour, the Catwoman. Act two follows the Carthage-Caroline wedding reception, an event marked by a strong visual repetition, with its curious proliferation of "brides." Besides the real bride, Caroline, in wedding attire and veil, Carthage's mother appears "in what looks extremely like a wedding dress, white, a white hat, with a bit of a veil trailing off it, white shoes, tights, bag, etc."(47). Young Josie attends wearing her communion outfit which also has a "veil, buckled shoes, handbag"(41) and which is, inevitably, all white. Hester finally and vengefully appears wearing a wedding gown bought for her by Carthage years previously, "veil, shoes, the works" (54). In the third act, in rage at being forced to leave her home, Hester terminates any possibilities of return by burning the house, farm animals and buildings. She is about to kill herself when young Josie enters and begs her mother not to leave her. Hester refuses to perpetuate the trauma of abandonment inflicted upon her by her own mother and slashes her daughter's throat and then, unlike Medea, cuts her own heart out before an audience of horrified neighbours.

It is evident when one regards each play's schema in this manner that Carr's tragedies depend heavily on the modalities of repetition for their structures and for dramatic impact. Her use of ghost figures, myth and repeated motifs focus a sense of claustrophobic constriction. The space given to "new" actions or patterns seems minimal and the role of the unexpected would appear to be deliberately undercut by Carr's mid-play revelations of the heroines' deaths in *The Mai* and *Portia Coughlan* and by her use of the Medea myth in *By the Bog of Cats*.... The characters' identities are greatly determined by their compulsion to return, to repeat the past, a compulsion which ultimately relates to a desire to control and order their destinies.

In the three plays this compulsion is marked by an obsessional relation to an ever receding other. The central characters recapitulate their various woes and wants and culminate in thanatotic capitulation. Carr's heroines are all mature women; the Mai is thirty nine and in the course of the second act "celebrates" her fortieth birthday, similarly Portia Coughlan's drama occurs on her thirtieth birthday and the day following, and Hester Swane is forty and the action of the play is set on her deathday. These characters are essentially conservative, wishing to evade new, perhaps unpredictable or uncontrollable experiences and favouring a return to a previous, often illusory state of affairs. Each is a mother and yet for each their offspring are not focal points of their desires or identities. Each is driven by an obsessional hunger which can, it seems, neither be controlled nor sated. Each struggles with a man in her life who is either absent or uncommitted. Each is bound by the legacy of the past.

In addition to the role of repetition, a number of the thematic strands are closely woven through the question of tragic destiny and closure in the plays. Among Carr's favoured themes are predestination or predeterminacy, heredity, illusion and choice. They are developed in various aspects of the drama, not least through Carr's use of names which becomes increasingly deliberate and meaningful from *The Mai* to *By the Bog of Cats...*, thus belying her growing tendency to underpin their narratives with mythology.

As in folkloric narrative traditions, names indicate character and bear multiple significances as stigma or stigmata. Characters, then, inhabit the role invoked by their names. For instance, in *The Mai* Grandma Fraochlán's name emerges as a cipher to a whole family's intricate and unfortunate history of (self) deception. The name is equivocal, functioning to anchor her amid all her flights of fancy to a place of origin and as an implicit reminder of the social stigma of her illegitimacy. "tha on'y bastard an Fraochlán in livin' memory" (60) is given the island's name in place of a father's name as a means of maintaining a façade of respectability or legitimacy. The name also facilitates a symbolic contraction rendering grandmother and island synonymous, both sites of origin, mapping the fertility of the woman (the *über* mother of the play) onto the land. This name with its various resonances encodes a history that mars the future generations of women in the play while men continue to be absent. Thus, the seed of the Mai's destiny is to be found in the name which marks her grandmother's identity.

The stigmatic quality of names is also in evidence in *Portia Coughlan.* "Portia" explicitly solicits references to choice and the act of choosing. This allusion to *The Merchant of Venice* is reinforced by the arrangement of characters in the play. Portia, a "lady richly left" has three "suitors" of importance: Gabriel, Raphael and Damus. Again the names are worth unravelling. Raphael, her husband who is a cripple, is named rather ironically after the archangel who in Hebrew legend personifies the power of healing. Gabriel, also shares the name of an archangel, though one associated with the manifestation of Divine justice and punishment. However, the play appears partially to reverse the relation between choosers and the chosen of *The Merchant of Venice*. Simultaneously, Portia's freedom remains ambivalent for whether she is marked as the predestined or chosen twin or is marked by a congenital abnormality is unclear. Whether Portia has chosen Gabriel or vice versa her bond with him is, it seems both her destiny and her torment.

In *By the Bog of Cats...* Carr's use of names as vehicles is carried further. The inferences solicited by the names of characters in the play are still more transparent. Hester Swane is doubly marked. Her life span is yoked with that of a black swan which also lives by the bog—"Swane means swan"(22) as her mother has declared. She objects to her own name, "What sourt of a name is Hester? Hester's after no wan"(61), thus stressing the necessity of genealogy, of a reference to make her name signify. Yet while "Hester" is severed from her immediate heredity of the bog, inevitably the name intertextually aligns her with Hawthorne's Hester Prynn of *The Scarlet Letter*, a fallen woman with an illegitimate child. Hester's scarlet letter will ultimately take the shape of her own heart, cut out of her chest in the play's final scene. Questions of legitimacy and naming also arise in regard to her daughter Josie. Josie is named after Hester's mother but her surname, is contested by her paternal grandmother. Josie straddles both identities and lineages, maternal and paternal, as both a Kilbride and a Swane. It is Carthage Kilbride, though, who bears a name which is excessively burdened with negative connotations, recalling Aeneas's fateful affair with Dido, queen of Carthage and her subsequent suicide. Carthage is as ill-fated as his namesake city—his precious possessions become a pyre, his child is slaughtered and the woman who ought to have been his bride (like Dido) kills herself. The echo of the word "carnage" in his name seems highly appropriate by the play's finale.

The stigma of names complements a concern for genealogy and the notion of heredity as destiny that is foregrounded in narrative terms by the testimonies of different generations of characters in the plays. In each the present is haunted by the past and seems determined by its spectral legacy. In *The Mai*, a span of four generations of women is represented. The oldest, Grandma Fraochlán, provides an archive of fantasies and far-fetched stories, passed on to her by her mother "The Duchess," many of which hinge upon her father's fluid identity; an exotic mysterious Spanish/Moroccan/Tunisian sailor. The proliferation of myths of origin to supplement "reality" is crucial to the course of the play. Grandma Fraochlán's difference is underlined not only by her refusal to be separated from an oar—a totem of her dead husband—but also by the language she uses, which is a curious mixture of heavily accented Donegal English tempered with the sentiments of popular romance. In addition, her frequent use of the word "sublime" is replete with associations with English Romanticism, and coupled with her opium habit, serves to align her with escapism and the imagination. Reared on (necessary) fantasies she perpetuates her own mother's flight from the mundane. But this flight from mundanity and, more precisely, stigma is not without consequence, for veiled anxiety about illegitimacy leads her to force her favourite daughter Ellen into a destructive marriage. In turn the Mai and her sisters Connie and Beck are all marked by their mother's premature death and their grandmother's idealisation of sexual carnality and passion over maternal love. Finally, the character Millie demonstrates the same deliberate retreat to fantasy with regard to her child's paternity, the same indifference to her offspring and the same bleakness about the possibility of ever breaking what is cast as a fixed cycle of tragedy.

Portia Coughlan similarly delineates a territory of corrupted relationships in which an atmosphere of foreclosure is conjured through genealogy. Not only does Carr's presentation of Belmont valley suggest a limited, rural and, above all, brutal world but the sub-plot of incest serves to heighten the sense of claustrophobia, violence and predeterminacy which dominate the characters' fates. As in *The Mai*, generations of characters appear on stage. Portia is the last in a three-generation line of poisoned marriages and her parents' hidden and inadvertent incest resurfaces like an hereditary disease. Portia associates her dead twin with her essence/origin. As proof she relates a fantasy memory of how they were "lovers" in their mother's womb and how they came into the world holding hands. Significantly, her mother Marianne's memory differs—Gabriel "came out of the womb clutchin' [Portia's] leg and he's still clutchin' it from wherever he is" (62). The echoes of the legend of Romulus and Remus, where twinship involves a struggle for dominance and ultimately survival, cast into doubt the authenticity of Portia's alternative version.

This thread of predeterminacy continues in *By the Bog of Cats…*, which further develops heredity as destiny in terms of poisoned, brutal and tragic "love" relationships. From the start the play is beset with bad omens. When Hester first appears, at dawn, dragging the corpse of a black swan, she meets her own death, in the form of the supernatural figure of the Ghost Fancier. The Ghost Fancier warns her of the bad luck incurred by interfering with swans, especially black ones. We later learn of the "curse" Josie Swane placed on Hester as an infant, committing her to the care of the black swan and binding their fates and life spans. The Ghost Fancier is, as he apologetically puts it, "too previous" (14), she will not die until dusk. Hence from the first act and scene Hester's destiny is foretold. Hester has been wandering the bog and has, albeit temporarily, abandoned her seven-year-old daughter, just as her mother, Josie Swane had done. When young Josie first appears she is singing a song about haunting the bog which we later learn is one of her grandmother's creations. Hester is psychologically scarred by her mother's negligence and unexplained disappearance. She is also, notably, stigmatised by her heredity, both as a traveller and as the daughter of such a malevolent member of the local community. Her hunger for security and fear of being abandoned again is reflected in the jealous and possessive nature of her relationships with Carthage and her daughter.

In addition to the significances of naming and heredity to Carr's dramatisation of her heroines' identities, tragic destiny is articulated through Carr's use of stories within each play. The folk tales of Owl Lake and the Belmont river facilitate a metonymic shift where the protagonists are doubled in other "fictions." In the former, an abandoned lover cries a lake of tears and drowns, in the latter a socially ostracised woman is punished by the community but is finally saved from suffering by the river god who revenges himself on the people with a flood. In both cases the characters of the Mai and Portia may be transposed to the roles of Coillte, in the story of Owl Lake, and the tortured woman of Belmont Valley, respectively. The multiple titles of the story of Owl Lake might suggest, as Donald Morse has noted, "an English misreading of the Irish name," but also perhaps a reiteration of the same story in different forms which reflects upon notions of heredity elsewhere in the play.[69]

The legend of Coillte echoes the Mai's hopeless pursuit of Robert. In the tale it is Coillte's "unnatural" impatience which leads to her demise. Her desire is contrary to natural order, (the seasons) and therefore destroys her. Similarly, the woman of Belmont valley is impaled because she is different, just as Portia is tortured by her special bond with Gabriel. Both women are "unnatural" and suffer as a result. The story is rich with sexual connotations; impaling, penetration, sex, torment. The riverbank has been the stage where much of Portia's sexual life

---

[69] Morse, "'Sleepwalkers along a precipice,'" 114.

has been played out. It is where she and Gabriel "made love all the time … from the age of five"(68), where they danced naked, where Portia first saw Raphael, where she has carried on her long-term affair with Damus, the affair which first ruptured her relationship with Gabriel, and where she chooses to meet Fintan. Like the woman of the legend, Portia is tormented, impaled upon her memories of Gabriel and just as the woman is carried off to a merciful death by the river, Portia seeks release in its waters.

Throughout *By the Bog of Cats…* Hester seeks the "story" of her mother which is revealed in fragments. She cannot wholly recall this narrative alone, but desperately needs it to define her own identity. Snatches are supplied by different characters but Hester wishes to tailor their unsatisfactory versions to her own needs. She is unable to reconcile the contradictions and create a story of her mother which is positive and comforting. The idealisation she desires is undermined since "what [she can] remember doesn't add up" (21). The Josie Swane she wants to remember—the Josie Swane who "[made] up songs for every occasion," who was invited everywhere to sing at funerals, weddings, harvests, the Josie who took her daughter with her on those "singin' sprees" (65)—cannot be reconciled with the mother who abandoned her. Throughout the play, Hester's ideal Josie is continually dismantled and destroyed. None of the other characters can affirm or validate Hester's fantasy. As Monica warns her towards the end of the play, "She's not comin' back […]. This waitin' is only a fancy of yours […]. You up on forty, Hester, and still dreamin' of storybook endin's, still whingin' for your Mam" (65). As with Portia Coughlan, Hester's memory betrays her and ontological wholeness can never be achieved. Like the Mai, she wishes to control her illusory destiny, in which the separation between her self and her mother/origin would no longer exist. In all three plays these "fictions" metonymically echo the characters' anxieties concerning identity and the threat of annihilation and indicate a desire to make sense of and by implication to master their fates.

In each of the plays it is evident that origins are supposed to determine destiny and yet in each play the problematic nature of origins is stressed. Carr's use of multiple strategies to develop the notion of destiny and the inevitable, all of which have some ontological dimension in every case reveal a lack which is amended through simulation—illusion, fantasy, false memory, story. Therefore, although the dramas seem to open the traumatic unstable space of subjectivity, they always achieve a "destined" closure.

Desire, Identity & the Inevitable
From the above readings it should be clear that Carr abandons a theatre of realism "employing instead various fantastic stage techniques and set pieces—such as the presentation of events in a non-chronological sequence, the use of mythic and/or prophetic narratives, [...] violent shifts of subject, and [a] sometimes arbitrary mixture of times, people, and places"[70] in her attempts to tell tragic stories on stage. On the other hand one might argue that this involves little real disruption of conventional character, narrative devices or relatively linear plot development. Carr's avowed interest in destiny means that character and character development are substantial elements in her work. Characters are woven through dialogue and storytelling. Colourful, often archaic language and strong midlands accent are used to lend authenticity to not only the setting, but also the narrative. The rough texture and imagery of the characters' speech accentuates the physical violence in the plays, though it often seems overburdened with the weight of dialect, poetic and symbolic significances.

In each play, then, destiny is heavily determined, even over determined, by myths of origin and citations, resulting in a relentless stress upon the inevitable. It is hardly surprising that McGuinness can assert that Carr's "characters die from a fatal excess of self-knowledge [rather than the more conventional

---

70 Morse, "'Sleepwalkers along a precipice,'" 115.

lack of it]. Their truth kills them. And they always knew it would."[71] The tragic genres cited and deployed by Carr foreground closure through the self-fulfilling prophecies of inescapable destiny.

Carr's contemporary reproductions of "tragic drama" might be thought of as simulacra which fulfil, among other things, a desire for age-old stories explicating a relatively stable, universal human nature and narrative closure. The mixture of such notions of identity and ontology, and the plethora of textual devices woven into each play at times seem to tax their structures to such an extent, however, that it could be argued that Carr's theatre is perpetually poised between tragedy and melodrama.

Both *On Raftery's Hill* and *Ariel* illustrate this problematic equilibrium. The former is a harsh tale of incest and insanity that continues to "reinscribe her Midlands society in terms of fateful ancient tragedy,"[72] but also departs from this particular tragic model somewhat—there are no brutal deaths or suicides, and the focus is dispersed rather than tightly fixed upon a single central character. The play might well be seen as a graphic updating of the gloom of Eugene O'Neill's *Desire Under the Elms* and *Long Day's Journey into Night*. Similar to the plays discussed above, Carr puts multiple generations of a single family on stage. The characters are sketched broadly. The head of the household, Red Raftery, is a brutal and theatrically cruel farmer who, when not stabbing his own cows or strangling baby hares in what can only be described as fits of sheer maliciousness, torments his own family. Shalome, his mother is senile and repeatedly appears dressed in her wedding gown attempting to escape the house. Dinah, Ded and Sorrel are Red's offspring and each is scarred by his savagery: Dinah is revealed to be Sorrel's mother; Ded is insane as a result of the trauma of having to assist at Sorrel's birth; while Sorrel, just

---

71 McGuinness, *The Dazzling Dark*, ix-x.
72 Claudia Harris, "Rising Out of the Miasmal Mists: Marina Carr's Ireland," *The Theatre of Marina Carr*, 222.

before she is to marry, is raped by her father and then rejects her fiancé. While the play deploys a bleak sense of humour principally through the eccentricities of Shalome, the capitulation of the daughters of Red Raftery to their incestuous destiny is far more brutally pessimistic than any of Carr's dramas to date. One specific complicating factor is that *On Raftery's Hill* seems more closely aligned with an actual social context and immediate issues than her previous work. Claudia Harris reviews the debate that surrounded the American premiere of the play and the discomfort many felt at what they perceived to be "an inappropriately dark view of rural Ireland."[73] More problematically, as Mic Moroney describes, though Carr's language is still "coarse, lyric vinegar," *On Raftery's Hill* seems peopled with characters who have begun to solidify into types, bearing "all Carr's hallmarks and caucus-race characters of hardened strange women, addled old birds and sacrificial lambs."[74]

A comparable tension is evidenced by responses to *Ariel* and by the text itself. Again citing a classical "source," Euripides's *Iphigenia at Aulis*, Carr transposes elements of that narrative onto a tale of political corruption in present day Ireland. The play attempts to tell a story of epic premodern proportions set in the present day, but fails to build a convincing tragic foundation, principally because of the utter disjunction between the mythic and the contemporary elements. The play, as O'Toole notes, fails to create "a sense of necessity" for its plot.[75] The mixture of primal myth, intense emotional pitch and contemporary social comment topples the play into melodramatic excess that won laughter rather than awe from audiences at its premiere.[76]

---

[73] Harris, "Rising Out of the Miasmal Mists," 226.

[74] Mic Moroney, "The Twisted Mirror: Landscapes, Mindscapes, Politics and Language on the Irish Stage," *Druids, Dudes and Beauty Queens*, 251.

[75] O'Toole, rev of *Ariel*, by Marina Carr, *Irish Times* 4 Oct. 2002 (online).

[76] See Harvey O'Brien's review of the play at the Dublin Theatre Festival 5 Oct. 2002, and Nick McGinley's review 7 Oct. 2002 available online at <www.rte.ie/arts/2002/1007/ariel.html>.

While tragedy and melodrama may be considered antithetical, they may also be productively viewed as gradations on a scale, as is illustrated by the excessive tendencies of Carr's work. Referring to the work of Peter Brooks (*The Melodramatic Imagination* [1976]), Richard Murphy describes "melodrama as a response to a specifically modern crisis, namely the general process of 'desacralisation' which has been operating since the Enlightenment and which has eroded the sacred myths of Western thought and belief, affecting in particular their explanatory and cohesive power."[77] Carr's comments regarding her role as a writer and the deterioration of particular types of belief suggest that she too is responding to a comparable sense of crisis, although one that is conditioned by postmodernity. Consequently, her method of doing so differs from the usual structures of melodrama which "play out the force of [...] anxiety with the apparent triumph of villainy, and [...] dissipates it with the eventual victory of virtue;"[78] however, the rejection of realism is just as forceful. Moreover, just as melodrama has been aligned with the fantastic, so too has Carr's drama been discussed in relation to its referencing of this mode.[79] Rather than a melodramatic play of good and evil, Carr prefers to pit predestination against arbitrary possibility.

As noted earlier Victor Merriman argues that these plays "operat[e] as spectacle," and is critical of Carr's work because the "content which appears to be quintessentially Irish is overlaid with tropes and conventions deriving from Greek cosmology [... and that] the resources of the most successful Irish theatre companies have been deployed [...] to the extent that their theatricality [...] overpowers engagement with their

---

[77] Richard Murphy, *Theorizing the Avant-Garde: Modernism, Expressionism and the Problem of Postmodernity* (Cambridge: Cambridge University Press, 1999) 147. Murphy is citing Peter Brooks, *The Melodramatic Imagination. Balzac, Henry James, Melodrama and the Mode of Excess* (New Haven: Yale University Press, 1976) 16 and following.

[78] Brooks, *The Melodramatic Imagination*, 20.

[79] See Murphy, *Theorizing the Avant-Garde*, 145-46, Morse "'Sleepwalkers along a precipice'" and Sihra "A Cautionary Tale."

significance as dramatic art."[80] The problem with this approach is that it condemns the theatricality of productions rather than examining the implications or dimensions of spectacle in Carr's work. It also assumes that spectacle may function to obscure the authentic or real message of that work. What the above close readings demonstrate is that the spectacles of simulated origins and ontologies are intrinsic to the structure of Carr's drama from this period. Jean Baudrillard's four "successive phases of the image" would seem of relevance here. The first phase is when the image "is the reflection of a profound reality," in the second "it masks and denatures a profound reality," in the third "it masks the absence of a profound reality," and in the fourth "it has no relation to any reality whatsoever: it is its own pure simulacrum."[81] While Carr seems to want to claim the first, described by Baudrillard as "representation [...] of the sacramental order,"[82] it is, arguably, rather of the order of simulation.

In its efforts to reassert the sacred as tragic destiny, Carr's drama then tends towards a "semiotic overloading,"[83] a feature also remarked in Sarah Kane's work. This takes the shape of a kind of hysterical drive towards the hyper production of determining and authenticating devices that are primarily nostalgic. If these plays can be said to stage the theatrical spectacle of the self, then this spectacle is conditioned by what might be called a performative textual hysteria in which the proliferation of signs of destiny can be read as symptoms. Hysteria should not be interpreted as a pejorative term here, rather it is descriptive of the mechanisms at work in the plays.

"[H]ysterics suffer from reminiscences," claim Sigmund Freud and Joseph Breuer; so too do Carr's heroines.[84] However,

---

80 Merriman, "'Poetry Shite,'" 152.

81 Jean Baudrillard, *Simulacra and Simulation*, trans. Sheila Faria Glaser (1981; Ann Arbor: University of Michigan Press, 1994) 6.

82 Baudrillard, *Simulacra and Simulation*, 6.

83 Murphy, *Theorizing the Avant-Garde*, 166.

84 Sigmund Freud and Joseph Breuer, *Studies on Hysteria, Project for a Scientific Psychology* vol. 1 (London: Hogarth, 1966) 7.

as is widely acknowledged, hysterical symptoms cannot be cured by locating and reproducing a primal scene of trauma since it is impossible to distinguish simulated from "real" memories.[85] Similarly, in Carr's plays the attempt to reinstate destiny and some unitary narrative of the selfhood is conditioned by simulation.

Authentic Reproductions

To conclude, a contentious authenticity can be seen to permeate both Carr's work and image in myriad and often conflicting ways. With regard to her public persona, some of the authenticating or authorising gestures are her own, while some are produced by her commentators and critics. With regard to the plays discussed here, the term "authentic reproduction," though ripe with paradox, seems particularly appropriate the ways in which Carr draws upon different traditions and stereotypes.[86] The reproduction of aspects of various dramatic traditions, in contrast to the methodology of a playwright like Martin McDonagh for instance, provides a legitimising connection with moral values and dilemmas, which might be understood as inevitable and authentic. These reproductions fulfil a yearning for timeless stories and narrative closure at a time "when the real is no longer what it used to be."[87] Within the plays, however, the duplicities of nostalgia are critically present and identity, amidst a plethora of fantasy and false memory, is structured by the failure to locate any ontological plenitude.

---

[85] Elisabeth Bronfen, *The Knotted Subject: Hysteria and its Discontents* (New Jersey: Princeton University Press, 1998) 32-33.

[86] See Graham *Deconstructing Ireland*, 132.

[87] Baudrillard, *Simulations*, 12-13.

David Greig
Time-Space Compressions

The world's waiting for us. We've only to take our place in it.[1]

Although one of Scotland's most important younger playwrights, David Greig has yet to receive his due in terms of critical consideration. In an introduction to *Plays 1*, Dan Rebellato notes the significance of globalisation to Greig's work, how the plays are structured by questions of citizenship in an apparently borderless world.[2] Greig's drama, like Carr's and McPherson's diverges from an In-Yer-Face aesthetic, yet like Ravenhill's the effects of postmodern globalisation on identity and a sense of place underpin it. It is all the more ironic then that Greig has been, in many ways, left off the map of the 1990s new writing scene by some of the most influential books surveying theatre of the period. The reasons for this are several. First, as a Scot, Greig has for some time slipped through the cracks in surveys of British theatre and has been left to Scottish theatre criticism. As one reviewer noted, before *The America Pilot*, *Pyrenees* and a revival of *The cosmonaut's last message to the woman he once loved in the former Soviet Union* appeared on stages in London and Stratford in 2005, "Greig had never quite managed to climb out of the tartan box that the London

---

[1] David Greig, *Victoria* (London: Methuen, 2000) 20.
[2] Dan, Rebellato, Introduction, *Plays: 1*, by David Greig (London: Methuen, 2002) xii-xiv.

establishment had put him in."[3] Certainly now such narrow stereotyping seems on the wane and Greig's achievements as a playwright and theatre practitioner are starting to attract broader recognition. Second, his methods have not been provocative in a visceral or sexually shocking fashion (*San Diego* excepted), thus do not easily fit the popular conventions of experiential theatre. Finally, the sheer quantity and diversity of his work has made generalisations about it a challenge.[4]

Greig began writing for theatre in the early 1990s (*A Savage Reminiscence* was produced in Bristol in 1991), when he also co-founded the Suspect Culture Theatre Group with Graham Eatough. Since then his work, which is both copious and varied, has extended in a number of directions. In collaboration with Suspect Culture he has been involved in numerous productions including *Stalinland* (1992), *Stations on the Border/Petra's Explanation* (1994), *One Way Street* (1995), *Airport* (1996), *Timeless* (1997), *Mainstream* (1999), *Casanova* (2001), *Lament* (2002) and *8000M* (2004). He has produced pieces for radio (*Nightlife* [1996], *Copper Sulphate* [1996], *Swansong* [2000], *The Commuter* [2001]) and plays for children (*Danny 306 + Me Forever* [1999] and *Dr Korczak's Example* [2001]). Among his translations and adaptations are *Candide 2000* (2000), *Oedipus* (2000), *Caligula* (2003) and *When the Bulbul Stopped Singing* (2004). As playwright his work comprises, *Europe* (Traverse, 21 October 1994), *The Architect* (Traverse, 23 February 1996), *The cosmonaut's last message to the woman he once loved in the former Soviet Union* (Paines Plough Tour, Ustinov Studio Theatre Royal Bath, 15 April 1999), *The Speculator* (9 Mercat de la Flors, Barcelona, 29 June 1999 in Catalan, in English Royal Lyceum Theatre Edinburgh, 16 August 1999) and *Victoria* (Royal

---

[3] Leo Benedictus, "I really, really, really … hate jobs," *Guardian* 12 Apr. 2005. (online).

[4] In 2005 when Greig's work finally won recognition in London several reviewers noted that at the age of 36 Greig had produced 37 plays. See Benedictus (cited above) and Nick Curtis, "Cosmic Landing on the London Stage," *Evening Standard* (London) Apr. 2005 (online).

Shakespeare Company at the Pit, Barbican, 17 April 2000). Greig has continued to be extremely prolific and increasingly successful since the 1990s with plays like *Outlying Islands* (Traverse and Royal Court, 2002), *San Diego* (Royal Lyceum, 2003), *Pyrenees* (Paines Plough, The Chocolate Factory, London, 2005), *The American Pilot* (RSC at The Other Place, Stratford-upon-Avon, 2005) and *Yellow Moon* (Citizens' Circle Glasgow, 2006), and he is currently dramaturge of the National Theatre of Scotland.

Responses to Greig's work have generally been positive. Cerebral, allusive, sensitive, intelligent, intellectually stimulating are regularly among the adjectives used by reviewers to describe it. These qualities might serve to align him with the subtleties of McPherson's dramaturgy, while a core interest in the political potential of theatre links Greig with his contemporaries Ravenhill and Kane. Nevertheless, what might distinguish Greig, apart from his prodigious output, is the way his work is widely regarded as belonging to a theatre of ideas—reflective, allusive and articulate—in other words, the reverse of a theatre of sensation or provocation. Critical essays have tended to focus on a cluster of ideas represented largely by Greig's first volume of plays. In addition to the deep "imprint of globalisation," Rebellato also attends to the issue of national identity in Greig's work.[5] Other commentators have, similarly, been drawn to questions of identity, though within the broader context of the political transformation of Europe after the fall of Communism. Thus, Janelle G. Reinelt has interpreted *Europe* in terms of the troubled identity and politics of a "New Europe."[6] Peter Nesteruk has explored the "two opposing poles of identity exchange" in this same play. These poles destructive and affirmative, exclusive and cosmopolitan delineate the extremes of self-identification and present the

---

[5] Rebellato, Introduction, xiii.

[6] Janelle G. Reinelt, "Performing Europe: Identity Formation for a 'New' Europe," *Theatre Journal* 53.3 (2001): 365-87.

problem as a Brechtian *Lehrstück*.[7] Anja Müller, in partial opposition to Nesteruk's interpretive model, "propose[s] a distinction between residual and migratory characters in *Europe*,"[8] to facilitate a more nuanced reading of displacement and the conceptual heterogeneity of the continent as it is staged. Finally, Peter Zenzinger also deals with Greig's perspective on the New Europe, specifically how he extends "an imaginative (re)creation of the continent from a Scottish artist's point of view,"[9] in the plays *One Way Street: Ten Short Walks in the Former East*, *Europe* and *The cosmonaut's last message*.

A common component to most of these responses to Greig's drama has been the issue of identity in the contemporary world where disjunction and dislocation seem to prevail. Here, Zygmunt Bauman's assertion (cited above with respect to Mark Ravenhill's work) that postmodern society is marked by the impossibility of being or feeling at home, of being perpetually "out of place"[10] seems apt. Indeed, Greig's work is repeatedly peopled with characters at odds with their place, in both an interior and exterior sense. *Europe, The Architect, The cosmonaut's last message* all probe precisely this dilemma, be it in the paranoia and racism of those left behind by geopolitical change, the destruction of the modernist architectural dream, or those literally or metaphorically lost in space. A similar sense of displacement and contradictory continuity is explored in the epic historical play *Victoria*. In contrast to the bleak view of

---

[7] Peter Nesteruk, "Ritual, Sacrifice, and Identity in Recent Political Drama—with Reference to the Plays of David Greig," *Journal of Dramatic Theory and Criticism* 15.1 (2000): 32.

[8] Anja Müller, "'We are also Europe:' Staging Displacement in David Greig's Plays," *Staging Displacement, Exile and Diaspora in Contemporary Drama in English*, CDE 12, ed. Christoph Houswitschka (Trier: Wissenschaftlicher Verlag Trier, 2005) 158.

[9] Peter Zenzinger, "David Greig's Scottish View of the 'New' Europe: A Study of Three Plays," *Literary Views on Post-Wall Europe: Essays in Honour of Uwe Böker*, ed. Christoph Houswitschka et al. (Trier: Wissenschaftlicher Verlag Trier, 2005) 262-3.

[10] Zygmunt Bauman, *Postmodernity and its Discontents* (Cambridge: Polity, 1997) 93.

humanity offered by many of his contemporaries in the 1990s, Greig has often been credited with staging a vision of hope and the possibility of communication. This vision however, I would argue, is tempered with strong ambivalence and, as with several of the other playwrights in focus here, an unresolved openness. Broadly, two key aspects of Greig's work will be explored throughout this chapter. The first is the political dimension to the plays and the backgrounds against which Greig is working, theatrically and philosophically. The second, imbricated with the first, is the issue of space and time in a globalised and postmodern context. This, in Greig's work, is manifest in the ways in which the plays are structured, attitudes to plot, character and intertexts, the use of spatial metaphors and the motif of communication.

"The possibility of change": Political Theatre[11]
As is evident from the foci of the critical articles mentioned above, Greig's work is regularly read within some notion of the political. In fact Greig himself has reasserted the validity of political theatre—in his contribution to *State of Play*, he challenges the idea that "writing about politics might in some way be prehistoric." Political theatre, he maintains, "poses questions about society to which it does not already know the answer," it resists stasis; it opens a window to transformation.[12]

Such a statement serves to position him, like Ravenhill, within the lengthy tradition of the social problem play on the British stage, in addition to suggesting an affinity with Brechtian theatre as has been noted by Nesteruk. A century earlier, George Bernard Shaw inspired by Ibsen's naturalism, argued that the foundation required for modern plays was "not romance but a really scientific natural history."[13] Ironically,

---

[11] David Greig in *State of Play: Playwrights on Playwriting*, ed. David Edgar (London: Faber and Faber, 1999) 66.

[12] Greig, *State of Play*, 66-68.

[13] George Bernard Shaw qtd. in Bentley *The Playwright as Thinker* (New York: Meridian, 1955) 7.

despite his lip service to scientific objectivity, Shaw's own work soon departs from naturalism thus defined, and his method of taking the sentimental structures and situations of melodrama and inverting them, is ultimately less conditioned by realistic representation than by didacticism.[14] Shaw's work is founded upon a belief in progress and the possibility of improving humanity through enlightened education and social policy. Of especial relevance to Greig's theatre is the way in which Shaw's plays thematically situate social issues centre stage, while disrupting melodramatic forms with the objective of challenging his audience's beliefs and values.

Similarly, of course, Brecht perceived theatre as instrumental, "a tool for the reordering of human existence."[15] And as is well-known, his work is structured by a keen awareness of storytelling as performative and of the effect it may, or should, have on its audience:

> We need a type of theatre which not only releases the feelings, insights, and impulses possible within the particular historical field of human relations in which the action takes place, but employs and encourages those thoughts and feelings which help to transform the field itself.[16]

In reaction to the symbolism of the expressionist stage, Brecht's Epic theatre was to reinstate place and period on stage, but also to invert the conventions of dramatic theatre in its attempt to address contemporary political problems and ethical dilemmas. As already mentioned, Greig's *Europe* in particular has been likened to a Brechtian *Lehrstück*. The *Lehrstücke* represent Epic theatre in its most concentrated form where a problem is posed and debated from different perspectives. Language is

---

[14] Christopher Innes, *Modern British Drama: The Twentieth Century* (Cambridge: Cambridge University Press, 2001) see chapter 2.

[15] Marvin Carlson, *Theories of the Theatre* (1984; Ithaca: Cornell University Press, 1993) 392-3.

[16] Bertolt Brecht, "A Short Organum for the Theatre," trans. John Willett, *Modern Theories of Drama*, ed. George W. Brandt (Oxford: Clarendon, 1998) 233, 238.

unadorned, plot is simple, character two dimensional.[17] Greig's work often shares a similar, though obviously not identical methodology. Due to their brevity, however, the *Lehrstücke* omit an important element to Brecht's narrative practice that Greig's theatre preserves. In Epic theatre the story is to be composed of episodes, each with its own movement or *gest*, and these "parts of the story have to be carefully set off one against another by giving each its own structure as a play within a play."[18] Such juxtapositional logic is crucial to the shape of Greig's drama and the articulated, disjunctive narratives it presents. The result is that themes are explored, as in Brechtian theatre, from various perspectives. Finally, though it is obviously a point of debate, Brechtian theatre at its best attempts to remain open to interpretation, to pose questions rather than to definitively answer them. Clearly, a similar premise is foundational to Greig's comments cited above about political theatre.

The heyday of political drama in the UK and Ireland was indisputably the 1970s and 1980s and some of the contexts for this have already been discussed in the opening chapter. The apparent dissolution of the polarised politics of the 1970s and 1980s, which segued into something troublingly diffuse and contradictory, has meant that political drama has itself been forced to undergo both redefinition and transformation. With the collapse of communism, the acceleration of globalisation and the changes wrought by postmodernity, issues of identity, the nation-state, power, justice and the politics of emancipation have been increasingly problematised. For young writers in the 1990s, according to Ian Rickson an artistic director at the Royal Court, politics became a matter of "privatised dissent,"[19] a rather dispiriting prospect for many, though one that dovetails

---

[17] See Keith A. Dickson, Introduction, *Fünf Lehrstücke*, by Bertolt Brecht (London: Methuen, 1969).

[18] Brecht, "A Short Organum for the Theatre," 245.

[19] Ian Rickson cited in Aleks Sierz, *In-Yer-Face Theatre: British Drama Today* (London: Faber and Faber, 2000) 39.

with Lyotard's oft-cited claim that the postmodern condition is marked by "incredulity towards metanarratives."[20]

As Klaus-Peter Müller remarked of 1990s theatre, "[i]t has become conspicuously more difficult to define political plays, because of the strong effects of both postmodernism and political reality" to the extent that,

> the most striking characteristic of the new plays written by young, unknown playwrights is their outspoken depiction of a remarkably rude, violent, and destructive world and their lack of suggesting alternatives or ways of changing such a world and of stopping the destruction of human life. There is a strong element of pessimism often mixed with a strange sense of relish in the destructive and dehumanising worlds depicted.[21]

Greig's work remains detached to a significant degree from explorations of onstage violence or laddish masculinity in crisis. He sees the contemporary withdrawal from ideology as the logical outcome of the collapse of both the left and the right. Such a disavowal of the political, in his view, results in a "culture of stasis" and disempowerment.[22] In a changed political context, political theatre evidently must also be redefined. It seems pertinent, as Müller also observes, that Edward Bond's 1970s pronouncements on human nature, good and evil are anathema to the 1990s new wave. Greig may not baldly declare as Bond has done, "we have rewrite human consciousness,"[23] but among the elements he identifies in a political theatre for the present are "the possibility of change," "the possibility of fantasy," "the individual changing individual circumstances," "desires changing" and, ultimately, the

---

[20] Jean-François Lyotard, *The Postmodern Condition*, trans. Geoff Bennington and Brian Massumi (1979; Manchester: Manchester University Press, 1984) xxiv.

[21] Klaus-Peter Müller, ""Political Plays in England in the 1990s," *British Drama of the 1990s*, eds. Bernhard Reitz and Mark Berninger (Heidelberg: Univeritätsverlag C. Winter, 2002) 15.

[22] Greig, *State of Play*, 68.

[23] Edward Bond, "A Note on Dramatic Method," *The Bundle or New Narrow Road to the Deep North* (London: Methuen, 1978) xv.

possibility that "the person's beliefs may change."[24] Greig's drama cannot be simply mapped onto Shaw's modernist commitment to social progress or human perfectibility or onto Brecht's theatre of alienation or distanciation. Nevertheless, his comments with regard to a political theatre for today suggest an attitude to the role of culture as a space of communication and social critique that is deeply indebted to these antecedents.

Space-Time: Equivocating Modernity, or Anarchy Playing Post?
The experience of space and time have been crucial to much of critical work cited throughout this volume both directly and indirectly. Admittedly this is a vast area of multidisciplinary enquiry, what follows is a constellation of references that seem particularly relevant to an exploration of these issues in Greig's work. As suggested by Debord, Lyotard, Baudrillard and Jameson among others, postmodernity entails a changed attitude to these co-ordinates, though, unsurprisingly, opinions as to the nature of such change remain conflicting and heterogeneous. Thus, in his *Commentary on the Society of the Spectacle* (1988), Debord concludes that "The society whose modernisation has reached the stage of the integrated spectacle is characterised by the combined effect of five principal features: incessant technological renewal; integration of state and economy; generalised secrecy, unanswerable lies; an eternal present."[25] Jameson strikes a similar note when he argues that postmodernity involves "the fragmentation of time into a series of perpetual presents."[26] If time has accelerated then paradoxically, according to such theorising, it would also seem to have been rendered static.

---

[24] Greig, *State of Play*, 68.

[25] Guy Debord, *Commentaires sur la Société du Spectacle* (Paris: Éditions Gérard Lebovici, 1988) §V. See Len Bracken, *Guy Debord: Revolutionary* (Venice CA: Feral House, 1997) 198.

[26] Fredric Jameson, "Postmodernism, or the Cultural Logic of Late Capitalism," *Postmodernism A Reader*, ed. Thomas Docherty (New York: Harvester Wheatsheaf, 1993) 85.

Globalisation correspondingly seems to have altered the space of the world, in which the significance of the nation-state has shrunk and deterritorialisation is "one of the central forces [...] bring[ing] labouring populations into the lower-class sectors and spaces of relatively wealthy societies."[27] Contradictorily, globalisation involves a certain homogenisation of space (in the shape of franchised fast food restaurants, multinational chains of clothing shops, supermarkets and hotels in urban centres) and simultaneously the production of new neighbourhoods and new senses of locality both material and virtual.[28] Marc Augé characterises what he refers to as supermodernity in terms of excess: an "overabundance of events, spatial overabundance, the individualisation of references." Our experience of space "is expressed in changes of scale, in the proliferation of imaged and imaginary references, and in the spectacular acceleration of means of transport" as well as, importantly, the proliferation of "non-places" which are divorced from traditional notions of "culture localised in time and space."[29] Again, what is evident are apparently diametrically opposed tendencies of homogenisation and diversification, global connectedness and disjuncture, contraction and proliferation.

For such intensification David Harvey employs the concept of time-space compression to articulate the "processes that so revolutionise the objective qualities of space and time that we are forced to alter, sometimes in quite radical ways, how we represent the world to ourselves."[30] These processes are, inevitably, rooted in nineteenth and twentieth century modernity. As has often been observed the optimism of the modern project faded following World War I. Nevertheless, as

---

[27] Arjun Appadurai, *Modernity at Large: Cultural Dimensions of Globalization* (Minneapolis and London: University of Minnesota Press, 1996) 37.

[28] See Appadurai, *Modernity at Large*, chapter 9.

[29] Marc Augé, *Non-Places: Introduction to an Anthropology of Supermodernity*, trans. John Howe (1992; London: Verso, 1995) 40, 33-34.

[30] David Harvey, *The Condition of Postmodernity: An Enquiry into the Origins of Cultural Change* (Cambridge MA and Oxford: Blackwell, 1990) 240.

Harvey notes, Enlightenment ideals had promised human progress on a grand scale through the amassing of knowledge for the betterment of human society, the advancement of science and technology as a means overcoming poverty, scarcity and natural catastrophe, and liberation from superstition through "rational forms of social organisation and [...] thought."[31] While attitudes to progress may have altered between the wars, already urbanisation, industrialisation, systems of transportation, literacy, the rise of technology, and especially communication technologies, had transformed the individual's experience of the world. Mechanisation in the workplace, the development of rail networks, urban transport systems, radio, telegraph and telephone meant that speed, mobility, as well as new senses of fragmentation and simultaneity became key aspects of modern existence. Meanwhile, the erosion of local knowledge and sense of long-term community foundational to rural experience for many, gave way to various grades of urban alienation where an individual is in almost constant, random contact with strangers be it on public transport or in apartment housing. And as already noted, associated with these developments is the creation of new types of place and "non-place."

Postmodernism is often criticised for its indifference to or, better still cannibalising of, history. Yet modernity and modernism with its fascination for novelty and innovation is already founded upon an ambivalent relation with the past. Harvey points to how modernity is predicated on what is conceived as a necessary rupture with what has gone before:

> If modern life is indeed so suffused with the sense of the fleeting, the ephemeral, the fragmentary, and the contingent, then a number of profound consequences follow. To begin with, modernity can have no respect for even its own past, let alone that of any pre-modern social order. The transitoriness of things makes it difficult to preserve any sense of historical

31 Harvey, *The Condition of Postmodernity*, 12 and following.

continuity. If there is any meaning to history, then that meaning
has to be discovered and defined from within the maelstrom of
change, a maelstrom that affects the terms of discussion as well
as whatever it is that is being discussed. Modernity, therefore,
not only entails a ruthless break with any or all preceding
historical conditions, but is characterised by a never-ending
process of internal ruptures and fragmentations within itself.[32]

Perhaps among the most crucial of these "internal ruptures" is
the above mentioned faltering belief in the metanarrative of
progress, the tension between universalist and anti-universalist
world views and the consequent turn towards relativism,
perspectivism and reflexivity. These qualities, though often
treated as belonging to the postmodern, as Harvey, Bertens and
Anthony Giddens among others have remarked, they are
intrinsic to modernity.[33] Yet perspectivism may serve different
ends. Brian McHale argues, with regard to the postmodern
novel, that the alteration is from an epistemological orientation
to an ontological orientation. Perspectivism may have served
the modernist as a means of broaching "a complex but
nevertheless singular reality," but for the postmodernist it
"foreground[s] questions as to how radically different realities
may coexist, collide, and interpenetrate."[34] Thus McHale frames
this as a shift from a cognitive to postcognitive interrogative;
the question is no longer "How can I interpret this world of
which I am part? And what am I in it?" but rather "Which
world is this? What is to be done in it? Which of my selves is to
do it?"[35]

Greig's drama time and again engages with the heritage of
modernity and the alleged anarchy of postmodernity in spatial
and temporal terms as can been seen in its references to

---

[32] Harvey, *The Condition of Postmodernity*, 11-12.

[33] See Bertens chapters 10 and 11 for an insightful overview of debates regarding
the postmodern as a social formation.

[34] See Brian McHale, *Postmodern Fiction* (London and New York: Methuen, 1987)
and Harvey, *The Condition of Postmodernity*, 41.

[35] Brian McHale, *Constructing Postmodernism* (London: Routledge, 1992) 32-3, 101.

ideology and history, tourism and travel, industrial development and building. Further, spatial concerns are formally linked with temporal ones through his use of collage to compose narratives. The matter of different coexistent realities recalls the opening question of the political in today's drama and the irreconcilable tension between a play of micronarratives and the evident need for judgement, justice and agency. In the selected plays from the 1990s, three nodes to this engagement are prominent: Greig's attention to space and places of belonging or of alienation; point of view, especially what Rebellato has called a "view from above" motif[36]; and finally a structural logic of juxtaposition and accidental encounter.

Europe, Greig's first play, presents a multi-perspectival treatment of the relation between location, history and identity. As a meditation on the nature of contemporary Europe and its changing dimensions, the play has attracted most commentary from scholars. This topicality provides another layer to the space-time dimension of the play, where the playwright intervenes in the political dilemmas of the present, opening the work to both timeliness and datedness. Reinelt in her analysis of the play discusses how the "New Europe" is "to date an unfilled signifier, an almost-empty term capable of great/little significance and power."[37] Equally, however, this "New Europe" remains entangled with the "Old" one in both its ruptures and continuities. Anja Müller concludes that "[i]f unity was the project of 'Old Europe,' 'New Europe' is marked by diversity" and argues that Greig's play ultimately challenges any simplistic notion of Eurocentrism or European hegemony.[38] Moreover, historians like Norman Davies have highlighted the plasticity and instability of the notion of Europe in the long-term[39]; the collapse of communism and subsequent redrawing

---

36 Rebellato, Introduction, xvii.
37 Reinelt, "Performing Europe," 365.
38 Müller, "'We are also Europe,'" 166.
39 See Norman Davies, *Europe: A History* (London: Pimlico, 1997).

of borders with the expansion of the European Union are but the latest manifestations of this conceptual and territorial malleability. It is in this contemporary territory of floating signifiers that the play's characters negotiate and renegotiate their identities. Greig's play likewise presents these conflicting elements simultaneously—they are neither temporally nor spatially distinct, but overlap, collide and interpenetrate.

Structured in episodic form, each of the play's twenty scenes bears a title in what can be seen as a clear reference to Brechtian theatre. Of these scenes, all but two—the silent arrival of Morocco and the sombre departure of Katia and Adele—are based on verbal exchange that unfolds a story. The action is set in "a small town on the border" in the heart of Europe.[40] As Anja Müller has discussed, Greig's play presents a spatial paradox—the town's position as simultaneously central and liminal[41]—which deconstructs any simple account of the community's identity, and, by implication, of contemporary European identity. This interpretation is reinforced by Greig's use of framing citations; the phrase taken from Jacques Derrida's *The Other Heading*—"Something unique is afoot in Europe, in what is still called 'Europe' even if we no longer know very well what or who goes by this name"—directly raises this question.[42]

The town's importance as a frontier crossing has vanished with the erasure of the border, to the extent that trains no longer stop at its station. Structurally this is underscored by the fact that fifteen of the scenes are concluded by the roar of a train passing, while two others are completed by buses departing or arriving. A chorus at the beginning of each of the two acts provides a metacommentary on the situation of the town. The

---

[40] David Greig, *Europe* in *Plays 1* (London: Methuen, 2002) 5. All quotations from *Europe, The Architect* and *The cosmonaut's last message…* will be taken from this edition and will be cited in-text.

[41] Müller, "'We are also Europe,'" 156.

[42] See Jacques Derrida, *The Other Heading: Reflections on Today's Europe*, trans. Pascale-Anne Brault and Michael B. Nass (Bloomington and Indianapolis: Indiana University Press, 1992) 5.

chorus makes space for the voice of community; it also positions the play formally just beyond the bounds of a purely naturalistic drama. The identity of the town has been traditionally derived from "our soup, for our factory which makes light bulbs and for being on the border" (5)—ironic markers, perhaps, of culture reduced to cuisine, illuminating industry and geopolitical location. However, by act two the minor, but relatively stable, historical identity of the place has been eroded as the border which has given it meaning no longer exists and the factory has been downsized; it has become unrecognisable, as the chorus states "it isn't our place any more" (48). Significantly, the redefinition of the town, which has become "meaning less" or, to an extent, a "non-place," involves the naming of it in the media: "They said the name of our town, politicians and sociologists all across the continent said its name" (89). The result of the publicity is short-lived and is rendered ambivalent as once again semantic slippage occurs: "it wasn't a name any more but a condition, not a place but an effect" (89). While the play concludes with the assertion by its most objectionable character that "we're also Europe," what Europe might be, or who "we" are remains deliberately unresolved.

The play's characters comprise two father daughter couples, Sava and Katia, Fret and Adele, Adele's husband Berlin, his former co-workers at the factory Billy and Horse, and their childhood friend Morocco. The opening scenes are marked by the arrival of a somewhat bedraggled Morocco in his hometown and the discovery of the refugees, Sava and Katia, in the waiting room of the now defunct train station. The random movement of apparent outsiders into this space which is both static ("History has washed across [it]" (6)) and changing, provides the main catalyst for the action. Nesteruk, Müller and Zenzinger in their readings of the play note how the characters may be grouped according to various principles interconnecting identity with place: insiders and outsiders, locals and foreigners, cosmopolitan and parochial, residual and migratory types. Notably, however, these different identities cut across and interpenetrate each other.

Multiple perspectives on self and place are juxtaposed. At first the stationmaster, Fret, attempts to evict the foreigners from his station. The antagonism of his attitude, however, melts as he discovers a kindred spirit in Sava—they both share a love of railways and a similar sense of an old and inherently "civilised" Europe. Adele is fascinated by the strangers because she longs to travel, but has only ever imagined doing so by watching the trains that pass through the station. Morocco, a mysterious entrepreneurial trader, returns in an apparent welter of nostalgia for his homeplace, but later confesses to Katia "nothing's more of a prison than a home" (71). Katia refuses to identify (with) the place she comes from by denying its existence, "The place I came from isn't there anymore. It disappeared. […] Its name was taken off the maps and signposts" (41). After a consultant visits the factory, the workers are told that they had "been living in a dreamland" (9). Consequently, Berlin, Horse and Billy are made redundant. Billy decides to leave, describing his hometown as "a dirty, nothing place […] a place to die" (23-4). Berlin and Horse stay and, for want of better activities, get involved with local neo-fascist skinheads. Morocco assists Katia in obtaining papers which enable her to leave, but is vengefully beaten by his former friends for fraternising with a foreigner. Adele chooses to go with Katia, while Sava decides to stay with Fret. The play culminates with opposing attitudes expressed through the characters' actions: Adele and Katia are last seen on an international train that carries them to a new set of possibilities, new places and future identities; Berlin and Horse remain rooted in their home soil looking back to the past with nostalgia, they "defend" this territory by firebombing the train station, killing Fret and Sava and, momentarily, putting their town on the map.

In *Europe* the view from above motif may broadly be connected with a more general attentiveness to perspective throughout the work, be it literal or metaphorical, in terms of height or depth. Adele's scaling the roof of the station to get a better view of the trains and thus imagine their destinations foreshadows Greig's more developed and complex use of this motif in *The Architect*, *The cosmonaut's last message* and *Victoria*. However, in a less literal fashion, both Morocco and Katia articulate attitudes to identity and place that have depth of experience which are opposed to the flatness or superficiality of the retrograde nationalist identity latterly adopted by Berlin and Horse.

In *The Architect* themes of space and identity are developed even more explicitly in relation to perspective. Like *Europe* the play's cast is small, consisting primarily of a middle class nuclear family; the plot emerges as an assemblage of short scenes arranged in two acts. The bourgeois nuclear family in ruins is collated with the heritage modernist architecture and the remnants of the ideal of the architect as a god-like designer of social space. The worlds of Leo Black, the eponymous architect, his wife, Paulina and their adult children, Dorothy and Martin, are offset against each other to reveal an utter lack of coherence or shared emotional territory. Encounters with three external characters Sheena, a woman who lives in an estate designed by Leo, Billy, an unemployed youth and Joe, a truck driver, again facilitate multiple views and catalyse the play's action. Leo has spent much of his professional life designing homes, so it is bitterly ironic that not only is his own home life collapsing despite his refusal to acknowledge it, but that one of his award winning designs is now up for demolition. At the play's conclusion Leo abandons his attempt to make the illusory centre hold; the family is seen as utterly alienated from each other, engaged in fragmented activities, while Leo chooses to be destroyed with his doomed architectural creation, unfortunately named Eden Court.

The play opens with Leo optimistically attempting to persuade Martin to work for him by showing him a model of the latest building project he has been involved in. Although the visual image of the model commands the spectator's and reader's attention and introduces the play's central spatial metaphor, a less prominent temporal dimension to this exchange is also worth noting. Leo's offer to engage Martin as an apprentice is a bid for continuity, which promises an eventual generational transfer, father to son, of his values, ideals and business. Notably, just as the daughters Katia and Adele in *Europe* reject their fathers' values, Martin spurns this heritage, severing links with what his father represents.

Greig exploits the image of the architectural model twice in the play, once in each act. The effect of the models on stage is to draw attention to space, perspective and scale. The models serve as representations of and designs for (social) space, as well as bringing on stage, in miniature, places that exist or will exist in the world outside. They also facilitate ironic and reflexive discussion of the role of architecture in creating places and non-places. In the opening scene, Martin, responding to his father's eulogy, describes the model as "flat." The model is of a car park, with a tower (not yet built either in miniature or reality) and high security walls. The disjuncture between Leo's idealistic vision and the scale model of a typical urban non-place ironically undermines the former.

The second instance where a scale model appears is in act two where yet again Leo attempts to explain and defend his vision, this time of the Eden Court estate to resident Sheena Mackie. As with the model of the car park, discussion is orientated around the difference between the pristine world of the plan and the constructed space of the final product. Martin's facetious comment that he could make "the models look real. Cover the walls in graffiti [...] put little models of dossers under the bridges" (102), is echoed by Sheena's remark that the towers should not be surrounded by green but by brown felt as the latter would be realistic (164). The optimistic vision expressed by the architectural plans is deconstructed and debunked by those familiar with the grim social realities of the end product.

The models, and the constructions they represent, suggest parallel realities, a motif developed in particular in the scenes tracking the movements of the Black offspring. Dorothy and Martin are seen seeking arbitrary sexual experiences with strangers—Martin in public toilets, Dorothy hitchhiking on the motorway. Dorothy meets Joe, a truck driver toward whom she makes some thwarted sexual advances. Martin is pursued by Billy, a resident of Eden Court, after a random sexual encounter in a public lavatory. Dorothy and Martin's attempts to escape the space of family might be interpreted as bids to forge other spaces of identity, yet they are rendered highly ambivalent in two important respects: the places in which they accidentally find themselves, the interior of a truck, a roadside café, the toilet, a gay bar and the roof of a tall building, are anonymous or generic, temporary or transitory. The prevailing impression is of disconnection and displacement—each character is adrift ontologically and physically.

As mentioned earlier, the hub connecting these fragmentary perspectives is a view from above, be it from the roof of a building or more abstractly as Rebellato puts it as "a view of ourselves, which is perhaps inevitably an aerial view, as members of a society, a community."[43] Importantly, in *The Architect* the motif of height and overview is enmeshed with attitudes to self and space that are closely bound to the modernist intertexts Greig is citing, discussion of which will be undertaken further on.

Juxtaposed micronarratives, each with its own *gest*, form the basis of *The cosmonaut's last message*. These stories, though initially apparently disconnected, are gradually revealed as nodal points in a loose web-like plot structure. An initial spatial opposition is presented by the Soviet cosmonauts, Oleg and Casimir, who orbit the earth on a mission that seems to have been forgotten, and the remaining characters wandering randomly below. Various trajectories are traced, motivated by

---

43 Rebellato, Introduction, xix.

accidental encounters. Casimir's daughter, Nastasja who works as an erotic dancer in London and dreams of being a film star, is having an affair with Scottish civil servant, Keith. Keith, who is on the verge of a life crisis, bumps into Eric, a World Bank official, in Heathrow while waiting for a plane. After several whiskies Keith gives Eric Nastasja's address and, inspired by Eric's opinions on conflict resolution, leaves his life behind by staging his own suicide. Following his disappearance Keith's wife, Vivienne, a speech therapist, is interviewed by a young policewoman, Claire, who is incidentally also one of their neighbours. Suspecting Keith's new tie, which has a Cezanne painting as a pattern, might be a clue to his whereabouts, Vivienne sets off to Provence to find him. Eric, likewise, sets off to find Nastasja, rescues her from the where club she works, and installs her as his mistress (along with her friend Sylvia from whom she refuses to be parted) in a flat in Oslo, near his workplace. Vivienne does not find Keith, but meets Bernard, a former space scientist who suffered a stroke and is now UFO spotter. He speaks little English, she little French, but somehow they communicate. Bernard has intercepted Casimir's attempt to communicate on his monitoring system, but believes it is a message from another life form. Oleg, finding the prospect of continuing alone following Casimir's death, while trying to repair the ship's communication system, too unbearable destroys the ship. Bernard sees the explosion and suffers a second stoke. Vivienne rushes to his aid, but he can no longer speak. Eric sends Sylvia to find Keith to retrieve a cassette Keith has made of Nastasja breathing. The play concludes with Sylvia entering a bar in the West Highlands where Keith is hiding, and inviting him to talk.

Similar to the plays previously discussed, *The cosmonaut's last message* takes shape around various character pairings; though in this instance a doubling effect is achieved by actors performing more than one role. In this way metaphorical affinities are suggested between the identities of Keith and Bernard, Vivienne and Sylvia, Nastasja and Claire, Erik and the various proprietors of an airport café, a bar in Provence, a pub in the Scottish Highlands. As Zenzinger notes, the setting of the play is overtly cosmopolitan, with scenes located in Scotland, London, Oslo, Provence and outer space, while other geographical locations are mentioned as characters attempt to communicate with each other. Yet there is little sense of meaningful identification with place, rather what is repeatedly emphasised is a sense of disjunction between place and identity. Casimir and Oleg meticulously record their position in the ship's log, but they are severed from earth not only by their distance from it but also temporally, as Oleg resignedly notes "[t]he time lines have diverged" (253). Keith and Vivienne in their "comfortable middle-class home in Edinburgh" (209) also are specifically located and yet disconnected from the world beyond their living room. They sit indoors, with the heating on and shutters closed on a warm summer evening, imagining a hostile, violent world outside. Like the cosmonauts, their communication lines (in this case the television reception) are down and to venture outside their capsule (in their view) might be fatal. Vivienne's accidental meeting with Claire ironically illustrates completely different attitudes to place and identity. Though the land around the house is owned by Vivienne, she has little sense of proprietorship; Claire in contrast, has planted a garden though she has no claim to the land. Claire's loathing of waste, a word repeated throughout the scene, extends to Scotland more generally. She and her husband go camping on Skye because "it's the most beautiful place in the world. And it's in Scotland [...]. It's a shame to waste it." (233) Similarly Claire is studying Gaelic, "[b]ecause it would be a waste not to learn another language. And it's Scottish too. So it'd be a waste if nobody speaks it. A waste of all those place names. A waste of all that poetry" (233). Claire's uninvited cultivation of Vivienne's garden is discreetly juxtaposed with this other laying claim to a space of a unified and unproblematic national identity, which is later openly critiqued when Keith attempts to speak Gaelic in a pub in the West Highlands. He is told by the proprietor "[i]t's my language [...]. Mountains we can share. Place names we can share. But leave me my language" (298). Vaguely reminiscent of the treatment of identity and place in *Europe*, this exchange suggests the complexities of insider/outsider, migrant/residual identity formations, in this instance in contemporary Scotland.

Zenzinger remarks with justification how a "sense of 'metaphysical homelessness' [...] permeates the play, sustained by a symbolism that occasionally tends to be somewhat heavy-handed."[44] Nastasja, when she is abandoned by Keith, is comforted by Sylvia who tells her that "[m]en think the entire world is contained in their eyes [...] they think you disappear when their eyes leave you" (250). As the cosmonauts observe the earth from space, repeatedly the earthbound characters either discuss the heavens or look up. Nastasja scales the roof of the Oslo flat to better see the sky, while the more subtle oppositions of Highlands, Lowlands, North and South intersect with the ever-present theme of point of view.

Victoria in some respects is distinct from the texts collected in *Plays 1* in that it is a form of history play structured in three interconnected movements.[45] In contrast to much of the new writing of the 1990s, the play deliberately calls for a large cast (fourteen actors). However, like Greig's other work, and like much new drama of the 1990s, the play is composed of numerous short scenes; in *Victoria* a compendious seventy two in all. And more so than the other plays under discussion, *Victoria* is located temporally and spatially in Scotland. Nevertheless, the currents of modernity and globalisation flow through the treatment of historical change, and similarly multiple perceptions of self and place are juxtaposed. Set in an unnamed "rural place on coast of Scotland," the play takes three specific periods—1936, 1974 and 1996—over three seasons, autumn, spring and summer, and across three

---

44 Zenzinger, "David Greig's Scottish View of the 'New' Europe," 276.
45 David Greig, *Victoria* (London: Methuen, 2000). All quotations are from this edition and will be cited in-text.

generations of characters, to form an epic triptych of twentieth century Scotland. Like the seasonal shifts, each period is characterised by a set of ideas or views that distinguishes it. The three parts are hinged together in a number of ways. A sense of generational continuity and discontinuity is wrought by the introduction of new characters in the community in parts two and three, along with the reappearance and disappearance of characters in each section. Each of the play's main characters appears in two periods, while the character Oscar appears in all three. In each section a character named Victoria is introduced, who voices a pivotal attitude to place and identity, while in the concluding scene views of the three Victorias are interleaved. Death also features in each part—in the first, Oscar's murder of David, in the second, the helicopter crash and in the third, Oscar's death—and in each instance serves to catalyse the plot. Verbal echoes, in which characters from different periods reiterate phrases spoken earlier, disrupt the naturalistic tone of the dialogue, pointing to a poetic symmetry and patterning of work as a whole. However, the overarching symbol of the play is the mountainous landscape in which this community exists and which the principal characters struggle to come to terms with.

In each part of the triptych, identities and world views are delineated by attitudes to place. In the first, entitled "The Bride," class distinctions are foregrounded. The characters are clearly divided in three groups—the aristocratic residents of the estate (Lord Allan, his son David), their guests (an assortment of "invaders" composed of a group of prosperous, pretentious lowlanders and David's English fiancée, Margaret) and locals. David, the laird of the estate, has returned from Europe brimming with the fervour of Nazism and a sense of his own degeneracy. The rugged grandeur of the landscape, to which he lays claim, stands in sharp contrast to David's sense of himself as an effete and "damaged specimen" (26). The guests, who are little more than caricatures, come to consume the landscape, to profit from the mountain air and some inept deer stalking.

Margaret, in opposition to their romantic appropriations of place, immediately dreams of modernisation projects that would, in her view, bring the community up to date and out of isolation. Finally, in the third group, Victoria, the minister's daughter, longs to escape the mountains, sea, forest and "a weight of oldness" (20), to emigrate with Oscar, a prospective student and her lover to Argentina, while farm worker Euan prepares to fight in the Spanish Civil War.

In the second section, "The Crash," only fragments of the old social strata remain and further erosion of these is foregrounded. Margaret and her son Jimmy still reside in the Red House, though Jimmy has no respect for the heritage it represents. Ultimately the Red House is sold to the highest bidder, Euan, entrepreneur son of Oscar and Shona. Disruption occurs when a helicopter of American oil speculators crashes into the mountain. Vicky, a geologist from Illinois, is the only survivor. She responds to the place with a strong sense of déjà vu, claiming to have "recognised it straightaway" (81). Here again, Greig's use of accidental encounter is at the core of the play's structure. The crash brings together an unlikely couple, Euan and Vicky, a relationship that enables Euan to shape the future of the community and its environment.

Finally, in "The Mountain," the landscape has become a site of contestation. Euan, now the owner of a quarry, wishes to mine the mountain for his granite business. Euan's views on the utility of the environment are opposed by a camp of protestors represented by Annie. Euan's wife, Vicky, who in part two was his saving grace is now, in his view, a liability due to her quirky obsession with "regression therapy" and reincarnation. Oscar has died, though his ghost haunts Euan and the record of his experiences during the Spanish Civil War are pored over by his granddaughter, Victoria. In a direct echo of the original Victoria's desires in "The Bride," young Victoria wants to shake off "the weight of oldness," to escape the mountain and "all that made [her]" (172). This rejection of home and its heritage is mirrored by Old Victoria's return after decades in Argentina, and her recognition that despite her flight she has remained bound to home like "a stone half in the ground" (180). The play concludes with three generations of Victorias against the backdrop of a determining landscape from which they can never wholly detach themselves.

Throughout the play the landscape and environment provide the unifying frame. Repeatedly characters remark upon the air, the sea, the forest and, above all the mountains, though clearly their significance differs from one period to another, one character to another. Nevertheless, in each period, the mountain is the critical space, facilitating a sense of perspective and a fixed point of reference. The stalking party of part one and the collection of the corpses of deer from the mountainside, is echoed in part two when the locals are employed assembling the remnants of the helicopter and its passengers from the same territory, and in part three where young Victoria and Billy burn Oscar's remains up on the mountain. In *Victoria* no single character manages a "view from above," they find themselves inevitably in the shadow of the mountain, rather the tripartite, epic historical form of the play provides a long range perspective. Oscillation between acceptance and rejection of this environment is maintained throughout Greig's exploration of its role in shaping the characters' identities. Place emerges as defining, but also imprisoning; those who attempt to escape, to "walk into some new life" (172), find that they are held by what they wish to leave behind, a predicament illustrated by the recurring image of a stone protruding from the earth.

In each of these plays, Greig's interest revolves around modes of representing experiences of space and time at points where the legacy of modernity meets the conditions of postmodernity. Time after time collages of micronarratives and patterned images are used as a means of exploring a topic from multiple angles. Perspective, place and position are to be found in various permutations, however, one notable feature of all of these plays is the tension between movement and stasis, between itineraries and itinerants.

Perpetual Motion: Tourists & Vagabonds

If modernity has been characterised by movement and a discourse of progress, then postmodernity realigns the restlessness of modernity and exacerbates what Harvey calls time-space compression. As briefly noted earlier with regard to Mark Ravenhill's *Faust Is Dead*, mobility and disorientation, seem to typify contemporary Western society. I wish to return to Zygmunt Bauman's *Postmodernity and its Discontents* in more detail here as the figures of tourist and vagabond as "the metaphors of contemporary life,"[46] and his elaboration of the functions and implications of these figures of mobility chime with central concerns in Greig's work in which forms of dislocation, physical and ontological, are constants. Bauman contends that identity now is shaped by the absence of a sense of time-space as "solid" or "durable." In contrast:

> modern men and women lived in a time-space with *structure* [...]. In that structured world one could be lost, but one could also find one's way and arrive exactly where one aimed to be. The difference between getting lost and arriving was made of knowledge and determination: the knowledge of the time-space structure and the determination to follow, be what may, the chosen itinerary.[47]

Such a sense of purpose or belonging has been replaced by a refusal either to commit to a single vocation, or to allow "the past to bear upon the present." Bauman sees this as a move "[t]o abolish time in any other form but of a loose assembly, or an arbitrary sequence, of present moments; to flatten the flow of time into a *continuous present*." Consequently: "The hub of postmodern life strategy is not making identity stand—but the avoidance of being fixed."[48] And, of course, the figure of the tourist might be considered a prime example of this evasion, forever in a place but never of it, never at home. What separates

---

[46] Bauman, *Postmodernity and its Discontents*, 93.
[47] Bauman, *Postmodernity and its Discontents*, 86-87.
[48] Bauman, *Postmodernity and its Discontents*, 89.

tourists from vagabonds, for Bauman, is "the degree of freedom [they] possess in choosing [their] life itineraries."[49]

Movement and stasis are motifs threaded through each of the plays and are always knotted to questions of identity and identification. A sense of home is continuously problematised. In *Europe* this is particularly clear and has already been extensively explored by several critics. Bauman's tourist-vagabond spectrum might be used to add further nuances to the interpretations of identity formation in the play. The characters Fret and Sava from this perspective must be aligned with a modern, rather than postmodern, stance. They adhere to a structured sense of time-space in which certain values are conceived to be durable, and itineraries (not only in Bauman's sense of a life project, but in their belief in the railway and its timetables as a testament to European civilisation) are, or rather were, predictable. The other characters in *Europe* can be seen to move along the tourist-vagabond spectrum in one direction or another. As Bauman stresses, neither tourists nor vagabonds need actually move far, rather these labels signify attitudes to identity and dislocation. Thus Katia is initially a vagabond, in the sense that her movement is the result of the "inhospitable"[50] nature of her world rather than free choice. She critically responds to Adele's naïve cliché, "travel broadens the mind" with a violent image of its destructive effects on the self:

> It doesn't broaden the mind, it stretches it like skin across a tanning rack … a pegged skin out to dry. Each thing you see, each thing the continent coughs up for you stretches it tighter until you can't keep all the things you've seem in the same mind and the skin rips down the middle. (53)

By the play's conclusion, however, Katia has become more empowered (if her scepticism about the joys of tourism remains), her journey with Adele is a matter of her own

---

49 Bauman, *Postmodernity and its Discontents*, 93.
50 Bauman, *Postmodernity and its Discontents*, 92.

choosing and her status is ensured by the papers she has acquired. Morocco, at first seems to be a self-proclaimed tourist figure, constantly on the move in pursuit of business. He articulates an attitude to home rooted in nostalgia and fantasy, which is, significantly, "gratifying and consoling as long as it remains a *prospect*."[51] If this dream of home is translated into a reality, as noted earlier, it becomes a prison. Morocco's confident self-identification as a tourist gives way to a more ambivalent and vulnerable vision of his character by the play's conclusion. Adele's hunger to roam Europe is balanced by the fates of Berlin and Horse who suffer discontinuity and dislocation caused by political and economic transformation. Once again like Bauman's vagabond figure, these characters represent sinister alter egos, revealing the unacceptable, but ever present, side to the uncertainties of contemporary identity.

A similar disjunction is evident in *The Architect*. While Leo identifies with a life project of the modernist architect of social space, his children and wife illustrate disconnection and various types of refusal to commit. So for instance, Martin indulges a blatantly abstract fantasy of becoming an apprentice to a deaf carpenter in the mountains while he rejects both Leo's practical offer of an apprenticeship in his firm and Billy's offer of a relationship. Dorothy responds to any encounter that suggests a need for emotional engagement with nausea, while Paulina's fixation with pollution and disease lead her to self-isolation.

In *The cosmonaut's last message* no character is rooted or at home. One notable effect of the peripatetic dynamic of the play is that different places are rendered equal since they have little effect on, or meaning for, the identities of the characters. It is deeply ironic that it is a typical non place, the transitional space of a Heathrow airport terminal, in which soul searching conversations and gems of wisdom are exchanged, despite the play's other more meaningful locations. If Oleg and Casimir's

---

[51] Bauman, *Postmodernity and its Discontents*, 92

mission originally might be seen as a heroic modern destiny, notably this project has been forgotten by the world below. Their years in orbit in the non-space of their ship leave them with nothing more than nostalgia and fantasy, and eventually these retreats become just as confining as the spaceship itself. The remaining characters in the play pursue personal journeys or are launched on seemingly accidental paths; some of these are blatantly illusory and fanciful, others are a means to deny or evade realities. The enduring impression is of identities divorced from a coherent singular sense of vocation or belonging. So for instance, Nastasja, though convinced she could be a film star, finds herself working as an erotic dancer in a basement in London and is unable even to find out "where the film people go" (228). Her destiny is determined by the actions of others, her astronaut father, Keith and, finally, Eric. Indeed her ambitions are quickly discarded when Eric offers to take her away from the club and to Oslo. Less superficially Keith, following literally Eric's suggestion that "the chaos of [...] li[fe] can be simply left behind" (239), abandons his marriage, his affair and the rest of his established life. Eric seems closest to having a vocation, as he tells Keith they are both,

> Species—servant, genus—civil. We are the people who maintain order [...]. We serve. We civilise. It's not a job people admire, it's boring, maybe even despicable but people like us [...] are the bulwark against the flood (238).

Yet even the figure of Eric might be viewed through Bauman's model—he is powerful precisely because he is free to choose, his job involves international travel, he can shop extravagantly in London, he can rescue Nastasja from her underground and underworld prison on a whim. Like the ideal tourist he follows his desire and moves on once it is sated, as he tells Nastasja, "the only way to get rid of desire. Is to possess the thing you want. When you have it, you no longer want it. Then you're truly free" (270). Implicitly such a consumerist modus operandi applies not only to Nastasja, whom Eric quite obviously wishes to own, but similarly to his involvement in peace negotiations in the Middle East and work on a landmine treaty.

Victoria's more specific focus upon home and nation in a Scottish context is less explicitly compatible with Bauman's compass of contemporary rootlessness. Pertinently, the play's setting is removed from the usual co-ordinates of postmodern urban aimlessness and ontological instability. Yet, here too it is clear that Greig in considering the imprint of the past on the present, proposes a complex web of responses to place. As he says in the introductory note to the play, his interest lay in the ways in which "in smaller places [...] history is refracted and revealed in a different way [to how it is in urban centres], its effects inscribed more subtly on the landscape, and in sharper relief on the lives of the people."[52] In the unnamed coastal village, the lynchpin characters are depicted coming to terms with history in different ways. Victoria of part one, flees the confines of rural Scotland for the supposed freedom of the new world, but is seen in part three accepting the trauma of self-exile. Vicky's fascination with regression and reincarnation marks an attempt to recover a distant point of origin as a means of making sense of the present. In contrast, young Victoria in part three, rejects the weight of the past, in the shape of her grandfather's diary, which is thrown on his makeshift funeral pyre. Her words echo those uttered by the oldest Victoria sixty years previously, suggesting the futility of such a rejection and a discreetly recursive view of history. In *Victoria*, therefore, the characters' refusal to allow "the past to bear upon the present,"[53] is recurrent but thwarted.

Hauntings & Recursions

In the introductory chapter to this book, I referred to Marvin Carlson's notion of the haunted stage and the ways in which theatre recycles and reformulates images and ideas. In his work

---

[52] Greig, *Victoria*, 6.

[53] Bauman, *Postmodernity and its Discontents*, 89.

from the 1990s Greig is repeatedly drawn to the ghosts of modernity that flit through the nebulous zones of postmodernity. Indeed, overlapping elements of modernity and postmodernity are especially prominent in his use citations and references. Modernity's legacies surface in three of the plays under discussion quite openly. Fret's homage to the glories of the European railway system, takes the form of a vivid anthropomorphic metaphor—"Steel and tracks and trains like blood muscle and arteries holding the continent together" (53). As Rebellato comments, this phrase recalls fascistic (as well as futuristic) imagery and "the infamous apologia for Mussolini, that at least he made the trains run on time."[54] Yet the intertext appears in a scene in which Fret and Sava connect with each other in what Zenzinger describes as "rhapsodic antiphonic chant" celebrating a common civilisation, metonymically represented by the rail network.[55] This positive vision of Europe as a cradle of civilisation, a model of progress, where at some fundamental level, "We speak the same language, we think the same way" (52), is one of modernity's most valued metanarratives.[56] Its negative underside is, of course, presented by Katia who recalls the brutality of the Yugoslav war from which she and her father are fleeing, and by Horse and Berlin's neo-fascist racism. Throughout the play, the rail system functions as an extended metaphor providing a problematic image of the European body politic. Significantly, the system is represented as no longer cohesive or comprehensible to even its most faithful adherents; Fret complains that the railway timetables have ceased to be intelligible, "Four hundred pages and none of it makes sense. Times, stations, trains … They've no relation to anything. Meaningless … they might just as well be foreign" (11-12). As Zenzinger points out, "Greig shows the two old men out of touch with the 'new' Europe [and] plays on

54 Rebellato, Introduction, xvi.
55 Zenzinger, "David Greig's Scottish View of the 'New' Europe," 270.
56 Zenzinger, "David Greig's Scottish View of the 'New' Europe," 270.

the postmodern idea that language has no external reference"[57] by means of this episode.

Such contradictory currents course through discourses of modernity. As Malcolm Bradbury and James McFarlane observe, "modernism" is

> an extraordinary compound of the futurist and the nihilistic, the revolutionary and the conservative, the naturalistic and the symbolistic, the romantic and the classical [...] the celebration of a technological age and a condemnation of it; an excited acceptance of the belief that the old regimes of culture were over, and a deep despairing in the face of that fear; a mixture of convictions that the new forms were escapes from historicism and the pressures of time with convictions that they were precisely the living expression of those things.[58]

In *Europe, Victoria* and *The Architect*, Greig harnesses the tensions, intrinsic to the modern project, between creation and destruction, celebration and condemnation, but with reference to the present. This heritage, elliptically present in *Europe*, is more explicitly a feature of *Victoria*. Despite the remote setting of the play, its characters are touched by the fierce ideological battles of early twentieth century and more muted ones later. The three quotations that preface the play set the tone for each of its movements. The verse by John Cornford suggests an attitude that interlocks with the opinions expressed by a number of characters in part one—the sense of the present moment as a swift moving, destructive force, but simultaneously brimming with potential just as history like "roaring sands" must be mastered and "sw[ung] to its final course." A feeling of expectation and excitement is voiced by Victoria who is bent on leaving Scotland and tries to persuade Oscar to come away with her:

---

[57] Zenzinger, "David Greig's Scottish View of the 'New' Europe," 271.
[58] Malcolm Bradbury and James McFarlane, *Modernism: 1890-1930* (Harmondsworth: Penguin, 1976) 46.

World's moving. People moving, we've only to cross the sea.
Same sea we're looking at. The world's waiting for us, we've
only to take out places in it. You and me. Just to see ourselves in
a place that isn't here. The thought of it's like breathing again.
Like waking up. (20)

Similarly, the sense of being on the cusp of momentous change
is evident in David's fascination with Nazi ideology, which
demonstrates with remarkable precision the opposing forces
described by Bradbury and McFarlane, and which he allies to
the natural purity of the Scottish landscape:

I am a national socialist. I believe in the nation. In the
aristocracy of working men. Mountains, sea and forest [...]. The
forces are gathering [...]. The forces of the north, the pure,
against the forces of the degenerate, the civilised, the carriers of
disease. There will be a fire. A magnificent fire. (29)

If this political dimension is absent from Victoria's desires,
likewise Margaret, David's fiancée, only partially grasps the
implications of David's assertion that he is a "modernist"—for
her simply, "[i]f being a modernist means wanting things to
become more modern then I'm a modernist too" (48). Her
progressive and unsentimental vision of a modernist future
entails a causeway to connect the village with the outer world
and a society in which everything is taken care of by civil
servants; ironically, in the following part of the play, the social
transformation envisioned by Margaret involves her own
displacement from her seat of privilege. In contrast, Euan,
having listened to David's Nazi fervour and having been
rejected by Victoria, commits himself to fighting fascism in the
Spanish Civil War and, as is revealed later in the play, loses his
life in Spain.

These dramatic modern dichotomies and violently emotive
beliefs have been left behind in part two of the play, set thirty
six years later. A nostalgic note is struck by the second

prefacing citation--part of a poem by Sorley Maclean mourning the lost generations of rural Scotland:

> ... I will go down to Hallaig
> to the Sabbath of the dead,
> where the people are frequenting,
> every single generation gone.

Victoria, Euan and Gavin are among those who are gone; Shona, Callum, Margaret and Oscar have remained. Margaret's progressive modernism has paled into aristocratic conservativism. She resents Oscar's proposal to buy the Red House in order to transform it into a community college, she wonders if the work the Allan family over the centuries "carr[ies] any weight" (71). The dilapidated state of the property and her son Jimmy's attitude strongly point to the end of such an era. The energies of part one, have dissipated — individualism and confusion are now the key notes. Vicky survives the helicopter crash, but abandons her colleague. Oscar, once feckless and carefree, has become a cantankerous socialist haunted by his past deeds. But the socialist metanarrative he has espoused, summed up in his story of his first day in Madrid (which later is revealed to be Euan's memory, not his), no longer presents any clear purpose or justification for his past actions. Shona can only advise his to "[b]est think it's a dream. Path you're given's the one you've to walk. All the other paths are dreams" (122). The determining destiny of the pre-war period is replaced with a sense of the accidental. As Oscar says to Vicky, "[s]ome people survive for no reason. Chance. We do our best for each other in the face of chance" (106).

In part three the heritage of modernity is a distant and abstract notion for the youngest generation of characters. Young Victoria's response to Oscar's diary is one of incomprehension, "I can't get it to mean anything" (158). Her boyfriend David, by contrast, is excited by the story's potential as a profitable publication. Victoria feels nothing at her grandfather's funeral and is without direction. Her ruthlessly businesslike father, Euan, critically remarks: "I see no—forward movement in your life," to which she answers "Forward to what?" (144). If the quotation from Henrik Ibsen—"There really are times when the entire history of the world seems to me like one great shipwreck from which the only imperative is to rescue oneself"—is regarded as the motif in this final section of the play, it best describes young Victoria's ambivalent and postmodern attitude to the past. She attempts to exorcise the past by partially fulfilling Oscar's wish to be cremated and his ashes scattered in Spain. However, during the improvised cremation on the mountainside she burns not only Oscar's remains, and her money, but also his diary. It is tossed in the flames as a gesture of liberation. "I read it. Just history" (180) says Victoria, as she sets out in wilful ignorance to repeat it.

The Architect too summons the legacy of modernist idealism in its treatment of urban architecture. The play solicits reference to Ibsen's *The Master Builder* (1892), mirroring but updating the plot which traces the destiny of the artist from confident self-assertion to doubtful disillusionment and self-destruction. Greig's drama plays with multiple echoes of *The Master Builder*. Like Solness, Leo Black's character is initially defined by obstinacy, self-mythologising and delusion, and similarly he faces a mid-life challenge to his authority. Aline Solness is characterised by a sense of duty and conventionality that emanates from a profound selfishness, Greig's Paulina is a remarkably similar character. A comparable tension exists between the master builder and the architect's task of designing residential buildings and their desire to force people to adapt to their creations. If Solness is destroyed by the arrival of Hilde Wangel. Leo Black's demise is set in motion by Sheena Mackie and the ruin of both is depicted in terms of a fall. Borrowings and quotations from *The Master Builder* are scattered through *The Architect*. The lines "houses for people" and "homes for human beings" provide obvious threads connecting the plays. Less obviously perhaps, Martin's sardonic nicknaming of his father as "boss" is reminiscent of Brovik's bitter reference to Solness as "the boss" at the beginning of *The Master Builder*, Kaja's trembling adoration is found modified in Dorothy's nausea, just as Ragner's hatred of his boss might be linked with Martin's distain for Leo. And Solness's green jacket migrates in *The Architect* to a shop window display and is then stolen by Billy for Martin.

Yet, sandwiched between *The Master Builder* and *The Architect* is a most important intertext that extends the citation of Ibsen in a new direction and facilitates Greig's critical reflection on the present. Explicitly, Leo Black is the spokesman for a modernist architectural project. For Harvey, the role of the modernist artist was, in part, circumscribed by a kind of "creative heroism,"[59] and such a posture is perhaps most clearly in evidence in the field of modernist architecture. As Mies van der Rohe claimed in 1920s, architecture "is the will of the age conceived in spatial terms."[60] Exemplified by Le Corbusier's vision of mass housing as "machine[s] for living,"[61] the ambition was to create rationally ordered space, from which would emerge a rationally ordered society. Greig's character Leo Black is a belated defender of such an ideal, and significantly his award-winning creation is a socially dysfunctional wasteland. Black's modernist monument, (modelled, as he proudly declares, on Stonehenge) is demolished at the play's conclusion, its residents having campaigned to be rehoused. The reference here might be traced to the demise of grand modernist building. Harvey relates how:

> With respect to architecture, for example, Charles Jencks dates the symbolic end of modernism and the passage to the postmodern as 3.32 P.M. on 15 July 1972, when the Pruitt-Igoe housing development in St. Louis (a prize-winning version of Le Corbusier's "machine for modern living") was dynamited as

---

[59] Harvey, *The Condition of Postmodernity*, 17.

[60] Mies van der Rohe qtd in Harvey, *The Condition of Postmodernity*, 21.

[61] Le Corbusier, *Towards a New Architecture*, trans. Frederick Etchells (1923; New York: Dover, 1986) 4.

an uninhabitable environment for the low-income people it housed.[62]

Black resents the residents' complaints, obstinately refusing to help because "[he] won't see good ideas blown up just because some people can't see beyond their own misery" (168), though in the end he, like modernist architecture, is forced to accept their will. However, like as loyal captain, he prefers to go down with his ship, than to attempt to conform to a postmodern context. This context is represented in the play through Martin, Dorothy, Billy and Joe, but it too shadowed by considerable ambivalence. Leo's ill-fated masterpiece is an attempt to create a meaningful social space with its conceptual reference to the pre-modern Stonehenge and vision of urban community linked through shared public space, linked by balconies and walkways, and it is an ostentatious failure. Martin and Dorothy, and their companions Billy and Joe are wary of such grandiose visions of social purpose, yet they find no substantial or meaningful replacement. Their wanderings through the metropolis and along the motorways linking urban spaces are fundamentally lonely, fragmented and aimless.

Inexorable Connections & Ephemeral Communication
The cosmonaut's last message concludes with an invitation to communication, and indeed if Greig's work is to be regarded as engaging with contemporary conditions of existence in a globalised world, then communication is a vital part of its political import. "Globalisation," Rebellato observes, "is often described not only as a form of economic expansion but an expansion of consciousness. [...] The conduit of this sensibility is [...] the expansion and acceleration of our global transport and communication networks."[63] Yet as illustrated above in a world of time-space compressions, meaningful interaction is often short circuited. The ephemerality of communication

---

[62] Harvey, *The Condition of Postmodernity*, 39.
[63] Rebellato, Introduction, xiii.

recurs in each the plays I have discussed, but is perhaps most deliberately explored in *The cosmonaut's last message*. Zenzinger, noting the "pervading Beckettian influence" in this play, contends that "the lack of, and the attempts at establishing communication can be made out as the main strand in [its] intricate thematic pattern [...], suggesting that regardless of whether political borders are raised or torn down, other barriers even more difficult to overcome exist."[64] Certainly the existential dilemma faced by Casimir and Oleg in outer space recalls Beckett's drama. Like Krapp, Oleg's thwarted attempts to record his "last message" implies the insufficiency of language to express his feelings or to capture his memories, underscored by the doubt that the message will ever reach its destination. Greig's opening citation, an excerpt from Edwin Morgan's poem, "Thoughts of a Module," with its telegraphic tone, grammatically confused sentences and machine persona, thematically points to the complexities of communication in a technological age. Technology, while seeming to connect characters, most often constitutes yet another barrier or layer of interference—the spaceship's communication system, televisions and radios regularly produce nothing but static. Vivienne's profession as a speech therapist is ironically undermined by her inability to talk with her "closest" companion, her husband. Their conversation at the beginning of the play is remarkable precisely because it is so inept and stilted. Vivienne's response to Keith's new tie is symptomatic of their mutual remoteness: "The things you get. One gets" (216). Her immediate self-revision marks a linguistic withdrawal, an awkward re-establishing of safe distance. Similarly, Nastasja's ropey command of English, Bernard and Vivienne's parallel conversation in different languages, the stroke victim's inarticulacy, Claire's fatal lack of interpersonal skills, Eric's peace negotiations keep communication and its difficulties in the foreground of the play.

---

[64] Zenzinger, "David Greig's Scottish View of the 'New' Europe," 274.

Simultaneously, characters in each of the plays here discussed are unavoidably and inevitably connected with each other. Safe distances are never entirely sustainable. Greig's "geography of the imagination"[65] is one where, despite themselves, people are linked in rhizomatic patterns, and exchange and transformation, though difficult or even unlikely, can occur. In seeking this possibility, Greig's theatre provides few easy resolutions, but poses some provocative and lingering questions.

[65] David Greig, "Internal Exile," *Theatre Scotland* 3.11 (1994): 8-9.

Evasion or Engagement?

The augmentation of the contradictory and problematic phenomena of postmodernity and globalisation is the defining feature of the context in which the new drama of the 1990s emerged. As a direct result of these forces, the UK and Ireland are culturally a good deal more contiguous and interconnected than at any other time in the twentieth century. Simultaneously, accelerated technological, political and economic change destabilised senses of value, identity and distance in ways that are reflected in and refracted by the new drama.

The ambivalence of such an altered context, for many critics, is manifest in the allegedly questionable energies of the decade's theatre. Thus one of the main criticisms of 1990s new playwriting has been its failure "to engage with significant public issues," that form is privileged over content, or that superficiality takes precedence over depth.[1] Yet such criticism must be modulated if one looks beyond the popularised and provocative hub of the "in-yer-face sensibility."[2] The "new aesthetic" was, according to Aleks Sierz, typified by "experiential confrontation," shock effects and lack of moral closure.[3] Nonetheless, relationships between such a "new aesthetic" and its theatrical and theoretical predecessors, signal its fundamentally intertextual, even recursive, nature. As Piet

[1] Vera Gottlieb, "Lukewarm Britannia," *Theatre in a Cool Climate*, eds. Vera Gottlieb and Colin Chambers (Oxford: Amber Lane, 1999) 212.

[2] Aleks Sierz, *In-Yer-Face Theatre: British Drama Today* (London: Faber and Faber, 2001) 233.

[3] Sierz, *In-Yer-Face Theatre*, 243-4.

Dufraeye remarks, "it is ironic that the question as to how theatre codes have recently been extended bears a millennial urgency to it, harkening back to the radical changes of theatre around the previous millennial turnover in the early years of the twentieth century."[4] Time and again "provocative theatre sets up a complicitous dynamic between stage and audience" that all too easily topples over into superficiality and is subject to early exhaustion of effect.[5] Undeniably, provocation is a dimension to the dramaturgies of some, but clearly not all, of the playwrights discussed here; rather, as the novelty of the 1990s wears off, it is evident that such a sensibility is a part of a much more extensive and intricate web of cultural and dramatic negotiations of postmodern conditions in the final decade of the century and, inevitably, continue beyond it. These conditions, as has been argued variously by the theorists cited in this work, involve the erosion or dissolution of particular social and political values, the advance of globalisation and the reconfiguration of the local, and a crisis not only of representation, but of ethics. Consequently, they solicit new perspectives on the affinities and associations, influences and objectives to be found in contemporary drama and, in particular, among the new generation of playwrights who appeared in the 1990s.

Attempting to map a concept of postmodernism, Ihab Hassan refers to "a number of related cultural tendencies, a constellation of values, a repertoire of procedures and attitudes" among an extremely heterogeneous list of philosophers, historians, literary theorists, architects, artists, writers and musicians. No school or movement or paradigm can adequately comprehend all the elements that have

---

[4] Piet Dufraeye, "In-Yer-Face Theatre? Reflections on Provocation and Provoked Audiences in Contemporary Theatre," *Extending the Code: New Forms of Dramatic and Theatrical Expression*, CDE 11, eds. Hans-Ulrich Mohr and Kerstin Mächler (Trier: Wissenschaflicher Verlag Trier, 2004) 79-98. 79.

[5] Dufraeye, "In-Yer-Face Theatre?" 94.

contributed to notions of the postmodern.[6] Similarly, the creative diversity of 1990s drama precludes interpretation in terms of a single paradigm, school or movement. Rather Hassan's "constellation" model provides a means by which the attitudes, values and practices of the playwrights in focus here might be analysed in relation to the received discourses of postmodernity. The range of their dramatic practices reflects the contradictoriness of responses to postmodern conditions—both thematically and formally, their procedures and attitudes hinge upon citation and intertextuality; narrative ambiguity and fragmentation; performative identities; and, to a lesser degree, spectacle. David Greig explores the contentious spaces of modernity and postmodernity, where interconnectedness persists even when communication seems impossible. Mark Ravenhill's work scrapes at the surface of contemporary political and moral disorientation. Martin McDonagh engages in a frenetically provocative production of fictionalised local identities. Sarah Kane's work attempts to cut through to some absolute core of intensity to assuage ontological incertitude, while a similar concern seems to generate both Marina Carr's equivocal reinscription of destiny and Conor McPherson's ambivalent performative narratives. Clearly traceable are a panoply of strategies, ludic, traumatic, violent, that highlight ontological uncertainty or the construct (or constructedness) of identity and which is allied with a strong focus upon minor, personal and fractured narratives. In addition, questions concerning the *true* or the *authentic* repeatedly resurface alongside a propensity to self-conscious textuality and, at times, ironic intertextuality.

That said, the work of these six writers is not simply commensurate with the radical disruptions of theatre-as-representation attempted by postmodern, or postdramatic,

---

6 Ihab Hassan, "Toward a Concept of Postmodernism," *Postmodernism: A Reader* ed. Thomas Docherty (New York: Harvester Wheatsheaf, 1993) 147. Excerpted from Ihab Hassan, *The Postmodern Turn* (Columbus: Ohio State University, 1987).

theatre—as discussed by Johannes Birringer, Elinor Fuchs, Marvin Carlson or Hans-Thies Lehmann, among others. Neither the posthuman nor the postdramatic have been (fully) processed by such theatre, though at times they may be ephemerally perceptible. Notably, the convention of the fourth wall often remains unchallenged. Also preserved is the play-as-text, and as intertext. Although Kane tends toward the dissolution of character in her final plays, character is generally maintained, if tested and distorted, throughout the remaining work considered here. What is perhaps most striking is how perception and the construction of narrative are foregrounded to the extent that this becomes the plays' ambivalent message, displacing unambiguous moral or political points. Ultimately the new drama of the 1990s—as exemplified by the plays of Carr, Kane, Greig, Ravenhill, McPherson and McDonagh—is marked less by revolutionary transformations of form or an explicit politics, than by the critical potential of ethical ambivalence, performative story-telling and stylistic appropriation, that involves both evasion and engagement.

Bibliography

Adorno, Theodor W. *The Jargon of Authenticity*. 1964. Trans. Knut Tarnowski and Fredric Will. Evanston Ill: Northwestern University Press, 1973.

Ansorge, Peter. *From Liverpool to Los Angeles: On Writing for Theatre, Film and Television*. London: Faber and Faber, 1997.

Appadurai, Arjun. "Modernity at Large: Cultural Dimensions of Globalization." *Minneapolis and London: University of Minnesota Press, 1996.*

Aristotle, *Poetics*. Trans. Ingram Bywater. New York: Modern Library, 1954.

Armand, Louis, ed. *Avant-Post: The Avant-Garde Under "Post"-Conditions*. Prague: Litteraria Pragensia, 2006.

Artaud, Antonin. *Theatre and its Double*. 1938. Trans. Victor Corti. London: Calder, 1993.

Augé, Marc. *Non-Places: Introduction to an Anthropology of Supermodernity*. Trans. John Howe. London: Verso, 1995.

Barker, Howard. *Arguments for a Theatre*. 1989. Manchester: Manchester University Press, 1993.

Barthes, Roland. *Image, Text, Music*. Trans. Stephen Heath. London: Fontana, 1977.

Baudrillard, Jean. *Jean Baudrillard: Selected Writings*. Ed. Mark Poster. Cambridge: Polity, 1988.

Baudrillard, Jean. *Simulations and Simulacra*. 1981. Trans. Sheila Faria Glaser. Ann Arbor: University of Michigan Press, 1994

Baudrillard, Jean. *Simulations*. 1981. Trans. Paul Foss, Paul Patton and Philip Beitchman. New York: Semiotext(e), 1983.

Bauman, Zygmunt. *Postmodernity and its Discontents*. Cambridge: Polity, 1997.

Benjamin, Walter. *Illuminations*. 1955. Ed. Hannah Arendt. Trans. Harry Zohn. New York: Harcourt Brace Jovanovich, 1968. 217-252.

Bentley, Eric. *The Brecht Commentaries 1943-1986*. New York: Grove, 1987.

Bentley, Eric. *The Playwright as Thinker: A Study of Drama in Modern Times*. New York: Meridian, 1955.

Bertens, Hans. *The Idea of the Postmodern: A History*. London: Routledge, 1995.

Birringer, Johannes. "Interacting: Performance and Transmediality." *Monologues: Theatre, Performance, Subjectivity*. Ed. Clare Wallace. Prague: Litteraria Pragensia, 2006. 297-325.

Birringer, Johannes. *Theatre, Theory, Postmodernism*. Bloomington and Indiana: Indiana University Press, 1991.

Blau, Herbert. "The Oversight of Ceaseless Eyes." *Around the Absurd: Essays on Modern and Postmodern Drama*. Eds. Enoch Brater and Ruby Cohn. Ann Arbor: University of Michigan Press, 1990. 279-291.

Blau, Herbert. "Universals of Performance; or Amortizing Play" *By Means of Performance: Intercultural Studies of Theatre and Ritual*. Eds. Richard Schechner and Willa Appel. Cambridge: Cambridge University Press, 1990. 250-272.

Blau, Herbert. *To All Appearances: Ideology and Performance*. London and New York: Routledge, 1992.

Bolger, Dermot, ed. *Druids, Dudes, and Beauty Queens: The Changing Face of Irish Theatre*. Dublin: New Island, 2001.

Bort, Eberhard, ed. *The State of Play: Irish Theatre in the 'Nineties*. Trier: Wissenschaftlicher Verlag Trier, 1996.

Bracken, Len. *Guy Debord: Revolutionary*. Venice CA: Feral, 1997.

Bradby, David and Annie Sparks. *Mise en Scène: French Theatre Now*. London: Methuen, 1997.

Bradwell, Mike, ed. *The Bush Theatre Book*. London: Methuen, 1997.

Brandt, George W., ed. *Modern Theories of Drama: A Selection of Writings on Drama and Theatre*. Oxford: Clarendon, 1998.

Brater, Enoch and Ruby Cohn, eds. *Around the Absurd: Essays on Modern and Postmodern Drama*. Ann Arbor: University of Michigan Press, 1990.

Brecht, Bertolt. "A Short Organum for the Theatre." 1948. Trans. John Willett. *Modern Theories of Drama: A Selection of Writings on Drama and Theatre*. Ed. George W. Brandt. Oxford: Clarendon, 1998. 232-246.

Brecht, Bertolt. "Short Description of a New Technique in Acting which Produces an Alienation Effect." 1940. Trans. John Willett.

The Twentieth Century Performance Reader. Eds. Michael Huxley and Noel Witts. 2nd Edition. London: Routledge, 2002. 93-104.

Brecht, Bertolt. "The Modern Theatre is the Epic Theatre: Notes to the Opera *Aufstieg und Fall der Stadt Mahagonny.*" 1930. Trans. John Willett. *Modern Theories of Drama: A Selection of Writings on Drama and Theatre*. Ed. George W. Brandt. Oxford: Clarendon, 1998. 224-231.

Bronfen, Elisabeth. *The Knotted Subject: Hysteria and its Discontents*. Princeton NJ: Princeton University Press, 1998.

Brook, Peter. "The Culture of Links." *The Intercultural Performance Reader*. Ed. Patrice Pavis. London and New York: Routledge, 1996. 63-66.

Brook, Peter. *The Empty Space*. 1968. London: Penguin, 1990.

Brooks, Peter. *Reading for the Plot: Design and Intention in Narrative*. Cambridge MA and London: Harvard University Press, 1984.

Brooks, Peter. *The Melodramatic Imagination: Balzac, Henry James, Melodrama and the Mode of Excess*. New Haven: Yale University Press, 1976.

Bürger, Peter. *Theory of the Avant-Garde*. 1974. Trans. Michael Shaw. Foreword Johen Schulte-Sasse. Theory and History of Literature, Vol. 4. Minneapolis: University Press of Minnesota, 1984.

Buse, Peter. *Drama + Theory: Critical Approaches to Modern British Drama*. Manchester: Manchester University Press, 2001.

Buxbaum, Martin. "'It's All Politics, Stupid!': David Hare and Mark Ravenhill's Latest, *Via Dolorosa* and *Some Explicit Polaroids.*" *(Dis)Continuities—Trends and Traditions in Contemporary Theatre and Drama in English*. Eds. Margarete Rubik and Elke Mettinger-Schartmann. CDE 9. Trier: Wissenschaftlicher Verlag Trier, 2002. 47-56.

Cahn, Steven M., ed. *Classics of Western Philosophy*. 4th ed. Indianapolis and Cambridge: Hackett, 1995.

Callahan, John M. "The Ultimate in Theatre Violence." *Violence in Drama*. Ed. James Redmond. *Themes in Drama* Vol. 13. Cambridge: Cambridge University Press, 1991. 165-175.

Callens, Johan. "Sorting Out Ontologies in Mark Ravenhill's *Faust (Faust Is Dead).*" *Mediated Drama Dramatized Media*. Ed. Eckart Voigts-Virchow. CDE 7. Trier: Wissenschaftlicher Verlag Trier, 2000. 167-178.

Cardullo, Bert and Robert Knopf. *Theater of the Avant-Garde 1890-1950: A Critical Anthology*. New Haven and London: Yale University Press, 2001.

Carlson, Marvin. *Performance: A Critical Introduction*. London and New York: Routledge, 1996.

Carlson, Marvin. *The Haunted Stage: The Theatre as Memory Machine*. Ann Arbor: University of Michigan Press, 2001.

Carlson, Marvin. *Theatre Semiotics: Signs of Life*. Bloomington and Indiana: Indiana University Press, 1990.

Carlson, Marvin. *Theories of the Theatre: A Historical and Critical Survey from the Greeks to the Present*. 1984. Ithaca, NY: Cornell University Press, 1993.

Carr, Marina. "Dealing With the Dead." *Irish University Review* 28:1 (1998): 190-196.

Carr, Marina. *Ariel*. Meath: Gallery, 2002.

Carr, Marina. *By the Bog of Cats…* . Meath: Gallery, 1998.

Carr, Marina. *On Raftery's Hill*. Meath: Gallery, 2000.

Carr, Marina. *Plays I: Low in the Dark, The Mai, Portia Coughlan, By the Bog of Cats…*. London: Faber and Faber, 1999.

Carr, Marina. *Portia Coughlan*. Meath: Gallery, 1998.

Carr, Marina. *The Mai*. Meath: Gallery, 1995.

Carr, Mary. "Don't Myth it: The Responsibilities of the Critic towards New Companies." *Irish Theatre Forum* 1.2 (1997) <http://www.ucd.ie/~irthfrm/seciss.htm>.

Chambers, Lilian and Eamonn Jordan, eds. *The Theatre of Martin McDonagh: A World of Savage Stories*. Dublin: Carysfort, 2006.

Chambers, Lilian, Ger Fitzgibbon and Eamonn Jordan, eds. *Theatre Talk: Voices of Irish Theatre Practitioners*. Dublin: Carysfort, 2001.

Connor, Stephen. *Theory and Cultural Value*. Oxford: Blackwell, 1992.

Counsell, Colin. *Signs of Performance: An Introduction to Twentieth Century Theatre*. London and New York: Routledge, 1996.

Crimp, Douglas. "Appropriating Appropriation." *Image Scavengers: Photography*. Ed. Paula Marincola. Philadelphia: Institute of Contemporary Art/ University of Pennsylvania Press, 1982. 27-34.

Cummings, Scott T. "Homo Fabulator: The Narrative Imperative in Conor McPherson's Plays." *Theatre Stuff: Critical Essays on Contemporary Irish Theatre*. Ed. Eamonn Jordan. Dublin: Carysfort, 2000. 303-312.

Debord, Guy. *The Society of the Spectacle*. 1967. Trans. Donald Nicholson-Smith. New York: Zone, 1995.

Derrida, Jacques. *Margins of Philosophy*. 1972. Trans. Alan Bass. Chicago: University of Chicago Press, 1982.

Derrida, Jacques. *Writing and Difference*. Trans. Alan Bass. London and Henley: Routledge and Keegan Paul, 1978.

Devine, T.M. *The Scottish Nation 1700-2000*. London: Penguin, 2000.

Docherty, Thomas. *Postmodernism: A Reader*. New York: Harvester Wheatsheaf, 1993.

Dromgoole, Dominic. *The Full Room: An A-Z of Contemporary Playwriting*. London: Methuen, 2002.

Dufraeye, Piet. "In-Yer-Face Theatre? Reflections on Provocation and Provoked Audiences in Contemporary Theatre." *Extending the Code: New Forms of Dramatic and Theatrical Expression*. CDE 11. Eds. Hans-Ulrich Mohr and Kerstin Mächler. Trier: Wissenschaflicher Verlag Trier, 2004. 79-98.

Edgar, David, ed. *State of Play: Playwrights on Playwriting*. London: Faber and Faber, 1999.

Edgar, David. *Contemporary British Dramatists*. London: British Council, 1992.

Elam, Kier. *The Semiotics of Theatre and Drama*. London and New York: Methuen, 1980.

Elsom, John. *Post-War British Theatre*. 2nd ed. London, Boston and Henley: Routledge and Keegan Paul, 1979.

Emeljanow, Victor. "Grand Guignol and the Orchestration of Violence." *Violence in Drama*. Ed. James Redmond. *Themes in Drama* Vol. 13. Cambridge: Cambridge University Press, 1991. 151-163.

Esslin, Martin. *Antonin Artaud: The Man and His Work*. 1976. London: Calder, 1999.

Esslin, Martin. *Brecht: The Man and His Work*. 1959. New York: Anchor, 1971.

Esslin, Martin. *The Field of Drama*. London: Methuen, 1988.

Esslin, Martin. *The Theatre of the Absurd*. 1961. Harmondsworth: Pelican, 1968.

Eyre, Richard and Nicholas Wright. *Changing Stages: A View of British Theatre in the Twentieth Century*. London: Bloomsbury, 2000.

Foster, Hal, ed. and intro. *The Anti-Aesthetic: Essays on Postmodern Culture*. 1983. New York: New Press, 1998.

Freud Sigmund. *The Interpretation of Dreams*. 1900. Trans. James Strachey. New York: Avon/Basic, 1965.

Freud, Sigmund. "Psychopathic Characters on the Stage." *Art and Literature* Vol. 14 Penguin Freud Library. 1904. London: Penguin, 1990. 120-127.

Freud, Sigmund. "The Theme of the Three Caskets." *Art and Literature* Vol. 14 Penguin Freud Library. 1913. London: Penguin, 1990. 234-247.

Freud, Sigmund. "The Uncanny." *Art and Literature* Vol. 14 Penguin Freud Library. 1919. London: Penguin, 1990. 336-376.

Freud, Sigmund. *Civilisation and its Discontents.* 1930. Trans. James Strachey. New York: Norton, 1962.

Fuchs, Elinor. *The Death of Character: Perspectives on Theatre after Modernism.* Bloomington and Indiana: Indiana University Press, 1996.

Furay, Julia and Redmond O'Hanlon, eds. *Critical Moments: Fintan O'Toole on Modern Irish Drama.* Dublin: Carysfort, 2003.

Gottlieb, Vera and Colin Chambers, eds. *Theatre in a Cool Climate.* Oxford: Amber Lane, 1999.

Graham, Colin. *Deconstructing Ireland: Identity, Theory, Culture.* Edinburgh: Edinburgh University Press, 2001.

Greig, David. "Internal Exile." *Theatre Scotland* 3.11(1994): 8-10.

Greig, David. *Plays 1.* Intro. Dan Rebellato. London: Methuen, 2002.

Greig, David. *Victoria.* London: Methuen, 2000.

Grene, Nicholas. "Black Pastoral: 1990s Images of Ireland." *Litteraria Pragensia* 10.20 (2000): 67-75.

Grene, Nicholas. *The Politics of Irish Drama: Plays in Context from Boucicault to Friel.* Cambridge: Cambridge University Press, 1999.

Harvey, David. *The Condition of Postmodernity: An Enquiry into the Origins of Cultural Change.* Cambridge MA and Oxford: Blackwell, 1990.

Hassan, Ihab. "From Postmodernism to Postmodernity: The Local/Global Context." <www.ihabhassan.com/postmodernism_to_postmodernity.htm>.

Hassan, Ihab. "Toward a Concept of Postmodernism." *Postmodernism: A Reader.* Ed. Thomas Docherty. New York: Harvester Wheatsheaf, 1993. 146-156.

Hayman, Ronald. *British Theatre since 1955: A Reassessment.* Oxford: Oxford University Press, 1979.

Huber, Werner. "Contemporary Drama as Meta-Cinema: Martin McDonagh and Marie Jones." *(Dis)Continuities—Trends and Traditions in Contemporary Theatre and Drama in English.* Eds.

Margarete Rubik and Elke Mettinger-Schartmann. CDE 9. Trier: Wissenschaftlicher Verlag Trier, 2002. 13-23.

Huber, Werner. "The Plays of Martin McDonagh." *Twentieth-Century Theatre and Drama in English: Festschrift for Heinz Kosok on the Occasion of his 65th Birthday.* Ed. Jürgen Kamm. Trier: Wissenschaftlicher Verlag Trier, 1999. 555-571.

Hughes, Declan. "Who The Hell Do We Think We Still Are? Reflections on Irish Theatre and Identity." *Theatre Stuff: Critical Essays on Contemporary Irish Theatre.* Ed. Eamonn Jordan. Dublin: Carysfort, 2000. 8-15.

Hutcheon, Linda. "Irony, Nostalgia, and the Postmodern." University of Toronto
<www.utlink.utoronto.ca/www.utel/criticism/hutchINP.html>.

Hutcheon, Linda. *A Poetics of Postmodernism. History, Theory, Fiction.* London and New York: Routledge, 1988.

Hutchinson, David. *The Modern Scottish Theatre.* Glasgow: Molendinar Press, 1977.

Huxley, Michael and Noel Witts, eds. *The Twentieth Century Performance Reader.* 2nd Edition. London: Routledge, 2002.

Innes, Christopher. *Avant-Garde Theatre 1892-1992.* London: Routledge, 1993.

Innes, Christopher. *Modern British Drama 1890-1990.* Cambridge: Cambridge University Press, 1992.

Innes, Christopher. *Modern British Drama: The Twentieth Century.* Cambridge: Cambridge University Press, 2002.

Jameson Fredric. *Postmodernism, or The Cultural Logic of Late Capitalism.* London: Verso, 1991.

Jordan, Eamonn, ed. *Theatre Stuff: Critical Essays on Contemporary Irish Theatre.* Dublin: Carysfort, 2000.

Jordan, Eamonn. "Pastoral Exhibits: Narrating Authenticities in Conor McPherson's *The Weir.*" *Irish University Review.* 34.2 (2004): 351-368.

Kane, Sarah. *Complete Plays.* Intro. David Greig. London: Methuen, 2001.

Kaufmann, Walter. *Tragedy and Philosophy.* New York: Doubleday Anchor, 1969.

Kiberd, Declan. *Inventing Ireland: The Literature of the Modern Nation.* London: Jonathan Cape, 1995.

Kilroy, Tom. "A Generation of Playwrights." *Theatre Stuff: Critical Essays on Contemporary Irish Theatre*. Ed. Eamonn Jordan. Dublin: Carysfort, 2000. 1-7.

Kuhns, Richard. *Tragedy: Contradiction and Repression*. Chicago: University of Chicago Press, 1991.

Kurdi, Mária. "The Helen of Inishmaan Pegging Eggs: Gender, Sexuality and Violence." *The Theatre of Martin McDonagh: A World of Savage Stories*. Eds. Lilian Chambers and Eamonn Jordan. Dublin: Carysfort, 2006. 96-115.

Kurdi, Mária. *Codes and Masks: Aspects of Identity in Contemporary Irish Plays in an Intercultural Context*. Frankfurt: Peter Lang, 2000.

Lacan, Jacques. *Écrits: A Selection*. Trans. Alan Sheridan. New York and London: Norton, 1977.

Lacan, Jacques. *The Four Fundamental Concepts of Psycho-analysis*. 1973. Ed. Jacques-Alain Miller. Trans. Alan Sheridan. Intro. David Macey. London: Vintage, 1998.

Lachman, Michal. "Happy and in Exile? Martin McDonagh's 'Leenane Trilogy'." *Engaging Modernity*. Eds. Michael Böss and Eamonn Maher. Dublin: Veritas, 2003. 194-206.

Leeney, Cathy and Anna McMullan eds. *The Theatre of Marina Carr: "Before Rules was Made."* Dublin: Carysfort, 2003

Lehmann, Hans-Thies. *Postdramatic Theatre*. 1999. Trans. Karen Jürs-Munby. London and New York: Routledge, 2006.

Lenz, Peter. "Anything New in the Feckin' West?: Martin McDonagh's *Leenane Trilogy* and the Juggling with Irish Literary Stereotypes." *(Dis)Continuities—Trends and Traditions in Contemporary Theatre and Drama in English*. Eds. Margarete Rubik and Elke Mettinger-Schartmann. CDE 9. Trier: Wissenschaftlicher Verlag Trier, 2002. 25-38.

Lester, Gideon. "Reign of Terror: The Peculiar Charms of the Grand Guignol." American Repertory Theatre. 13 Jan. 1997. <http://www.fas.harvard.edu/~art/caligari1.html>.

Llewellyn-Jones, Margaret. *Contemporary Irish Drama and Cultural Identity*. Bristol: Intellect, 2002.

Lonergan, Patrick. "Globalisation and Irish Theatre." Critical Interventions Series—Irish Writers Centre. 2002. <http://www.writerscentre.ie/anthology/plonergan.html>.

Luckhurst, Mary. "Contemporary English Theatre: Why Realism?" *(Dis)Continuities—Trends and Traditions in Contemporary Theatre and Drama in English*. Eds. Margarete Rubik and Elke Mettinger-

Schartmann. CDE 9. Trier: Wissenschaftlicher Verlag Trier, 2002. 73-84.

Lyotard, Jean François. "Answering the Question: What is Postmodernism?" *Postmodernism: A Reader*. Ed. Thomas Docherty. New York: Harvester Wheatsheaf, 1993. 38-46.

Lyotard, Jean François. "Note on the Meaning of 'Post-'" *Postmodernism: A Reader*. Ed. Thomas Docherty. New York: Harvester Wheatsheaf, 1993. 47-50.

Lyotard, Jean-François. *The Postmodern Condition: A Report on Knowledge*. 1979. Trans. Geoff Bennington and Brian Massumi. Foreword Fredric Jameson. Manchester: Manchester University Press, 1984.

MacLean, Marie. *Narrative as Performance*. New York: Routledge, 1988.

Maufort, Marc and Franca Bellarsi, eds. *Crucible of Cultures: Anglophone Drama at the Dawn of a New Millenium*. Brussels: Peter Lang, 2002.

Maxwell, D.E.S. *A Critical History of Modern Irish Drama, 1891-1980*. New York: Cambridge University Press, 1984.

McAvinchey, Caoimhe. "Theatre—Act or Place?" *Theatre Stuff: Critical Essays on Contemporary Irish Theatre*. Ed. Eamonn Jordan. Dublin: Carysfort, 2000. 84-88.

McCullough, Christopher. *Theatre and Europe 1957-95*. Exeter: Intellect, 1996.

McDonagh, Martin. *A Skull in Connemara*. London: Methuen, 1997.

McDonagh, Martin. *The Beauty Queen of Leenane*. London: Methuen, 1996.

McDonagh, Martin. *The Cripple of Inishmaan*. London: Methuen, 1996.

McDonagh, Martin. *The Lieutenant of Inishmore*. London: Methuen, 2001.

McDonagh, Martin. *The Lonesome West*. London: Methuen, 1998.

McDonagh, Martin. *The Pillowman*. London: Faber and Faber, 2003.

McDonald, Marianne. "Classics as Celtic Firebrand: Greek Tragedy, Irish Playwrights and Colonialism." *Theatre Stuff: Critical Essays on Contemporary Irish Theatre*. Ed. Eamonn Jordan. Dublin: Carysfort, 2000. 16-26.

McGuinness, Frank ed. *The Dazzling Dark: New Irish Plays*. London: Faber and Faber, 1996.

McHale, Brian. *Constructing Postmodernism*. London: Routledge, 1992.

McHale, Brian. *Postmodern Fiction*. London and New York: Methuen, 1987.

McMillan, Joyce. "Ireland's Winning Hand." *Irish Theatre Magazine* 3.15 (2003): 15-23.

McMullan, Anna. "Irish Women Playwrights since 1958." *British and Irish Women Dramatists since 1958: A Critical Handbook*. Eds. Trevor R. Griffiths and Margaret Llewellyn-Jones. London and New York: Open University Press, 1993,

McMullan, Anna. "Marina Carr's Unhomely Women." *Irish Theatre Magazine* 1.1 (1998): 14-16.

McPherson, Conor. *Plays: Two*. London: Nick Hern, 2004.

McPherson, Conor. *Shining City*. London: Nick Hern, 2004.

McPherson, Conor. *The Weir and Other Plays*. New York: Theater Communications Group, 1999.

Merriman, Victor. "Decolonisation Postponed: The Theatre of Tiger Trash." *Irish University Review* 29.2 (1999): 305-317.

Merriman, Victor. "Settling for More: Excess and Success in Contemporary Irish Drama." *Druids, Dudes, and Beauty Queens: The Changing Face of Irish Theatre*. Ed. Dermot Bolger. Dublin: New Island, 2001. 55-71.

Miller, J. Hillis. "Narrative." *Critical Terms for Literary Study*. Eds. Frank Lentricchia and Thomas McLaughlin. Chicago: University of Chicago Press, 1990. 66-79.

Miller, J. Hillis. Tropes, Parables, Performatives: Essays on Twentieth-Century Literature. *Durham, N.C.: Duke University Press, 1991*.

Morash, Chris. *A History of Irish Theatre 1601-2000*. Cambridge: Cambridge University Press 2002.

Moroney, Mic. "The Twisted Mirror: Landscapes, Mindscapes, Politics and Language on the Irish Stage." *Druids, Dudes and Beauty Queens*. Ed. Dermot Bolger. Dublin: New Island, 2001. 250-275.

Morse, Donald. "'Sleepwalkers along a precipice': Staging Memory in Marina Carr's *The Mai*." *Hungarian Journal of English and American Studies* 2.1 (1996): 111-121.

Müller, Anja. "'We are also Europe': Staging Displacement in David Greig's *Europe*." *Staging Displacement, Exile and Diaspora in Contemporary Drama in English*. CDE 12. Ed. Christoph Houswitschka. Trier: Wissenschaftlicher Verlag Trier, 2005. 151-168.

Müller, Klaus-Peter. "Political Plays in England in the 1990s,." *British Drama of the 1990s*. Eds. Reitz, Bernhard and Mark Berninger. Heidelberg: Universitätsverlag C. Winter, 2002.15-36.

Murphy, Richard. *Theorizing the Avant-Garde: Modernism, Expressionism and the Problem of Postmodernity.* Cambridge: Cambridge University Press, 1999.

Murray, Christopher. *Twentieth-Century Irish Drama: Mirror up to Nation.* Manchester: Manchester University Press, 1997.

Nesteruk, Peter. "Ritual, Sacrifice, and Identity in Recent Political Drama—with Reference to the Plays of David Greig." *Journal of Dramatic Theory and Criticism* 15.1 (2000): 21-42.

Nietzsche, Friedrich. *The Birth of Tragedy.* 1872. Trans. Francis Golffing. New York: Doubleday Anchor, 1956.

Orr, John. *Tragic Drama and Modern Society: Studies in Social and Literary Theory of Drama from 1870 to the Present.* London: Macmillan, 1981.

Pavis, Patrice, ed. *The Intercultural Performance Reader.* London and New York: Routledge, 1996.

Pavis, Patrice. *Dictionary of the Theatre: Terms, Concepts and Analysis.* Trans. Christine Shantz. Toronto and Buffalo: University of Toronto Press, 1998.

Pavis, Patrice. *Theatre at the Crossroads of Culture.* Trans. Loren Kruger. London and New York: Routledge, 1992.

Pilný, Ondřej. "Martin McDonagh: Parody? Satire? Complacency?" *Irish Studies Review* 12.2 (2004).

Pilný, Ondřej. "Staging Ireland: Identity and Irony in Modern Irish Drama." Diss. Charles University, 2001.

Pilný, Ondřej. *Irony and Identity in Modern Irish Drama.* Prague: Litteraria Pragensia, 2006.

Poggi, Valentina and Margaret Rose, eds. *A Theatre that Matters: Twentieth-Century Scottish Drama and Theatre.* Milan: Unicopli, 2001.

Raab, Michael. "The End of a Wave: New British and Irish Plays in the German-speaking Theatre." *(Dis)Continuities—Trends and Traditions in Contemporary Theatre and Drama in English.* Eds. Margarete Rubik and Elke Mettinger-Schartmann. CDE 9. Trier: Wissenschaftlicher Verlag Trier, 2002. 39-46.

Rabey, David Ian. *English Drama Since 1940.* London: Longman, 2003.

Ravenhill, Mark. *Plays 1.* Intro. Dan Rebellato. London: Methuen, 2001.

Rebellato, Dan. *1956 And All That: The Making of Modern British Drama.* London and New York: Routledge, 1999.

Reinelt, Janelle G. "Performing Europe: Identity Formation for a 'New' Europe." *Theatre Journal* 53.3 (2001): 365-87.

Reinhelt, Janelle G. and Joseph R. Roach, eds. *Critical Theory and Performance*. Michigan: University of Michigan Press, 1992.

Reitz, Bernhard and Mark Berninger, eds. *British Drama of the 1990s*. Heidelberg: Universitätsverlag C. Winter, 2002.

Roche, Anthony. "Women on the Threshold: J.M. Synge's *The Shadow of the Glen*, Teresa Deevy's *Katie Roche* and Marina Carr's *The Mai*." *Irish University Review* 25.1 (1995): 143-62.

Roche, Anthony. *Contemporary Irish Drama: From Beckett to McGuinness*. Dublin: Gill and Macmillan, 1994.

Rockett, Kevin, Luke Gibbons and John Hill. *Cinema and Ireland*. London: Routledge, 1988.

Sartiliot, Claudette. *Citation and Modernity: Derrida, Joyce and Brecht*. Oklahoma Project for Discourse and Theory. Norman and London: University of Oklahoma Press, 1993.

Saunders, Graham. *"Love Me or Kill Me"*: *Sarah Kane and the Theatre of Extremes*. Manchester: Manchester University Press, 2002.

Schmidt, Kerstin. *The Theater of Transformation: Postmodernism in American Theatre*. Amsterdam and New York: Rodopi, 2005.

Scholes, Robert and Robert Kellogg. *The Nature of Narrative*. Oxford: Oxford University Press, 1966.

Shank, Theodore. "Framing Actuality: Thirty Years of Experimental Theater, 1959-89." *Around the Absurd: Essays on Modern and Postmodern Drama*. Eds. Enoch Brater and Ruby Cohn. Ann Arbor: University of Michigan Press, 1990. 239-272.

Sheehan, Paul. *Modernism, Narrative and Humanism*. Cambridge: Cambridge University Press, 2002.

Shellard, Dominic. *British Theatre since the War*. New Haven and London: Yale University Press, 2000.

Sierz, Aleks. *In-Yer-Face Theatre*. <http://inyerface-theatre.com>.

Sierz, Aleks. *In-Yer-Face Theatre: British Drama Today*. London: Faber and Faber, 2001.

Sihra, Melissa. "A Cautionary Tale: Marina Carr's *By the Bog of Cats....*" *Theatre Stuff: Critical Essays on Contemporary Irish Theatre*. Ed. Eamonn Jordan. Dublin: Carysfort, 2000. 257-268.

Singleton, Brian. "Am I Talking to Myself? Men, Masculinities and Monologue in Contemporary Irish Theatre." *Monologues: Theatre, Performance, Subjectivity*. Ed. Clare Wallace. Prague: Litteraria Pragensia, 2006. 260-277.

Spencer Robinson, Herbert and Knox Wilson. *Myths & Legends of all Nations*. New York: Bantam, 1950.

Steiner, George. *The Death of Tragedy*. Oxford: Oxford University Press, 1961.

Stephenson, Heidi and Natasha Langridge. *Rage and Reason: Women Playwrights on Playwriting*. London: Methuen, 1997.

Stevenson, Randall and Gavin Wallace, eds. *Scottish Theatre since the Seventies*. Edinburgh: Edinburgh University Press, 1996.

Stevenson, Randall. "Border Warranty: John McGrath and Scotland." *International Journal of Scottish Theatre* 3.2 (2002).

Stevenson, Randall. "Home International: The Compass of Scottish Theatre Criticism." *International Journal of Scottish Theatre* 2.2 (2001).

Stewart, Bruce. "'A Fatal Excess' at the Heart of Irish Atavism." *IASIL Newsletter*, 5.1 (1999): 1-2.

Storm, William. *After Dionysus: A Theory of the Tragic*. Ithaca, NY: Cornell University Press, 1998.

Styan, J.L. *Modern Drama in Theory and Practice 3: Expressionism and Epic Theatre*. Cambridge: Cambridge University Press, 1981.

Tönnies, Merle. "The 'Sensationalist Theatre of Cruelty' in 1990s Britain, its 1960s Forebears and the Beginning of the 21st Century." *(Dis)Continuities—Trends and Traditions in Contemporary Theatre and Drama in English*. Eds. Margarete Rubik and Elke Mettinger-Schartmann. CDE 9. Trier: Wissenschaftlicher Verlag Trier, 2002. 57-72.

Vandevelde, Karen. "The Gothic Soap of Martin McDonagh." *Theatre Stuff: Critical Essays on Contemporary Irish Theatre*. Ed. Eamonn Jordan. Dublin: Carysfort, 2000. 292-302.

Verhaeghe, Paul. *Does the Woman Exist? From Freud's Hysteric to Lacan's Feminine*. Trans. Marc du Ry. 1996. London: Robus, 1997.

Voigts-Virchow, Eckart. "Sarah Kane, a Late Modernist: Intertextuality and Montage in the Broken Images of *Crave* (1998)." *What Revels are in Hand? Assessments of Contemporary Drama in English in Honour of Wolfgang Lippke*. Eds. Bernhard Reitz and Heiko Stahl. CDE Studies 8. Trier: Wissenshaftlicher Verlag Trier, 2001. 205-220.

Wallace, Clare, ed. *Monologues: Theatre, Performance, Subjectivity*. Prague: Litteraria Pragensia, 2006.

Wallace, Clare. "'A Crossroads between Worlds": Marina Carr and the Use of Tragedy" *Litteraria Pragensia* 10.20 (2000): 76-89.

Wallace, Clare. "Authentic Reproductions: Marina Carr's Drama and the Inevitable" *The Theatre of Marina Carr: "Before Rules was Made."*

Eds. Anna McMullan and Cathy Leeney. Dublin: Carysfort, 2003. 43-64.

Wallace, Clare. "Dramas of Radical Alterity: Sarah Kane and Codes of Trauma for a Postmodern Age." *Extending the Code: New Forms of Dramatic and Theatrical Expression.* Eds. Hans-Ulrich Moher and Kerstin Mächler. CDE 11. Trier: Wissenschaftlicher Verlag Trier, 2004. 117-130.

Wallace, Clare. "Tragic Destiny and Abjection in Marina Carr's *The Mai, Portia Coughlan* and *By the Bog of Cats...*" *Irish University Review* 31.2 (2001): 431-449.

Wallace, Clare. "Versions and Reversions: The New Old Story and Contemporary Irish Drama" *Engaging Modernity: Readings of Irish Politics, Culture and Literature at the Turn of the Century.* Eds. Michael Böss and Eamonn Maher. Dublin: Veritas, 2003. 112-120.

Waters, John. "The Irish Mummy: The Plays and the Purpose of Martin McDonagh." *Druids, Dudes and Beauty Queens.* Ed. Dermot Bolger. Dublin: New Island, 2001. 30-54.

Watt, Stephen. *Postmodern/Drama: Reading the Contemporary Stage.* Ann Arbor: University of Michigan Press, 1998.

Williams, Raymond. *Modern Tragedy.* London: Chatto and Windus, 1966.

Wood, Gerald C. *Conor McPherson: Imagining Mischief.* Dublin: Liffey, 2003.

Zenzinger, Peter. "David Greig's Scottish View of the 'New' Europe: A Study of Three Plays." *Literary Views on Post-Wall Europe: Essays in Honour of Uwe Böker.* Ed. Christoph Houswitschka et al. Trier: Wissenschaftlicher Verlag Trier, 2005. 261-282.

Zimmermann, Heiner. "Martin Crimp's *Attempts on her Life*: Postdramatic, Postmodern, Satiric?" *(Dis)Continuities—Trends and Traditions in Contemporary Theatre and Drama in English.* Eds. Margarete Rubik and Elke Mettinger-Schartmann. CDE 9. Trier: Wissenschaftlicher Verlag Trier, 2002. 105-124.

Index